PAVLOVIAN APPROACH TO PSYCHOPATHOLOGY

History and Perspectives

PAVLOVIAN APPROACH
TO PSYCHOPATHOLOGY

HISTORY AND PERSPECTIVES

Edited by

W. H. GANTT, L. PICKENHAIN,
CH. ZWINGMANN

1966

PERGAMON PRESS

OXFORD · LONDON · EDINBURGH · NEW YORK
TORONTO · SYDNEY · PARIS · BRAUNSCHWEIG

EDITION LEIPZIG

Pergamon Press Ltd., Headington Hill Hall, Oxford
4 & 5 Fitzroy Square, London W. 1
Pergamon Press (Scotland) Ltd., 2 & 3 Teviot Place, Edinburgh 1
Pergamon Press Inc., Maxwell House, Fairview Park, Elmsford, New York 10523
Pergamon of Canada, Ltd., 207 Queen's Quay West, Toronto 1
Pergamon Press (Aust.) Pty. Ltd., 19 a Boundary Street,
Rushcutters Bay, N.S.W. Zoll, Australia
Pergamon Press S. A. R. L., 24 rue des Écoles, Paris 5^e
Vieweg & Sohn GmbH, Burgplatz 1, Braunschweig

First edition 1970

Library of Congress Catalog Card No. 77-99994

PRINTED IN GERMANY
08 013016 X

CONTENTS

Part III

Experimental Neuroses and Clinical Applications of the Conditioned Reflex Method

INTRODUCTION

IN THE twentieth century we have seen the greatest expansion of science in the whole history of the human being. By far the most spectacular achievements have been in the physical sciences, especially those which concern the unlocking of previously hidden sources of energy, viz. atomic as well as the application of energy through the development of machines. While these developments have made possible an easy life for a part of the world, they have posed a threat not only to all forms of civilization and culture, but to all life.

During this same century, the study of medical science and mental science has shown marked advances. Medicine has eliminated many of the virulent and prevalent diseases. That part of medicine which deals with the higher nervous activity, † though it has not kept pace with the physical sciences, has laid the basis for an objective study of the part of mental life which can be reduced to its measurable aspects. The investigator has begun a scientific study of higher nervous activity comparable to the study of a physical science. He has therewith provided the only acceptable alternative to the soul searching and other speculative approaches (like the psychoanalytic one) which are still, though only sectlike, persued in some countries.

To understand the progress in this field, it is necessary to trace the developments from the beginnings, to have examples from those who have been concerned in the research through their significant articles. This volume aims to supply such an historical survey.

The advice that Bertrand Russell gives to students of philosophy seems pertinent here:

> The student who wishes to acquire an elementary knowledge of philosophy will find it both easier and more profitable to read some of the works of the great philosophers than to attempt to derive an all-round view from handbooks. ‡

The understanding of science depends upon seeing it in historical perspective. Such a view shows whence we have come, and to some extent, where we go. It can spare us a repetition of the errors of our predecessors. The investigators themselves are usually more capable of giving a clear account of their concepts, data, and discoveries than those who come after them, although they may not see so accurately their own errors.

---

† Higher nervous activity, a term used by Pavlov, has the advantage of being a more precise functional term. And it is actually the higher nervous activity rather than the mental and subjective that is being recorded. The distinction is important.

‡ B. Russell in The Problems of Philosophy, Oxford University Press, London, 1967.

The study of behavior has been approached by two fundamentally different methods since the turn of the century. At that time Thorndike in America and Pavlov in Russia instituted methods of study in the higher animals,
"learning" and the "higher nervous activity" (HNA). These methods grew
out of the philosophy and the procedures which were used in the disciplines
of these two researchers. Thorndike's methods involved the use of the "voluntary" muscular system, the gross movements, while Pavlov's were based
on gastrointestinal secretions innovated by the autonomic system. The subsequent developments have been related to these two methods—in procedure and in concepts.

Pavlov says:

> The Americans, judged by the book of Thorndike, set out on this new
> path of investigation in quite a different manner from us. From a passage
> in Thorndike one may conjecture that the practical American mind applied
> to everyday life found that it is more important to be acquainted with the
> exact outward behavior of man than with guesses about his internal states
> with all their combinations and changes. With these considerations concern-
> ing man, the American psychologists proceeded to their laboratory experi-
> ments on animals. From the character of the investigations, up to the pre-
> sent, one feels that both the methods and the problems are derived from
> human interests.
>
> I and my co-workers hold another position. As all our work developed
> out of physiology, so it has continued directly in that path. The methods
> and the conditions of our experimentation, as well as the scheme of the
> separate problems, the working up of the results, and finally their systema-
> tization—all this has remained in the realm of the facts, conceptions and
> terminology of the central nervous system. This approach to our subject
> from both the psychological and the physiological sides enlarges the sphere
> of the phenomena under investigation.†

The methods which I. P. Pavlov and his followers have developed since
the turn of the century for analysing higher forms of nervous activity in
animals and humans, as well as the findings and insights these methods
have produced, have been applied to an ever-increasing extent during the
past decades in laboratories and clinics outside the Soviet Union; this has
been true in capitalist and socialist countries alike. Thus, conditioned reflex
methods for analysing neurophysiological events are in broad use in major
laboratories today in France, Japan, the U.S.A. and many other countries.
In the field of psychosomatic medicine, continually greater support is being
gained for the fundamental notions of cortico-visceral physiology and pathology (Bykov and Kurzin). In psychiatry, methodological aspects of
Pavlovian physiology have been employed by various schools. Advances of
this sort have been evident in many international conferences and symposia.
The Moscow Colloquium on Electroencephalography of Higher Nervous

† I. P. Pavlov, Lectures on Conditioned Reflexes, Vol. I, tr. W. H. Gantt,
New York, International Publishers, 1928, p. 40.

Activity (1958), the Pavlovian Conference on Higher Nervous Activity held in New York in 1960 (sponsored conjointly by The New York Academy of Sciences and The Academy of Medical Sciences of the USSR), the Setschenov Memorial Conference on Brain Reflexes (sponsored by the International Brain Research Organization, IBRO) held in Moscow in 1963, and the Fourth World Congress of Psychiatry held in Madrid in 1966, serve as milestones in this development.

The introduction of Pavlovian concepts and methods into the U.S.A. was promoted in particular by one of the editors of this book, W. Horsley Gantt, Professor Emeritus at Johns Hopkins University in Baltimore and founder of the Pavlovian Laboratories at the Johns Hopkins University and at the Veterans Administration Hospital, Perry Point, Md., who worked for several years in Leningrad under the direct supervision of Pavlov. Since the 1930's Gantt has continued the investigations on higher nervous activity in animals which he began in Leningrad, extending these studies to humans. He and his co-workers have done much to create the basis for Pavlovian concepts being introduced into the clinic.

Many symposia and publications in recent years have been devoted to this important question of introducing the Pavlovian approach into clinical work and applying it to psychopathological phenomena. For the most part, only highly specialized topics have been dealt with, for example in the excellent monograph by Astrup, *Schizophrenia, Conditional Reflex Studies* (1962). To the present time, however, a comprehensive but brief account in English of the basic fundamentals for applying Pavlovian concepts to clinical and psychopathological areas has been lacking. And here lies the purpose of the book, namely to provide the interested reader, whether physician, psychologist or student, quick access to original materials otherwise published in diverse sources, and to present him with examples of the results achieved so far.

The present volume of collected papers offers historical and scientifically systematic evidence to show that the Pavlovian physiology of higher nervous activity represents a highly useful foundation for understanding human psychopathological processes and that to an increasing extent, the diagnostic and psychotherapeutic procedures developed from it have been employed in clinical work. No attempt is made to outline the newest lines of research in the physiology of higher nervous activity carried on in the USSR and other socialist countries (this research is characterized by its utilization of social-psychological thought-models and the most modern technological methods) since this would exceed the limits of the present volume.

Particular emphasis is placed upon elucidating the methodological starting point of the Pavlovian-oriented approach. Pavlov himself expounded this again and again in his own writings (I. P. Pavlov, "The Discovery of the Conditioned Reflex", pp. 15–19; I. P. Pavlov, "An Attempt to Undertsand Physiologically the Symptoms of Hysteria", pp. 20–34).

The viewpoint he discusses here has been fundamental to an introduction of Pavlovian concepts into the clinic. It rests upon the assumption that human psychological phenomena of both a normal and psychopathological nature are influenced by biological as well as social factors; these are seen as conjointly determining a single, unified state which represents the environmental conditions of the individual; biological and social factors are thus not differentiated in principle, but only on the basis of methodological approach. The major findings and arguments in support of this view are presented by Pickenhain ("The Higher Nervous Activity of Man," pp. 126–49) and by Sarkisov, Bassin, and Banstchikov ("The Significance of Neurophysiological Terms for Psychopathology," pp. 55–65). Although the methodological standpoint which is manifest here is not as clearly expressed in the other contributions to this book, it is more or less implicit to all of them. Each of the authors has clearly aimed at achieving an exact scientific basis for the psychopathological conceptions he advances, carefully avoiding all speculative-mystical notions such as those propounded by certain psychoanalytical schools.

The historical section, constituting the first major portion of the book, begins with an essay by Wolman (pp. 9–14), who emphasizes the necessity of psychology advancing from the level of pure description to that of philosophical generalization, since only then can it be elevated from empiricism to the rank of science. This is followed by two papers by Pavlov, in which the author characterizes his initial approach, indicating the applicability of his findings and theoretical insights to the area of human psychopathological phenomena (pp. 15–34). The influence which the work of Pavlov exerted as early as 1916 upon the development of behaviorism in the U.S.A. is attested to in an article by Watson, "The Place of the Conditioned Reflex in Psychology" (pp. 35–46). In his "Presidential Address", Gantt discusses the importance which the insights of Pavlovianism will have for the psychiatry of the future.

In the second major section of the book several physiological systems and mechanisms which Pavlovian research has shown to play a significant role in the development of psychosomatic disturbances and psychopathological symptoms are examined closely. In a contribution concerning cardiac and vascular components of reflexes conditioned to food, pain, and other stimuli (pp. 69–94) Gantt deals with the important problem of the vegetative components of conditional reflexes. Referring to his own experimental results, he indicates that under certain conditions a dissociation between various components of the conditional reflex can occur, and that this points to a method for the experimental reproduction of functional-pathological circulatory ailments.

An excerpt from the classical work of K. M. Bykov, "Brain Cortex and Internal Organs", is presented as an example of the participation of interoceptive processes in conditional-reflex events. The development of conditional reactions of the kidney on the basis of stimulation of stomach and intestinal receptors, as well as the interplay of exteroceptive and interoceptive stimuli in relation to conditional reflexes of the kidney, are examined carefully (pp. 95–108).

In two further articles Gantt concerns himself with the role of sexuality and with the relationship between constitutional and individually acquired factors in the development of abnormal behaviour ("Psychosexuality in Animals", pp. 109–20) as well as considering the importance of phylogenetic factors for an understanding of environmental reactions ("Acquired Vestibular Balancing Responses", pp. 121–25). Finally, at the close of the chapter Pickenhain discusses the second signaling system, possession of which is characteristic of the human being ("The Higher Nervous Activity of Man", pp. 126–49). An understanding of Pavlov's concept of the second signaling system is essential if one is to transfer to human behavior the experimental findings concerning higher nervous activity which have been obtained in animal experiments. Such transfer can enable one to gain insight into the specifically human reactions of a neurotic and psychopathological nature.

The third major section of the book presents papers dealing with the laws involved in producing experimental neuroses in animals, as well as with the clinical application of conditional-reflex methods. In an article by Broadhurst ("Abnormal Animal Behavior", pp. 153–222) a comprehensive summary is given of those studies regarding the generation of experimental neuroses in animals which were published up to 1960. The four papers that follow (Birch and Demb, "The Formation and Extincton of Conditioned Reflexes in Brain-damaged and Mongoloid Children". pp. 223–34); Alexander, "Differential Diagnosis between Psychogenic and Physical Pain", pp. 235–49); Lindsley, "Characteristics of the Behavior of Chronic Psychotics as Revealed by Free-Operant Conditioning Methods", pp. 250–71); Gantt, "Measures of Susceptibility to Nervous Breakdown", pp. 272–83) represent examples of the use of conditional reflex methods for diagnostic purposes in working with psychopathologically altered individuals. Finally, a rather lengthy contribution by Wolpe ("The Experimental Foundations of Some New Psychotherapeutic Methods", pp. 284–304), who has had vast experience in this field, is devoted to the application of conditional-reflex techniques to psychotherapy.

The concluding portion of the book contains an article by Gantt ("The Physiological Basis of Psychiatry: The Conditional Reflex", pp. 305–27) in which the author again draws attention to the fact that the methods developed by Pavlov and his followers, together with the fundamental laws of higher nervous activity which they discovered, form the physiological basis for vast developments in the field of psychiatry.

With this the volume ends, having shown to what a considerable extent our present knowledge of the course and development of psychopathological phenomena can be interpreted in terms of the normal and pathological physiology of higher nervous activity. What an advantageous starting-point for further research was achieved in the conceptions developed by Pavlov and his followers is clearly demonstrated. The book will surely prompt many readers to delve further into studies of the physiology and psychopathology of higher nervous activity, and to pursue with interest those investigations being conducted in this field.

If the title of this book speaks of the "Pavlovian approach", this should not reflect a dogmatism on the part of the editors. The name was merely applied to honor the great initiator of a direction of scientific search and of a method of search which provided the theoretical and practical foundations for research into the newest areas of scientific endeavor.

In reprinting the original articles it was necessary to carry out a few deletions (e. g. of several non-essential diagrams and of various remarks contemporary in nature). These done were with consent of the authors and do not alter the basic content of the articles. The undersigned thank all authors and publishers for their cowurtesy in granting us the right to reprint the original papers.

Perry Point, Md., Leipzig, Frankfurt on the Main, July 1969

H. W. Gantt
L. Pickenhain
Ch. Zwingmann

PART I

HISTORY AND FOUNDATIONS

1

THE NEED FOR A PHILOSOPHY†

B. B. WOLMAN

MODERN science has broken away from philosophy. Instead of leaning on speculative philosophy, modern physicists have developed their own frame of reference and their own conceptual system. Neither Einstein, Maxwell, nor Eddington could rely on the philosophical systems of Leibniz, Kant, or Bergson. Yet the spectacular development of empirical research required fresh hypotheses and new and bold theories.

In their search for clarity and refinement in the development of concepts and theories, the philosophically minded scientists found reliable support in scientifically minded philosophers. Most of the traditional areas of philosophy are now harnessed for the use of science. The new philosophy is primarily a philosophy of science. This philosophy is not a prolegomena to science but rather an *epilegomena* of the sciences. Philosophy is no longer the proud queen of the sciences but the useful serviceman, the dependable repairman of the sciences. It analyzes the formal content of propositions and checks research methods and concept-formation. The philosophy of science does not prescribe truth, but it checks and analyzes the methods by which the sciences proced in their search for truth.

The cooperation between scientists and scientists of science, or philosophers, has been beneficial for both. Scientists need a check-up of the tools they use, formal logical analysis of their premises, examination of their research methods, detailed scrutiny of their observational and experimental procedures, and finally, a rigorous critique of their concept-formation and construct- and model-building. The development of theories requires advice from men competent in the formal sciences. Philosophers, by the nature of their discipline, can help to make science more logical, more consistent, more precise.

Conversely, philosophers need the empirical body of scientific data to apply their formal rules of implication, their syllogisms, axioms, calculus of classes, and other techniques. Scientists supply the propositions to be analyzed, examined, verified, deduced, and inferred from. Close cooperation between philosophers of science and philosophically minded scientists pro-

† From Chapter I by Benjamin B. Wolman, of *Scientific Psychology* edited by Benjamin B. Wolman, consulting editor, Ernest Nagel, Copyright © 1965 by Basic Books, Inc., Publishers, New York.

duces *science without naiveté and logic without metaphysics* (Nagel, 1956; Wolman, 1960a).

This rapprochement requires a great deal of work on both sides. Philosophers of science must become fully acquainted with the methods and problems of the particular branch of science they intend to serve. Scientists must examine carefully their specific area of research and cautiously elaborate the specific problems.

This has happened in physics. Einstein, de Broglie, Eddington, Jeans, Planck and Schrödinger carefully examined the problems faced by *physicists*. Their epistemological and methodological inquiries revolved around problems created by the nature of physical science and its subject matter—the physical world. Theoretical physicists developed their own philosophy of science guided by and related to the peculiar problems in their research area. Einstein developed an epistemological system related to physics; nothing of that kind has been done in psychology.

Unfortunately, *some psychologists have adopted concepts and research tools from areas alien to their own research area*. Too often psychologists wear a hat borrowed from the physical sciences, although psychology by the very nature of its subject matter is miles apart from physics. Psychology, the study of the behavior of certain organisms, is a specific branch of the biological sciences. The biological sciences, as a study of certain processes of certain objects, are a specific branch of physical sciences. The physical sciences deal with the entire universe.

It is a dubious procedure to apply indiscriminately the rules of a class to a subclass on the assumption that these rules will explain all the processes of the subclass. To be sure, human beings are physical bodies, and the laws of physics and chemistry apply also to them; no man could ever be jailed for a violation of the laws of gravitation or electromagnetism. Yet, as Fenichel (1945) put it, "Mental phenomena occur only in living organisms. The general laws that are valid for life phenomena are also valid for mental phenomena: Special laws that are valid only for the level of mental phenomena must be added".

Human behavior cannot be reduced to and wholly interpreted in terms of physical laws. Nor can the behavior of the experimental rat, cat, dog, or monkey be reduced to physics or chemistry. There are additional variables, discovered by the biological sciences and nonexistent in the nonorganic part of the world: consider birth, sex, reproduction, assimilation, digestion, respiration, growth, and death.

Unfortunately, many modern psychologists are inclined to abandon biology and join the physicists. One form of this practice is an extreme and radical *methodological reductionism*. Instead of developing methods and concepts derived from human life, they imitate the methods and concepts of physical science. More generally, methodological reductionism introduces into one area of research methods and concepts coined in another. In a sec ond form, *theoretical reductionism*, they reduce psychological propositions to propositions of other sciences.

Quite naturally, one is prone to transfer his observations from the physical world to human beings, and from humans to everything else. Were men exactly the same as all other things, such a "transfer" would be justified. Despite the obvious differences, some authors have practised *anthropomorphism*, whenever they ascribed their nature to nonhuman objects, and *reimorphism* whenever they ascribed physical nature to themselves. Both types of "morphism" have certainly not promoted the cause of scientific inquiry.

Unfortunately, both tendencies are very much alive in contemporary psychology. When psychologists describe "anxiety", "frustration", or "nervous breakdown" in rats or servomechanisms, at least the language of scientific propositions in comparative psychology becomes suspect; and so does the validity of generalizations which stem from fitting a human hat on a rat's little head and then returning it to the human being.

The impressive precision and achievements of physical science tempt psychologists to view men and their activities in terms of mechanics, electromagnetism, or other physical concepts. Being human, psychologists fall prey to many temptations, including the fantasy of the golem or robot. Certainly, one can program a computer in such a way as to prove his theory. Computers are more obedient than rats and more cooperative in research than hospitalized patients. One wonders whether students of medicine would abandon the study of the organism and dissect statues or electric wires to prove the validity of a theory in anatomy or physiology.

Actually, no psychological theory can ever be finally and completely proven. Every set of observable data can be interpreted in more than one way; obviously, human behavior, largely unobservable and hidden from observation and known only through inference, leaves even more freedom in its interpretation. Unfortunately, some psychologists seem to insist on final and conclusive evidence. For lack of it, they resort to the null–hypothesis method as if this were the best medicine for the troubled research worker. Yet Rozeboom (1960) has raised the most serious doubts about the null–hypothesis as a method of inference. Needless to say, the common practices (significance levels 1–5) prove little if anything at all.

Dazzling statistical techniques are no guarantee of proper scientific procedure. Schlaifer (1959) pointed to the common error that occurs "when the statistician delivers a carefully computed solution of the wrong problem". A considerable part of quite precise research in abnormal psychology deals with irrelevant issues in an inconclusive way, probably because the research problem was incorrectly stated.

The "right problem" must be derived from painstaking study of the behavior of a single case. Psychological processes are too complex to be studied by oversimplified and uncritical generalities. Certainly the case study method and uncontrolled observation easily become anecdotic and even misleading. But a controlled observation and/or controlled experimentation must be *preceded* by the most meticulous naturalistic observation of and experimentation with single cases. Because of the high variability of human behavior, the careful study of individual cases is a necessary first step. Observational or experimental case study will *disclose* the variables to be isolated, variated, and controlled in further research. The meticulously conducted case study will point to the relevant problems. Quantification is the indispensable language of science, but it must come at a later stage, after identical elements have been isolated and put into distinct classes.

The men who have contributed most to the development of psychology as a science are undoubtedly Freud, Pavlov, and Piaget. They did not use high-powered statistics, nor did they try to validate their generalizations or theories by correlations, null hypotheses, chi square, and the like. Freud, Pavlov, Piaget, and scores of other workers in psychology started from the most detailed case-study observations and experimentations. They drew generalizations, and developed general theories on the basis of relatively small numbers of patients, dogs, and children.

The most intimate knowledge of the individual case is a priceless virtue in all biological sciences. Neurologists, biochemists, histologists, physiologists—all start from the single case. The greatest scientific discoveries in biological science have been attained by this method.

It is patent that no science can stop at the single case. Comparison, abstraction, measurement, classification, generalization, and correlation, as well as postulates, constructs, deduction, and equations, are legitimate tools in any scientific inquiry. Psychologists must study the tools they use in relation to their empirical data and in regard to their specific problems: Do we psychologists really see what we see and how do we see? To what extent does the observer become a determinant in results of observation when he observes another human?

The quantum theory or the corpuscular theory of light will not make us more sophisticated, more precise workers in our field. Psychology needs its own sophistication, its own precision, its own philosophical refinement.

Theoretical physicists today combine physics with the philosophy of science. Some graduate schools of physics teach the history and philosophy of physics; psychologists seem to be more concerned with the history and philosophy of physical problems than with the history and philosophy of problems specifically psychological.

Physical science gained depth and clarity by philosophical analysis of itself as a science. A similar development is suggested for psychology. While empirical research goes on, analysis of methods and theory-formation requires the help of what was called logic, epistemology, semantics, and so on, presently included in the modern philosophy of science. Philosophically minded psychologists and philosophers interested in psychology must re-examine the specific problems of psychological science. A new branch of the philosophy of science, applied specifically to psychology, is needed, not a science of physical science, ill-translated into psychology. We need a philosophy that has grown up in psychological laboratories and clinics—*a science of psychological science.*

REFERENCES

ABRAHAM, K. (1955) *Selected Papers on Psychoanalysis*, New York, Basic Books.

ALLPORT, G. W. (1960) *Personality and Social Encounter*, Boston, Beacon Press.

ALLPORT, G. W. (1961) *Pattern and Growth in Personality*, New York, Holt, Rinehart and Winston.

BARKER, R. G., DEMBO, T., and LEWIN, K. (1941) Frustration and Regression: An Experiment with Young Children, *Univ. Iowa Stud. Child Welf*, **18**, No. 1.

BRIDGMAN, P. W. (1927) *The Logic of Modern Physics*, New York, Macmillan.

BRIDGMAN, P. W. (1936) *The Nature of Physical Theory*, Princeton Univ. Press.

COHEN, M. R., and NAGEL, E. (1934) *An Introduction to Logic and Scientific Method*, New York, Harcourt, Brace and World.

DEESE, J. (1958) *The Psychology of Learning*, New York, McGraw-Hill.

DILTHEY, W. (1883) *Einleitung in die Geisteswissenschaften*, Vol. 1, Leipzig.

DOLLARD, J., DOOB, L. W., MILLER, N. E., MOWRER, O. H., and SEARS, R. R. (1939) *Frustration and Aggression*, New Haven, Yale Univ. Press.

EINSTEIN, A. (1931) Maxwell's influence on the development of the conception of physical reality, in *James Clerk Maxwell: Commemoration Volume*, London, Cambridge Univ. Press, pp. 66–73.

EINSTEIN, A. (1959) Reply to criticisms, in P. A. Schilpp (ed.), *Albert Einstein: Philosopher-Scientist*, Vol. 2, New York Harper, pp. 663–88.

ESTES, W. (1960) Learning theory and the new "mental chemistry". *Psychol. Rev.* **67**, pp. 207–23.

FARRELL, B. A. (1954) The scientific testing of psychoanalytic findings and theory, in H. Brand (ed.), *The Study of Personality: A Book of Readings*, New York, Wiley.

FEIGL, H. (1951) Principles and problems of theory construction in psychology, in W. Dennis (ed.), *Current Trends in Psychological Theory*, Univ. Pittsburgh Press, pp. 179–213.

FENICHEL, O. (1945) *The Psychoanalytic Theory of Neurosis*, New York, Norton.

FREUD, S. (1950) *Beyond the Pleasure Principle*, New York, Liveright.

GANTT, W. H. (1958) *Physiological Bases of Psychiatry*, Springfield, Ill., Charles C. Thomas.

GUTHRIE, E. R., and HORTON, G. P. (1946) *Cats in a Puzzle Box*, New York, Rinehart.

HALVERSON, H. M. (1938) Infant sucking and tensional behavior, *J. Genet. Psychol.* **53**, pp. 365–430.

HILGARD, E. R. (1956) *Theories of Learning*, 2nd ed., New York, Appleton-Century-Crofts.

HULL, C. L. (1943) *Principles of Behavior*, New York, Appleton-Century-Crofts.

HULL, C. L. (1952) *A Behavior System*, New Haven, Yale Univ. Press.

ISAACS, S. (1933) *Social Development in Young Children*, London, Routledge and Kegan Paul.

KIMBLE, G. A. (1961) *Hilgard and Marquis Conditioning and Learning*, New York, Appleton-Century-Crofts.

KOCH, H. L. (1935) An analysis of certain forms of so-called "nervous habits" in young children, *J. Genet. Psychol.* **46,** pp. 139–70.

LEWIN, K. (1935) *A Dynamic Theory of Personality*, New York, McGraw-Hill.

LEWIN, K. (1936) *Principles of Topological Psychology*, New York, McGraw-Hill.

LIPPITT, R. (1940) An Experimental Study of the Effect of Democratic and Authoritarian Group Atmospheres, *Univ. Iowa Stud. Child Welf*, **16,** pp. 44–195.

MAIER, N. R. F. (1949) *Frustration: The Study of Behavior Without a Goal*, New York, McGraw-Hill.

MOWRER, O. H. (1960) *Learning Theory and Behavior*, New York, Wiley.

NAGEL, E. (1956) *Logic without Metaphysics*, Glencoe, Ill., Free Press.

NAGEL, E. (1959) Methodological Issues in Psychoanalytic Theory, in S. Hook (ed.), *Psychoanalysis, Scientific Method, and Philosophy*, New York Univ. Press, pp. 38–56.

NAGEL, E. (1961) *The Structure of Science*, New York, Harcourt, Brace and World.

NORTHROP, F. S. C. (1959) Einstein's conception of science, in P. A. Schilpp (ed.), *Albert Einstein: Philosopher-Scientist*, Vol. 2, New York, Harper, pp. 385–408.

PAVLOV, I. P. (1927) *Conditioned Reflexes*, London, Oxford University Press.

PAVLOV, I. P. (1928) *Lectures in conditioned reflexes*, New York, Liveright.

POINCARÉ, H. (1908) *La Science et l'Hypothèse*, Paris, Flammarion.

RAZRAN, G. (1957) The dominance-contiguity theory of the acquisition of classical conditioning, *Psychol. Bull.* **54,** pp. 1–46.

ROZEBOOM, W. W. (1960) The fallacy of the null–hypothesis significance test, *Psychol. Bull.* **57,** pp. 416–28.

SCHLAIFER, R. (1959) *Probability and Statistics for Business Decisions: an Introduction to Managerial Economics under Uncertainty*, New York, McGraw-Hill.

SKINNER, B. F. (1931) The concept of the reflex in the description of behavior, *J. Gen. Psychol.* **5,** pp. 427–58.

SKINNER, B. F. (1950) Are theories of learning necessary? *Psychol. Rev.* **57,** pp. 193–216.

SKINNER, B. F. (1953) *Science and Human Behavior*, New York, Macmillan.

SPENCE, K. (1960) *Behavior Theory and Learning*, New York, Prentice-Hall.

2

THE DISCOVERY
OF THE CONDITIONED REFLEX†

I. P. Pavlov

More than 20 years ago I began these experiments independently, passing to them from my former physiological work. I entered this field under the influence of a powerful laboratory impression. For many years previously I had been working on the digestive glands. I had studied carefully and in detail all the conditions of their activity. Naturally I could not leave them without considering the so-called psychical stimulation of the salivary glands, i.e., the flow of saliva in the hungry animal or person at the sight of food or during talk about it or even the thought of it. Furthermore, I myself had demonstrated a psychical excitation of the gastric glands.

I began to investigate the question of psychic secretion with my collaborators, Drs. Wolfson and Snarsky. Wolfson collected new and important facts for this subjects; Snarsky, on the other hand, undertook to analyse the internal mechanism of the stimulation from the subjective point of view, i.e., he assumed that the internal world of the dog—the thoughts, feelings, and desires—is analogous to ours. We were now brought face to face with a situation which had no precedent in our laboratory. In our explanation of this internal world we diverged along two opposite paths. New experiments did not bring us into agreement nor produce conclusive results, and this in spite of the usual laboratory custom, according to which new experiments undertaken by mutual consent are generally decisive. Snarsky clung to his subjective explanation of the phenomena, but I, putting aside fantasy and seeing the scientific barrenness of such a solution, began to seek for another exit from this difficult position.

After persistent deliberation, after a considerable mental conflict, I decided finally, in regard to the so-called psychical stimulation, to remain in the role of a pure physiologist, i.e., of an objective external observer and experimenter, having to do exclusively with external phenomena and their relations. I attacked this problem with a new co-worker, Dr. Tolotchinov, and from this beginning there followed a series of investigations with my highly esteemed collaborators, which has lasted for more than 20 years.

† By permission of *International Publishers Co. Inc.*

15

When I began our investigations with Dr. Tolochinov, I was aware that in the extension of physiological investigation throughout the whole animal world (in the form of comparative physiology), dealing with other animals in addition to those common to the laboratory (dogs, cats, rabbits, and frogs), the physiologist is obliged to abandon the subjective point of view, to endeavour to employ objective methods, and to try to introduce an appropriate terminology (the doctrine of tropism of Jacques Loeb, and the objective terminology of Beer, Bethe, and Uexküll). Indeed, it would be difficult and unnatural to speak of the thoughts and wishes of an amoeba or infusorian. But our study concerned the dog, the intimate and faithful companion of man since prehistoric times. And I take it that the most important motive for my decision, even though an unconscious one, arose out of the impression made upon me during my youth by the monograph of I. M. Setchenov, the father of Russian physiology, entitled *Cerebral Reflexes* and published in 1863. The influence of thoughts which are strong by virtue of their novelty and truth, especially when they act during youth, remains deep and permanent even though concealed. In this book, a brilliant attempt was made, altogether extraordinary for that time (of course, only theoretically, as a physiological outline), to represent our subjective world from the standpoint of pure physiology. Setchenov had made at that time an important physiological discovery (concerning central inhibition) which deeply impressed European physiologists. That was the first Russian contribution to this important branch of natural science, which just previously had been remarkably advanced through the successes of German and French physiologists.

The great effort which this discovery demanded, and the joy which it brought, mixed perhaps with personal emotion, gave rise to the ideas expressed by Setchenov, which are certainly those of a genius. Afterwards, it is interesting to note, he referred to this theme in the same resolute manner he used at first.

Some years after the beginning of the work with our new method I learned that somewhat similar experiments on animals had been performed in America, and indeed not by physiologists but by psychologists. Thereupon I studied in more detail the American publications and now I must acknowledge that the honour of having made the first steps along this path belongs to E. L. Thorndike (1898). By two or three years his experiments preceded ours, and his book must be considered as a classic, both for its bold outlook on an immense task and for the accuracy of its results. Since the time of Thorndike, the American work (Yerkes, Parker, Watson, *et al.*) on our subject has grown. It is purely American in every sense—in collaborators, equipment, laboratories, and publications. The Americans, judged by the book of Thorndike, set out on this new path of investigation in quite a different manner from us. From a passage in Thorndike's book one may conjecture that the practical American mind applied to everyday life found that it is more important to be acquainted with the exact outward behaviour of man than with guesses about his internal states with all their combinations and changes. With these considerations concerning man, the American psychologists proceeded to their laboratory experiments on animals. From the character of the investigations, up to the present, one feels that both the methods and the problems are derived from human interests.

I and my co-workers hold another position. As all our work developed out of physiology, so it has continued directly in that path. The methods and the conditions of our experimentation, as well as the scheme of the separate problems, the working up of the results, and finally their systematisation—all this has remained in the realm of the facts, conceptions and terminology of the central nervous system. This approach to our subject from both the psychological and the physiological sides enlarges the sphere of the phenomena under investigation. To my deep regret, I know absolutely nothing about what has been done on this question in America during the last four or five years; up to this time it has been impossible to obtain American literature on the subject here, and my request last year to go to America to learn of the recent work was not granted.

Some years after we started, the problem was also taken up by Bechterev here and by Kalischer in Germany. In our work we used an inborn reflex upon which all nervous activity is modelled, *viz.* the food reflex and the defensive reflex against acid, the secretory component of which we had observed. Bechterev used instead the defensive reflex against destructive (painful) irritation of the skin in the form of a movement reaction. Kalischer, however, employed as we did the food reflex, concentrating on the motor reaction. Bechterev designated as "associative" these new reflexes which we called "conditioned", while Kalischer called the whole method the *Dressurmethode* (training method). If I may judge from what I saw in the physiological literature during my five weeks' stay in Helsingfors this spring (1923), the objective examination of the behaviour of animals has already attracted the attention of many physiological laboratories in Europe — in Vienna, Amsterdam, etc.

About myself I shall add the following. At the beginning of our work and for a long time afterwards we felt the compulsion of habit in explaining our subject by psychological interpretations. Every time the objective investigation met an obstacle, or when it was halted by the complexity of the problem, there arose quite naturally misgivings as to the correctness of our new method. Gradually with the progress of our research these doubts appeared more rarely, and now I am deeply and irrevocably convinced that along this path will be found the final triumph of the human mind over its uttermost and supreme problem—the knowledge of the mechanism and laws of human nature. Only thus may come a full, true and permanent happiness. Let the mind rise from victory to victory over surrounding nature, let it conquer for human life and activity not only the surface of the earth but all that lies between the depth of the seas and the outer limits of the atmosphere, let it command for its service prodigious energy to flow from one part of the universe to the other, let it annihilate space for the transference of its thoughts —yet the same human creature, led by dark powers to wars and revolutions and their horrors, produces for itself incalculable material losses and inexpressible pain and reverts to bestial conditions. Only science, exact science about human nature itself, and the most sincere approach to it by the aid of the omnipotent scientific method, will deliver man from his present gloom, and will purge him from his contemporary shame in the sphere of interhuman relations.

The freshness of the subject, in addition to the hope just expressed, should inspire all workers in this new field. The work advances along a wide front. Much has been accomplished during the 25 years since its beginning made by Thorndike.

My laboratories have contributed not a little to this progress. Our investigations have continued unbrokenly up to the present time. A slackening of the work was caused in 1919 and 1920 owing to extraordinary difficulties (cold, darkness, starvation of the experimental animals, etc.). Since 1921 the conditions have improved, and now they approach normal except for lack of instruments and literature.

Our data increases, the outline of our research becomes larger, and gradually there looms up before us a general system of the phenomena in this new field—in the physiology of the cerebral hemispheres, the organ of the highest nervous activity.

These are at present the main features of our work. We are becoming better and better acquainted with the fundamental mode of conduct with which the animal is born—with the congenital reflexes, heretofore usually called instincts. We observe and intentionally participate in building new reactions on this fundamental conduct, in the form of so-called habits and associations, which now increase, enlarge, become complicated and refined. According to our analysis, these are also reflexes, but conditioned reflexes. Step by step we approach the inner mechanism of these reflexes, become more accurately informed about the general properties of the nervous masses in which they move and have their being, and with the hard and fast rules by which they are governed. There pass before us several individual types of nervous systems highly characteristic, strongly expressed, showing us the different aspects and properties of nervous activity upon which is based the whole complicated behaviour of animals. And even more than this! The results of animal experimentation are of such nature that they may at times help to explain the hidden processes of our own inner world.

Such is the situation as I conceive it.

REFERENCE

THORNDIKE, E. L. (1898) *Animal Intelligence – An Experimental Study of the Associative Processes in Animals*, New York, Macmillan

AN ATTEMPT TO UNDERSTAND PHYSIOLOGICALLY THE SYMPTOMS OF HYSTERIA

I. P. Pavlov

The Academy of Sciences of the U.S.S.R., Leningrad, 1932. Dedicated to my esteemed and respected comrade Alexei Vasilievich Martuinov, on the fortieth year of his scientific, professorial, and practical activity by the grateful author

ALTHOUGH hysteria is classified by all clinicians as a psychiatric disease, wholly or predominantly—a psychogenic reaction to the surroundings—the objective study of higher nervous activity by the conditioned reflex method has very much advanced, broadened and deepened. Therefore, I do not consider it very risky to attempt to understand physiologically, and to analyse such an intricate pathological picture as hysteria in all its manifestations.

Thus this will be a physiological explanation of the so–called psychical phenomena, which is an aspiration of conditioned reflex investigations.

Unfortunately, some physiological introduction is necessary here. Even on my native soil, the concept of conditioned reflexes is not well known, and the study has developed so rapidly that many of the most important facts have not yet been published, appearing here for the first time.

I

The conditioned reflexes which accumulate progressively during the individual life of animals and man, are formed within the cerebral hemispheres—the highest section of the central nervous system. They are a further complication of the usual unconditioned reflexes, which are present in the central nervous system from birth.

The biological meaning of the conditioned reflex consists in the fact that the few external stimuli which elicit the unconditioned reflexes in special conditions (temporal coincidence) are combined temporarily with the innumerable phenomena of the environment, so that they become signals for these stimuli. Thus, the functions of all organs, which are effects of unconditioned stimuli, enter into a more subtle and exact interrelation with increas ingly more and more parts of the environment. The doctrine of conditioned reflexes, or the physiology of higher nervous activity, studies the dynamic laws of these reflexes during both normal and pathological life.

We must assume that the activity of the cerebral hemispheres and of the whole central nervous system with their two processes – excitatory and inhibitory—is regulated by two fundamental laws: the Law of Irradiation and Concentration of each of these processes and the Law of Reciprocal Induction. Experiments carried out during normal activity of the cortex suggest the conclusion that these processes irradiate instantaneously from the point of origin, when a weak stimulus intensity is used, but concentrate when the stimulus intensity is strong enough. If the intensity is extremely strong, they irradiate again. When the processes of excitation and inhibition concentrate, they induce the opposite process in the periphery during the action, as well as at the site of the activity after it has finished.

Thanks to the irradiation of the excitatory process, summation of reflexes occurs. A wave from a new excitation, having spread, summates with the existing local excitation, kinetic or potential, in the latter case becoming a hidden focus of excitation. In the cerebral hemispheres on account of the complex structure and great reactivity, the irradiated process leads to the elaboration of a temporary conditioned connexion—an assocation. While a summated reflex is momentary and transitory, the conditioned reflex is gradually reinforced to become a chronic manifestation—a characteristic process of the cortex.

With the concentration of the excitatory process along the whole extent of the central nervous system, inhibition appears—the Law of Induction. The point of concentrated excitation is surrounded by the process of inhibition—a phenomenon of negative induction, seen with unconditioned as well as conditioned reflexes. The inhibition is deeper, broader and lasts longer the stronger the excitation and the less the positive tone of the surrounding nervous tissue. Negative inhibition acts between small points, as well as between large divisions of the brain. This inhibition is external, passive and unconditioned, as we call it. Formerly this was referred to as a conflict of nerve centres.

In the cerebral hemispheres in addition to the above form of inhibition, there is another one but there is reason to think that the same physico-chemical process underlies both. At first, there is the inhibition which continuously corrects the conditioned connection. It operates when the conditioned stimulus, as signal, is not accompanied by the signalled agent and it depresses the excitation appropriately. Furthermore, it splits and differentiates the positive conditioned agents from the innumerable similar, but negative ones. In these conditions, it arises by itself, increases gradually, and may continue to develop by itself. This inhibition may be connected also with each indifferent external stimulus, when its influence coincides with it within the cortex for some time. Then, this stimulus also begins to evoke the inhibitory process in the cortex. This special cortical inhibition together with the conditioned connection is, as we have shown, very important for adaptation to environmental conditions, because it always analyses the excitations originating from these conditions. We have called this kind of inhibition internal or active inhibition. But it might also be called "conditioned". Secondly, in the cortex, an additional, special form of inhibition is observed. As a rule, the effect of the conditioned stimulus, all other conditions being unchanged, is in parallel to the physical intensity of the eliciting stimulus. But this is valid only up to a definite limit upwards (and possibly also downwards). Above this limit the effect does not increase any more, but rather diminishes. We think that a stimulus of such a strength no longer evokes an excitation, but rather an inhibition. We explain the whole phenomenon in terms of the cortical cell having a limit of ability within which to work, beyond which a functional disturbance arises. The inhibition which we have described protects this limit in the case of supramaximal stimulation. This inhibition is the greater, the more supramaximal the stimulus is. In these cases, the effect of stimulation either retains its maximal level (which is more usual) or it decreases when the stimulation is too strong. This inhibition may be called transmarginal or ultramaximal inhibition.

The limit of ability of the cortical cells is not constant, showing both acute and chronic fluctuations: during exhaustion, hypnosis, disease and senility the limit constantly falls, and the environment is now more often "transmarginal" with resulting inhibition. Also, when the excitability is raised, normally or artificially, as with chemicals, then the more the formerly submaximal and maximal excitations are converted into ultramaximal, leading to inhibition and a general lowering of the conditioned reflex activity. There remains the unsolved question of how the last two cases of inhibition are related to the first universal type of negative induction? If they are actually only a variation, how does this inhibition become a peculiarity of the cortex? Probably, frontier (i.e. ultramaximal) inhibition is nearer to the inborn external passive inhibition than to the internal active form, as it arises immediately and without elaboration or training.

Both of these cortical inhibitions spread over the nervous tissue. Most experiments related to this spreading were carried out with respect to the first kind of cortical inhibition—internal inhibition. In these experiments, we can say, the inhibition was spreading before our eyes.

There may be no doubt that this spreading and deepening inhibition constitutes different degrees of the hypnotic state, and that spreading maximally down the brain it induces normal sleep. Already, in our experimental subject (the dog), the heterogeneity and great number of different degrees of hypnosis have proved more interesting. But at the beginning, one could hardly differentiate them from the wakeful state. In considering the intensity of inhibition, the equalizing, paradoxical, and ultraparadoxical phases must be specially mentioned. During these phases, conditioned stimuli of different physical intensity do not evoke effects of different magnitude according to their intensity, as is observed during the wakeful state, but evoke equal or even inverse effects. In some phases, the inverse force may be so great that only the inhibitory stimuli give a positive effect while positive stimuli give an inhibitory one. In respect to the extent of the inhibition, functional subdivisions are observed in the cortex as well as in other parts of the brain. In the cortex, the motor region especially is often isolated from the remaining part of the cerebral hemispheres. This process is accompanied by a similar, marked functional dissociation within the motor region itself.

Unfortunately the results of our experiments have not been brought into correlation with the so-called sleep centres of the clinicians and certain physiologists. But it cannot be doubted that there exist two mechanisms of sleep, and one must distinguish between *active* and *passive* sleep. The former proceeds from the cerebral hemispheres and is based upon active inhibition, spreading from its origin to the underlying parts of the brain. Passive sleep originates as a result of decreased excitatory impulses falling upon the highest parts of the brain, not only on the cerebral hemispheres but on the underlying subcortex.

The excitatory impulses may be external, reaching the brain through the external receptors, or internal, conditioned by the work of the viscera and coming to the higher parts of the brain from the central nervous regions regulating the vegetative activities. The first type—passive sleep—has long been known from the clinical report of Strümpell; it is analogous to a recent fact from the experiments of Speransky and Galkin, when after peripheral destruction of three receptors (the auditory, visual and olfactory) the dog falls into a profound and chronic sleep lasting for weeks or months. The second type—passive sleep—is the clinical one, leading to the recognition of the so-called sleep centre of the clinicians and certain experimentalists. We have an analogous example in the muscle tissue. Under special physiological conditions the skeletal muscle contracts actively and relaxes actively— under a stimulation of two special nerves, the excitatory and the inhibitory.

Precisely during the concentration of the excitatory and inhibitory processes, the opposite process appears, as an effect of the law of reciprocal induction. The concentration point of inhibition is surrounded to a greater or smaller extent, by a process of increased excitability. This is the phenomenon of positive induction. Positive induction is observed in both unconditioned and conditioned reflexes. The increased excitability arises immediately, or after a limited period, during which the inhibition gradually concentrates. It exists not only during the actual duration of the inhibition, but also after it, and sometimes even for an extended time. The positive induction occurs between single cortical points, as well as between larger cerebral sections.

Now I shall touch upon certain facts significant for the physiological analysis of the symptoms of hysteria. The connexions of the organism with

the surroundings through the conditioned signals are the more perfect the
more the cerebral hemispheres analyse and synthesise the signals corresponding to the extreme complexity and continued fluctuations of the
surroundings. Synthesis is accomplished by the process of conditioned connections.

Analysis, differentiating the positive conditioned signals from the inhibitory, is based upon the process of reciprocal induction; the separation of
the various positive agents, i.e., unions with the various unconditioned reflexes, occurs by virtue of the process of concentration (recent experiments
of V. V. Rikman). Thus for an exact analysis a certain tension is required of
the inhibitory as well as of the excitatory process.

Of specific significance for the physiological study of hysteria are our
facts relating to the types of nervous systems. First we have the very strong
animal, albeit unbalanced, in which the inhibititory process is considerably
weaker than the excitatory. In the face of difficult problems necessitating
great inhibition, these animals lose nearly altogether the inhibitory function
(a special neurosis) and become extremely restless and agitated, sometimes
with periodic drowsy or depressive states. In their general behaviour they
are aggressive, animated, undisciplined. We call such animals excitatory or
choleric.

Next follows the strong but balanced type where both processes stand at
the same level. This is why it is impossible to produce a nervous disturbance in such animals through giving hard tasks. This type occurs in two
forms: the quiet (phlegmatic) and the very lively (sanguine).

Finally there is the weak inhibitory type in which both processes are insufficient especially the inhibitory—a type easily produced experimentally
and particularly subject to neuroses. They are in constant fear and anxiety.
They cannot endure intense external stimuli in the form of positive conditioned stimuli, nor much normal excitation (food, sexual), nor a prolongation of the inhibitory process, nor a collision of the nervous process, nor a
complex system of conditioned reflexes, nor finally a change in the stereotype of the conditioned reflex activity. Under such circumstances the conditioned reflexes become weaker and chaotic, and many of these animals fall
into the hypnotic state. Separate pathological points in the cerebral hemispheres may be easily produced in them which, when touched, result
in a rapid deterioration of the conditioned reflexes. If judging by the external behaviour, it is not always appropriate to call these animals melancholic, they may nevertheless be placed in the group of melancholics, i.e.,
with those animals who seem to be constantly inhibited. Explaining these
types from the point of view of a balance between excitation and internal
inhibition, we feel that in the weak type on account of the weakness of
the internal inhibition, the external inhibition (negative induction) on the
other hand predominates and determines the whole external behaviour,
hence the name of this type—the weak inhibitory.

In concluding the physiological part I should call attention to the following difficulty, especially important for understanding some of the extraordinary symptoms of hysteria. Not only from the skeletal motor apparatus proceed centripetal, afferent impulses from every element of movement to the motor area of the cortex, making possible the exact control of movement by the cortex, but indeed from the other organs and even from the individual tissues, whence the cortical control is over them. At present this intricacy—and it must be connected with the higher parts of the central nervous system—has a wide biological significance once it is proven that leucocytosis, immunity and other organic processes can be conditioned, although we do not yet know exactly the nervous connections, participating directly or by some indirect way. Only this latter possibility of action from the cortex is voluntarily utilized and expressed by us very rarely under exceptional, artificial or abnormal circumstances. The cause of this is, on the one hand, that the activity of the organs and tissues other than the skeletal musculature is automatically regulated chiefly by the lower parts of the central nervous system, and on the other hand, marked by the main function of the cerebral hemispheres directed to the intricate relations with the external environment.

II

Let us return to hysteria. The general clinical descriptions of hysteria include those concerning the basic characteristics of the condition as well as the special symptoms. Some clinicians speak of a reversion to the instinctive, i.e., emotional and even reflex life, others describe the disease as resulting from suggestibility and autosuggestion with the consequent so-called stigmata of hysteria (analgesia, paralysis, etc.); some see the disease primarily as voluntary—a retreat into illness. Some ascribe to it fantasy—an absence of reality in the relation to life; others consider hysteria as chronic hypnosis; and finally there are those who propose a diminished function of psychical synthesis or a destruction of the integrated "inhibition". One may presume that together these symptoms include the whole symptom-complex of hysteria.

First one must recognise hysteria as a production of a weak nervous system. Pierre Janet states that hysteria is a psychical disorder belonging to the immense group of diseases resulting from weakness and exhaustion of the brain. If this is true, then the described characteristics of hysteria as a weakness related chiefly to the higher part of the central nervous system and especially to the cerebral hemispheres (the most reactive of its parts) are comprehensible in the light of the physiology of the higher parts of the central nervous system as it is represented by the knowledge of the conditioned reflex.

Usually the cerebral hemispheres, as the highest organ of correlation of the organism with the surrounding medium and consequently a continual controller of supplementary functions, constantly restrain the other parts of the brain with their instinctive and reflex activity. Hence with the strained and weakened cerebral activity, there goes a more or less chaotic function of the subcortex, deprived of its corresponding relation to the cortex. This is a generally known physiological fact seen in animals after extirpation of the cerebral hemispheres, in adult people under the influence of various narcotics, and in small children during the transition from the waking state to sleep. Thus speaking in the above established physiological terms, the waking active state of the cerebral hemispheres consists in the continual analysis and synthesis of the external stimuli, the active surroundings, and produces negative induction in the subcortex, i.e., generally restrains its functions, freeing selectively only that of its work requiring a conditioned place and time. Conversely, the restraining, inhibitory state of the cerebral hemisphere liberates, it seems, positive induction of the subcortex, i.e., intensifies its general activity. Consequently (this is a justifiable physiological basis) in the hysterical patient during acute restraint of the cortex under the influence of intolerably strong stimulations (and on account of its weakness these are numerous)—there resulted various affective splits and convulsive seizures, now in the form of more or less definite instinctive and reflex actions, now completely chaotic, correspondingly localized by the mobilization of inhibition in the cortex and subcortex, now in the neighbouring, now in the more distant parts.

But this is an extreme and active expression of the illness. When the inhibition spreads deeper into the brain we have another extreme, but passive state of hysteria in the form of profound hypnosis and finally complete sleep lasting not only hours but for many days (lethargy). This difference between extreme states is probably determined not only by the various degrees of weakness of the processes of excitation and of inhibition in the cortex but by the established relations between the cortex and subcortex, now changing acutely and chronically in the same individual, now connected with different personalities.

Besides the fact that a varying, chronic, cortical weakness is the basis for the manifestation of the above described extraordinary states of the organism, this weakness inevitably conditions a constant special state of the hysteric. This is *emotionability*.

Although the life of animals as well as our own is directed to the basic tendencies of the organism—food, sexual, aggressive, investigative, etc. (functions of the underlying subcortex)—nevertheless for the perfect agreement and correlation of all these tendencies in connexion with the general circumstances of life, there is a special part of the central nervous system which measures every separate tendency, correlates them and secures their advantageous realisation in connexion with the environment. This of course is the cerebral hemispheres. There are two methods of action. After a preliminary survey, so to speak (sometimes arising almost instantaneously), of the given tendency of the cerebral hemispheres and its transmutation, in the proper degree and at the corresponding moment, into the corresponding motor act or behaviour by means of the motor cortical area—this is the reasoned action; and the action (perhaps directly through the subcortical connexions) under only the influence of the tendency without that preliminary control—this is the affective, emotional action. In the hysteric it is this second action that predominates and by a well understood nervous mechanism. The tendency arises as the result of an external or internal stimulus. To it corresponds the activity of the known point or region of the cerebral hemispheres. This point under the influence of emotion, subsequent to irradiation from the subcortex, is heavily charged. With a weak cortex this is enough to produce an intense spreading negative induction excluding the control of the rest of the cerebral hemispheres. But there, in those parts representing other tendencies, are the representatives of the surroundings, traces of past stimulations and experiences. Here is connected another mechanism. The strong stimulation of emotion raises the excitability of the cortex, quickly leading to stimulation to the limit and beyond the limit of its capacity. Therefore the negative induction summates with the ultramaximal inhibition. Thus the hysterical patient lives, more or less, in an unreasoned and emotional life directed by the subcortical rather than by the cortical functions.

Suggestion and autosuggestion stand in direct relation with the above mechanism of the hysteric. What is suggestion and autosuggestion? They are a concentrated excitation of a definite stimulation, sensation or its trace, a representation, now in evoked emotion, i.e. excited from the subcortex, now produced from without, now arising from an internal connexion, an association, excitation, having been given a predominant, "illegitimate" and irrepressible significance. It exists and acts, i.e. passes over into movement in one or another motor act because it is reinforced by all the associations, i.e. by the connexions from many present and past stimulations and representations. This is an established and logical act if occurring in the normal healthy cortex; but because it exits in a weak cortex with a lowered tonus it becomes concentrated and is accompanied by an intense negative induction, cutting it off, isolating it from all foreign, unnecessary influences. Such is the mechanism of hypnotic and posthypnotic suggestion. In hypnosis and in the normal cortex we have a diminished positive tonus as a consequence of irradiated inhibition. When on such a cortex a word or order of the hypnotiser is directed to a definite point this stimulus concentrates the excitatory process in the corresponding point and is immediately accompanied by negative induction, which causes it without the slight opposition to spread over the whole cortex; this is why the word or order iscompletely isolated from all influences and is made an absolute, irrepressible, fatally-acting stimulus, even after the subject has returned to the waking state.

3 PAP

The mechanism is exactly the same, varying only in degree, arising in old age as the excitatory processes of the cortex naturally decrease. In the brain which is yet strong the external and internal stimulations concentrate to some degree (extremely only exceptionally) in a definite cortical point or region, accompanied of course by negative induction, but thanks to the strength of the cortex it is not complete and at some distance inhibition is extending. Therefore together with the chief excitation another one is acting to a certain degree to evoke the corresponding reflexes, especially the old established "automatic" ones. Ordinarily in our behaviour we react not singly, but complexly, to fit the ever present contents of our environment. In old people the matter is altogether different. Concentrating on one stimulus, we exclude other collateral and simultaneous stimuli by negative induction, because they often do not suit the circumstances, are not complementary reactions in the given setting.

Let me give a minor incident of this. I look at some object which I need, take it and do not see anything touching or near it—this is why I unnessarily strike against surrounding objects. This is erroneously called senile distraction, on the contrary it is concentration, involuntary, passive, defective. Thus the old man, dressing and at the same time thinking about something or talking to someone, goes out without his cap, takes the wrong article, leaves his clothes unbuttoned, etc., etc.

In consequence of foreign and unpremeditated suggestions and also of autosuggestion the life of the hysteric is replete with every possible eccentricity and invention.

Let us begin with a war neurosis, common since the First World War. War as a continued serious threat to life naturally creates the fear impulse. Fear represents certain physiological symptoms which in those having a strong nervous system either simply do not appear, are suppressed or quickly dissipated, but in weak people they last for some time making them unfit for further military participation, thus freeing them from the necessity of endangering their lives. These symptoms may disappear of themselves in time, but in the weak nervous system precisely on account of this weakness, the reinforcement of their mechanism is added. The symptoms of fear become connected, associated, with security to life by the law of conditioned reflexes. Hence the existence of these symptoms is invested with a positive emotional colouring and they are repeatedly reproduced. Then, according to the law of irradiation and summation from the cortex, they reinforce and intensify the lower centers of reflex symptoms of fear on the one hand, and on the other hand being emotionally charged, in the weak cortex accompanied by strong negative induction, they thus exclude the influence of other representations which might oppose the representation of the conditioned pleasantness or desirability of these symptoms. Therefore sufficient justification does not remain for us to say that in the given case there is an intentional simulation of symptoms. It is an example of fatalistic physiological relations.

Such cases in hysterics and in ordinary life are numerous. Not only the threat of war but many other dangers for life (fire, railraod wrecks, etc.), the countless blows of fate as the loss of loved ones, disappointment in love and the other vicissitudes of life, economic reversals, and the devastation of one's beliefs and faith, etc., and in general hard living conditions: an unhappy marriage, the struggle with poverty, the destruction of the feeling of self-respect, etc., evokes at once or finally in the weak person the strongest reaction with various abnormalities in the form of somatic symptoms. Many of these symptoms having arisen in a moment of strong excitation are imprinted on the cortex for a long time or permanently, like many intense stimulations in normal people (kinesthetic similarly to all others). Different symptoms, capable of acting in the normal subject, are in them obliterated, in consequence of a fear that they might be abnormal, or ackward, harmful or even only indecent; or conversely, for some advantage, or simply for the sake of an interest, by the same mechanism as in the above war case, emotionally reinforced they become more and more intense and extensive (on account of irradiation) and stable. Obviously in a weak person who is a living invalid incapable in a positive way of demanding attention, respect, good will, the motive to obtain these will function to continue and reinforce the pathological symptoms. Hence the flight, the will to be sick as a most characteristic feature of hysteria.

Together with these positive symptoms are also negative ones, i.e., those produced in the central nervous system not by the process of excitation but by the process of inhibition, such as analgesia and paralysis. They demand especial attention, and several clinicians, e.g. Hoche in a recent article, consider certain hysterical symptoms absolutely incomprehensible. But this is illogical; for these symptoms are not different from the positive. Do we normal subjects always restrain our definite movements and words, i.e., send the inhibitory impulse to the proper areas of the cerebral hemispheres? In the laboratory as I have pointed out in the physiological introduction, we continually elaborate with the positive conditioned stimulations also inhibitory. In hypnosis by a word-stimulus we produce anesthesia, analgesia and inability to move and in some instances paralysis. But the hysterical patient often can and must be considered under the ordinary circumstances of life as chronically hypnotized to a certain degree; for to his weak cortex usual stimuli are ultramaximal and are accompanied by an overflow of transmarginal inhibition just as we see it in the paradoxical phase of our hypnotized animals. Then in addition to the established inhibitory symptoms, similar to the positive ones arising at the moment of a severe nervous trauma, these inhibitory symptoms can be produced in the "hysteric-hypnotized" subject by suggestion and autosuggestion. All representation of an inhibitory effect, whether from fear, interest or of an advantage to be gained, is concentrated and intensified repeatedly in the cortex as a result of the emotionality of the hysterical patient just as in hypnosis the command of the

hypnotizer evokes and establishes these symptoms for a long time, while
finally the more intense waves of excitation in any case do not touch these
inhibitory points.

By the same mechanisms autosuggestion in hysteria brings up many
other symptoms both ordinary and extraordinary.

Any slight feeling of indisposition or unusual difficulty in any organic
function is accompanied in the hysteric by the emotion of fear of a serius
illness, and this is enough, by the above mechanism, not only to support but
to intensify them to an extreme degree, making of the subject an invalid.
Only in this instance the cause of its spreading and dominating action in
the cortex is not a positively coloured sensation as in the war neurosis but a
negative one. Of course the nature of the physiological process is unimpor-
tant. One of the peculiar cases of hysterical autosuggestion is that of ficti-
tious pregnancy with the corresponding changes in the mammae and increased fat in the abdominal wall, etc. This is an additional confirmation of
what was stated in the first part of the article concerning the representations
in the cortex of not only the activities of all the organs but even of the individual tissues. At the same time the extreme emotionality of the hysteric
lends support to this hypothesis. In the given case it is true the powerful
maternal instinct acting by autosuggestion provokes, in an extreme degree
in some components, such a complex and special state of the organism as
pregnancy. To this group belong the states and stigmata of the various
religious ecstatics. It is an historical fact that the Christian martyrs not only
endured but joyfully faced torture and died praising Him in whose name
they were sacrificed – a proof of the power of autosuggestion, i.e., the strength
of the concentrated excitation of a definite area of the cortex accompanied
by marked inhibition of the rest of the cortex, representing, so to speak, the
basic interests of the whole organism, its integrity and its existence. If suggestion and autosuggestion are so strong that they can annihilate the or-
ganis mwithout the slightest physiological resistance from the organism, then
from the adduced possibilities of influence by the cortex on the internal processes, from the physiological point of view it is easy to understand how suggestion and autosuggestion can destroy the integrity of the organism by
means of the just proven trophic innervation.

Therefore is not the extreme opinion of Babinsky in error (although in
general correctly appraising the basic mechanism of hysteria) that one should
consider only as hysterical symptoms those either evoked or removed by
suggestion? Such a conclusion omits the exceptional force and irrepressible
act of the given emotional motivation which cannot be produced intentionally
by suggestion, the more so because the true hidden source of this motivation
is not evident.

Finally it is necessary to discuss the fantasy, the breach from real life
toward a fanciful one that the hysteric shows. There is reason to believe that
these symptoms are connected one with the other. As is shown by the obser-

vations of Bernheim and others on hypnotised normal subjects as well as by ours on dogs, we must recognise many phases of the hypnosis, passing from one hardly distinguishable from the waking state to full sleep.

In order to comprehend thoroughly these degrees especially in the human being it seems to me necessary to mention the following fact, which not only has never been solved, but never even been clearly stated.

Life definitely reveals two categories of people—artists and thinkers. Between them is a marked difference. The artists, including all types, as writers, musicians, painters, actors, etc., comprehend reality as a whole, as a continuity, a complete living reality, without any divisions, without any separations. The other group, the thinkers, pull it apart, kill it, so to speak, making out of it a temporary skeleton and then only gradually putting it together anew, piecemeal, and thus try to give it life in order that they might also succeed. This difference is especially prominent in the so-called eidetic imagery of children. Here I remember an astonishing case that occurred forty to fifty years ago. In a certain family with an artistic leaning there was a child two or three years old whose parents among other things diverted him and also themselves by giving him to pick over a collection of twenty or thirty photographs of their relatives, writers, artists, etc., naming each one to him. The result was that he called them all correctly. What a general amazement there was when accidentally he also named them correctly, taking them in his hand from the nurse. Evidently in this case the cerebral hemispheres receive the visual stimuli exactly as the variations of intensity of the light in a photographic plate, just as a phonographic record is made from sound. Indeed this is, some may think, a characteristic of all types of artists. Such a whole creation of reality cannot be completely attained by a thinker. This is why it is so exceedingly rare that there is united in one person a great artist and a great thinker. They are usually represented by separate individuals. Of course the average person occupies a middle position.

It seems to me that there are strong physiological reasons, although not entirely convincing, to understand the matter thus. In the artist the activity of the cerebral hemispheres flowing through the whole mass, involve least of all the frontal lobes, concentrating chiefly in the remaining parts; in the thinkers, however, the converse is true.

The total integrity of the higher nervous activity I represent thus. In the higher animals, including man, the first mechanism for the complex correlation of the organism with the surroundings is the neighbouring subcortex with its intricate unconditioned reflexes (our terminology), the instincts, urges, affections, emotions (the usual terminology). These reflexes, i.e. inborn activities, are called out by only a few unconditioned external agents. Hence the limited orientation in the milieu and with it a weak adaptation. The second step in the correlation is made by the cerebral hemispheres, but without the frontal lobes. Here arises with the help of the conditioned connexions, associations, a new principle of activity; the signalisation of a few unconditioned external agents by numberless other agents, constantly analysed and synthesised, making possible an extremely varied orientation in the same milieu and a much greater adaptation. This constitutes a unified signaling system in the animal organism and the primary in the human. In the latter there is added, possibly especially in the frontal lobes, which are not so large in the animal, another system of signalisation, signalling the first system—*speech*, its basis or fundamental components being the kinesthetic stimulations of the speech organs.

Here is introduced a new principle of higher activity (abstraction—and at the same time the generalisation of the multitude of signals of the former system, in its turn again with the analysis and synthesis of these new generalised signals), the principle of the conditioning limitless orientation in the surrounding world and of creating the highest adaptation of the human—science both in the form of a humanitarian empiricism as well as in its specialised form. This second system of signalisation and its organ—the very last attainment in the evolutionary process—should be particularly fragile, supported in the first instance by overflowing inhibition, once it has arisen in the cerebral hemispheres in the primary degrees of hypnosis. Then instead of the usually predominant (in the waking state) function of the second signalising system, there arises the activity of the first system, primarily and more stably as fantasies and day dreaming, but further and more definitely as sleep, dreaming, and drowsiness, freed from the regulating influence of the second system. Hence the chaotic character of this activity depending chiefly upon the emotional influence of the subcortex.

On considering all the above facts, from the physiological point of view it is easy to understand the clinical expression applied to hysteria, destruction of psychical synthesis (Pierre Janet) or splitting of the "inhibition" (Raymond). Instead of a united and equally reciprocating activity of the three above mentioned systems in hysteria we have a continued separation of these systems with a marked disorganisation of the natural and lawful correlations, when in connexion with and in obligatory co-dependence of the work of these systems is the healthy personality, the integrity of our "inhibition".

As a final result, due to the weakness of the cerebral hemispheres in the hysteric there is a continual manifestation in different combinations of three special physiological phenomena: the readiness with which the hypnotic state occurs because even the habitual daily stimulations are ultramaximal and are accompanied by transmarginal overflow of inhibition (paradoxical phase), the extreme fixation and concentration of the nervous processes in separate points of the cortex, thanks to the predominance of the subcortex, and finally the extraordinary intensity and extension of the negative induction, i.e. inhibition in consequence of the reduced positive tonus of the other parts of the cortex.

In conclusion I shall mention the hysterical psychoses, a case (hysterical *puerilism*) which was demonstrated to me. A woman of 40 or more years became ill from shocks arising in her family life. At first the husband was suddenly arrested, and then some time after the husband had returned the child was taken away. After an attack of tetanus with a prolonged paresis she became puerile. She behaved as a child although she did not show general mental, ethical, and social deterioration. Looked at more closely, there is absence only of the more stable and constant accompaniments of our behaviour, the particular movements, words and thoughts, inhibitions which differentiate the adult from the child. Does not our growth consist in that, under the influence of education, of the religions, social, and governmental requirements, we gradually inhibit, restrain ourselves from doing what is not permissible, prohibited by, the above forces? Do we not in the family, with friends, conduct ourselves in all relations otherwise than in different situations? Indeed these are living universal experiments which undoubtedly prove this. Do we not see constantly how a person under the influence of strong emotion, of predominating higher inhibitions, speaks and does that which he would not allow himself to do when undisturbed and which he bitterly regrets when the effect vanishes? And is this not obvious among the intoxicated, where there is a marked exclusion of inhibition, so well expressed in the Russian proverb—to the drunk man the sea is only knee deep?

Does this state pass over into the normal? Perhaps and perhaps not. During youth, according to the psychiatrists, this may linger for hours and days, or may continue longer. In the given case this state was one of relative calmness and satisfaction. Here may act the nervous mechanism described above in the form of escape through illness from the burdens of life, finally becoming an ineradicable habit. But on the other hand, the disturbed, tensed inhibition may irrevocably weaken, vanish.

From the physiological point of view can hysteria in general be treated? Here all depends upon the type of nervous systems. The predominating and most stimulating impression from our work with the conditioned reflexes on dogs is that it can. This opens wide possibilities for the training of the cerebral hemispheres, but of course there is a limit. Once we have an extremely weak type, here in the presence of the exclusive setting of the experiment (as we say in the laboratory) it is possible to improve and regulate the general conditioned reflex activity of the animal but no more. There can be no question of transformation of the type. But as the separate hysterical symptoms, being general physiological reactions with extremely strong stimulations, from the severe shocks of life, are encountered in the more or less strong types, here a complete return to normal is possible; however only when the series of these shocks and extreme tensions do not exceed a limit.

While it is with absorbing interest that one reads the brilliant article of Kretschmer on hysteria, showing a decided inclination of the author toward a physiological conception of the hysterical symptoms, the recent paper of Hoche in the January, 1932, number of the *Deutsche Medizinische*

Wochenschrift produces a strange impression. Really do not contemporary physiological data cast the sligtest ray into the mechanism of hysteria, actually does the clinic and physiology "stand before hysteria as before a closed door"? Oddly enough Hoche's point of view is as follows: Assuming hysterical analgesia and paralysis are the fundamental features of the disease, he asks the advocates of the theory of the pathological force of motives in hysteria, why does not the intense indignation of some of his readers and listeners against his opinion of this theory make them insensitive to pain, as if he gave them a severe electric shock? Then follows another similar instance. Why for example, do people not cure themselves by a strong desire to be rid of their disease, their neuralgia? But here I recall from my student days the following fact, astonishing to me and many others. A young woman underwent a plastic operation on the nose, which had been frightfully disfigured by some process. To the amazement of all present, in the middle of the operation the patient calmly repeated the words said by the surgeon. Evidently she was hardly anesthetised (general narcosis). The same woman attracted attention to herself by the insensitiveness shown during the daily dressings of the operated area. Obviously the intense desire to be free of the disfigurement, probably connected with the sexual emotions, made her insensitive to the trauma of the operation under the influence of the hope and faith in its success. When after the operation, especially at first, the crude and comical artificial nose bitterly, cruelly disillusioned her, the same emotion made her now, on the contrary, very sensitive to every manipulation no matter how carefully performed.

Such cases are not rare in common life nor in history. As their basis one must always consider either, in the strong healthy subject, a complex of intense emotion and overpowering cortical associations under the influence of a dominant negative induction for the rest of the cerebral hemispheres, or, with the weak nervous system, the above described hysterical mechanism.

THE PLACE OF THE CONDITIONED
REFLEX IN PSYCHOLOGY

J. B. WATSON

SINCE the publication 2 years ago of my somewhat impolite papers against current methods in psychology I have felt it incumbent upon me before making further unpleasant remarks to suggest some method which we might *begin* to use in place of introspection. I have found, as you easily might have predicted, that it is one thing to condemn a long-established method, but quite another thing to suggest anything in its place. I wish in my remarks tonight to report what progress has been made in this direction.

Probably the first question you will insist upon my answering is: "Why try to find a substitute for introspection? It is a pretty good method after all and has served us well." Rather than stop at this tempting place to enter into a controversy, I shall call your attention to the naturalness of such a quest on the part of the students of animal psychology. The truth of the matter is that animal psychologists have become somewhat intoxicated with success. Finding that an amoeba will orient more quickly to certain rays of light than to others, and that a blind, anosmic rat can learn to thread its way through a maze, they begin to look at man with a covetous eye: "After all", they argue, "man is an animal; he moves in response to stimuli in his environment, or to the stimuli offered by the displacement of tissue within his own body. Furthermore, he moves in characteristic ways. Why cannot we study his behavior in the same way that we study the behavior of other animals, modifying our methods to suit this new genus?"

We all admit that many problems in the two fields are similar if not identical. This is especially true of sensory problems. All of us alike wish to determine the various groups of stimuli to which our human or infra-human organism will respond; the various amounts of stimulation necessary to produce these responses, and the bodily areas upon which stimuli must impinge in order to be effective.

Now the animal psychologist has met with a certain degree of success in answering such questions. When we contrast animal psychology in 1900 with animal psychology in 1915 we are forced to admire the enormous strides which have been made in defining problems, in evaluation methods, and in refining apparatus. In 1900 we were content to study by crude methods the elementary features of habit formation in a few easily handled vertebrates. 1916 finds us prepared to carry out on animals as low in the scale as the worm far more delicately controlled experiments than were dreamed of in 1900. The present time likewise finds us prepared to undertake upon the higher vertebrates problems in behavior which in 1900 could hardly have been formulated in behavior terminology. In 1900 who thought of comparing visual acuity in different animals by the use of methods as delicate as those we use on the human being? Or who was bold enough then to assert that in a few years' time we should be using methods for studying vision, audition, and habit formation which are more refined than those which have been employed in the study of the human subject? We must admit, I think that, in the infra-human realm, at least, these years of constant effort have given the animal psychologist a right to look with yearning eyes at this proud genus *Homo*, the representatives of which he finds roaming everywhere, eating any kind of food and from almost any hand, and so resistant to climatic changes that only the lightest kind of covering is necessary to keep them in good condition. Such in part are the motives which have led the animal behaviorist to push into gatherings to which he has not been especially invited. Whether we should condemn his enterprising spirit or accept him depends upon how he behaves after admittance. If he can justify his position by deeds, I believe he will be accepted, while possibly not to complete fellowship, at least as an individual who will not bring discredit upon his fellow scientists.

The behaviorist, while meeting not theoretical difficulties in his attempts thus to universalize his methods, does, at the very outset of his studies upon man, meet with very practical ones. In sensory problems when we ask such simple questions as, what is the smallest vibration difference between two tones that will serve as a stimulus to reaction in this particular man, or whether sweet and bitter can be reacted to differently by him, we find that there is no objective method ready at hand for answering them. We know how to employ objective methods in answering such questions with animals. But the animal methods are admittedly slow, and, from the standpoint of the human subject, cumbersome. Some years ago I suggested that we ought to begin to use human subjects in our so-called "discrimination boxes". As might have been surmised, no one took my advice. This was due inpart at least to man's upright position, his size, and I might add, his general unwillingness to work under the conditions which must be maintained in animal experimentation. One can scarcely blame the human subject for objecting to being kept for long stretches of time in a home box, the door to which opens from time to time permitting him to pass to the right or left of a partition, and ultimately to reach one or the other of two differently colored surfaces below which he finds a food trough. That which makes the situation still more humiliating to him is the fact that if he has "backed" the wrong color he receives a stone in the guise of an electric shock, in place of the bread which he seeks.

I suggested this rather hopeless method of investigating the sensory side of human psychology because of the increasing desire on the part of many psychologists to see psychology begin to break away from the traditions which have held her bound hand and foot from the establishment of the first psychological laboratory. I believe that the time is here when the most conservative psychologists are willing to give a lenient hearing to even crude experimentation along lines which may possibly yield an objective approach to sensory problems. This belief has emboldened me to describe briefly our work at Johns Hopkins University upon the *conditioned reflex*.

Conditioned Reflexes

In discussing the subject of conditioned reflexes it is customary to make a distinction between (A) *conditioned secretion reflexes* and (B) *conditioned motor reflexes*. Whether there is any genuine distinction between the two types depends, I think, upon what ultimately will be found to be true about the *modus operandi* of the glands (i.e. whether under such conditions muscular activity is essential to glandular activity or whether control of the glands can be attained independently of the muscles through nervous mechanisms).

A. Conditioned Secretion Reflexes

Before taking up the conditioned motor reflex, with which I am most familiar, I wish briefly to call your attention to one of the most widely known conditioned secretion reflexes, viz., the salivary. The conditioned salivary reflex is well known in this country thanks to the summaries of the researches in Pavlov's laboratory made by Yerkes and Morgulis, and more recently by Morgulis alone. In brief, this method, which has been under experimental control for some eighteen years, depends upon the following fact. If food (or some similar salivating agent) which produces a direct salivary reflex, and, e.g., a flash of light, are offered jointly for a number of times, the light alone will come finally to call out the salivary secretion. To bring this 'reflex' under control it is necessary to fix upon some method for observing the flow of saliva. This is accomplished usually by first making a salivary fistula, and later attaching a glass funnel to the opening of the duct of the gland. The total flow of saliva may then be measured directly or the individual drops registered graphically. The use of food for arousing the direct flow of saliva has proved to be slow and not very satisfactory. Most of the work has been done by using acid (dilute HCl). The acid produces a salivary flow immediately and with great sureness.

The conditioned salivary reflex has at present no very wide sphere of usefulness or applicability. In the first place, it can be used upon but few animals. Up to the present time it has been used largely upon dogs. Even when used upon these animals, the method has very serious limitations. The use of acid for any appreciable time produces stomatitis, according to Bur-makin. This makes it almost impossible to carry out investigations which extend over long periods of time. Unless some strong saliva-producing agent is used, the reflex quickly disappears and cannot easily be reinforced. In its present form the method (which calls for operative treatment of the subject) cannot be used, of course, on man. Dr. Lashley has been making some tests looking towards an extension of the method. He is experimenting with a small disc grooved on one surface, so as to form two concentric but non-communicating chambers (Figure 1). The outer chamber, by means of a

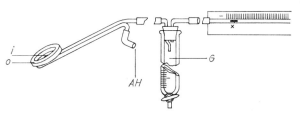

Fig. 1. Apparatus for measuring salivary secretion in man (devised by K. S. Lashley). o, Outer chamber connecting with vacuum pump, through tube at *AH*. When a vacuum is created, the disc clings to the inner surface of the cheek. i, inner chamber which is placed over opening of parotid gland. Saliva flows into graduated flask *G* where the total flow of saliva can be measured. Another system of measurement is offered by reason of the fact that when a drop of saliva falls into *G*, air is forced out through a second opening in the flask. When a slender glass tube containing a drop of mercury is attached to this opening, the mercury drop is forced forward a short distance at each drop of saliva. A suitable scale placed behind the glass rod enables one to read and record the number of drops of saliva which fall during any part of the total reaction. (*Sialometer* is an appropriate name for this instrument.)

slender tube, communicates with a vacuum pump. When the air is exhausted the disc will cling to the inner surface of the cheek. The inner chamber, which is placed directly over the opening of the salivary gland, is likewise supplied with a slender tube which passes out through the mouth. The saliva passing out through this tube can be recorded in different ways. It is too early to make any predictions concerning the usefulness of such a method.

Of the possibility of extending investigation to other forms of secretion, little at present can be said. The work of Cannon, Carleson, Crile, and others, has opened our eyes to the extent to which glandular and muscular activity are called into play in the simplest forms of emotional response. The human psychologist has too long subordinated everything to the obtaining of a vocal response from the subject, while the animal psychologist has too long subordinated all to the obtaining of response in the muscles used in loco-motion. Both have failed to work out methods for observing the finer changes that go on in that large class of actions that we call emotional. Until recent years we have been lacking proper indicators of such changes. I believe that the conditioned secretory reflex, in one form or another, can be made useful in these fields.

While recognizing the importance to all psychological students of Pavlov's work on secretion reflexes, our own work has centered around the conditioned motor reflex of Bechterev, since we find for his method an immediate and widespread usefulness.

B. The Conditioned Motor Reflex (Bechterev)

The *conditioned motor reflex*, while familiar in a general way to everyone, has not, so far as I know, engaged the attention of American investigators. This is not surprising in view of the fact that all of the researches have appeared in Russian and in periodicals which are not accessible at present to American students. At least we have not been able to obtain access to a single research publication. The German and French translations of Bechterev's *Objective Psychology* give the method only in the barest outline. Bechterev's summary was the only guide we had in our work at Hopkins.

We may give a few examples from daily life of conditioned *motor* reflexes. In the moving-picture tragedies the suicide of the villain is often shown. Usually the hand only of this unfortunate individual is displayed grasping a revolver which points towards the place where his head ought to be. The sight of the movement of the hammer on the revolver brings out in many spectators the same defensive bodily reaction that the noise of the explosion would call out. Again, we find in persons recently operated upon numerous reactions, such as deep inspirations, cries of pain, pronounced muscular movements, the stimuli to which are the cut and torn tissues themselves. For many days after the disappearance of the noxious stimuli, the reactions will appear at the slightest turn of the subject's body or even at a threat of touching the wound. Similar instances of this can be seen in many chronic cases. In such cases the charitable physician characterizes the patient as having "too great a sensitivity to pain." The patient, however, is not shamming in the ordinary sense: conditioned reflexes have been set up and the subject makes the same profound reactions to ordinary attendant stimuli that he would make to the noxious stimuli themselves†.

For almost a year Dr. Lashley and I have been at work upon the production and control of these reflexes. We are not ready to give any detailed report of the results. Our efforts have been confined rather to the general

---

† I wish I had time here to develop the view that the concept of the conditioned reflex can be used as an explanatory principle in the psychopathology of hysteria and of the various "tics" which appear in so-called normal individuals. It seems to me that hysterical motor manifestations may be looked upon as conditioned reflexes. This would give a *raison d'être* which has hitherto been lacking.

features of the method. We find little in the literature upon such important points as:

1. Technique of method;
2. Subjects upon which the method may be used;
3. Present range of application of method.

1. Technique of Method

As Bechterev's students affirm, we find that a simple way to produce the reflex is to give a sound stimulus in conjunction with a strong electro-tactual stimulus. Bechterev's students use the reflex withdrawal of the foot: the subject sits with the bare foot resting on two metal electrodes. When the *faradic* stimulation is given the foot is jerked up from the metal electrodes. The movements of the foot are recorded graphically upon smoked paper.

We modified this method slightly in our first experiments. We found that the reflex appeared more surely and quickly if the subject lay on his back with his leg raised and supported by a padded rod under the knee. This position leaves the muscles of the lower leg in a more flexible condition. As a further modification we placed one electrode having a large surface under the ball of the foot and a second electrode only one sixteenth of an inch in width under the great toe, and then strapped down the foot across the instep. When the electrical stimulation was given the great toe was raised from the narrow metal strip (toe reflex). This device made the recording of the reflex somewhat easier. While the use of the foot is fairly satisfactory it is inconvenient for general laboratory work. We found that the reflex appears in the finger as readily as in the toe. So satisfactory and convenient is this last method that we have adopted it in all of our later work with human subjects (Figure 2). A bank of keys is provided which enables the experimenter (he is in a different room, of course, from the subject) to give at will the sound of a bell coincidently with the current, or separate from the current.

In beginning work upon any new subject we first sound the bell alone to see if it will directly produce the reflex. We have never yet been able to get the reflex evoked by the bell alone prior to the electro-tactual stimulation. We give next the bell and shock simultaneously for about five trials; then again offer the bell. If the reaction does not appear, we give five more stimulations with the bell and current simultaneously etc. The conditioned reflex makes its appearance at first haltingly, i.e. it will appear once and then disappear. Punishment is then again given. It may next appear twice in succession and again disappear. After a time it begins to appear regularly every time the bell is offered. In the best cases we begin to get a conditioned reflex after fourteen to thirty combined stimulations.

We have found several refractory subjects: subjects in which even the primary reflex will not appear in the toe when the current is strong enough to

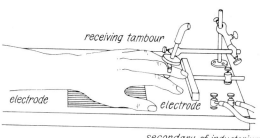

Fig. 2. Method of recording finger movement and of giving faradic stimulation. A large electrode is placed under the hand, and a small electrode under the finger. When key, in the experimenter's room, is pressed down by the operator, the secondary current from the inductorium causes the finger to rise from the small electrode. A receiving tambour, to the face of which a saddle-shaped button has been shellacked, enables a graphic record to be made of such movements

induce perspiration. Whether this is due to atrophy of the toe reflex through the wearing of shoes, or to some other cause, we have never been able to determine. In such cases, however, we can rely upon the breathing which we record simultaneously with the reflex toe or finger movement. The breathing curve is very sensitive and a conditioned reflex appears very plainly upon its tracing.

Some General Characteristics of the Reflex

It is interesting at this point to treat of certain characteristics of the reflex.

First, as regards the similarity and difference between the conditioned reflex and the primary reflex upon which it is grafted. However much they may differ so far as the central nervous pathway is concerned, the general and coarser motor features are closely similar. One watching the movements of a subjcet first beginning to show a conditioned reflex cannot tell whether he is being stimulated by the bell alone or by the bell and punishment combined. The conditioned motor reflex is usually sharp, quick, and widespread, the whole body as a rule being brought into the reaction at first. Gradually, the reflex becomes more circumscribed.

Second, as regards persistence of the reflex; after the reflex has once been thoroughly established it carries over from one day's experiments to the next for an indefinite period. Sometimes a single punishment at the beginning of a day's work is necessary to cause the reflex to make its appearance. We are not able to state over how long a period of time the unexercised reflex will persist. In one case we trained one subject thoroughly in May to the bell, then did not test him again until October. The reflex did not appear on the first ringing of the bell alone, but after the first administration of the combined stimuli (at which the subject disrupted the apparatus although the induction shock was very weak) the conditioned reflex appeared regularly to the bell alone.

Third. We had hoped to make some statements concerning the reaction times of the fundamental and the conditioned reflex. While we are at work upon this problem, we are not ready to make any report as yet.

Fourth. We know that the conditioned motor reflex can be made to undergo reinforcement and inhibition by factors such as those Yerkes has made us so familiar with in his work on the mutual relations of stimuli in the reflex movements of the leg of the frog. A few examples of the role such factors play in the control of the reflex may be of interest. Take first the fatigue of the reflex. A well-trained subject will react regularly for an indefinite period of time to a stimulus given at an interval of 4–5 sec. If now we give the stimulus, i.e., the bell, every 2 sec for a short time, he may react for the first three times and then fail. If the interval is then lengthened, or a rest period introduced, the reflex will again appear. It will be seen later that we utilize this principle of fatigue in setting up differential reactions. Oftentimes before the conditioned reflex is thoroughly set up, it will, after a time, begin to decrease in amplitude. Whether the time is increased is not known. When the reflex is beginning to vanish it can be strengthened in a variety of ways, the most usual way being the introduction of the current, but it can be reinforced also by throwing in simultaneously with the bell some other form of stimulation. I have dwelt at some length upon this subject for fear some might advance the view that the conditioned reflex is nothing more than the so-called "voluntary reaction." The fact, in addition to those cited above, which makes such a view less easily held, is the ease with which the conditioned motor reflex can be set up in animals. The strongest argument against such a point of view is the fact that it apparently can be set up on processes which are presided over by the autonomic system. To test this, we have made a series of experiments having for their object the establishment of a pupillary reflex by the combined stimuli of a very strong light and a sound (bell). We found that the diameter of the pupil under constant illumination with fixation is very steady after the first 5 min; consequently it is possible to make measurements upon the pupil. To ordinary stimulations (sounds, contacts, etc.) there is a slight but not constant change in diameter (at times changes follow evidently upon intra-organic stimulation). But to such stimulation the pupil may respond either by dilation or constriction. In the short time which we had for training subjects we found two individuals in which, after 15–20 min' training, the sound alone would produce a small constriction of the pupil in about 75 per cent of the cases. In two subjects no such reflex could be built up in the time we had to devote to them.

The use of the pupil is thus not very satisfactory: first because it is very difficult to obtain the reflex in it; second, because, due to the fact that we have to induce the fundamental reflex by light, it is not possible to use light as a form of secondary stimulation; and third, because the method is very uncomfortable for the subject. Indeed the long training necessary to produce the reflex in refractory cases would probably be actually injurious to the eyes. Our interest in establishing a conditioned pupil reflex was entirely theoretical.

We have also made one brief attempt to establish the reflex on the heart beat; but on account of the fact that respiratory changes show so markedly on the tracing of the heart, we have been unable to convince ourselves that we have produced a genuine conditioned reflex.

Finally, we had hoped to combine this work with the so-called psychogalvanic reflex in such a way as to produce a method which would yield quantitative results. It seemed a reasonable train of argument to suppose that the sound of an ordinary bell would not cause changes enough in the bodily resistance (or E.M.F.) to produce galvanometric deflections; but on the other hand, that the sound of the bell joined with the faradic stimulation of the foot (punishment) would produce an emotional change sufficient to show. We argued further that if punishment and bell were then given together for a sufficient number of times, the bell alone would come finally to produce bodily changes sufficient to show on the galvanometer and we would thus have our conditioned reflex. The only fault to be found with such a train of reasoning is that it does not work out when put to practical test. In the first place the bell, as we expected, does not produce observable changes (nor do other ordinary stimuli), but, and this was unexpected, neither does the combined stimulus of bell and electric shock. Violent stimulations such as the bursting of an electric light bulb, burning the subject with a cigarette, tickling with a feather, etc., do, in our set-up (which contains no battery), produce anywhere from 10 to 100 mm deflection. Furthermore, the movement of the galvanometer does not start until an appreciable time after the stimulus has been given; sometimes not until 3 or 4 sec afterwards (showing that effect is a glandular change). Another difficulty is that after a deflection has been obtained the original reading of the galvanometer cannot again be duplicated (resistance of the body not going back to the same point). It was largely because of these factors that we temporarily discontinued our experiments in this direction.

Method of Using Reflex to Obtain Differential Reactions

As I have sketched the method of using the conditioned reflex, it is suitable for working out many problems on reinforcement, inhibition, fatigue, intensity of stimulation necessary to call out response under different conditions, etc. The method, however, has a much wider sphere of usefulness. If we take a subject in whom such a reflex is established to a bell or a light, he will react to any sound or light not differing too widely in physical characteristics. By continued training it becomes possible to narrow the range of the stimulus to which the subject will react. For example, if we train on a given mono-

chromatic light, using red until the reflex is well established, and then suddenly exhibit green or yellow, the reflex appears. The sudden throwing in of
the green light will often cause the reflex to fail the next time the red light
is given. We proceed then to differentiate the reflex. As was suggested above
we bring about differentiation by punishment with the positive stimulus
(red in this case) but never with the negative stimulus (green). The second
step in the process of bringing about differentiation consists in exhausting
the reflex to the negative stimulus (using the factor of fatigue). This can
usually be done by giving the negative stimulus four or five times at intervals of about 1–2 sec. After the reaction to the negative stimulus disappears
we 'rest' the subject for a few seconds, and then give the positive stimulus. If this procedure is continued long enough the differential reaction is
finally perfected. The differential reaction can be so highly perfected that
it becomes possible to use it with great accuracy in determining difference
limens on human subjects. So far we have tested it out in the fields of light,
sound, and contact with very encouraging results.

As may readily be seen, this extension of the method gives us the possibility of objectively approaching many of the problems in sensory psychology.
We give no more instruction to our human subjects than we give to our animal subjects. Nor do we care what language our subject speaks or whether
he speaks at all. We are thus enabled to tap certain reservoirs which have
hitherto been tapped only by the introspective method. The data which we
collect in this way, while they have no bearing upon a Wundtian type of
psychology, serve (as far as they go) every practical and scientific need of a
truly functional psychology.

2. Subjects upon Which the Method May be Used

The range of subjects upon which the motor reflex method may be used
is wide. We have tried it out in all upon eleven human subjects, one dog
and seven chickens. The adult human subjects used were chosen largely,
but not wholly, from among the graduate student sof psychology and biology.
Three of the subjects used had never had any psychological training. As
might be expected, the ease with which the method may be used is not dependent upon the previous psychological training of the subject. We give
the subjects no instructions or explanations of the purport of the experiment.
It is unreasonable to suppose, however, that the adult psychologically trained subjects do not get drift of what is expected of them as the experiment
proceeds. Whether the bodily set or emotion which results from this plays any
role in the ease with which the reaction may be obtained has not been determined. On the whole I am inclined to think now that students of physics
will prove to be our best subjects since they have been trained to make fine
observations of small differences in physical stimuli, without at the same

time trying to make crude observations of the stimulations arising from the laryngeal or other vocal organs.

Since we began to use the finger in place of the toe we have had only one subject fail to show the conditioned reflex (a graduate student of psychology). This subject also failed to give the conditioned toe reflex. We failed to obtain the great toe reflex (conditioned) upon one other subject, when we first began our work early in the year. We have had not an opportunity of retesting this individual with the finger reflex.

Whether the method can be used widely with children has not been determined. In the course of 20 min we obtained the reflex several times upon an 8-year-old boy. When first punished he cried and showed some reluctancy toward having the experiment continue. One of the experimenters then sat in the room with him, and, under promise of a moving picture show after the experiment, the series was completed with smiling fortitude. When once we get the reflex established thoroughly to the bell, our troubles with children ought to be over, since we can proceed to build up second-order reflexes, i.e., the bell may be used in place of the electric shock.

Much to our regret we have not been able during the year, to find time to try the method out in pathological cases. We hope that during the coming year we may be able to try the method out thoroughly, especially upon cases to which language methods are not applicable.

3. Present Range of Applicability of Method

At the expense of possible repetition I shall enumerate some of the uses to which the method may be immediately applied.

(1) To all forms of experimentation on light, size, form, visual acuity, etc. It is apparently the only method which will enable us to study visual after-images in animals.

(2) It is apparently the only existing method of testing auditory acuity, differential sensitivity to pitch, range of pitch, timbre, etc., in any reasonable length of time.

(3) It affords us, by reason of the fact that the stimuli may be given serially, a method of testing the role of olfaction. We know nothing now concerning olfactory acuity, differential sensitivity to olfactory stimuli, classification of stimuli, the effect of such stimuli on the emotional life of the animal, etc. Nor is it very feasible to carry out such experiments by the discrimination method.

(4) The method gives a reliable means of testing sensitivity to temperature and to contact and to the fineness of localization of such stimuli—factors which likewise cannot be determined by methods now in use.

When we recall that the reflex method can be used upon man, without modification, in solving many of the above and similar sensory problems,

we must admit, I believe, that it will take a very important place among
psychological methods. It may be argued, however, that this method is
useful only in yielding results upon very simple sensory problems. Although
I cannot here enter into the wider applications of the method, I am sure that
its field will be a larger and wider one than I have indicated. I feel reasonably
sure that it can be used in experimentation upon memory, and in the so-
called association reaction work, and in determining the integrity of the
sensory life of individuals who either have no spoken language or who are
unable for one reason or another to use words—I have in mind deaf and
dumb individuals, aphasics, and dementia praecox patients of the "shut in"
type. If indications can be trusted the method ought to yield some valuable
results on the localization and method of functioning of the various neural
pathways.

In conclusion, I must confess to a bias in favor of this method. Time may
show that I have been over-enthusiastic about it. Certainly I have attempted here to evaluate a method which possibly cannot be evaluated properly
until many investigators have had opportunity to subject it to prolonged
tests.

5

THE FUTURE OF PSYCHIATRY†

W. Horsley Gantt

Pavlov's Contributions

THE success of Pavlov rests upon his powers of observation, his ability to formulate clearcut questions to Nature and to design appropriate experiments to answer them, his skill as a surgeon and his physiological intuition, his boldness in establishing definite theories on the basis of the laboratory facts, and his willingness to relinquish these theories in the face of new data.

Pavlov was not a philosopher. He was not concerned with problems of the universe nor of the spirit. At the same time Pavlov was emphatic in not denying the importance of art in all its forms, human aspirations, and religion. But he did not think the methods of science at a time when there was much confusion relating to the highest and most complex phenomenon that we know—our subjective and psychic life. And this confusion persists today!

Pavlov devised a method to measure quantitatively an aspect of the higher nervous activity. This he did through the use of the salivary conditional reflex. From the laboratory data he formulated laws, not appreciated or understood, but which are being confirmed today by neuro- and electrophysiology. Objections were made to his idea that excitatory and inhibitory processes spread through the brain (irradiation and concentration) in a matter of minutes. Physiology did not know of so low a movement in the nervous system. But Evarts this morning reported an effect lasting some seconds after the stimulus, in the "evoked potentials".

Pavlov described the orienting reflex—a response to a novel stimulus. This reaction is only now beginning to be understood and worked on. During Pavlov's lifetime, only six articles were listed in the bibliography from his laboratory on the subject, and I do not know of others until quite recently. Our research and that of others on the orienting response is the basis for learning and indicates that it plays a prominent role in characterizing personality and the status of the psychiatric patient. Robinson in my laboratory was the first to report that the orienting response has a definite car-

† By permission of Grune & Stratton, Inc., New York, from: The Future of Psychiatry, by H. Gantt, New York 1962 pp. 93–102.

diac component. Grastyán from Hungary, who was in Magoun's laboratory, reported that the hippocampus is responsible for the inhibition of the orienting response, viz., for the adaptive function of this response.

Pavlov recognized differences in the reactivity of his dogs which he classified into the four temperaments of Hippocrates. The normal animals occupied a central position of increased or decreased reactivity—the sanguine and the phlegmatic. The two pathologic groups of choleric and melancholic corresponded to manic and depressive patients. Recently Krasutsky in Chernigovsky's laboratory in Leningrad has defined types more clearly through the use of reaction to drugs and exploration of genetic factors which may be obscured by the acquired responses to the human through experience. And psychiatrists in Kiev have been able to predict and prevent manic psychoses through biochemical studies. Along these lines lies the promise of a real preventive psychiatry.

One aspect of Pavlov's work has been unfortunately almost completely neglected both in Russia and abroad, viz., the social factor. Of course social influences have been observed by many psychiatrists, e.g. in the excellent articles of Dr. C. Michailová in Prague, and in the report of Dr. Rioch this morning. Pavlov's observations outlined a fruitful field for experimental work which has gone unnoticed by both his pupils and others.

In the 1920's Pavlov noted that certain dogs were greatly influenced by the person who worked with them. He thought that this relation held only for a given type of dog, those having the guarding instinct as in the police types, and with those people who were especially authoritative toward the dog. He could reproduce the effect through putting some of the experimenter's clothing in the room with the dog.

Owing to lack of a delicate measure for the effect of one individual on another, Pavlov had to rely only on gross motor behavioral changes. But by the use of the very delicate cardiovascular response, we have shown that this is a function of all dogs, and even a function omnipresent throughout Nature. Though perhaps more definite in certain dogs it is by no means confined to them. Our results will be mentioned later.

The experimental neurosis was produced in Pavlov's laboratory, at first accidentally, by what he called the collision of the excitatory and inhibitory processes. Since then here and abroad frustrating episodes have been used to produce neurotic behavior. Many factors are operative in addition to that of the difficulty of sensory discrimination. Pavlov, during the last decade of his life when he began to take up the study of the psychiatric patient, mphasized what he considered a chief difference between the human and other animals was the existence of the language function. This he called the second signalling system, a new development in Nature. Language represented a higher order of conditional reflexes; words became the signals of primary signals. The relationships in this system add a tremendous complexity to the conditional reflexes, and present a liability for disturbance as well as the basis for the special human achievement—his brilliant successes and his tragic failures.

Between the ages of 80 and 86, during the last 6 years of his life, Pavlov attempted to apply his laboratory findings to the clinic, explaining schizophrenia and paranoia by what he saw in his dogs. Noting that paranoias had been described as homosexual, he saw that in castrated dogs the conditional reflexes once formed were very stable and showed a difficulty in adaptation.

Some of the pupils of Pavlov, notably Bykov, have shown that many of the functions of the viscera as well as of the endocrine glands and metabolic processes, can be conditioned, e.g. urinary secretion, biliary formation, thermal control, egg production. Thus the viscera participate in the adaptation to the external and the internal environments. In the last two decades we have made a special study of the cardiac conditional reflex in several animals—penguin, opossum, dog, as well as in the human. In spite of Pavlov's early recognition of the importance of the cardiovascular system in acquired responses, he never used it as a measure of the conditional reflex because of its multitudinous connections with other bodily functions, and hence little work was done in this area. Since 1940 we have made a systematic study of the participation of the cardiovascular system in the life experiences of the individual.

We were at first impressed by the parallel between the cardiac and the salivary changes in the excitatory as well as in the inhibitory conditional reflexes. They seemed to obey the same laws and to be parallel in their quantitative relationships. Furthermore, owing to the sensitivity of the cardiovascular system, these responses revealed inner mechanisms not evident in the secretory or in the motor conditional reflexes.

The cardiac conditional reflex forms much quicker than the specific motor or salivary components of both the pain and the food reflexes, often after one experience (reinforcement of the conditional stimulus by the unconditional stimulus, e.g. one instance of bell and the food), while the movement or the appearance of the secretion to the bell may require 30–100 reinforcements. Paradoxically, the disappearance of the cardiac conditional reflex may occur much later than the loss of the salivary or of the motor conditional reflexes. The heart rate conditional reflex is not only not lost by the passage of time, but it may not be possible to extinguish it as can be done with the other conditional reflexes by repeating the conditional stimulus without the unconditional stimulus, e.g. the bell without the food. In some dogs the acquired cardiac responses may last for 8 or more years after the other components have dropped out. This split in function is what we call *schizokinesis*. Though it is revealed by the cardiac conditional reflex, it represents in my view an innate lack of adaptability in the organism evident in the cardiovascular function by extension to other organs. It is the opposite to the function of perfect adaptation and balance described by Claude

Bernard as maintenance of a constant *milieu intérieur* and by Cannon as homeostasis.

This rigidity of the cardiovascular system—and to some extent of the respiratory system—may be responsible for the persistence of blood pressure changes to the traces of old emotional stimuli and situations, long after their occurrence and even when they are forgotten. Externally the body may appear calm and unperturbed, while internally, as seen in the blood pressure and heart rate, there may be violent agitation. Dr. Hohman and some other psychiatrists share my view that schizokinesis is an important feature in the development of behavior disturbances.

The cardiovascular system does not always correspond to the statement of the poet:

> And if the wine you drink, the lips you press,
> End in what all begins and ends in yes,
> Think then that yesterday you were not more,
> *Tomorow you will not be less.*

But this contemplative adaptation may not be attainable. With the philosophizing facility of the highest cortical processes, one may forget his reverses, but with his visceral processes he fortunately or unfortunately remembers; his heart keeps beating to the old rhythm. Closer to the physiology of the cardiac conditional reflex are the words of another poet: "The heart that has loved never forgets, but as truly loves on to the end."

Pascal stated a physiologic truth we see revealed today: "The heart has reasons that reason knows not of."

The heart remembers and reacts in the absence of momevents or even conscious memory. The teaching of Freud about the "unconscious" and of Kubie in the concept of the "preconscious" may be relevant here.

Other functions of importance for psychiatry have to do with the development and elaboration of processes in the nervous system on the basis of past experiences but in the absence of repetition of the situations. This may be in a positive, curative direction, as when a patient continues to improve after brief psychotherapy, or in a negative elaborated on the basis of old experiences but also without their repetition. The reinforcement is internal.

The experimental evidence for this function has appeared frequently in our work, but space does not permit to summarize it here. The development of new symptoms in the dog Nick over three or four years after experimentation was discontinued is an example. It has been fully reported in my *Experimental Basis for Neurotic Behavior*. Examples also are many in Nature, as in the development of plants from seeds, of the adult from a fertilized ovum. New relationships may be formed within the nervous system, such as we get in external-internal relationships in learning. There may be internal learning. That new connections can be formed between nerve centers is against current neurologic concepts, but the recent work of Jerzy Rose demonstrates the possibility of new anatomic connections in the cortex after damage by radiation.

This function of development of new functional connections on the basis of old experiences in their absence, as well as a wider range of similar phenomena is what I call *autokinesis*.

We have shown that the conditioning process is primarily a central phenomenon and that the periphery plays a minor role. That the cardiac conditional reflex is due to central excitation and not muscular tension is proven by many experiments in our laboratory, e.g. the persistence of heart rate and blood pressure in the conditional reflexes undiminished after paralysis by crushing anterior nerve roots, use of curare, and when the dog is standing perfectly quietly (work of Newton, Stephens, Dykman, Cruet, Royer).

A potent factor in both normal and abnormal behavior is, as I have mentioned earlier, the social one. This we have investigated through the study of the influence of one individual on another using the heart rate as a measure. We have referred to this as "social factor" or "effect of person."

The dog is an especially favorable subject to reveal the effect of person because (1) of his very responsive and labile cardiovascular system, and (2) because of his special relationship to the human being.

The presence of the experimenter can be conditioned in a dog as shown by the heart rate. This effect depends upon what the person is doing, whether standing before the dog or petting him. In nearly all dogs tactile stimulation of rubbing behind the ears causes a marked deceleration. In a catatonic dog, V_3, the heart rate has dropped from 165 (dog alone) to 20 when the experimenter is sitting near the dog; on another occasion the heart ceased beating for 8 sec and the blood pressure dropped from 140 to 70 (Newton and Royer).

Also in normal dogs the presence of the person in the room may obscure the effect of a strong conditional reflex, e.g. of the bell in producing the food reflex. And if two conditional stimuli are presented simultaneously—a conditional stimulus for the presence of the person though the person is actually absent, and the conditional stimulus for food—the dog may react to the signal for the person and not to the signal for the food (Royer).

The person dissipates anxiety when he is petting the dog. G. H. Lewes about 100 years ago in his *Physiology of Everyday Life* spoke of food as the prime mover of the human and other animals. Today we see that the influence of person is ordinarily much greater than the desire of food. Even during famines, human cannibalism is rare; while millions of people were starving in Russia in 1920–21, there were only a few isolated instances.

It is interesting that in the nineteenth century before science had conquered Nature as it has today, in the period of materialistic theories such as of Malthus the emphasis was on food, the chief goal, whereas today we recognize the greater potency of the social factor. Even though material things may seem to be the most important, usually their power rests on the value given to them by society rather than the intrinsic stimulating quality. The chromium on the car, the price label, and even the thought of the food itself is often more closely related to the effect of person than to the unconditional stimulus value of the food. For example, even dogs will often starve before eating their kind.

It would be interesting to hear from Dr. Ogden Lindsley, who was a war prisoner in Germany on very short rations, about the relative values of food and of the effect of person. From his statement to me, that after catching a German chicken, when his weight was reduced from 180 to 120 lb he divided the chicken among twenty comrades, would seem to answer the relative strength of the food and social factors, even in a semi-starved person. We have, of course, to allow for the orientation and special character of Dr. Lindsley.

The "effect of person", the social factor of one individual on another, is universal probably throughout the whole animal kingdom. It rests upon an innate, unlearned response, though the life experiences may add to and complicate the inborn response.

In the application of the principle to the human, Pavlov (as well as some psychiatrists) invoked the idea of what he called the paradoxical phases, viz. of the reversal of the usual effect of the conditional reflex when the situation is changed from normal to a very difficult emotional one. This law seems to explain some abnormal behavior, as pointed out by Sargant, Leo Alexander, Fabing.

For a few moments I would like to move into the field of the higher criticism with Dr. Rioch. I shall comment on only one aspect of his fascinating and informative report here. What I have to say should not obscure my respect for his wisdom, his philosophy, nor my indebtedness to his advice to me through the years.

I refer to his comparisons of the brain to physical systems, e.g. that the forebrain acts as an analog rather than a digital computer† and the handling of "information" by the nervous system.

I think Dr. Rioch is by no means a mechanist and that he has spoken against the so-called mechanistic point of view.

In a former generation the brain was compared to a telephone system, the conditional reflex, to the making of telephone connections. This view has been derided as naive and mechanistic. (Pavlov has been donned a mechanist, though he used very sparingly any analogies to machines.)

Mechanisms in Different Eras

In the nineteenth century the connections in the brain were compared to telephone switches, in the twentieth century we have advanced by gradual steps through electronics into the highest forms of calculating machines.

---

† Another expert, Dr. Warren McCulloch, tells me he doubts wether the forebrain acts like an analog computer.

The comparisons have kept pace with the advance of the mechanistic devices.

But is the principle any different from what we had before? Up until the beginning of the twentieth century, the telephone was the highest kind of mechanism for comparison that we knew of. Now with the advance of our knowledge concerning machines we adjust the comparison accordingly—to fit the most complex machines with which we are acquainted. In previous generations, physical systems were also invoked to compare with or explain human action—the humors of the blood, astrology. But is this process other than adorning the old manikin in new clothes to keep in style? Are we any the less mechanistic than were our peers of a previous era?

This process of keeping up with the Joneses has been followed also by our psychiatric patients.† In times past they were in league with the Devil, their preoccupations were voices from God, then it became the radio which was directing them, and now it is radioactive dust—or in the case of a former professor of psychiatry the isotopes of cobalt were scattered in his shoes by the FBI.

I am not against the use of mechanistic analogies as long as we do not *equate* the inanimate mechanism with the living process. There may be some aid in comparing the organism with a machine, but let us not fool ourselves that because the dress is modern the manikin is any different.

I do not deny the value of making physical analogies as long as we recognize them for what they are, as very superficial and imperfect explanations. Nor do I negate the fact that the living organism does not contradict any law of Nature found for physical systems. But the organism employs its own methods, and it seems to me that the total behavior of even simple organisms invokes principles different from any conceivable machine. The myriad integrations are beyound our comprehension of a machine, though perhaps any one of them may be similar to what we see outside of living protoplasm. Science may unravel any single mechanism, but the integration of all into a homeostatic system, is a living function. Schizokinesis, important as it is, is only an exception to the successful integration.

In the twenty first century, the mechanism which we use for comparison with the living processes may be the antigravitational forces of the expanding universe or the reverse curves of saddle shaped space. These may satisfy the mode of the new era, but will they be any less mechanistic?

The characteristics of an investigator, of a true seeker after knowledge in the experimental sciences, must remain the same now as in the past. First there is the keen power of observation, the perception and collection of facts. Pavlov considered this so important that he had placed above the new laboratory in Koltushi the words "Observation and Observation". Secondly, one should strive toward some kind of appropriate method of quantitative

† I am endebted to Dr. Leo Alexander for this simile.

measurement in units that are universally recognizable by trained observers.

The question of what to measure is a crucial one requiring intuition and
careful judgment. Often, it is less important what we measure than the precision of the measurement; the various measurements may be only different
aspects of the same underlying reality. One or another of these aspects may
provide special advantages. Thus for light, you may measure its wavelength,
its thermal properties, its brightness, or its potential energy; they are all
aspects of the same thing.

After the facts have been collected and measured by an appropriate
method, the ability of the investigator is required to see from them a governing law. Previous to the establishment of a law, a theory has to be proposed
to test the validity of the investigator's suppositions.

Science depends for its progress, fortunately, upon a few brave young men
somewhere, crazy enough not to be discouraged by criticisms or dogmata,
not afraid to be out of style with whatever is current—reflexology, electronics, cybernetics, feedback, games and computers, biochemical paradigms
or obscure complexes. It depends on those who, by careful observation and
resolved thinking, are willing to collect new facts, throw them into the hop-
per, come out what will—who have a sense of humility, respect, and understanding of the work of others and of the scientific achievements of the past,
upon which foundation these new seekers after knowledge must build.

6

THE SIGNIFICANCE OF NEUROPHYSIO-
LOGICAL TERMS FOR PSYCHOPATHOLOGY

S. A. Sarkisov, F. V. Bassin and V. M. Banstchikov

Now we proceed to the next great problem wich, in terms of methodology, is especially important for psychiatry. This is the question in which way and to what extent the main theoretical conceptions of Pavlovian doctrine influence modern psychopathology.

In the foreign literature, one can often find the opinion that by introducing into neurophysiology terms such as "feed back" or "comparison" (of the actual and the expected effect of function), regulation on the basis of the "probability prognosis", information content and codification of signals, such classical terms as "temporary connection", "conditioning", "signal meaning" of a stimulus, and so on must be gradually superseded. Critics of the Pavlovian doctrine claim that such a development would be unavoidable, because the classical terms are more "global" and less logically exact than the conceptions which arose later, and which are more differentiated and nearer to the ideas of the modern cybernetics, mathematics, and biophysics. This objection is especially emphasized when the application is discussed of Pavlovian terms to the phenomena of pathological derangement of the most complex forms of psychical activity such as consciousness. Critics have pointed out that the interpretation in terms of the Pavlovian school of such psychopathological phenomena as catatonic stupor, hallucinations, hypochondriacal sensations, obsessional symptoms, amnestic disturbance of consciousness, and so on, disregards obvious differences in the clinical picture. According to the classical theory in physiology, the nervous mechanisms underlying these different psychopathological phenomena are assumed to be one and the same—an increase in the processes of inhibition.

Therefore, these critics believe that the mechanisms postulated by Pavlovian doctrine are insufficient to explain the qualitative differences between psychopathological phenomena, and that the theoretical categories it describes are not differentiated enough to accomodate the real causes of the polymorphic pictures observed in the psychiatric clinic. And some of our ideological opponents claim that in many other fields there is a similar inadequacy of Pavlovian categories to explain clinical phenomena.

What can be answered to such objections? Here, we think it would be useful to point out some philosophical statements which are important in the correct application of physiological terms in psychopathology.

Most probably, protective inhibition and other non-specific changes in the functional state of nerve centres postulated by the theory of higher nervous activity, can develop accompanying psychopathological symptoms of completely different aetiology and character. But does this justify the conclusion that these non-specific physiological changes, just because of their frequent occurrence, thereby loose any importance in explaining features of psychological disturbance? Such a conclusion would be completely unfounded.

In the first place, in investigating any pathophysiological or psychopathological phenomenon, we shall find effects caused by specific factors (i.e. with respect to aetiology, pathogenesis and dynamics) and others caused by more general factors. Factors of the second type are no less important than specific factors in revealing the nature of the phenomena under study. But we must clearly distinguish which parts of the phenomena in question may be caused by one or the other. To assume that the non-specific factors could give a complete explanation of the specific features of any psychopathological syndrome would be as serious a methodological mistake as to disregard the general, nonspecific background on which the observed changes occur.

Here we are touching on the problem of which factors determine the psychical function, a question prominently treated in our philosophical literature. For the moment, we only wish to explain why the physiological factors must appear as non-specific ones if the problem of the determinants of psychological activity is treated on the basis of dialectical materialism.

We have already mentioned that we consider the Pavlovian doctrine a strict example of the dialectical materialistic approach in biology. This means that the Pavlovian approach to the phenomenon of consciousness as a function of the brain does not veil the fact that each conscious act is a phenomenon determined by social factors. These have arisen on the basis of such results of historical social development as labour, generalization, and language, and in this respect are indirectly based on the whole prehistory of mankind.

Nevertheless, the dialectical materialistic conception of the nature of consciousness does not exist merely of the assumption of its social origin.

From the standpoint of Marxism–Leninism, it is important to understand that conscious perception of external reality by a subject is in no way similar to the passive process of reflection in a mirror. This fact was especially stressed by V. I. Lenin. Each conscious act arising only because man separates himself from the surrounding objective world, is possible only by the existence of a defined relationship between the perceiving subject and the world of objects, and consequently by the inseparable connection between consciousness and this relationship. In this respect, we must return to the basic statement of Karl Marx—"My consciousness, this is my relation to my surroundings"—where he stated the really vital characteristic of consciousness. This is its fusion with the totality of all concrete needs and motives of the social life of man and, consequently, the unvoidable, principal, permanent *causal dependence* of consciousness on the world of objects, social needs, and motives.

These classical philosophical statements are decisive for a methodologically correct understanding of the characteristic role which physiological factors play in explaining normal psychological processes as well as the pathogenesis of psychopathological syndromes. According to the dialectical materialistic approach, each psychological process independent of its character, modality, origin and content, *is produced by brain mechanisms and only by these*. But the underlying causes, which in an analysis of this process prove to be its moving forces, on which it "depends", are connected *not only with the brain, but also with different extracerebral influences and, in addition, with factors of social environment*. From our point of view, this fact is of principal importance.

On this basis, it becomes clear that everything said on the "general character" of the Pavlovian categories concerns the philosophically adequate application of physiological terms to the process of revealing the nature of consciousness. Because each act of consciousness is determined by cerebral, as well as by social factors, and because no act of consciousness is determined by physiological factors alone, it is impossible to "reduce" consciousness to its physiological basis. Consciousness is realized only by the brain, but its nature may not be explained *only on the basis of physiology*. Hence physiological terms, applied to a causal analysis of consciousness, may only be explaining categories of a "general" character, *without giving informations which could sufficiently explain the social features of consciousness*. This is valid for the theoretical categories elaborated by the Pavlovian school, as well as for any other physiological terms which are adequately applied in the philosophical sense.

From all this we must reject the assumption that the classical Pavlovian categories, owing to their general "global" character, would be inappropriate for revealing the nature of consciousness. But we must also consider that other, essentially more serious, critical remarks are made against the legitimate application of these categories. These critics not only emphasize their general character, but claim an incompatibility between the laws and mechanisms of brain function, established on the basis of the classical Pavlovian doctrine, and newer methodical approaches and terms. We shall consider these arguments later. Now we wish to discuss these views in more detail in connection with questions of psychopathology.

The philosophy of dialectical materialism has shown that it is impossible to "reduce" normal consciousness to its physiological basis and therefore that the explanatory role of physiological terms in the theory of consciousness is principally restricted. But what about cases in which consciousness is deranged by pathological processes within the brain? Are not cerebral (pathophysiological, biochemical, and so on) processes decisive under these clinical conditions in explaining, all features of the psychopathological syndrome? May not the derangement of consciousness in such case (unlike the origin of consciousness) be completely "reduced" to its physiological basis? May not the relationship between the "cerebral" and "social" factors in the pathology of consciousness be qualitatively different from their relationship during development and in the normal activity of consciousness. May not, therefore, cerebral factors have an essentially greater explanatory value under clinical conditions than in normal cases?

These aggressively formulated questions, which sometimes appear in the literature, require principal answering.

It is beyond doubt that a pathophysiological cerebral process, depending on its character, localization, and so on, may produce defined psychological changes. In these cases, it is the immediate and specific cause of these changes. But does the structure of the psychopathological syndromes consist only in the immediate expression of this cerebral process? Is it not essentially more intricate? Besides the immediate "primary" symptoms of cerebral destruction, there are factors which originate in the "reaction of the personality" to these primary changes. Of course, each of these secondary, reactive components of the psychopathological syndrome, like the primary changes, *is realized by cerebral mechanisms and only by these.* When we ask about the determinants and causal conditions, i.e. what they "depend" on, then we must return to the question we have already analyzed above relating to the theory of normal consciousness. Normal consciousness is realized by brain only; but it may not be "reduced" to its physiological basis, because other factors participate in its origin and in its determination. This general scheme, formulated by the philosophy of dialectical materialism, has universal validity, and we cannot disregard it if we are dealing with clinical problems. The psychopathological syndrome originates on the basis of a cerebral process. Each of its components is realized by cerebral mechanisms. Among these components are some which are only determined by cerebral factors, and others where, owing to the social nature of every act of consciousness, their determination is much more intricate — sometimes deeply rooted in the system of highly developed social needs and motives.

This interpretation reminds us that even in the most advanced cases of psychological derangement, the social character of the remaining elements of consciousness does not disappear. *Even though diminishing more and more consciousness does not cease to be a "relationship"* (in the sense used by

Karl Marx). This assumption demonstrates the great humanism contained in the dialectical materialistic approach to the problem of psychological derangement. It requires that even in the most deranged psychiatric patient, we should see above all the human being. It also acknowledges that in psychopathology, as in psychology, it is impossible to "reduce" the phenomena of consciousness to their physiological basis.

But the interpretation of the general, non-specific character of the physiological factors, as determinants of consciousness, does not only result from philosophical premises. It is also emphasized by the results of modern psychopharmacology.

It is well known that every substance injected into the blood finally affects the fundamental nervous processes. Therefore, during treatment, the psychopathological syndrome depends on the dynamics of the fundamental nervous processes. But this dependence is intricately mediated by many additional factors, which are connected with the functional organization of single neurones, with the individual history of the particular brain system in question and with the "traces" accumulated during the individual's development. For that reason, there is the remarcable fact, whose significance was stressed by Rochlin (1962) that an antagonistic therapeutic effect from psychopharmacological substances is not caused in every case by great differences in the chemical structure of these agents. For instance, the general sedative effect of the phenothiazine derivatives does not exclude profound differences between the clinical effects of the various agents of this group, although the chemical formulae of these substances remains essentially similar.

Here we do not wish to touch upon the very difficult question to what extent these differentiated relationships between the chemical structures of psychopharmacological substances and their therapeutic effects may indicate that these substances change only definite syndromes, and not nosological characteristics. Such an analysis would lead us away from the fundamental question treated here. These psychopharmacological experiences confirm our previous statement that in explaining the dynamics of both the normal and the pathologically changed consciousness, we must consider not only physiological, but also many other factors. Therefore we can by no means regard the physiological categories as factors which may explain *all* features of consciousness completely.

We have outlined how to solve the question of what significance physiological terms have in psychopathology when we approach this problem from the methodological position of Pavlovian doctrine. Leaving these positions, one naturally comes to a completely different interpretation of the importance of physiology for psychiatry and to a completely different interpretation of the relationship between the cerebral, extracerebral and social factors in psychosis. We shall now outline this alternative (and we may really call it an "alternative"!) to the Pavlovian approach in a little more detail.

We shall do so, analysing the address by Henri Ey during the 1961 International Congress of Psychiatry in Montreal. The considerations set forth in this speech are typical in many respects.

On the fundamental question of the essential nature of psychological derangement, Henri Ey, a distinguished psychiatrist of Western Europe chooses an eclectic approach, which at first sight might seem to be a genuinely broad one. According to him psychological derangement simultaneously represents the totality of disturbances caused by lesions in defined brain systems, changes in the ability to adapt to environmental conditions, the appearance of degradation symptoms in psychological processes, which are followed by disturbances in the basis of existence itself (the "mode of existence"), in the basis of perception and in the reactability of the psychiatric patient. To understand the very intricate picture of psychological derangement arising in this way, Ey regarded it as necessary to use different methods. He admits the phenomenological approach, looking at the psychopathological phenomenon as a type of "symbolic expression", behind which the real experiences are veiled. He admits also the existential, i.e. deeply irrational approach to the psychopathological phenomena, based on the theories and methods of "hermeneutics" which were developed by Heidegger, Binswanger, Wyrsch, Sartre, and others. He includes the psychoanalytical schema, according to which the "unconscious" dominates the consciousness, thus replacing the normal connections of the subject with the external world by symbolizations and internal connections of an intrasubjective type, with an analysis of the disturbances of conditioning and of behavioural stereotypes. He regards it as equally important to study the effects of local cerebral damage, to investigate the appearance of laws of gestalt psychology in the picture of psychological derangement and to analyse the influence of "interpersonal" social factors on psychiatric illness.

Such an eclectic joining of different methodological points of view and types of investigation sometimes even excluding one another, only imitates richness and flexibility of interpretation. In reality, it unmasks the great inconsistency of the whole theoretical construct.

It is highly characteristic that Ey does not even ask the question how the results of these different approaches can be brought together to the problem of psychosis, assuming that they are realized in any way during the investigation (or "empathy"). He does not in the least reveal how it would be possible to relate, for example, the results of the phenomenological analysis of schizophrenic symptoms to the results obtained by investigating disintegrated conditioned dynamic stereotypes. Or how to combine the existential approach, which denies every rational understanding, with the acknowledgement of the cerebral causation of psychological derangements, and so on. And this is in no way the result of any intellectual negligence in the way these ideas were proposed by Ey.

One cannot assume that Ey, who is certainly a penetrating thinker, does not apprehend, that the lack of a method to introduce such a synthesis involves one of the most dangerous viewpoints which can arise during scientific work – that it will be impossible to generalize the results obtained by the different analytical procedures. Obviously, it is impossible that Ey does not see this situation. Therefore, if he still puts these qualitatively different approaches side by side without raising the fundamental question of how to combine the results obtained by their different methods, then this must have significant causes. Let us try to analyze these causes now.

Why does the question which we regard as fundamental not exist at all for Ey, i.e. analysis of the relationship between the results obtained by approaching the psychopathological structure as a phenomenon which is caused by cerebral as well as social factors? To what final conclusions must one come on the nature of psychosis, when as many different types of psychosis as methods of investigation have been used?

When Ey would put at the head of his schema a question on the integration of results obtained by different methods of psychiatric research which he favours, then he must logically raise also the question of the relationship between the different factors determining the development and derangement of consciousness, and particularly of the relationship between cerebral and social factors. But one cannot deal with the last problem while disregarding the question of which psychopathological phenomena depend on one or the other oft he two factors, and so on. In other words, when Ey does not restrict himself to the mere enumeration of psychopathological syndromes, and would proceed to an analysis of the connections existing between them and to a description of the hierarchy of their interrelations, then this would mean a radical break with eclecticism, and a change to a viewpoint which in its development would lead him to positions very near to those held by modern soviet psychiatry, oriented to Pavlovian doctrine.†
But this is impossible while remaining within the framework of those general psychiatric conceptions which Ey relies on. Indeed, he does not even regard it as a deficiency of his general interpretation that is is impossible to determine from it the inner connections between, for example, the existentialist conception of the nature of schizophrenic derangement and the conception based on the study of the higher nervous activity of the schizophrenic patients. Rather, he appears to regard it as completely impossible to combine such different aspects of philosophy and supposes that according to the nature of the things, a synthesis would be primarily inaccessible.

† In this connection, not to complicate the logic of the discussion, we disregard an evaluation of the different methods used by H. Ey. It does not seem necessary to stress that H. Ey, as long as he is oriented to existentialism, psychoanalysis and phenomenology, in his conclusions will never approach to conceptions of the soviet psychiatry, even if he would change from the mere enumeration of psychopathological syndromes to an analysis of their causes and connections.

But we think that the conscientiousness of a scientist will oblige Ey to aggree with us that taking the way proposed by him, psychiatric science will cease to be an organized system of knowledge at all. Thus, in effect, we are confronted with a refined, idealistic procedure, which disregards the study of objective reality by scientific knowledge and also disregards the question of the objectivity of our knowledge. Instead of this, it presents a kaleidoscope of procedures from which everybody may choose what he intuitively prefers.

We think that we do not falsify or simplify Ey's position. Moreover, this example demonstrates very clearly the end to which disowning the methodological procedures connected with Pavlovian doctrine leads. This disowning also implies giving up the possibility of generalizing the results.

Ey's position is, indeed, an "alternative" to that approach to psychopathology which results from the dialectical materialistic study of the nature of consciousness and which is only realized by Pavlovian doctrine. Whereas we cannot imagine any investigation of the nature of any psychopathological syndrome without refering to physiological data, which are taken as factors participating in the construction of the syndrome in a non-specific way, Ey does not even admit the need to relate the cerebral basis of the psychological derangement logically to the other aspects in which this derangement is expressed. This clearly means leaving the methodological positions which have been traditional for scientific medicine.

This judgement on the situation which arises when one leaves the methodological principles, regarded by us as fundamental, may seem too strong. Therefore, we shall mention some additional proofs, which may demonstrate that nowadays, the alternative to our philosophical position is a gradual transition to a pure irrationalism, which displays an essentially more crude and vulgar character than was characteristic for the idealistic conceptions of only a few decades before.

As we have already mentioned, an essential role is played in Ey's theory by existential procedures. This is not by mere chance. Existentialism is a philosophical doctrine which very deeply influences modern psychiatry in western Europe, especially in such countries as Western Germany, Switzerland, England, Spain, and also the conceptions of many psychiatrists in the Latin American countries and the United States. Originating as a conception not immediately connected with problems of the psychiatric clinic, but as a manner of thinking, stemming from the ideas of Kierkegaard and Heidegger, existentialism was enthusiastically received by those who had already treated the problems of the pathology of consciousness from the position of idealistic phenomenology. Characteristic above all of the existentialistic procedure is the highly developed intuitivism, and in this respect, it naturally must completely deny any scientific approach in its general meaning. Reducing the term psychosis to a change in the "structure of existence", which allows only an irrational approach denying the right to confront the "I" and the "world", i.a. to differ between the "subject" and the "object", as differentiated elements of the world, and regarding psychiatric illness as a conditional, pragmatic category, existentialism in its very essence means giving up every investigation based on the use of logical categories and, strictly speaking even the refusal of the very idea of "investigation" at all. In fact, it is a system in which the intellect, as a weapon to recognize the world and especially the world of the psychiatric patient, is considered not to be competent and to be replaced by such categories as "empathy", "enlightenment", and so on.

When the history of the foreign psychiatry of our epoch is written, the author will certainly dwell on the deeper causes which, in the middle of the twentieth century, resulted in such a propagation of these reactionary, non-scientific, irrational conceptions, destroying in all respects the sound basis of psychiatry. One of these causes will doubtlessly be the fact that an adequate philosophical, methodological basis was lacking for modern foreign psychiatry.

It is highly characteristic and very instructive for the history of culture that those methods of thinking in which an adequate philosophical basis is lacking display a progressive loss of the elementary fundamentals of the scientific approach. Our attitude to psychoanalysis in all its orthodox or "neo"-form is well known. During recent years, many papers have been published in our literature, pointing out the specific grounds which induce soviet psychiatry to reject the doctrine of Freud and his school. Therefore, we will not dwell on these arguments. But one characteristic feature in the development of the psychoanalytical conception which has emerged during recent years must be stressed.

The followers of psychoanalytical theory have always reacted very strongly when their critics, especially soviet scientists, have pointed out that they ignore the most elementary requirements of any type of scientific analysis. Answering this criticism, the advocates of Freudian theory have emphasized Freud's tendency to determinism, which brought him to introduce the term "unconscious", the claimed experimental conformation of Freud's hypotheses, apparently reached during recent years, and so on. Their answers have shown an effort to demonstrate in any way the objectivity and scientific foundation of their position.

In a discussion between one of us (F. V. Bassin) and the well-known French follower of psychoanalytical theory, Charles Brisset, he made the following statement on the principal peculiarities of psychoanalysis:

> This knowledge is not demonstrable experimentally. Naturally technical procedures stimulated by Pavlovian ideas, may demonstrate the correctness or falsity of respective psychoanalytical hypotheses (e.g. experiments of Hebb on repression). But in this field, the scientific conviction is not based on experimental proofs, as in the field of natural sciences. The limited possibilities of undertaking experimental proofs in the field of inter-

personal relations determine the special character of the proofs used. The point is that we must understand and not explain. We are working in a field of science of historical order. Personality means history . . . Conformity between a defined group of scientists on these questions may arise on the basis of confidence in the spirit of criticism, and on the basis of mutual control, by which time corrects experience and interpretation. The facts are even so in the matter of psychoanalysis.

And later on, Brisset (1961) emphasizes: "everybody has the right not to believe the psychoanalysts, but nobody has the right to demand proofs from them, which are strange to the character of their knowledge."

We have cited this long quotation to demonstrate how deeply the spirit of irrationalism, the spirit which denies the very possibility of a deterministic approach ("we must understand and not explain") has penetrated the conceptions of psychiatrists in western Europe. Dilthey, who founded the alternative to the marxist conception, regarded history, in contrast to the natural sciences, as a field in which it is impossible to derive any objective laws and in which, therefore, no causal interpretation at all may be carried out. Therefore, he assumed that history may be only "understood". When Brisset approaches the experiences of the neurotic and hysterical patient in the same way, then this means that *he denies any possibility of explaining these experiences causally.* Among other things, it is very difficult to understand how, considering this approach, anyone can defend the theory and therapeutic practice of psychoanalysis; but this, we believe, is finally a personal matter for Brisset. For us, in this respect, it is only important that such an approach produces apparently the deeply pessimistic irrationalism that inevitably brings on the denial of the possibility of obtaining a scientific knowledge at all.

Now we see clearly to what consequences one is brought by following the "alternative" to those methodological positions proposed by Pavlovian doctrine. In the modern struggle of ideologies, the Pavlovian doctrine is deeply connected with optimistic rationalism, which is convinced of the possibility of understanding the world rationally and of disclosing the nature of the world scientifically and without any limit. This is the basis of the whole philosophy of dialectical materialism. Therefore one can nowadays say with conviction that denying the basic methodological positions of Pavlovian doctrine means resigning any possibility of reaching a real scientific philosophy.

Summarizing, we wish to state the following. The importance which the fundamental theoretical categories of Pavlovian doctrine have, now as ever, for psychopathology, stems from the dialectical materialistic approach to the problem of consciousness and to the role this approach principally ascribes to physiological factors. To deny the conceptions of soviet psychiatry on the relationship between neurophysiological and social factors, determining the structure of the psychological derangement, means the simultaneous denial of a deterministic interpretation. It can lead only to a far-reaching distortion of the very basis of a scientific approach to psychiatry at all, as is demonstrated by the papers and formulations of distinguished foreign psychiatrists.

REFERENCES

BRISSET, Ch. (1961) Réponse au professeur Bassine, *Rév. méd. psychosom.* Nr. **4,** 69.

ROCHLIN, L. L. (1962) *Problems in Psychopharmacology*, Moscow (Russian).

PART II
PHYSIOLOGICAL SYSTEMS

7

CARDIOVASCULAR COMPONENTS
OF THE CONDITIONAL REFLEX TO PAIN,
FOOD AND OTHER STIMULI†

W. Horsley Gantt

Twenty years ago when I was impressed by some of the difficulties in the field of conditional reflexes I questioned ten physiologists and cardiologists whether there could be any cardiac conditional reflexes, and if there were, whether the response would be different for excitation and inhibition. It was interesting that seven of the ten cardiologists and physiologists whom I asked to make a random guess, predicted that there would not be any cardiac conditional reflexes. That was in 1939.

We have known for a long time about the cardiac changes which accompany emotional states. To what extent cardiac changes occur as adaptive learned responses to the same degree that the salivary and motor components occur in the conditional reflex is another question.

If one goes back to the classical writings of some of the great authors, such as Darwin, he will often find information shadowed and outlined, general truths that hold up later and which are very useful to the experimenter. In Darwin's work on the emotional expressions, one now sees many instances of cardiovascular changes which were discovered by general observational methods, but which would certainly fall into the category of cardiac conditional reflexes. Some years later we had the theoretical formulation of James and Lange. I believe Lange actually made some experiments on the vasomotor changes in emotions and James propounded the theory that these physiologic changes preceded the subjective feelings that went with our emotions.

Notations in the writings of Sherrington also gave a general indication of the existence of cardiac changes in learned experiences. The cardiac conditional reflex has, moreover, been established in pigs in Liddell's laboratory by Moore and Marcuse in 1944[28], in rabbits by Kosupkin and Olmsted[26], as well as by a number of subsequent workers in Russia and elsewhere. Considerable work has been done on the respiratory conditional reflex; among these are the researches of Freedman[8], Krogh and Kellogg.

† By permission of *Physiologinal Reviews* Vol. 40, pp. 266–91, 1960

What I was interested in at the beginning of this work were the fluctuations induced by giving a very small amount of food, such as 1 gr. Would there be any cardiac conditional reflex to the signals of the food?

I want to say a word, first about the terminology "cardiac conditional reflex." We may use an organ as a specific target for a reaction, such as the salivary gland for food—i.e. by applying an adequate physiological stimulus to evoke the reaction. In the case of the cardiac reaction, since it, like the respiratory response, is a general response, it can either be one aspect viz. a general aspect of a conditional response, or it may be the reaction to an adequate stimulus, such as an electrical stimulus applied to the nerves to effect changes in heart rate.

In general, most of what I have to say has to do with the first aspect—i.e., the cardiac component of the conditional reflex, which is not based on a specific cardiac unconditional stimulus, but where the cardiovascular system participates in the inborn reaction and also in the conditional reflex.

My first interest was to ascertain whether there would be any change in heart rate accompanying the signal for a small amount of food which was fed to a hungry dog. That is, if you give signals which represent 10 gr, 5 gr, or 0.5 gr of food, the amount of food being a definite quantity to a given signal, would there be a corresponding quantitative change in the heart rate?

My reasoning at that time was that there probably would not be. In order to receive a small morsel of food the dog ordinarily stands perfectly still while he is listening to the tone signal for the food. He may make a slight movement of the head toward the place where he will get the food. In order to support such a small reaction, is it necessary, thinking teleologically, which we usually do in one way or another, is it necessary for there to be any very marked change in the cardiovascular state?

I was accustomed to think according to teleology—or if you want to give it a more dignified name, homeostasis—that there would not be any change in the heart rate while the dog was in the observably quiescent state in order to receive only a morsel of food. Then, after establishing whether there would or would not be any cardiac conditional reflex to the excitatory stimulus, the question was what would be the cardiac change to the inhibitory stimulus. The answer to that had a special interest for me, because I thought in that way we might be able to get a measure of inhibition below the control state. In the measure of salivary secretion you know that if there is any excitatory conditional reflex, you will get secretion. But if you have inhibition, there is no opportunity for reduction in the secretion below zero. A change in heart rate, since it could fluctuate below the control reading, might thus provide a measure of the inhibitory conditional reflex, which we cannot ordinarily get, either with the motor or with the salivary component.

Well, in brief, it turned out that there was not only a specific relationship to the excitatory and to the inhibitory salivary conditional reflex, but that there were, in general, parallels between the cardiac changes and the quantitative relations which we had found to exist for the salivary component of the reflex to food. I shall point out briefly what those parallels are. Pavlov had shown that the louder the tone used, even though accompanied by the same amount of food, the more marked the conditional reflex. I found that the larger the amount of food or the greater the intensity of the painful stimulation (up to a certain point), that is, the greater the unconditional stimulus, the larger will be the salivary conditional reflex or the movement. Moreover, the latent period is inversely proportional—as it has been shown with the simple physiological reflexes—to the intensity of the conditional reflex, whether it be produced by the intensity of the conditional signal, or whether it be related to the amount of the unconditional stimulus which reinforces it. In general, there was a parallel between the cardiac component, using heart rate, and later blood pressure, and the quantitative measures that we had found for salivation, for movement, and also for the extent of the respiratory response.

In the following pages I shall give a brief summary of the main principles governing the cardiac conditional reflex, which we have found since 1939, the beginning of our work with cardiac conditioning.

Although most of our work with cardiac conditioning has been done on the dog, we have also elaborated it in opossums and penguins, beginning with Hoffman's work 1939 [11], and in the human being. Cardiac conditional reflexes have been recognized in the human being for many years, though not precisely described under this term. George Burch (personal demonstration), Shmavonian [37], Mawardi, Bykov [4], and Traugott [40], and others have noted the existence of vasomotor reflexes in people. If the faradic shock used is weak, there may not be perceptible change in heart rate even to the shock, although there is in the psychogalvanic response and in respiration [36,1]. Cardiac conditional reflexes have been demonstrated in man to the signals for muscular exertion, as well as to faradic shock, by Peters and Gantt [34,35]. In eleven subjects the increase in heart rate to the signal (a light) for exertion (as measured by manuel pressure on a dynamometer) was from a control of 79 to 82 for the conditional reflex and 84 for unconditional reflex (one-sixth maximal exertion); from control of 78 to 82 for the conditional reflex and 94 for unconditional reflex (one half maximal exertion); and from control of 82 to 87 for the conditional reflex and 102 for unconditional reflex (with maximal exertion). Human subjects as well as dogs fall into two types: the majority show acceleration as a manifestation of the conditional reflex, a few show deceleration. In man cardiac conditional reflexes can be established to exertion as readily as to other unconditional stimuli.

Normal Heart Rate in the Dog

Normal unanesthetized dogs, in a quiet room alone, show a range of heart rates from 40 to 120 per min with a usual rate of 70 to 80 per min in most dogs. In pathological animals, the same subject will show a great fluctuation—from 12 to over 200 per min in dog V_3, and from 70 to 250 per min in dog Nick. Blood pressures, measured in only a few dogs, range from 100/80 mm Hg under normal circumstances to 250/180 mm Hg under stress. All of the above readings have been taken with apparatus attached, but with the dog otherwise quiescent and alone.

The heart rate of the dog is much more sensitive than that of the human being. First, there is a very definite respiratory arrhythmia, the rate increasing with inspiration, and decreasing during expiration [33].

Motor activity increases heart rate, but not to the same extent as emotional causes. The heart rates for three normal dogs under various conditions are shown in Table 1. The respiratory rate normally is 12–20 per min. As is well known, respiration increases markedly with panting. After sexual stimulation, and with petting, the respiration may slow to 4 per min.

In a dog at rest, making spontaneous movements from time to time, such as shifting weight from one foot to another, standing or sitting, an acceleration of heart rate precedes the movement, and during the movement the heart rate is already falling[33]. This phenomenon will be discussed later.

Comparison of Cardiac Fluctuations in Rate with Motor and Salivary Conditional Reflexes

Cardiac unconditional reflex can be produced by a specific adequate stimulus to the heart, such as the injection of acetylcholine, atropine, bulbocapnine, or the stimulation of the efferent fibers of the cardiac nerves, of the cerebral centers or the sinus caroticus. On the other hand, the change in heart rate accompanying general excitatory states may be conditioned to the signals (conditional stimuli) of those states. In the latter instance the heart rate is only part of a complex reaction. As is well known, the cardiovascular functions have manifold connections with the multitudinous activities of the organism. For this reason, it is essential in a study of the cardiac conditional reflex to isolate the animal from adventitious stimuli even more rigidly than in the ordinary experiment. Owing to these multitudinous connections of the heart, Pavlov in his studies rejected the cardiovascular system in favor of the salivary system, which responds to very few stimuli other than food. Although most of our work has been with the cardiovascular component based on nonspecific cardiac reflexes, in Russia cardiac conditional

TABLE 1. HEART RATES PER MINUTE DURING SEXUAL AND OTHER FORMS OF EXCITATION

MARCH 20, 1940

	Dog Sechs	Dog Billy	Dog Peik
Control	15:30 87	15:58 123	16:47 75
Positive food conditional reflex	103	125	118
Eating	80	144	118
Inhibitory conditional reflex	15:37 87	16:02 112	16:51 104
Control	15:42 90 (80–100)+	16:16 125	16:55 95
SEXUAL EXCITATION			
During orgasm	145 (120–170)+	154 (138–162)+	110
After orgasm but during erection lasting 4 min	90 (85–110)+	125	17:01 110 (90–110)+
Immediately after erection	88 (80–105)+	123	17:07 106 (94–118)+
Shaking dog violently	84	125	89
H.S. in room with dog	95	115	113

+ Minimum-maximum.

reflexes have been formed to some adequate cardiac stimuli by Russian workers and others [26, 38].

We shall designate any regularly occurring acceleration or deceleration of heart rate (HR), acquired in an individual as a result of his experience, i.e. owing to the juxtaposition of an unconditional stimulus such as pain which produces a change in heart rate with an accidental alteration of environment (conditional stimulus), as a cardiac conditional reflex (HR-CR). If this change in heart rate accompanies food, pain, sexual stimulation, presence of person, petting, etc., it is clear that the heart rate is not in the same category as a salivary conditional reflex. The latter is specific to food while the respiratory and cardiac changes, though acquired and therefore aspects of the conditional reflex, are generalized, supporting components of the state of excitation. Evidently innumerable chemical, physical and physiological changes occur in the organism with a conditional reflex, which are not specific to the particular conditional reflex, but are general and related to the unconditional excitation. The cardiac changes however become specific as regards excitatory and inhibitory conditional reflexes, and are specific quantitatively to many of the same factors that govern the quantitative specificity of salivary and motor conditioning [16].

The acquired changes in cardiovascular function, in my opinion, cannot be dispensed with under the term "action of the body as a whole." Not all functions of the organism fluctuate together; it is our scientific duty to find out which ones do and which ones do not.

In addition to our work on cardiac conditioning, the existence of a vasomotor conditional reflex has been demonstrated by Burch (personal demonstration) and by Bykov [4].

Relation of Cardiac Conditional Reflexes to Intensity of Conditional and Unconditional Stimuli

Pavlov has shown that the nature of the sensory stimulus, viz. whether auditory, visual, tactile or olfactory, determines the amplitude of the salivary conditional reflex. There is a definite hierarchy for dogs, auditory stimuli causing the most intense response [31]. I have shown that the conditional salivary reflex is dependent also upon the intensity of the unconditional stimulus—the amount of food or the intensity of the shock [12]. The same parallel was found in our work with the cardiac conditional reflexes.

As seen in Figures 1 and 2, an auditory conditional stimulus produced a change in heart rate from 120 to 135 per min, while a visual conditional stimulus produced a change from only 115 per min to 122 per min, both stimuli being reinforced by the same amount of food. A metronome reinforced by 2 gr instead of 5 gr of food produced a smaller heart rate conditional reflex than the auditory conditional stimulus reinforced by the larger

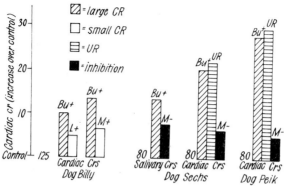

FIG. 1. Cardiac conditional responses to three different excitatory signals (*Bu*, buzzer; *L*, light; *M*, metronom) and to an inhibitory signal (*M*-) in three dogs. The salivary conditional responses are shown for comparison to excitatory and inhibitory signals in *dog Sechs*. The unconditional stimulus is the same for the excitatory stimuli (food).

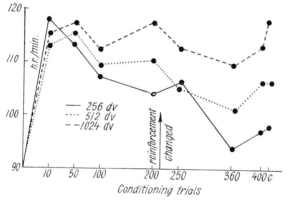

FIG. 2. Showing the gradual differentiation of the cardiac conditional responses based on three intensities of the unconditional stimulus (pain)

amount of food, viz. a change of 10 beats per min instead of 15. There was a parallel in the salivary conditional reflex, the metronome producing two-thirds the amount of saliva as did the other auditory conditional stimulus.

Experiments were conducted on three dogs (figs. 1 and 2) ranging in age from 1 to 11 years. In two of these, Billy and Sechs, the heart rates accompanying old stable food conditional reflexes elaborated three to six years previously were measured, and in the third dog, Peik, the cardiorespiratory changes were followed during the period of early conditional reflex elaboration. During the ten-second action of the conditional stimulus, all the animals showed an increase in heart rate: from 118 per min control to 131 per min during the conditional stimulus (Billy), from 85 to 102 per min (Sechs), from 81 to 110 (Peik). These figures represent the means of 15 to 35 readings. There was also a slight increase in heart rate accompanying a conditional inhibition: in Sechs 82 per min (control) to 88 per min (inhibition); in Peik 81 to 91 (means). The heart rate accompanying the unconditional reflex (the eating of the food) was approximately the same as the heart rate during the action of the conditional reflex. The respiratory rate was also increased during conditional (from 12 per min, control, to 18 per min, conditional), but very little change occurred during inhibition. It thus appears that there is an appreciable and constant change in the heart rate during conditional food excitation, and that a differentiation can be seen in the heart rate between excitation and inhibition as well as the differentiation formerly noted, and conventionally measured, in secretion and overt muscular movements [12].

Another group of four dogs were given three intensities of shock (unconditional stimulus) preceded by three tones of three different pitches, an octave apart. After 10 repetitions there was adaption in the cardiac conditional reflexes to the three tones, and also in the blood pressures, in proportion to the intensity of the shock which the tone signalized [6, 25] (Fig. 2).

Respiratory Conditional Reflexes

There is in general a parallel between the respiratory conditional reflex and the cardiac, the former usually showing acceleration as well as increased intensity. The respiratory conditional reflex is somewhat different with pain and with food stimuli. The cardiac conditional reflex, however, is independent of the respiratory conditional reflex [8].

As is common with conditional reflexes, the emotional and physiological state of the animal has a marked influence. In the pain conditional reflex, a function which is abrupt and nonperiodic, the fluctuation of the conditional reflex is not so marked as it is with the state of the organism in periodic functions such as eating and sexual activity. Satiation of the latter instances markedly diminishes or abolishes the conditional reflex related to that function. Our previous investigations showed that the salivary conditional reflexes were dependent upon the state of hunger of the animal, falling from a maximum to zero immediately after satiation. For example, the cardiac conditional reflex, measured in this laboratory for many years to study the inner emotional state of the animal, is parallel with the more specific external conditional reflexes. Several dogs with well-established conditional reflexes to food were allowed to eat to satiation after taking control salivary and cardiac measures to the conditional signals for food. An immediate decrease of the cardiac conditional reflex (CR) resulted from the satiation. The cardiac component of the unconditional reflex (UR) was only slightly affected (the animal would not eat after satiation unless the food were forced into the mouth). Satiation caused an elevation of control cardiac rate. For example, in Sechs the heart rates per minute were: control 85, CR 110, UR

110; after satiation: control 100, CR 108, UR 105; in Peik before satiation: control 65, CR 98, UR 95; after satiation: control 85, CR 95, UR 110. The cardiac component of the inhibitory conditional reflex was not affected. It is thus evident that not only the specific salivary conditional reflexes but the more generalized emotional conditional reflex components, presented by the heart rate, may be immediately abolished by a change of emotional state of the animal, while the unconditional reflexes are much less affected.

Both the respiratory and the cardiac conditional reflexes are diminished after satiation.

The Time Reflex

In order to establish a salivary and a motor conditional reflex to time it is necessary to give many repetitions of the unconditional stimulus at definite intervals. The heart rate conditional reflex, however, appears more quickly, as is shown in the figures given below for dog Skipper, in which the time reflex appeared several months before there was evidence in the motor activity, or in the restlessness or whining of the dog. In the following experiments, alternate excitatory and inhibitory conditional stimuli (two tones of 256 and 512 cycles, respectively) were given for 3 sec at 2-min intervals, tone 256 being followed by shock and tone 512 without shock. The heart rate not only increased to the positive tone and to the shock, but to the 10-sec and 5-sec periods before the excitatory tones, i.e. every 4 min. The average of 30 readings for the heart rate per minute of each item is as follows. For the excitatory tone: control, 107; 10–5 sec before excitatory tone, 124; 5–0 sec before excitatory tone, 128; cardiac conditional reflex during 3 sec of action of tone, 142; cardiac unconditional reflex during shock, 138. For the inhibitory tone, changes in heart rate per minute were small: control, 109; 5–0 sec before inhibitory tone, 111; during 3 sec of action of inhibitory tone, 115 [13, 19].

There is thus not only a cardiac conditional reflex to a signal but a cardiac change to definite time intervals when these are punctuated by regularly recurring signals. The heart is a kind of physiological clock.

In another dog in which shock was used as a stimulus, with regular alternation of tone 256 and tone 512 (5 sec duration at 2-min intervals), differentiation of cardiac conditional reflexes (heart rate) develops after 50 or more repetitions of the tones. A time conditional reflex appears first in the cardiac rate (after 150–300 repetitions), later in respiration and leg movements, but the cardiac conditional reflex is the most reliable and delicate measure of the time reflex. The heart rate (HR) is greatest during tone 256 and shock (100–200), drops within 15 sec (60–100), is lowest within 10 sec after inhibitory tone (512—), and rises gradually during the next 50 sec before the excitatory tone (256+). Only after 500 repetitions is there anticipatory anxiety evidenced by whining. Brain lesions (hemidecortication plus limbic lobe exstirpation on opposite side) impair or destroy time reflex but not differentiation measured by cardiac conditional reflexes to the two tones. Omission of the inhibitory signal (tone 512—) halfway between the two excitatory signals does not destroy the cardiac conditional reflexes to time. Thus the cardiac conditional reflexes are not only more delicate measures of adaptation to a situation than are the somatic movements, but they give a clear-cut picture of adaptation to time intervals not obtainable through other usual measurements.

Latent Period

The latent period of the cardiac conditional reflex is usually shorter than the latent period of the motor or the salivary conditional reflex. The latency depends upon the duration of the conditional stimulus and also upon the individual. If the duration is, for example, only 5 sec the acceleration of heart usually occurs in the next heart cycle, while if the duration of the conditional stimulus is 30 sec, the latent period may be much delayed [30, 36]

The Cardiac Component of the Orienting Reflex (HR-OR)

The effect of the stimulus itself, before it is made a signal for an unconditional reflex, is known as the orienting reflex (OR). Motor responses, salivation and changes in heart rate were taken as measures of the orienting reflex to neutral, auditory, and visual stimuli. As the neutral stimulus is repeated the initial changes in heart rate progressively decrease; in contrast, when the neutral stimulus becomes conditioned by reinforcement (with food or shock) the change in heart rate becomes greater and constant. The motor components of the orienting reflex (vocalization, movement of ears, turning toward stimulus, etc.) though less accurate indices than the cardiac changes, show a parallel pattern of extinction with repetition of the stimulus. The heart rate is the most significant index of the orienting reflex, showing a correlation among animals for different stimuli, and with the motor components. Furthermore, heart rate can be measured precisely. The cardiac reflexes (orienting and conditional) vary with each dog, some showing acceleration, others deceleration, but the pattern is similar for both the orienting and conditional reflex. The orienting reflex is subject to conditional inhibition by repetition; its reappearance later, after conditioning, is a symptom of nervous strain, probably a result of disinhibition of the conditional reflex from agitation. The sensitivity of the cardiac reflexes is shown by their correlation with the orienting reflex as well as by their almost immediate transformation into conditional reflexes when the signal is reinforced [36].

Although the orienting reflex has motor and respiratory as well as cardiac components, there is not a strict parallel among them—the heart rate sometimes being markedly increased when there is little movement and vice versa.

Development of the Cardiac Conditional Reflex

In Figures 3–7 from the work of Dr Gakenheimer, the development of the heart rate conditional reflex can be seen from the very beginning. Figure 3 indicates the appearance of the cardiac orienting reflex to a novel stimulus and its disappearance (extinction) after more than 100 repetitions. Figures 4–7 demonstrate the development of the heart rate-conditional reflex without differentiation (generalization), to both the excitatory and inhibitory tones, while there is motor differentiation (February 27, Figure 5) to be discussed later under "schizokinesis". With the continued experimentation, differentiation develops (March 17, Figure 6) and later (March 29, Figure 7) a definite time reflex [17, 22].

Anatomy

The anatomical structures concerned in cardiac conditioning may be considered *a*) under the centers in the central nervous system and *b*) in relation to the peripheral nerves—sympathetic or parasympathetic—which are chiefly responsible for conducting the impulses, and *c*) the hormonal secretions involved.

There has been considerable evidence that the gyrus cinguli is especially concerned with visceral functions (Kennard, Woolsey, et al.). For this reason we began a study in two dogs, Checkers and Crazy, in which the cortex was completely removed on one side and the gyrus cinguli on the other side; thus the dogs were deprived of one cortex and both gyri cinguli (work with Woolsey). These animals showed forced movements, spasticity, placing, hopping, tendon reflex differences, etc., on the two sides. However, they readily formed both cardiac and motor conditional reflexes to a faradic shock. The cardiac conditional reflex was quickly established after two or three repetitions of the stimulus, and as in the normal, much more quickly than was the motor conditional reflex. Cardiac differentiation, as well as a time reflex, was also obtainable, though the ability to establish the time reflex was somewhat impaired [12, 13, 23].

From these experiments it follows that the formation of the cardiac conditional reflex, both excitatory and inhibitory, as well as of the motor conditional reflex occours with very little impairment when both gyri cinguli have been extirpated.

Several dogs were used in the study of the relative role of the vagus and sympathetic nerves in the cardiac conditional reflex. These experiments have not been completed; at present only the vagus has been eliminated through giving large doses of atropine (0.15 mg/kg). In atropinized dogs with stable cardiac conditional reflexes, both excitatory and inhibitory, the heart rate under atropine accelerated to 200–75 per min. In spite of this tachycardia,

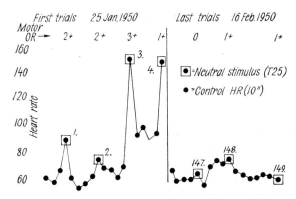

FIG. 3. Fig. 3–7 trace the development of the cardiac conditional response to faradic shock in dog Skipper from the beginning of experimentation in January to complete differentiation, March 29. In the first four trials of the novel auditory stimulus the cardiac reaction is seen as part of the orienting reflex. Three weeks later (right) the orienting reflex has been extinguished after 147 repetitions. 2-min intervals between CS

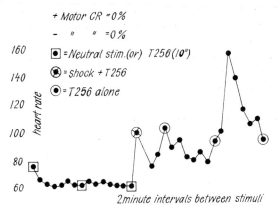

FIG. 4. Here we pass from the orienting reflex to the first reinforcement of the neutral signal (T 256). The reinforcement (pain) is given only once. We see the resting heart rate increase from a stable level at 60 to a rate of 80–160. After one stress reinforcement three things happen: a, heart rate level increases; b, rate becomes irregular; c, cardiac conditional response forms, but without conditional motor response

it was still possible to obtain a positive cardiac conditional reflex to the tone representing faradic shock and a differentiation in the heart rate to the tone representing no shock. These two tones (tone 256 and tone 512—) were given at exactly 2-minute intervals alternately; before atropinization, the heart rate of dog Skipper rose from 90 per min (control) to 150 per min during tone 256; during tone 512—, heart rate increased only 4 or 5 beats per min. Under atropinization, tone 256 gave a cardiac conditional reflex rise in

heart rate from 200 per min before the tone to 225 per min during the tone
[5]. Thus, eliminating the vagus through large doses of atropine markedly
reduced the response of cardiac conditional reflex but did not abolish it,
nor did it eliminate differentiation between the excitatory and inhibitory
tones. Since the upper limits of cardiac acceleration, during tone 256 under
atropine, are well below the capacity of the dog for cardiac acceleration, we
may conclude that both the vagus and the sympathetic nerves are involved
in the cardiac conditional reflexes, i.e. the changes in heart rate to the symbols of the life experiences, but that the vagus is probably the chief mediator
of the cardiac conditional reflex [5] (Fig. 8).

Mechanism

Antedating the work with the cardiac system, we had shown that central
nervous system excitation is essential for a conditional reflex to be formed.
With agents which produce the effect solely through peripheral action—either
on tissues or on nerve endings—reponses cannot be elaborated into a learned
reaction no matter how many repetitions are given. But the same response,
when it is a part of central nervous system activity, can be readily conditioned. It matters not whether the effect be available to consciousness or
whether it be mediated through the autonomic or through the somatic nerves.
The crucial factor is only whether it be peripherally or centrally produced.
Salivary secretion and prostatic secretion, induced by pilocarpine, hyperglycemia resulting from adrenalin injection, gastric secretion following
histamine injection cannot be elaborated into conditional reflexes[9]. But
the same reactions to agents producing central nervous system excitation

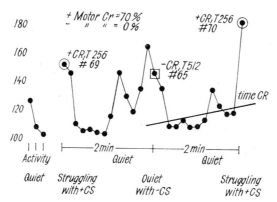

FIG. 5. After sixty-nine reinforcements, there is a definite cardiac and motor
conditional response, with excellent differentiation of the motor, but no differentiation of the cardiac. A time reflex begins to be apparent in the gradual increase of the heart rate 15–25 sec before the signal is given

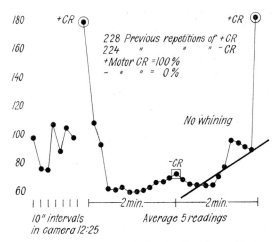

Fig. 6. A control heart rate, when the dog is first brought in, varies from 70 to 110, compared with 60 in Fig. 4. After 228 repetitions there is now perfect cardiac as well as motor differentiation. A time reflex is evident in the cardiac rate, but not in the movements or behavior of the dog

can be readily be conditioned. Thus salivary and gastric secretion as part of the food reaction, prostatic secretion as part of central sexual excitation, hyperglycemia when a component of an emotional state, can all be conditioned.

In order to test this principle for the cardiac system, we used acetylcholine and atropine as agents that effected a change in heart rate through action on the peripheral structures in the heart, probably at the nerve endings. Atropine was injected from another room by special technique to

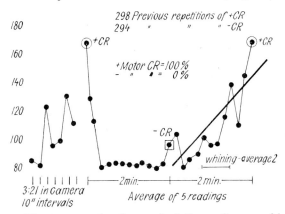

Fig. 7. Same as Fig. 6 except for the marked time reflex, combined now with motor components—whining and restlessness. The cardiac conditional response, however, is no greater than it was in fig. 6 before the motor components appeared

eliminate the presence of experimenter; a marked unconditional increase in heart rate to atropine could not be conditioned [25]. Using saline injection as a conditional stimulus, the results (average of 10 experiments) were as follows. Heart rates per min in dog Rhett: control 93 to 141 after atropine subcutaneously and control 116 to 106 after saline subcutaneously, 13th min after injection; dog Eliza: control 94 to 181 after atropine and control 103 to 93 after saline, 11th min after injection (Figure 8). Like other conditioned reactions, cardiac conditional reflexes result from central rather than from peripheral excitation [9].

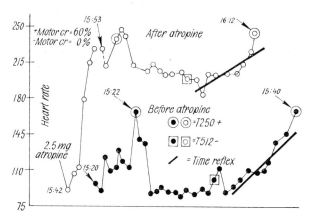

FIG. 8. The bottom line beginning at 15 : 20, ending at 15 : 40, shows the cardiac record taken before atropine; the top line, beginning at 15 : 42, shows the effect of atropine on the motor and cardiac conditional responses. Atropine increases the heart rate from 80–165 control to 215–50. The motor conditional responses are impaired in differentiation, and the cardiac conditional responses are much reduced. However, differentiation as well as the time reflex is still present after atropine, indicating that the sympathetic as well as the parasympathetic nerves are responsible for the cardiac conditional responses

In both secretory and somatic motor responses the peripheral action—secretion or movement—is also unnecessary for the establishment of the conditional reflex. Thus Light and Gantt paralyzed the leg of a dog by crushing the anterior spinal roots and trained the animal for motor conditional reflexes during the period of paralysis. Two months later after regeneration of the nerve and recovery of motor function, the unreinforced conditional stimulus elicited a conditional reflex [10, 27]. Whether this principle applies to the heart is now under investigation in this laboratory (work of Royer).

Role of Muscular Movement in the Cardiac Conditional Reflex

We have ample evidence that muscular excitation and coincidental movements play a relatively minor role in the cardiac conditional reflex. Although the motor and cardiac components are usually parallel, this is not always the case. In a study of heart rate and exertion, the heart rate generally increases while the muscular tension is falling, e.g. during an attempt by the human being to maintain maximal exertion on a dynamometer [34]. Again the heart rate is much greater with emotional states than in situations where there is considerable motor activity in the absence of emotion [35] (Table 1).

Using curare to block the motor component of both the orienting reflex and the conditional reflex to a faradic shock, the cardiac component (acceleration) was not eliminated, indicating that movement is not essential for the cardiac conditional reflex, and that it results from central excitation. Strong motor orienting reflexes during the control period were blocked completely by curare in four dogs, markedly depressed in two others, and moderately depressed in the remaining two. A bell produced average cardiac acceleration of 22 beats per minute in control series, with no diminution under curare in two dogs, 50 per cent decrease in five dogs, slight increase in one dog. Cardiac control orienting reflexes were 87 per cent acceleratory, compared with 83 per cent acceleratory during drug action (average of all eight dogs). All animals retained cardiac orienting reflexes under curare, although no orienting movements were made (schizokinesis).

In a study of the effect of curare on cardiac conditional reflexes to shock in eight dogs with doses of 0,86 to 2.17 units/kg or 2.25 to 4.50 mg, the cardiac conditional reflex was increased in 87 per cent of the cases without curare and 83 per cent under curare, there being no statistically significant difference [30]. Furthermore, curare does not eliminate the decrease in heart rate induced by petting the dog; during petting with the animal under curare heart rate decreased from 95 to 60 per min, compared with a decrease from 93 to 70 per min without curare (unpublished work of Newton).

Drugs

Although drugs may have a selectic action on one system or another, most drugs affect unequally the motor and the visceral responses, both conditional and unconditional. A study of two new drugs with marked therapeutic effect in some neurotic and psychotic patients, chlorpromazine and reserpine, reveals that they diminish both the motor and cardiac components of the orienting reflex, and especially the motor, but that they have less effect on either component of the conditional reflex to painful stimuli. A comparative study of the effect of chlorpromazine on motor and cardiac conditional reflexes indicates that there is a reduction of the motor conditional reflexes to 50 per cent or less, but there is very little change in the cardiac conditional reflexes. With reserpine the reduction of the motor conditional reflex was 40 per cent to 0 per cent, but there was also a very slight effect, or no effect, on the cardiac component of the conditional reflexes. The effect of these drugs may depend upon their specific action on the orienting reflex [25].

Morphine has an especially interesting influence on the motor conditional reflexes compared with the cardiac responses. In doses of 3–5 mg/kg, enough to produce drowsiness and ataxia, morphine abolishes the motor conditional reflexes to pain but has relatively little effect upon the cardiac conditional reflexes to pain, in spite of a lowering of heart rate from about 90 per min for control state to about 50 per min during morphine. This preferential action of drugs on the motor rather than on the cardiac component of the conditional reflexes reveals the mechanism which we have called schizokinesis, the relative stability of the cardiovascular responses compared with the more superficial component, viz. the motor or the salivary [39].

Meprobamate has the opposite effect from chlorpromazine and reserpine on conditioned responses: it markedly diminishes the cardiac component of the conditional reflex while leaving unaffected the motor component. This property of meprobamate would suggest its use in cardiac patients who are overreactive and anxious; by eliminating the excessive cardiac reactivity, without impairing the motor habits, it might alleviate cardiac stress [20].

Mescaline, which produces hallucinations and feelings of unreality in the human being, resembles meprobamate in its differential effect on motor and cardiac components of the conditioned response; it has a more pronounced action on the cardiac than on the motor component. Thus with doses of 35 mg/kg in dogs, the motor responses were only slightly diminished as measured by a decrease in amplitude and an increase of latent period, but there was complete inhibition of the cardiac components of the excitatory conditional reflex [3].

Drugs which have a specific effect on the heart can also be used for investigation to determine if this effect can be conditioned. We have previously mentioned that the effects produced by drugs acting peripherally cannot be conditioned. Bulbocapnine, on the other hand, produces not only catalepsy but an extreme exaggeration of the T–wave of the electrocardiogram. Using intravenous injection of saline plus tone as the conditional stimulus, the T–wave change appeared in the same exaggerated form as it did to the actual injection of bulbocapnine. The duration of the change was brief—only a few minutes. The catelepsy of bulbocapnine was also conditioned [32].

Serotonin (5-hydroxytryptamine) in doses of 15 mg/kg intravenously which do not produce physical symptoms, and 30 mg/kg, which caused physical distress—ataxia, lacrimation, dyspnea, diarrhea—produced a marked reduction in both cases to motor and cardiac conditional reflexes based upon food and auditory signals [2].

Psychopathology

Under this heading I shall discuss the principles relating to the establishment of acquired functional cardiac pathology and then devote some discussion to the production of tachycardia and hypertension.

Formation of the Cardiac Conditional Reflex

In previous studies with conditioning in dogs, it seemed remarkable that
so many repetitions were necessary for the appearance of the salivary or
motor components of the conditional reflex, while in the experience of the
human being we know that simple conditioning often occurs after one intense
experience. But a study of the cardiorespiratory components reveals that
in dogs the conditional reflex is formed on the visceral emotional level after
one reinforcement. This is apparent in the charts of the dogs Pedro, Skipper
and Crazy, although the motor components did not appear for several days.
In the process of elaboration of the cardiac conditional reflex to the stress of
a mild faradic shock to the foot, three characteristics are evident in the heart
rate: *a*) an elevation of the level of heart rate, which may never return to
the prestress level in that situation; *b*) a marked irregularity of heart rate in
contrast to a former stability; *c*) the occurrence of an increased heart rate to
the signal after only one reinforcement by the unconditional stimulus. In
our experiments the increase of heart rate to the signal *per se*, viz. the orienting reflex, is always extinguished by repetition of the signal alone before
conditioning begins. In a study of scores of dogs there has been only one animal in which we did not see a cardiac component of the conditional reflex
to shock.

Retention

In previous studies with the retention of motor and salivary responses
there has been little attention to the emotional and visceral components. On
the other hand the data of clinical psychiatry, while supporting evidence of
long retention, do not control the factor of intermediate reinforcement of
the original stiuation[16].

In several laboratory dogs, stable conditional reflexes were established to
food or to pain (faradic shock). In addition to the specific salivary and motor
components, the more general visceral components representing the emotional response (heart rate, respiration) were recorded in both normal and
pathological dogs. There was no repetition of the original conditional stimulus until the animal was brought in for a retention test. The criterion for
retention is the presence of the conditional reflex on the very first presentation of the conditional stimulus. In one dog there was perfect retention of the
motor conditional reflex ro faradic shock when the animal was tested after
an interval of 8 months, 2 years, and 4 years, with loss of differentiation after
4 years. In another extremely phlegmatic dog, after 16 months there was no

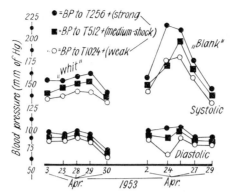

FIG. 9. Hypertension in two dogs, measured 13 months after cessation of experiments which formed hypertensive conditional reflexes to three signals for different intensities of shock. Note differentiation to the signals for the three intensities of shock, both in diastolic and systolic pressures, and retention of blood pressure, 130–170 in one dog, 150–225 in the other. Although there is no repetition of stress during the month shown in the record, hypertension increases instead of diminishing when dogs are returned to stress environment (autokinesis)

retention of the motor conditional reflex (pain), but some retention of the cardiac component and marked retention of the general emotional pattern [18, 21] (Figure 9). Thus retention in the dog of the motor, salivary and especially visceral (cardiac and respiratory) components of the food and pain reflexes may last for 10 or more years without practice. This is predominantly true of the cardiac conditional reflex mentioned above.

Extinction

Retention of cardiac conditional reflexes after attempts at extinction are even more striking. Extinction is the term used by Pavlov to designate the disappearance of the excitatory conditional reflex when the conditional stimulus is successively repeated without reinforcement by the food or shock which had formerly supported it. If the conditional stimulus is repeated without reinforcement at intervals of a few minutes, twenty to forty times daily, the secretory and motor components gradually disappear, but they may reappear on the next day in weakened form. After a number of days of such a procedure, extinction becomes complete for these components and normally the dog gives only the inhibitory response to the formerly excitatory conditional stimulus. If the cardiac conditional reflex is studied under these circumstances, the results are markedly different—depending upon the individual dog. In some dogs extinction of the cardiac conditional reflex, though more difficult than extinction of the salivary and motor components, can be accomplished, but in many animals extinction of the cardiac conditional reflex is impossible. Thus, in dog Peik although the salivary component disappeared in 1 or 2 days and did not reappear in either 1 month or 1 year, the cardiac conditioned reflex could not be extinguished and was greater after one year and continued undiminished after 4 years. Pathological as well as normal animals show a persistent retention without reinforcement—7 or 8 years with one dog, *Nick*, for cardiac, sexual and other visceral responses to situations of conflict. Emotional components of a conditional reflex (respiratory and cardiac) are retained much longer than the specific motor or secretory components; retention is even longer in pathological than in normal animals [12].

Thus by a study of the cardiorespiratory components we get a new insight into inhibition: We see the dog in a state of fractional inhibition in contrast to what we formerly thought of as complete inhibition. The fact that Pavlov considered inhibition as an active process may represent in its activity the residue of visceral emotional components left after extinction of the more observable and specific components such as salivary and motor. Here is the basis for schizokinesis [22, 22a, 25].

Effect of Person

The inclusion of cardiovascular measurements in conditional reflexes makes possible the detection of factors not hitherto easily recognized. Such a factor is the effect of one individual on another. This effect is both generic and specific. Thus all human beings when petting the dog, by rubbing him behind the ears, produce a marked slowing of heart rate, while the mere presence of a person usually accelerates the heart, depending upon the relationship of that particular person to the dog. The stimulus of the person can be used as a basis for forming conditional reflexes. In dogs it is one of the most powerful of stimuli and may even be more potent than the food stimulus. We have conducted numerous experiments, not only showing the effect of a person on other conditional reflexes, but establishing that signals of the person have a comparable effect to the person himself. Thus in a dog in whom the bell *per se* caused an acceleration of heart rate when the bell was used to precede the action of the person petting the dog (which always decelerates the heart rate), the bell then became itself a decelerator of the heart rate through its becoming a conditional signal for the petting (work of Dr. Joseph Stephens). This effect may be especially marked in pathological animals. For example, in the hyperreactive dog Nick the heart rate in the camera, where the stress was produced in the presence of one of the workers who had been associated with the dog was 147 per min, 123 per min with the same person outside of the camera and 97 per min when this person was petting the animal [12]. With the catatonic dog V_3, age 10 years, the heart rate was 160 per min in the room where the stress was produced but without any other stimulation applied; the rate fell to about 60 per min in the presence of the person and to 20–40 per min when this person was petting the animal [16, 22a] (Figure 10).

The effect of one individual on another is universal throughout the animal kingdom whether it be insect with insect, man with dog, dog with dog, or one human being with another. The imprinting of Konrad Lorenz and the work in Liddell's laboratory with infant goats and lambs may be based on some innate reaction to another individual. That these imprints may become very stable and unmodifiable in adult life reminds us of the phenomenon of schizokinesis described below [28].

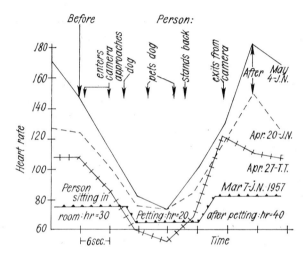

FIG. 10. Showing the effect of two people on the heart rate, taken 1 year apart. The heart rate level falls from 110 to 170 in the stress room as the person enters. Petting has a profound depression on every occasion. In the bottom line (March 7) the heart rate is 30–20—much lower than in the top three lines, because the person is sitting in the room with the dog throughout the record. V_3 is a markedly catatonic dog. The bottom line is not plotted to scale. Upper three records, 1956

Pathological Tachycardia and Hypertension Experimentally Produced

As pointed out before, the cardiac conditional reflex passes through several phases—an increase of the general level of heart rate, irregularity of rate, and a subsequent decrease with specific differentiation to excitatory and inhibitory conditional stimuli. However, the rate does not return to the pre-experimental level when the dog is placed in the experimental room, even though he is not being stimulated. The level often rises from about 50 beats per minute pre-experimentally to a resting level of twice that rate after once being conditioned. After the first phase of experimentation, the heart rate may follow different courses depending upon the individual and the unconditional stimulus employed (food, pain): (a) the rate may decrease as seen in dog Crazy, (b) the rate may become exaggerated to form a permanent tachycardia or (c) the rate may remain at a fixed level resistant to extinction as in dog Peik (schizokinesis).

Pathological tachycardia may ensue, as we have seen in a number of dogs [21, 25]. This tachycardia may exist without any motor activity indicative of the stress. In some dogs, e. g. Nick, the heart rate was regularly 175–225 per min in the "stress" room. In this dog there were a number of other pathological symptoms such as dyspnea, pollakiuria, negativism, extreme restlessness, gastric hyperacidity. The increase in heart rate was present not only to the room but to the people and even to the food used in producing the stress. The respiratory rate, mainly panting, was often 150–300 per min. The heart rate was higher to the stress situation than to a stimulus such as a cat clawing this dog's back—250 per min compared with 140 per min [12].

Conditioned hypertension may also be induced by conditioning. The method of Allen and Wilhelmj was used for recording; the dog was separated from the experimenter, and auditory signals for faradic shocks were employed. The blood pressure rise to the novel stimuli was eliminated by repetition before using faradic shock. In some dogs excitatory and inhibitory signals were used, in others, three excitatory signals representing three intensities of shock. There was differentiation in the blood pressure between the excitatory and inhibitory stimuli, as well as among the signals for different intensities. Thus in the dog Shep, tone 256—(reinforced by shock) gave an increase in blood pressure from 168/46 mm Hg control to 182/74 mm Hg during the tone, and tone 512–(inhibitory) caused practically no change (174/48 control to 176/54 during tone). The blood pressure, like the conditioned tachycardia, usually shows a tendency to decrease after some weeks as the dog becomes accustomed to the experiments. At the end of a 13 month period during which the dogs were not brought back to the experimental room, the conditioned hypertension remained (225/100 mm Hg in one dog). Furthermore in two dogs in which three tones an octave apart were reinforced by three intensities of shock (weak, medium, strong) there was differentiation in the blood pressure response to the three tones, both diastolic and systolic, as shown in Figure 9 [25]. Although blood pressure is much more difficult technically to record in the chronic experiment, these studies indicate that blood pressure like heart rate is readily conditioned, that it is specific to excitation and to inhibition, and that it is probably in delicate balance with the acquired signals for emotional events.

The marked difference—the early formation, and the extreme durability of the conditioned cardiovascular response, in contrast to the greater plasticity of the specific secretory or motor responses—is what we have called "schizokinesis" [18]. In this term I intend to include not only a difference between the more general emotional components of the acquired responses and the specific ones in a narrow sense, but in a broader way, the lack of perfect adaptation that exists in our biological systems.

The heart is doing one thing, out of adaptation to present reality, while superficially the individual may be in repose and undisturbed. But beneath, in the autonomic components of the response, there may be violent turbulence. Here may lie the explanation for the persistence of psychogenic hypertension to past experiences long forgotten [22, 22a].

By schizokinesis I mean not only the lack of a parallel between the general, emotional, visceral acquired responses and the specific motor habits, but the sum of all those maladaptations, such as evident inefficiency of the organism in meeting stress in the daily routine of life.

It is obviously difficult to decide upon an arbitrary mechanical analogy as to what is efficient for an organism and more so for groups of individuals. The meaning and purpose of life, the destiny of the race, the capabilities of the living structure, etc., may all be factors. These are too complex to discuss physiologically. But if one has a right to speak of homeostasis as balance, of psychiatric symptoms as useful for compensation, of the conditional reflex as a mechanism of equilibrium, then one has also a right to point out the failures of these mechanisms, viz. of schizokinesis. It is therefore with this relativity of viewpoint (relative to homeostasis) that I will discuss schizokinesis aud autokinesis.

Schizokinesis is seen in the marked difference between the specific conditional reflex and the visceral general component in (a) the speed of formation, the cardiac conditional reflex being formed quicker, often after one repetition,

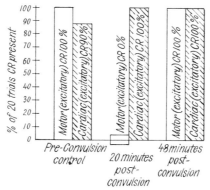

FIG. 11. A hippocampal stimulus not severe enough to cause loss of consciousness, abolishes the motor conditional responses for the next 30 min, but does not diminish the cardiac conditional responses (schizokinesis)

and (b) the greater stability of the cardiac conditional reflex. This visceral component may last years after the motor and salivary components have been extinguished, or they may resist extinction by strong agents, such as convulsions. See Figure 11 (experiments of Andy, Gliedman, and Gantt). The cardiac conditional reflex is present soon after an induced hippocampal convulsion, the conditioned motor response being lost [25]. Similar results have been obtained by P. Mac Lean.

Autokinesis

There is another process, seen especially in neurotic animals, viz. a development of symptoms from traces of past stimulations, their interrelations, and perhaps new internal elaborations. In our neurotic dogs we have seen the appearance of new symptoms—sexual, urinary, respiratory, cardiac—many years after cessation of the active experimentation but based upon those past stressful stimulations. Thus in dog Nick we could, after nine repetitions of a neutral light given in the room where the stress occurred 4 years previously, form an anxiety-like dyspnea as severe as the original dyspnea. In the human being with his much greater capacity for symbolization, there may occur on the basis of some past emotional disturbance, perhaps in childhood, and without conscious memory of the event, elaborations and developments to many associations of the original environment, related to language, people, etc. Thus hypertension which was produced to an original emotional situation may become chronic and permanent, and elaborated to many originally unrelated circumstances through the conditional reflex principle of generalization and association, as occurred with dog Nick and a light signal [12].

Autokinesis, as we see it in the laboratory, is most often abnormal and pathological, but it may also operate normally and therapeutically to improve cardiovascular adaptability. The mechanism of this internal elaboration is not known, but the fact exists. The work of Eccles [7] and Mountcastle (personal communication) furnishes some scientific basis for such internal new relationships between foci of excitation in the central nervous system.

Conclusion

The principle established by Claude Bernard, the ability of the organism to maintain a constant *milieu intérieur*, amplified by Cannon as homeostasis, expanded by the modern electronic physiologists as feedback, should be joined by the principles of pathology (schizokinesis) and the keystone of the living arch resting upon these two stones, viz. autokinesis, which may be either positive or negative. It is the study of the heart more than any other organ which has revealed to us these two new principles. To conclude our work on this veteran of the physiolygical systems, we may paraphrase in reverse the statement of Dr. Samuel Johnson ("we cannot see into the hearts of men, but their actions are open to observation"): *though the observed actions of men hide their real thoughts and feelings, these are revealed by the observations on their hearts.*

REFERENCES

1. ALEXANDER, L. (1959) Objective approach to psychiatric diagnosis and evalaution of drug effects by means of the conditional reflex technique, *Biological Psychiatry*, New York, Grune, pp. 154–83.
2. BIRK, L., CONTE, L., and GANTT, W. H. (1959) Inhibitory effect of serotonin (5-HTP) on retention of cardiac and motor conditional reflexes: schizokinesis, *Physiologist* 2 (3).
3. BRIDGER, W. H., and GANTT, W. H. (1956) The effect of mescaline on differentiated conditional reflexes, *Am J. Psychiat.* 113 (4)..
4. BYKOV, K. M. (1957) *Cerebral Cortex and Internal Organs* (ed. W. H. Gantt), New York, Chemical Publ.
5. DYKMAN, R. A., and GANTT, W. H. (1959) The parasympathetic component of unlearned and acquired cardiac responses, *J. Comp. Physiol. Psychol.* 52 (2).
6. DYKMAN, R. A., and GANTT, W. H. (1956) Relation of experimental tachycardia to amplitude of motor activity and intensity of the motivating stimulus, *Am. J. Physiol.* 185, p. 495.
7. ECCLES, J. C. (1958) Physiology of imagination, *Scient. Am.*, p. 135.
8. FREEDMAN, B. (1951) Conditioning of respiration and its psychosomatic implications, *J. Nerv. Ment. Dis.* 113 (1).
9. GANTT, W. H., KATZENELBOGEN, S., and LOUCKS, R. B. (1937) An attempt to condition adrenalin hyperglycemia, *Bull. Johns Hopkins Hosp.* 60, p. 400.
10. GANTT, W. H. (1937) Contributions to the physiology of the conditioned reflex, *Arch. Neurol. Psychiat.* 37, p. 848.
11. GANTT, W. H., and HOFFMAN, W. C. (1940) Conditioned cardio-respiratory changes accompanying conditioned food reflexes, *Am. J. Physiol.* 129, p. 360.
12. GANTT, W. H. (1944) *Experimental Basis for Neurotic Behavior*, New York, Hoeber,. 212 pp.
13. GANTT, W. H. (1946) Cardiac conditional reflexes to time, *Trans. Am. Neurol. Assoc.*, p. 166.
14. GANTT, W. H., HOFFMAN, W. C., and DWORKIN, S. (1947) The cardiac conditional reflex, *XVIIth Internat. Physiol. Congress*, Oxford, p. 15.
15. GANTT, W. H. (1949) Emotional state on acquired and inborn reactions: satiation on cardiac conditional reflexes and unconditional reflexes to food, *Fed. Proc.* 8, p. 52.
16. GANTT, W. H., and TRAUGOTT, U. (1949) Retention of cardiac, salivary, and motor conditional reflexes, *Am. J. Physiol.* 159, p. 569.
17. GANTT, W. H., GAKENHEIMER, W. A., and STUNKARD, A. (1951) Development of cardiac reflex to time intervals, *Fed. Proc.* 10, p. 47.
18. GANTT, W. H. (1952) Effect of alcohol on the sexual reflexes of normal and neurotic male dogs, *Psychosom.* Med. 14 (3).
19. GANTT, W. H. (1952) Experimental induction of psychoneuroses by conditioned reflex, in *Biology of Mental Health and Disease*, New York, Hoeber, pp. 508–14.
20. GANTT, W. H. (1957) Pharmacological agents in study of higher nervous activity, *Dis. Nerv. System* 18 (9).
21. GANTT, W. H., and DYKMAN, R. A. (1957) Experimental psychogenic tachycardia, in *Experimental Psychopathology*, New York, Grune, pp. 12–19.
22. GANTT, W. H. (1957) Normal and abnormal adaptations—homeostasis, schizokinesis and autokinesis, *Dis. Nerv. System* 18 (7).
22a. GANTT, W. H. (1953) Principles of nervous breakdown—schizokinesis and autokinesis, *Ann. New York Acad. Sc.* 56, p. 143.

23. Gantt, W. H. (1957) Anatomical control of the cardiac conditional reflex: role of the vagus in control of acquired disorders, *Trans. Am. Neurol. Assoc.* p. 142.
24. Gantt, W. H., Newton, J. E. O., and Stephens, J. H. Person as a factor in normal and abnormal behavior, *Psychosom. Med.* (in press).
25. Gantt, W. H. (1958) *Physiological Bases of Psychiatry*, Springfield, Ill., Thomas.
26. Kosupkin, J. M., and Olmsted, J. M. D. (1943) Slowing of the heart as a conditioned reflex in the rabbit, *Am. J. Physiol.* **139**, p. 550.
27. Light, J. S., and Gantt, W. H. (1936) Essential part of reflex arc for establishment of conditioned reflex: formation of conditioned reflex after exclusion of motor peripheral end, *J. Comp. Psychol.* **21**, p. 19.
28. Moore, A. U., and Marcuse, F. L. (1945) Salivary, cardiac and motor indices of conditioning in two sows, *J. Comp. Psychol.* **38** (1).
29. Newton, J. E. O., and Gantt, W. H. (1958) Cardiac conditional reflexes in the opossum, *Physiologist* **1**, (4), p. 55.
30. Newton, J. E. O., and Gantt, W. H. (1959) Independence of cardiac and motor orienting reflexes: schizokinesis, *Pharmacologist* **1**, p. 57.
31. Pavlov, I. (1941) *Lectures on Conditioned Reflexes* translated and edited by W. H. Gantt, New York, International Publ., vol. I, 414 pages.
32. Perez-Cruet, J., and Gantt, W. H. The conditional reflex electro-cardiogram to bulbocapnine—conditioning of the T-waves (in press).
33. Perez-Cruet, J., and Gantt, W. H. (1959) Relation between heart rate and "spontaneous" movements, *Bull. Johns Hopkins Hosp.* **105**, p. 315.
34. Peters, J. E., and Gantt, W. H. (1953) Effect of graded degrees of muscular exertion on human heart rate and the role of muscular exertion in cardiac conditional reflexes, *J. Gen. Psychol.* **49**, p. 31.
35. Peters, J. E., and Gantt, W. H. (1951) Conditioning of human heart rate to graded degrees of muscular tension, *Fed. Proc.* **10**, p. 104.
36. Robinson, J., and Gantt, W. H. (1947) The orienting reflex (questioning reaction): cardiac, respiratory, salivary and motor components, *Bull. Johns Hopkins Hosp.* **80** (5).
37. Shmavonian, B. M. (1959) Methodological study of vasomotor conditioning in human subjects, *J. Comp. Physiol. Psychol.* **52** (3).
38. Simonson, E., and Brozek, J. (1959) Russian research on arterial hypertension, *Ann. Int. Med.*, p. 120.
39. Stephens, J. H., and Gantt, W. H. (1956) The differential effect of morphine on cardiac and motor conditional reflexes—schizokinesis, *Bull. Johns Hopkins Hosp.* **98**, p. 245.
40. Traugott, N. N., Ballonov, L. Y., and Lichtko, A. E. (1958) *Evolutionary physiology, Acad. Sc. USSR, Moscow*, Vol. III.

8

CONDITIONAL-REFLEX CONNECTIONS OF THE KIDNEY†

K. M. Bykov

THE method of chronic experiment demands that the investigator should be specifically trained, as the procedure differs greatly from the acute experiment in which the investigator considers only one particular aspect of the process and is interested in isolating a complex phenomenon by concentrating his attention on that particular part of the process in the focus of his observation. Under the conditions of a chronic experiment, in additon to separately analyzing a single phenomenon, the development of a complex process is also observed as it runs its natural physiological course. The chronic experiment, therefore offers an opportunity for studying the architecture of the most complex functional phenomena and for penetrating into the very nature of the process under investigation. A synthesis of a process requires that the phenomena observed should be thouroughly analyzed at every stage of their development. For this purpose, a chronic experiment is sometimes combined with acute experiments. A knowledge of the complex regulating adjustments of the animal organism can only be gained under conditions of a chronic experiment on a sound and intact animal. Neither artificial nerve stimulation nor extirpation can give a true idea of a complex functional phenomenon in which the highest regulating and most sensitive apparatus participates.

One of the most essential conditions for adequately conducting the experiments is regularity. Any change in time for the daily test affects the course of the diuresis. As we shall see, temporal connections play an important part both in the origin and in the development of conditional reflexes.

It is necessary to emphasize the peculiarities of the chronic experiment because it determines the success of the investigation and makes possible the detection of the origin of a temporary connection which may be intentionally formed by the investigator, may develop independently in the course of the experiment, or may have even developed prior to the animal's being brought into the laboratory.

---

†By permission of Chemical Publishing Co., Inc., New York, from: *Cerebral Cortex*, by Bykov

Together with our collaborator, Alexeev-Berkman, we first attempted to form temporary connections with the activity of the kidneys and to study the properties of the conditional reflexes thus formed. Renal secretion was systematically investigated both under conditions of normal diuresis, independently of any special intake of liquids, and also when the intake of water was increased. In the second case, one of the experimental dogs was given injections of 100 cc of water per rectum. Before the experiments were begun, the procedure of injecting the water was repeated several times in order to avoid any unconditional reflex effect on the activity of the kidney by the stimulation of injecting the water, as well as any indirect effect resulting from a change in the cardiovascular system. The initial experiments served to establish that in 16–18 h after the last injection of water, urination was very slight, only a few cubic centimeters in 2 hr (Table 1).

TABLE 1. CONTROL SECRETION

Experiment of December 8, 1924			
Dog Norka placed in stand at 15 : 02			
Time	Cubic centimeters of urine each 15 min	Time	Cubic centimeters of urine each 15 min
15 : 17	0·6 ⎫	16 : 17	0·1 ⎫
15 : 32	0·4 ⎪ 1·5 cc	16 : 33	0·1 ⎪ 0·4 cc
15 : 47	0·3 ⎬ for 1 hr	16 : 47	0·1 ⎬ for 1 hr
16 : 02	0·2 ⎭	17 : 02	0·2 ⎭

The total quantity of urine spontaneously secreted was 1. 9 cc.

To stimulate urination, 100 cc of water, heated to body temperature, was given per rectum. The most striking feature was that as we proceeded with the experiment, the quantity of urine was found to increase from day to day, and diuresis became marked as soon as the dog was placed in the stand and the usual apparatus attached.

In a number of subsequent experiments, when the dog was given 100 cc water, administered per rectum, the quantity of urine secreted, increased as shown in Table 2.

Considerably intensified urinary secretion at a time when the water could not have yet produced hydremia, as well as the progressively increasing diuresis observed in every successive test, led us to assume that the very environment of the experiment had become a conditional stimulus for urinary secretion. This assumption was later fully confirmed by a number of special experiments. To exclude the effect of hydremia and to determine the role of all the different factors attending the actual injection of water into the rectum, we used a syphon enema in subsequent experiments (Figure 1).

TABLE 2. SECRETION AFTER ADMINISTRATION OF 100 cc WATER

Date of test January, 1925	Cubic centimeters of urine for 2 hr
2	6·4
6	14·3
7	17·3
8	22·0
18	22·5
20	28·2

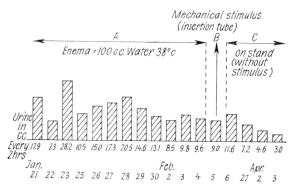

FIG. 1. Conditional-reflex diuresis to environment (dog Norka). A, diuresis after enema of 100 cc warm water; B, diuresis during introduction of the tube for the enema into the rectum without injection; C, diuresis during placing the dog in the stand without stimulation

The experiments represented by the diagram of Figure 1 show that 100 cc of water, introduced per rectum and instantly ejected, produced diuresis of the same, or even greater intensity than the introduction of water into the intestine and its entrance into the blood. In our experiments with the enema, we observed that renal secretion varied in different experiments, from 7 to 28 cc in 2 hr. Increased diuresis (spontaneous secretion) was produced by a mechanical stimulation of the rectum with a rubber tube and even by merely placing the animal in the stand. After the experiments, in which the animal was placed in the stand (where all the experiments were performed), had been repeated many times without, however, administering any enemas, diuresis gradually came down to the initial values observed at the beginning of our experiments.

The results of a number of experiments in which the dog Norka was placed in the stand without using any other stimuli that had coincided with the giving of an enema are listed in Table 3.

As can be seen from these experiments, when the dog was placed in the stand, diuresis returned to its initial value only after 2 months. Apparently,

TABLE 3. EFFECT OF ENVIRONMENT

Day of trial	Cubic centimeters of urine for 2 hr
February 6, 1925	11·6
February, 22 1925	7·2
April 2, 1925	4·6
April 3, 1925	2·8

the cortical connection formed was extinguished very slowly. A stable conditional salivary reflex dies out in the course of one experiment if the stimulation is repeated several times without being reinforced by the unconditional stimulus (feeding), but it is clear that the temporary connection formed to the secretion of urine disappears much more slowly.

Besides the environment of the experiments in which the animal was given the water injections, it was found that the action of any agent previously indifferent with respect to kidney activity, when combined with water infusion, could after some time produce considerable urination by its isolated action. Experiments on the formation of artificial conditional reflexes to diuresis were carried out on Norka and in another similarly operated dog, Koosachka.

When the temporary connections of the experiment to the environment were extinguished in both dogs, we combined the sounding of an organ pipe with water injection per rectum administered in a soundproof room. The tone was started a minute before the administration of water began and was interrupted a minute after it was completed. After the injections had been combined with the sound of the tone eleven times, the isolated action of the sound was tested without the injection. Under these conditions, Norka secreted 14.2 cc of urine in 5 hr instead of the usual 2 cc of spontaneous diuresis. Similarly intense diuresis was produced by the action of the sound in the other dog Koosachka. Then, after the stimulus by the sound was reinforced in the second dog another seven times by water injections, its isolated action gave 13 cc of urine in 5 hr.

In all the experiments previously described, it was not only the tone, but the total environment of the experiment which acted as a conditional stimulus. It sufficed to place the dog in the experimental room and to start preparations for administering the injection to increase the renal secretion. Against this novel background, the action of the sound produced greatly increased diuresis.

It was thus established that any agent which was in no way previously connected with the usual environment of the experiment could be made to act as a conditional stimulus.

The sound of the tone was then extinguished in the same way as the environment of the experiment had been extinguished before, and diuresis was once more reduced to its normal value. That the increased renal secretion brought about by the action of a signal, which was combined with injecting water (the unconditional stimulus) and which had previously been indifferent with respect to renal activity, can justly be regarded as a conditional reflex is confirmed by the possibility of forming a differential inhibitory reflex from this positive conditional reflex. Pavlov's experiments have demonstrated that if a stimulus applied repeatedly in the course of an experiment is reinforced by an unconditional stimulus, while another similar stimulus is left unreinforced, the second fails to produce a conditional reflex, owing to the development of an inhibitory state. In the experiments with the conditional reflexes developed in the kidney, the differentiation between the two stimuli was formed as follows: the animal was placed in a stand unlike the one where it had been given the water injections. On this new stand, no injections were administered, but in the other room where the experiments were usually conducted they were given as before. For a number of weeks, the experimental dog Norka was alternately placed first in one room and then in the other.

The first room was not connected with the action of the unconditional stimulus (water)—it was the *differentiating* room; while the second room in which the water injections had been always administered, i.e., in which the unconditional stimulus had been brought into action was the *active room.* Observations were carried out by different persons in the two rooms by placing the dog on the stand without administering injections. Thus, the complex stimulus of one room widely differed from that of the other. The results of the experiments are shwon in Figure 2.

It can be clearly seen from the diagram of Figure 2 that placing the animal in the active room produced marked diuresis while placing it in the differentiating room produced considerably less. It was evident that a differentiation between the two complex stimuli, i.e., between the environment of the one and of the other room was formed within the first few days of the experiment.

The differentiation is formed in precisely the same way as the inhibitory salivary conditional reflex. In the first experiments, the application of the

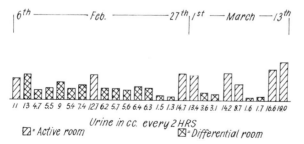

FIG. 2. Elaboration of differentiation to complex stimulus and experimental environment (dog Norka)

differential stimulus produced fairly abundant renal secretion, but later diuresis in the differentiating room gradually decreased, until it was reduced to values lower than those of spontaneous diuresis, whereas in the active room the quantity of urine, which was reduced by the first few applications of the differential stimulus, one more increased as the experiments were repeated. The decrease of diuresis caused by the action of the differential stimulus was followed by an increase in the urinary solids, while diuresis intensified by the effect of the active room is characterized by the secretion of urine low in solids. In the first case, the 4.3 cc of urine secreted during 5 hr of observation contained 5.4 per cent of solids, while in the second case the 17.3 cc secreted during the same period of time contained only 2.11 per cent of solids.

These experiments prove beyond doubt that in the one case, when the positive complex stimulus is in action, we have to deal with cortical excitation resulting in intensified diuresis and in the other, when a negative (differential) stimulus is in action, we observe cortical inhibition resulting in decreased diuresis.

In these experiments, complex stimuli were applied in both the active and the differentiating rooms. We shall now report an experiment carried out by Balakshina which illustrates the formation of a conditional reflex to a much simpler stimulus (Table 4). From this stimulus another stimulus was later differentiated.

TABLE 4. CONTROL

Experiment of December 4, 1933
Beginning of experiment: 10 a. m. with the dog Kenna

Time	Conditional stimulus	Cubic centimeters of urine each 15 min		
		Right kidney	Left kidney	
10 : 15	Horn 1 min	4.6	5·8	The dog stands quietly.
10 : 30	Horn 1 min	5·2	6·3	
10 : 32	Horn 1 min	—	—	
10 : 47	Horn 1 min	6·8	7·4	
11 : 02	Horn 1 min	8·2	9·0	
11 : 17	Horn 1 min	7·0	9·6	
11 : 32	Horn 1 min	10·9	12·6	
11 : 47	Horn 1 min	13·2	14·0	
12 : 02	Horn 1 min	9·8	10·2	
12 : 17	Horn 1 min	10·3	10·6	
12 : 32	Horn 1 min	7·4	8·2	
For 2 hours 27 min		83·4	93·7	
Total		177·1 cc		

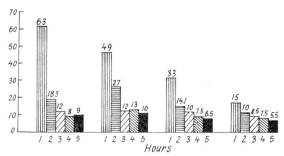

Fig. 3. Extinction of conditional–reflex diuresis (dog Jennia). The numbers over the bars indicate the quantity of urine secreted hourly

Balakshina succeeded in forming conditional–reflex anuria of the second order. An inhibitory conditional reflex to the noise of an inductorium was formed in the dog Aza and when the stimulus was found always to diminish diureses, Balakshina began combining the conditional reflex anuria with a preliminary stimulation caused by sounding a bell. After the bell had been several times reinforced by the sound of the inductorium and the reduced diuresis connected with it, then the isolated action of the bell began to reduce the secretion of urine below that observed in spontaneous diuresis.

Figure 3 shows the curve of diuresis in response to the conditional stimulus of the second order. A temporary connection of the second order is formed more slowly and the amount of urine secreted is smaller than to a conditional response of the first order.

A few more data on the formation of temporary connections to renal activity, obtained by Komendantova, are reported as follows: Komendantova gave the dog Jennia 450 cc water and 50 cc milk per os, 10 min after she had been placed in the stand. A few experiments sufficed to increase the diuresis considerably within the first hour after the dog had been placed in the stand. To prove that this was due to the temporary connection formed, Komendantova continued to place the dog in the stand for several successive days performing all the necessary preparations to administer the water without, however, actually giving it to the dog; this resulted in the extinction of the temporary connection which had been formed. Figure 3 shows the extinction of conditional–reflex diuresis.

After the *environmental* conditional reflex (cr) to diuresis had been extinguished, Komendantova proceeded to form an auditory cr reinforcing it by administering 200 cc water per rectum.

After twenty-three similar combinations, the isolated action of the bell clearly revealed the presence of a temporary connection. After the cr had been made stable, a differentiation to a less intense sound of the bell was formed. The experiments of December 31, 1937, and of January 21, 1938, in which the positive cs and the differentiated stimulus were respectively applied are recorded in Table 5.

TABLE 5. EFFECT OF POSITIVE AND NEGATIVE CONDITIONAL STIMULI ON CONDITIONAL
REFLEX DIURESIS

Time from beginning of test in min	Cubic centimeters of urine from both kidneys	
	Experiment of December 31, 1937	Experiment of January 29, 1938
5	3·00	3·00
10	3·00	3·25
	Conditional stimulus (bell, 1 min)	Less intense differential stimulus (i. e., weaker bell sounded for 1 min)
15	7·50	2·50
20	9·00	1·50
25	10·75	2·25
30	13·00	0·75
35	10·00	1·00
40	7·00	1·75
45	5·00	0·25
50	3·25	0·25
55	3·50	1·00
60	3·75	0·75
65	2·00	0·50
70	3·25	1·00
75	2·25	0·25
80	2·00	1·00
85	2·00	0·25
90	2·00	—
Total	92·25	21·25

In the first experiment, the quantity of urine secreted during $1^1/_2$ hours by both kidneys was 92.25 cc, while in the second experiment, when the negative stimulus was acting, the quantity secreted was only 21.25 cc.

It is evident that in the experiment of December 31, 1937, we were dealing with the stimulating effect of the cerebral cortex on the kidney, while in the experiment of January 29, 1938, the effect of the cortex on diuresis was inhibitory, causing inhibition not only of conditional diuresis, but also of spontaneous diuresis.

The inhibitory effect of the cortex was demonstrated by Balakshina on several animals; she formed an inhibitory diuretic conditional reflex leading to a stage of complete anuria. Conditional-reflex anuria has also been described by Leibson, in Orbeli's laboratory. Leibson obtained a reflex retention of urine by means of a painful stimulus (induction current) applied to the skin of the hind paws; the stimulation produced a violent motor reaction and an almost complete retention of urine.

In further experiments, Leibson succeeded in developing anuria by applying the isolated sound of the inductorium having coincided in time with the electro-cutaneous stimulation of the hind legs became a negative conditional stimulus of renal activity.

Balakshina effected retention of urinary secretion through the agency of the cortex in the following experiment, in which stimulation of the walls of one of the ureters, using a weak induction current passed through a specially constructed electrode, or a thermal stimulation of the mucous membrane of the ureteral orifice was used as an unconditional stimulus. The introduction of the electrode into the ureters produced no motor reaction in the animal. Stimulation of the ureters with a low induction current likewise produced no motor reaction but caused a retention of urine. The length and intensity of the urinary retention depended on the intensity of the stimulation applied to the ureters. The noise of the inductorium was used as a conditional stimulus.

The reaction to the sound of the inductorium was extinguished and after the stimulus had become indifferent, i.e. when it no longer produced any effect on renal secretion, Balakshina began combining it with electric stimulations of the ureter. As in the experiment of forming cr diuresis, in forming conditional anuria, 15-min portions of spontaneous diuresis were first recorded and only then was stimulation applied. After a few (6–8) stimulations of the ureter, the isolated sound of the inductorium was found to produce complete anuria. That this was no mechanical retention of urine caused by a spasm of the ureters is evidenced by the fact that, as a rule, retention developed gradually and the secretion of urine was gradually restored after the action of the conditional reflex had ceased. Mechanical retention, however, is characterized by a sudden onset of anuria.

In the same experimental dogs, Balakshina then formed differentiations from the cr anuria. Table 6 lists the values of the diuresis in response to the action of the positive conditional stimulus and to conditional inhibition which had been formed to urinary retention by stimulating the ureters. The data in this table are mean values of twenty experiments conducted on each of the dogs; each figure indicates the cubic centimeters of urine secreted by both kidneys during 2 hr.

TABLE 6. Conditioned Secretion

Dog	Normal spontaneous diuresis	Unconditional diuresis	Conditional reflex diuresis	Differentiation	Cr anuria (conditional inhibition)	Unconditional anuria
Kenna (1932–33)	84·0	206·0	176·3	92·4	—	—
Rosa (1933–34)	70·6	172·4	150·2	84·0	—	—
Aza (1934–35)	76·8	184·0	159·2	75·3	36·5	22·4

It may be seen from Table 6 that complete differentiation was not achieved in any one of the dogs. It was possible only to obtain a difference in urinary secretion in response to the action of the positive stimulus and to that of the inhibitory stimulus which clearly proved that a differentiation between the two stimuli had been formed. In all the investigated dogs, the effect of external inhibition, i.e., the action of sufficiently strong foreign stimuli (sound, light, etc.) applied during the action of the conditional stimulus, could be observed along with the positive conditional reflexes. The effect of the external inhibitory stimulus manifested itself in the disinhibiting action of the agent, when it was used against the background of cortical inhibition. Two experiments illustrate the effect produced by an external inhibitory stimulus on a newly formed conditioned diuresis and on conditioned anuria (disinhibition) (Figure 4, B and C).

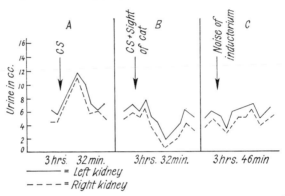

Fig. 4. A, conditional–reflex diuresis; B, external inhibition of conditional–reflex diuresis; C, disinhibition of conditional–reflex anuria under the influence of an external agent

It was possible even to form a conditional reflex retention of the second order against the background of a newly formed conditional inhibition. It is of interest to note that conditioned retention of the second order was more readily and more rapidly formed than conditioned diuresis of the second order. This interrelation between the intensity of the excitatory and of the inhibitory processes is apparently connected with the biological value of the stimulus.

That the kidney is very sensitive to cortical stimulation may be deduced from the rate at which conditional connections (positive reflexes of the second order and inhibitory reflexes of the first and the second order) are formed. The connections of the kidney with the cortex are extremely labile and varied, no less so than those of the salivary gland, the classical object of study of the Pavlovian school.

Our data indicate that it is the effector itself which determines the specific features of the temporary connection.

It should be likewise mentioned that indifferent external agents (auditory, visual, olfactory, etc.), unless they are unusually strong (in response to which no temporary connections were formed), fail to produce any appreciable effect on diuresis, whereas the conditional stimuli of the kidney itself or the conditional stimuli formed to another effector apparatus, such as food stimuli exercise a pronounced effect on the course of diuresis. These data concerning the cortical connections of the kidney lead us to believe that the kidney has a representation in the cerebral cortex.

It was of interest to test the possibility of forming temporary connections to diuresis by applying hormonal stimulations, acting on the kidney through the blood and important for the normal activity of the organism. In the experiments carried out by Borodavkina pituitrin was used as the stimulus. Pituitrin is known to affect diuresis by producing a change in the water balance.

Borodavkina determined the level of renal secretion while administrating 100 cc of water through a gastric fistula; she discovered a slight difference in the quantity of urine secreted by the right and left kidneys. The records of three experiments on the dog Tobik are presented in Table 7.

A subcutaneous injection of one ampule of pituitrin, administered against a background of a water load, produced the results shown in Table 8.

TABLE 7. Secretion of Urine Following Injection of 400 cc Water into the Stomach

Number of experiment	Cubic centimeters of urine for 1 hour	
	Left kidney	Right kidney
1	49·9	19·4
2	34·8	18·8
3	44·9	24·0

TABLE 8. Secretion of Urine Following Pituitrin Injection Given against the Background of 400 cc of Water Load

Number of experiment	Cubic centimeters of urine for 1 hr	
	Left kidney	Right kidney
1	1·5	3·9
2	11·9	1·2
3	13·5	6·9
4	12·4	6·8

In these experiments, there was clearly a marked inhibition of diuresis, due to the pituitrin. In the following experiments, recorded in Table 9, normal saline solution was substituted for pituitrin and injected against the background of a water load.

TABLE 9. CONDITIONAL–REFLEX DIURESIS ON NORMAL SALINE INJECTION
(DOG TOBIK)

Number of Experiment	Cubic centimeters of urine in 1 hr		Note
	Left kidney	Right kidney	
1	18·8	9·5	Cf. Table 7
2	18·5	3·2	
3	26·0	12·0	

It is obvious that the very pocedure of an injection came to be an inhibitory conditional stimulus, on the basis of the action of pituitrin on the kidney. Borodavkina succeeded in proving that the conditioned retention of urine could be disinhibited by means of any external agent. Sounding a whistle in the experiment that followed increased diuresis considerably, but then, in a subsequent experiment in which no whistle was used, the secretion of urine was once more decreased to the values observed in conditioned diuresis (Table 10).

TABLE 10. EXCITATORY AND INHIBITORY DIURESIS (DOG TOBIK)

Cubic centimeters of urine secreted from the left kidney in 1 hr	Cubic centimeters of urine secreted from the right kidney in 1 hr
Experiment with Sounding a Whistle	
39·8	20·6
Experiment without Sounding a Whistle	
26·2	12·0

These data prove that the external inhibitory agent disinhibited, to a great extent, the conditioned inhibitory diuresis.

The formation of conditioned diuresis has been lately experimentally produced by other laboratories, both in the Soviet Union and abroad. Grossman (1929) reports positive results in forming a temporary connection by administering daily water injection for a week. Marx, in attempting to reproduce the experiments previously made by Bykov and Alexeev-Berkman, failed to obtain a conditional renal secretion after twenty experiments with water injections. A study of his material reveals beyond doubt that no conditional reflex diuresis could possibly have been obtained under his experimental conditions, since he applied catheterization for the purpose of collecting urine. Most unfortunately the author was not acquainted with our work in the original and, therefore, was led to attribute the conditional reflex diuresis observed in our experiments to the direct reflex effect conveyed from the anus to the kidney, in spite of the fact that he is inclined to consider increased diuresis caused by merely placing the dog in the stand as being of the nature of a conditional reflex. In his other series of experiments, Marx gave the dogs bread in 400 cc. of water and milk, combining the intake of food with an auditory sound with the result that, in a number of cases, the isolated sound produced practically the same quantity of urine as the intake of water.

There are numerous observations described in medical literature where increased water metabolism was effected by means of hypnotic suggestion. The quantity of urine secreted owing to the effect of suggestion was the same as that caused by drinking large quantities of water. The same author (Marx, 1926) describes cases in which it was suggested that large quantities of water were being drunk and in which he had occasion to observe a change in water metabolism, analogous to that occuring when water is actually consumed in large quantities. I have already mentioned Platonov's experiments in which hypnotic suggestion affected the kidney. The experiments of Krasnogorsky in which he applied the conditional reflex method to treating enuresis nocturna are of no lesser interest.

Conditioned urinary secretion could be observed under laboratory conditions without any intentional formations of a temporary connection. In one of Scher's experimental dogs, conditional diuresis failed to be formed for a considerable length of time; the animal proved to have an extremely labile nervous system. The act of attaching the funnel for collecting urine sufficed to inhibit urination, and it proved very hard to elaborate a conditional reflex against this background by the action of any weaker agent. By the end of the experiment, however, before the dog was removed from the stand in order to be fed, an increase of spontaneous diuresis was often observed, a fact which was undoubtedly connected in time with the usual administration of water. Scher succeeded in confirming this in a series of special control experiments.

We could cite many more descriptions of medical observations, when any agent, coinciding in time with the intake of water, such as the sound of running water, the sight of water, and even phenomena less directly connected with drinking, stimulated micturition. Urination should, of course, not always be attributed to the process of renal secretion, for there are many well-known cases when the conditioned urination obtained (Bechterev, Krasnogorsky) depended on the muscular activity of the bladder and the sphincter and not on the secretion of urine by the kidney. Under the conditions of everyday life, the two phenomena may coincide and an intensified supply of urine to the bladder may become the stimulus for urination. We shall have the opportunity to prove the correctness of this assumption in dealing with the experiments devoted to the formation of interoceptive temporary connections.

It is our belief that the formation of temporary connections to renal activity is taking place continuously under normal conditions, but it is generally overlooked because of the fact that the conditional reflex part of this complex reaction of the organism is concealed or disguised by the action of unconditional stimuli and because we are in the habit of attributing the secretory activity of the kidney to stimuli directly acting on the kidney through the blood. Observations on diuresis in an acute experiment naturally fail to provide the opportunity for revealing the effect produced by the cerebral cortex on the kidney.

Similarly, observations on man which involve catheterization of the ureters practically exclude the possibility of establishing the dependence of urinary secretion on the higher parts of the central nervous system, owing to the inevitable inhibitory effect of catheterization.

In the same way as we fail to notice, in the course of the usual observations on the activity of the voluntary musculature developing under normal conditions, the reflexes causing flexion and extention, so with respect to an organ, such as the kidney, we fail to observe the effect produced by the cerebral cortex, which invariably manifests itself at any moment connected with changes occuring in the current reality of environment. Investigations conducted under conditions of the chronic experiment on a sound and intact animal have made it possible, by forming new artificial reflexes, to study the interrelation between the cerebral cortex and such an important organ as the kidney. Many pathological effects will be understood only after there has been obtained a precise knowledge of the regulating effect of the cerebral cortex on the complex functional activity of the kidney.

PSYCHOSEXUALITY IN ANIMALS†

W. Horsley Gantt

The facts that I have to report have one common feature with those of Dr Kinsey—they concern primarily the male. But while Dr Kinsey takes a telescopic view of thousands of subjects my view is a microscopic one of a lew individuals studied intensively throughout their lives—a view necessarily fimited and chiefly experimental.

The points that I shall emphasize are: (1) the profound effect of sexual excitation on other physiologic functions in the normal animal; (2) the reciprocal relations between these excitations, especially the inhibitory effect of sexual excitation on other excitations; (3) the definite relations between conflict arising outside the sexual sphere and sexual function.

The powerful drive of sexual excitation in normal animals is well known; how the male will brave prolonged deprivations and dangers for the one brief moment, often to die in the embrace of his mate. Witness the execution of the praying mantis by his consort, and of the drone after his nuptial flight, or the starvation of the male salmon before fertilizing the spawn.

Aside from these familiar examples, I shall cite two other observations from nature. My attention was first drawn to the inhibitory effect of sexual excitation in the giant woodcock which I hunted in the forests near Leningrad in the spring of 1926. This bird, somewhat larger than a grouse, dwells in the trees and is called by the Russians *glooharka* ("the deaf one") because of its oblivion to danger while singing its love song. Regardless of the noise the hunter makes, he may boldly walk towards the bird during the moments of singing, and arriving directly under the tree where the bird is sitting, may easily shoot him during the next burst of frenzied lovemaking.

I observed another example of the same inhibitory effect of sexual excitation later in an animal very lower on the zoologic ladder. During the spring of 1935–39 while walking over the grassy parks and golf courses of suburban Baltimore soon after sunrise, I became acquainted with some of the habits of the earthworm (the "fishing worm" of my boyhood days). These lowly benefactors of the art of agriculture are wont to emerge from their holes in the ground after nocturnal rain and before the sun becomes too strong. In the spring, from about March to May, the whole field is alive

† By permission of Grune & Stratton, Inc., New York, from: *Psychosexual Development in Health and Disease*, ed. by H. Gantt, New York 1949

with the nuptials of these creatures, soon after dawn. About one-fifth of the worm's length remains embedded in the soil while the other four-fifths is extended towards its neighbor who is similarly situated. During the copulatory act, the anterior third of the ventral surfaces of neighboring worms are applied to each other. Ordinarily, when the worms are not copulating, they are very alert; they withdraw into their tunnels at the approach of an intruder, detecting his footsteps several yards away, apparently through the tactile sense (they are less sensitive to air-borne noises, such as clapping of the hands). But during copulation they are as "deaf" as our friend the *glooharka*. Not only can they be approached, but one may, as with the *glooharka*, walk boldly up to them—and even prick them with a straw, especially if the pricking is done near the copulating end of the body—before they release their grasp and withdraw into their holes in the ground. The farther the prick from the copulating surfaces of the worm the sooner they withdraw, indicating a focus of inhibition in the more active areas of copulation. The one which is touched is the first to move, although the other partner also quickly withdraws once the clasp is broken. I have repeatedly performed these experiments with nearly uniform results. The picture of inhibition of the tactile sense and of the reaction to danger is so definite and striking in this simple organism that I feel it is an important fact in the comparative physiology of the sexual function. It is the same profound inhibition that we see during sexual excitation in lower vertebrates and mammals.

The clasp reflex in the frog during the mating season is another instance of the persistence of sexual excitation. Even though the animal is decerebrated, it continues its iron grip on the female, or on any object brought within reach; and it will continue to do so for several weeks, in spite of its mutilated and dying condition.

Beside the foregoing examples, I have measured repeatedly in the laboratory in normal animals both cat and dog, the reciprocal inhibition which exists between sexual and other forms of excitation. I submit below experiments demonstrating the immediate inhibitory influence of sexual excitation on both food excitation and rage.

A healthy vigorous tomcat 4 years old (Grumpet) was brought into a cage with a kitten about 6 months old. This tomcat would attempt to copulate indiscriminately with females (whether or not in estrus) or with kittens, even nearly grown males unless they were strong enough to escape or resist. In the adjoining cage was another tomcat (Cinder) recently brought into the laboratory. Grumpet lost a canine tooth during a battle and both cats were often seriously injured; they would likely have fought to death unless separated. Grumpet would usually challenge the other tom on sight. For the purpose of the experiment Grumpet was separated overnight from all other cats and deprived of food for the same time. He was allowed in the cage with the kitten; he attempted copulation by grasping the kitten by the scruff of the neck, mounting, and making copulatory movements (Table 1).

Table 1. Effect of Sexual Excitation on Food and Aggressive Responses

Time	Procedure
12 : 35	Grumpet (Tom I) put in with 6-month-old kitten
12 : 37	Copulatory movements, insertion, pelvic thrust
12 : 37–45	Second tomcat introduced during copulation. The copulatory movements were not disturbed by holding Tom II with head close Tom I, or by holding Tom II over Tom I so that his foot was touching back of Tom I.
12 : 45	Tom I removed from kitten
12 : 45–50	Refractory period for aggressive response in Tom I. During this time, Tom I will not fight Tom II, although Tom II is held close to Tom I, and Tom II is growling. Tom I forcibly sniffs, looks around for kitten, which has been removed from room.
12 : 51	Tom I begins to growl at Tom II who is now outside the room
12 : 53	Tom I slaps at Tom II through grating separating them
12 : 53–13 : 00	Tom I fights at Tom II through grating
13 : 01	Kitten brought back to Tom I's cage. Within 30 sec, Tom I mounts the kitten although he is only 18 in. from Tom II.
13 : 03	Tom I taken off kitten
13 : 03–08	Refractory period for aggressive responses toward Tom II. Tom I will not fight with Tom II although the kitten is placed tête-a-tête with Tom II, and only two feet away (separated by a grating). In 10 sec Tom I mounts kitten, paying no attention to Tom II, in spite of his proximity.
14 : 00	Tom I will not touch milk nor cheese offered him, although he usually takes them greedily. When the food is left in cage with Tom I, he eats it sometime during the night.

After Tom I and Tom II were allowed to fight with each other through the grating, Tom I mounted the kitten in from 10 to 30 sec after the fight.

In all of the above attempts of Tom I to copulate, except one, Tom I was unable to do more than make copulatory movements without insertion, owing to the resistance of the kitten.

The above experiment shows that there is a refractory period following sexual excitation in Tom I, during which Tom I does not show any aggression or reaction, and that this period lasts for 5 min (two observations). The refractory period for sexual stimuli following anger is, however, only 10–38 sec. These and other experiments demonstrate the greater intensity of the sexual excitation measured by the subsequent refractory period for food and aggressive stimuli, as compared to the intensity of the food and aggressive excitations measured by the refractory period following them toward sexual stimuli.

Thus the sexual excitation inhibits (1) for a short time, aggressiveness toward the other tom, and (2) for a much longer period, interest in food, despite the deadly enmity of the cats, on the one hand, and on the other, the enforced hunger of the animal. When Grumpet was allowed to copulate with a female, the results were similar.

Obviously the condition of the animal will affect these relationships. In Russia, during the famine which followed the revolution, I collected data showing that not only was there a marked decline in the birth rate, but that there was nearly universal amenorrhea, with diminished frequency of coition. The great decrease in love affairs was accompanied by a remarkable decline in the suicide rate. (Gantt, *Medical Review of Soviet Russia*, London 1927.)

A marked difference between the male and female cat is that the female's interest in food is not inhibited by the sexual excitation of copulation, for she, as well as a bitch, will accept food not only after coitus but even during the act! Dr. Beach tells me he has observed the same thing in dogs. (A hint for Dr. Kinsey when he extends his study to the female.) The female is, however, much more strongly oriented about the offspring than about the sexual act; she undergoes a great inhibition of conditional reflexes and of some unconditional reflexes post-partum, a fact which has been demonstrated several times in my laboratory with dogs. There is no disturbance of food conditional reflexes in either sex on the day following coitus in normal dogs.

The intensity of sexual excitation is likewise shown in its profound effect on respiration and heart rate. In a dog with anxiety, rapidly panting (over 100 per minute), the respiration becomes very regular after ejaculation and slows to 15 per min. In the human male after orgasm, the respiration also becomes very slow, deep and regular, sometimes decreasing to 4 or 5 per min for 5–10 min. Inspiration is fairly abrupt and very deep; expiration much slower, tapering off gradually, and followed by a long pause before the onset of the full inspiration. The change in the female is less marked.

Another indication of the intensity of sexual excitation appears in the heart rate. Figure 5 illustrates the acceleration of heart rate during food, sexual and other forms of excitation. Blood pressure would reveal even more striking changes.

Besides these normal relationships of this intense inhibitory effect of sexual arousal on the physiologic functions, I want to stress especially the psychopathologic relationship. We studied this by subjecting three dogs to the same procedure—that of giving them a difficult differentiation between two tones close together in pitch, both connected with food, one inhibitory, the other excitatory. We worked with these dogs, having them make this difficult differentiation for a year, and then we studied one of them for 11 years after we ceased experimentation with this difficult problem. The interesting result of these experiments was not so much the acute symptoms of neurosis that came about during the year of experimentation, but the fact that the development of these various nervous symptoms were related to and dependent on the original experimentation even though the dogs had been out of the experimental environment for several years.

I shall not take time to describe the acute symptoms†, which were like anxiety and varied in the different animals, but I shall tell you how they developed. One very interesting fact was the generalization: the animal not only reacted to the stimuli which were connected with the original difficult problem, but he reacted to any stimulus which might be used in the general environment, even though it was not presented until several years after the active experimentation had been discontinued. Thus, although the animal had never reacted to a light, if you used a flashing light in that room in which the difficulty was produced, the light itself would, after as few as ten repetitions, call out the same neurotic symptoms. When we give a light a few seconds before the tone it has no effect on respiration, although the tone has. But on the tenth trial, the tenth combination of light with the auditory stimulus, there is the same change to the light as to the tone. And where the light is used alone, after 1, 2, 3 and 4 sec—the tone having previously followed it in 5 sec—you see then after four seconds that the light itself after these few combinations in that environment will produce the same neurotic symptoms as the tone.

There was thus generalization of the neurotic reactions. Nick reacted not only to the specific stimuli we used but he had his own system of selecting stimuli, e.g. the people who worked with him. He gave the same reactions to these people and even though they were away from the original environment—200 miles out of Baltimore on a farm in Virginia—Nick would show the same anxiety symptoms as in the laboratory. When we would take the food that was used in the laboratory and show it to him on the farm he also gave the same pathologic reaction, often urinating and ejaculating.

After the experiments on the difficult problems were discontinued (2 years), we noticed other symptoms arising—respiratory, cardiac, urinary, sexual. The respiration was laboring and asthmatic, there was persistent pollakisuria—in the environment of conflict he would urinate as often as every 30 sec. One of the most interesting symptoms was the beginning of sexual erections, 2 years after the discontinuance of the experimentation. These occured almost every time the animal was brought into the experimental room, specifically to the stimuli that were used; they would also occur to the people that worked with him. When these same people came to see him at the farm, where these symptoms had gradually disappeared, they would reappear—he would urinate, and sometimes ejaculate when his former associates approached him.

† The details of these experiments have been given in my "Experimental Basis for Neurotic Behavior," Hoeber, N. Y. 1944.

There was another interesting fact that is perhaps more applicable to the dog than to the human being—that Nick would ejaculate not only to the person who worked with him, but to the members of the worker's family. I assume this was due to a general familial olfactory stimulus for the dog.

We know of pathologic ejaculations clinically in patients; we also know of it in other animals. Kluever has reported in monkeys and Jacobsen in chimpanzees that when they have a difficult problem they will sit and masturbate. Ischlondsky has frequently noticed that French children masturbate excessively during the period of examinations.

Sexual symptoms in this particular dog (Nick) can be classified in several ways. First the conflict produces *pathologic sexual reactions* to inadequate stimuli. The tone, the buzzer, and the food are not adequate stimuli, i.e. they are not specific stimuli for sexual erection. So in the neurotic animal these adventitious sexual reactions are aroused by inadequate stimuli. The second fact that we observed is paradoxically opposite to this, viz., that the environment in which the *neurosis* is produced has an *inhibitory effect on the reaction of the animal to adequate sexual stimuli*. If you confront the animal with a bitch in estrus in the neurotic enviromnent, he shows ejaculatio praecox and some evidence of impotence, instead of the pathologic sexual reactions occurring with his anxiety. Here you see apparently a state opposite to the first. Third, *sexual excitation has an inhibitory effect on the symptoms of anxiety.* This can be seen in the very exact time relationships in the acute experiment; and we can also see it in the chronic experiments, for we found that the animal, when put in a paddock with a dog in estrus, showed less anxiety for many days and even after the dog was in estrus, though the effect of this bitch gradually disappeared after the period of estrus.

Nick and Fritz are two dogs of different types, showing varying susceptibility to breakdown according to their previously determined temperaments. In Nick there was negativism to food after he had worked at this difficult problem for several months. He consistently refused food in the experimental room, although he ate greedily outside that environment. Even after several years' cessation of the experimentation, during his occasional visits to the experimental room Nick panted and pulled on his leash when he heard a tone formerly connected with the difficult differentiation. On these visits no problem was presented; he could get food whenever he wanted it. He revealed simply a development that occurred after the period of experimentation and persisted for 10 additional years until the end of his life.

Fritz, on the other hand, went through an acute breakdown, lasting only several months, during the period of experimentation. The condition did not become chronic.

During these later visits, on hearing the tone, Nick contrasted to Fritz in appearance. In Nick there was the sexual erection that the tone always produced—a prominent erection appearing within a few seconds after the onset of the tone. We could always count on Nick for a demonstration! This pathologic function of the sexual erections to the tone was not inhibited by the presence of other people during the experiment, as normal reflexes frequently are.

Figure 1 shows the spread of this conflict to other physiologic symptoms evoked by the person who passes in front of the window of the experimental room. At the beginning the heart rate is 100 per min, but soon after the person who has worked with the dog appeared in front of the window, the heart rate increases from 100 to 140. Another instance is shown by a control reading 1.8 sec before the person passes in front of the window, when the heart rate is 80 per minute, and 1.8 sec afterward—you can see the heart rate has risen to 133.

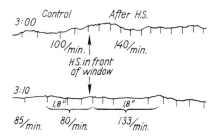

FIG. 1. Effect of experimenter on heart rate (Nick)

These marked changes in heart rate would be missed if we did not take very short periods. The heart rate accelerates in the next cycle after the stimulus, and the entire increase in heart rate may be over within a few seconds. Therefore if you do not take the rate for short periods, you will not see these effects, and you may not see any effect in the animal by any other measurement that we have used.

Figure 2 shows the irregular respiration of the animal in this environment of conflict. I want to emphasize particularly the effect of a person petting the dog—the smooth, deep respiration, the marked change, which you might call reassurance; that the presence of the person has on the animal. This is a social factor that we could demonstrate in many other ways.

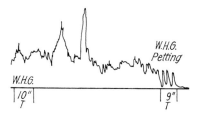

FIG. 2. Social factor and respiration

The respiratory records after sexual excitation and orgasm and after the social stimulus of petting are strikingly similar. The animal ordinarily shows a very rapid respiration in the environment of conflict—up to a 300 per min. In the neurotic environment, the respiration may be 210 per min—faster even than the heart rate. After orgasm the respiratory rate is only 20 per min; it is slow and deep, very much like it is when a laboratory worker faces the camera with the dog, affording him relief from the anxiety (Figure 3).

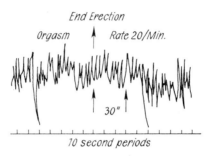

FIG. 3. Respiration in Nick during and after excitation

For a number of minutes after the orgasm, respiration continues to be very slow and deep.

In Figure 4 the inhibitory effects of this sexual excitation are seen on other functions—during sexual stimulation and some minutes later, the

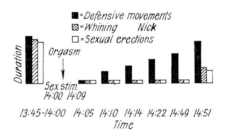

FIG. 4. Sexual excitation and anxiety

anxiety symptoms are completely inhibited to the stimuli which were used to bring them out originally. After sexual stimulation and orgasm there is a long "refractory" period lasting nearly an hour during which Nick does not give the usual anxiety-like symptoms to the tone. Normally there is whining, panting, struggling, backing away from the tone, and pathologic sexual erections, but these symptoms to the tone are completely absent during stimulation of the peripheral genitalia and they are very much diminished even one hour after the sexual stimulation.

Figure 5 shows in normal dogs the intensity of the sexual excitation measured by the heart rate. Here, for example, we see during sexual excitation in three dogs that they have a greater increase in heart rate during sexual excitation and orgasm, than they have to food stimuli and to eating, or to many other kinds of stimuli, such as a cat on the dog, clawing its back. The heart rate indicates the intensity of the excitation.

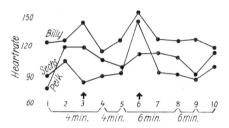

Fig. 5. HR and sexual excitation. (1) Control. (2) Excitatory food CR. (3) Eating. (4) Inhibitory CR. (5) Control. (6) During orgasm. (7) After orgasm but during erection lasting 4 min. (8) Immediately after erection. (9) Shaking dog violently. (10) HS in room with dog

In normal dogs there is no difference in the latent period of ejaculation and latent period of erection in the two environments (inside and outside of the laboratory room). However, in the neurotic dog, in the environment where the neurosis has been produced, the latent period of ejaculation and of erection is shorter, and the duration of the erection is reduced to about half. Here is the paradoxic effect—the *inhibition* of sexual erection to adequate stimuli and the appearance of erections to inadequate stimuli. The 2-year rest removed the effect of the experimental room in inhibiting sexual reactions to adequate stimuli. Shorter periods of rest were without effect.

An instance of how easily the sexual function can be inhibited by a slight and acute disturbance instead of the chronic condition seen in Nick is illustrated in Figure 6. When a male dog had to make a differentiation of which he was not yet capable between two lights, one excitatory, the other inhibitory for food, a disturbance resulted, hardly observable in the food conditional reflexes and in the sexual function: sexual erection to adequate stimuli (peripheral stimulation of the penis) was inhibited for several days and only gradually returned to normal.

Here in animals where there is no traditional taboo connected with overt expression of the sexual function, we see revealed not only the intensity of sexual excitation but its profound inhibitory effect on other functions, as well as the paradoxic fact of susceptibility of the sexual function to inhibition by conflict in other spheres. Although in the adult human, language and other means of interpersonal communication tend to obscure the focus of excitation, especially when this is sexual, man is endowed with the same

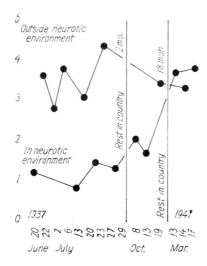

Fig. 6. Latent period of ejaculation. Effect of environment in labile dog on sexual reflexes (rest)

physiologic sytems—circulatory, respiratory, urinary, sexual—as the other mammals, and he obeys the same general biologic laws. Hence it is entirely within our right to believe that in man the sexual function may often assume the same dominant role†, both excitatory and inhibitory, as we can show experimentally it does in the earthworm, the bird, the cat and the dog.

Discussion

Several principles emerge from the experiments on Nick and other neurotic animals; first, the *spread* of the excitation from its origin in the food center to involve many physiologic systems—the respiratory, cardiac, urinary, sexual. Not only are these changes in some functions necessary components of the acute symptoms of the conflict, but the functions become stereotyped in a new way to emerge as definite and chronic respiratory, cardiac, urinary and sexual neuroses.

Unless we had been able to trace the development of each of these neuroses from its concept and to show the relation of each to the conflict in the food center, their origins would have remained enigmatic. The development in time i.e., the beginning of these symptoms at long intervals, 1–3 years after the experiments involving conflict had been discontinued, would further

† Not to be overlooked, however, in any explanation of the role of sexual excitation, is the special periodicity of the sexual function as well as its relation to other emotional states.

obscure the origin. A study of the sexual symptoms in Nick (see my *Experimental Basis for Neurotic Behavior*) indicates that a conflict in a functional center as unrelated to sex as is food, can spread to involve many functions of the organism even where there is no logical or understood connection between the functions. The *fact* is recognizable, but the *why* is at present as obscure as the *why* for the universal force of gravity. We may, however, make some teleologic or *a priori* suppositions, tentative and speculative, awaiting confirmation. The accumulation of inhibition of the specific and appropriate food conditional reflexes, secretory and motor, to the stimuli and the environment of the original conflict and the subsequent tension mounting during the life of the dog in the general environment may spill over into other physiologic systems resulting in activities of no apparent use to the organism but which nevertheless release the tension. Thus the sexual excitation, erection, and ejaculation, by expending some of the energy in the peripheral expression, may at least temporarily remove some of the inhibited excitation.

Observations have been made by Whitehorn in patients and by Hoffman and myself in dogs that are perhaps related to such a theoretic explanation, viz. the fact that in an individual, at least when a spontaneous movement is made, it is preceded rather than followed by an acceleration of heart rate. The nature of the spontaneous movements, i.e. whether the dog changes from sitting to standing or vice versa, or merely shifts his weight, is immaterial. First there is the cardiac acceleration, then the movement, or as Hoffman has put it, "first comes the heart rate and then the dog". From these observations of normal behavior, it appears that some natural excitation in the central nervous systems, expressed by an increase in heart rate, not only results in but rapidly expends itself in muscular movement. The confirmation of such an explanation, however, must await detailed experiments.

Another mechanism, or perhaps a different aspect of the same law, may be invoked as an explanation here. In a series of experiments from 1933 to 1936, I have shown that the advent of the unconditional reflex tends to inhibit the activity of the conditional reflex, both motor and secretory. Moreover, the unconditional reflex is followed by a period of quiescence, a kind of prolonged refractory period, during which the organism cannot be stimulated by conditional stimuli specific for the involved function. Thus, if one gives a tone as a conditional stimulus for food, then follows it by food, even if the dog has finished eating, there is a certain period of seconds or minutes during which the animal will not respond to this or even to other food conditional stimuli. This is not because the animal is satiated, for the same thing occurs with a smaller amount of food. Perhaps in a similar way the expression of symptoms, i.e. peripheral activity, may be followed by a period of rest during which the animal is not subject to further stimulation. Whitehorn has suggested such a possible advantage of neurotic symptoms.

The above theory of the mechanism of the relief of tension by activity must be considered at the present as unproven and a scheme for future critical experiments.

Finally, the comparative physiology of the cardiac, secretory and motor conditional reflexes reveals what may be a basic constitutional mechanism for nervous dysfunction on the higher level of behavior. Our studies show that the cardiac component is formed more quickly than the motor component of the conditional reflex to pain and that the cardiac component persists much longer.

The cardiac component is both more sensitive in appearing first and paradoxically more stable in persisting longer. Without reinforcement, it has endured as long as 2 years after the motor component has dropped out. If the cardiac acceleration represents the inner emotional aspect, and the motor conditional reflex the specific external component, we have the picture of an organism externally in adaptation to the environment but internally excited and reacting to the trace of a conditional stimulus which long since ceased to have its former significance. The animal has achieved external adaptation but emotionally it is maladapted. Thus there is a kind of cleavage between the outer specific muscular and the inner cardiac expression. Were it not for the fact that the specific secretory conditional reflexes behave more like the skeletal muscular ones, we would be tempted to put it on the basis of cerebrospinal somatic versus autonomic but, as the respiratory component also accompanies the cardiac, it seems to be a question of general emotional conditional reflex versus specific conditional reflex (secretory and motor). At any rate, there is this normal physiological cleavage, adaptive inhibition in the specific response with persisting excitation in the general emotional reaction. The latter may even become more pronounced than it was originally. Thus through this built-in principle of dysfunction, the organism tends to become a museum of archaic emotional responses, tied to the past internally while exhibiting freedom externally.

In our study of abnormal behavior we must reckon with this constitutional principle of dysfunction as well as with the acquired neurotic tendencies.

10

ACQUIRED VESTIBULAR BALANCING RESPONSES†

W. Horsley Gantt

Hans Löwenbach

AND

Clinton Brown

Problem and Procedure

THE problem which this study attempted to answer was whether reactions of equilibration based solely upon labyrinthine reflexes could be acquired as a result of individual experience, i.e. whether these responses could be conditioned. The vestibular response was studied in the human subject, in both normal and hemidecorticate dogs and in lower-order animals such as the pigeon, alligator and iguana.

Three methods for producing vestibular stimulation (and subsequent balancing or imbalancing adjustments) were available: caloric, rotational or tilting, and galvanic. The latter method was chosen because of its simplicity and the opportunity its use afforded for introducing measurable increments of stimulation even though it was recognized as the less desirable than other adequate stimuli. Subjects were blindfolded to exclude visual cues for balance or imbalance and were therefore forced to rely upon remaining proprioceptive and vestibular cues. In the dog, the head was enclosed in a mask-like covering and electrodes were inserted deep into the external auditory meatus. The passage of a brief d.c. current ranging from 3 to 8 mA between these electrodes resulted in an UR involving tilting of the muzzle, and with increased current—falling. Nausea was reported by the human subjects and the dogs displayed excessive salivation, and vomiting upon continued stimulation. There was an unusual reaction in a few of the experimental dogs marked by the appearance of a profound narcoleptic-like sleep with cataplexy and anesthesia.

Differentiation was accomplished by reversing the polarity of the current to the elctrodes, thus producing similar reactions but in an opposite direction. The CS was an auditory stimulus of 3–5 sec duration.

† By permission of *Trans. Am. Neurol. Assoc.* 1953

Stimulation of the vestibular response by tilting was performed on both dogs and humans.

The final phase of the study was concerned with the application of the above conditioning procedures to hemidecorticate dogs.

Results and Discussion

Alligator: US, 6 mA current; UR, jerk of head to positive ear, then movement to negative ear, variable movements of tail. Following experimental procedures there was a marked difference in neck muscle tonus, with an increase on the side of the negative ear. There was no evidence of conditioning after 300 trials to the auditory stimulus, neither in respiration, movement nor heart rate.

Iguana: US, 2.5 mA current; CS, 3 sec tone; UR, quick movement of head to the left with elevation of about 60°. After 400 reinforcements there was no evidence of CR formation. Some transient hypertonicity of neck muscles was noted which disappeared with a reversal of the polarity of current.

Pigeon: US, 0.5–1.0 mA; CS, 3 sec tone; UR, rotation of body in direction of the negative ear with a jerk to the positive ear. After five reinforcements a CR of struggling appeared; after thirteen reinforcements a jerk to the positive ear was noted, after twenty-six reinforcements there was a typical rotation to the side of the negative ear. While nystagmus and rotation were often present when the pigeon was placed in the experimental stand, after sixty-eight reinforcements the CS stopped or reversed the nystagmus.

Normal dogs: Using four dogs and galvanic current to produce the unconditional vestibular stimulation, the conditional responses to an auditory CS consisted of loss of balance and characteristic head and body movements. Differentiation was also attained by reversing the polarity of the current applied to produce opposite reflex movements which were conditioned to a new auditory stimulus. Two dogs used developed peculiar behavior in the form of prolonged sleep-like states and hypotonicity of the skeletal musculature. The conditioned vestibular responses persisted without additional training for at least 8 months.

Very striking was the type of sleep obtained as the result of the conditioning to the galvanic stimulus. In two of the dogs the sleep was so profound that it was impossible to awaken the dog by loud sounds, lifting him off the floor, pricking him with a hypodermic needle. However he would still give the CR to the conditional stimulus by raising his head. When the mask was removed the dog took several minutes to awaken during which time he walked around as if dazed.

Normal dogs were also subjected to tilting while blindfolded in an enclosed box, which was then displaced sharply through 10–20 degrees. The CS was

a 5-sec tone preceding the tilting. A response of leaning towards the side opposite from the tilting appeared early in the conditioning procedure and remained constant until the 50th trial when it gradually disappeared only to reappear after the 170th trial and remain constant until the 500th trial.

Hemi-decorticate dogs: Three dogs were used—Verulam, Crazy, and Vespucchi.

Verulam: Decorticated right gyrus ectosylvius (after Spiegel). US 2–10 mA, right ear negative. UR, elevation of the right ear, usually movement of the head to left. CS, auditory stimulus for 3 sec. The CR appeared to the tone signal after seven reinforcements. At first was amorphous in form with variable rotation to left and right and with random elevation of left and right ear. After twenty-two reinforcements, the CR approached duplication of the UR, but imperfectly. Experiments were terminated after sixty repetitions.

Crazy: Left decorticated with right gyrus cinguli extirpated (Woolsey), about 1943. US, 4–8 mA, CS, metronome (100 for one ear and 144 for the other). UR as above. This dog formed specific motor CRs (withdrawal of leg and cardiac CR to faradic shock to left forepaw) with, however, some impairment of time CRs. In 1953, vestibular conditioning to galvanic stimulation was attempted. After sixty reinforcements there was a generalized CR movement taking the form of crouching, variable movements of the head, but no clear-cut vestibular reaction. There was a generalized impairment of the CR function but no absolute loss in either motor, cardiac or vestibular systems.

Vespucchi: Left frontal motor area removed with resulting circus movements to the left. US, 4–8 mA with the right ear negative. UR, cessation of circus movements, going to right instead of left, violent struggling, occasional vomiting, elevation of the right ear. The CR appeared in a diffuse manner on the second trial and was apparently a duplication of the UR.

Human Subjects: Five subjects were used in all. The US was 2–8 mA for 5 sec. with a gradual reduction of current to zero through 20 sec. The UR appeared as swaying, turning or falling, usually to the negative side. The first appearance of the CR was from the 4th to the 22nd trial. The CR was generally in the same direction as the UR. The subjects were mostly unaware of their position after the turning to the US.

Tilting was employed with blindfolded subjects. The CR appeared after four to seven reinforcements and was in a direction opposite to the direction of the tilt. In this case the UR and CR were adjustive movements to maintain balance, while with galvanic stimuli, the UR and CR were inadequate adjustments to inadequately perceived vestibular cues. *Duplication* of the UR by the CR is seen, therefore in both situations.

It is therefore apparent that vestibular balancing mechanisms can be evoked and conditioned in the pigeon, normal and hemidecorticate dogs, normal and neurotic humans. In the reptiles only was there a failure in the evocation and conditioning of the vestibular responses. The CR formed differed from subject to subject in the ease of formation, specificity and intensity but in every case, the CR was essentially a *duplication* of the UR.

This similarity was found with both galvanic and tilting stimulation. The principle demonstrated here as in other studies involving simple conditioning is the simulation of the UR by the CR; regardless of whether the reaction is useful or harmful to the reacting organism. With more complex organisms and at more complicated levels of behavior, compensatory and delayed responses may occur as introspection and internal awareness allow the relay of the effect of an act into consciousness and consequent integration. The general rule of the duplication of the UR by the CR is not violated even in these cases.

In the dog, unilateral extirpation of the motor area or of the gyrus ecto-sylvius, or even of the whole cortex unilaterally with the opposite gyrus cinguli did not completely abolish the ability to form vestibular CRs, but there was an impairment in response roughly proportional to the amount of tissues removed.

Summary

An attempt was made to condition vestibular reflexes to auditory signals denoting a loss of balance. The US employed were either galvanic currents passed through the head and vestibular apparatus or mechanical tilting of the blindfolded subject. It was found that:

(1)   Reptiles showed some loss of balance but no evidence of conditioning after 400 repetitions.

(2)   Normal dogs and humans displayed an UR consisting of a rotation of the head about the cephalo caudal axis with the cathode side uppermost, a lowering of the forepart of the body, often falling to the anode side and occasional vomiting. These responses were conditioned to an auditory signal after a variable number of reinforcements and this CR persisted without practice for at least 8 months. The CR was a duplication of the UR, i.e. falling in the same direction, etc.

(3) Normal dogs and humans were stimulated by tilting of base. The UR was a compensatory movement toward equilibration. Extinction and differentiation were possible. The CR was a duplication of the UR.

(4) Conditioning was attempted with dogs having:
   (a) unilateral extirpation of the motor area;
   (b) unilateral extirpation of the gyrus ectosylvius;
   (c) complete unilateral hemidecortication and removal of the contralateral gyrus cinguli.

Vestibular CRs could be formed but were highly generalized in form. There was moderate impairment of CR in case (c) above.

11

THE HIGHER NERVOUS ACTIVITY
OF MAN

L. Pickenhain

During phylogenesis the higher nervous activity of man has developed from that of animals. Therefore the fundamental laws of the higher nervous activity of animals are essentially valid also for that of man. But, in addition, during the phylogenetic development of man to a social being new types of environmental relations have developed which have produced qualitatively new attributes of his higher nervous activity. This fact is best demonstrated by the existence of language and thinking. These functions correspond to the rapid development of the highest parts of man's central nervous system, especially of his cerebral cortex, which is the morphological basis of his highly differentiated behaviour. Despite its extreme complexity, which among other things has produced the specifically human attribute of the subjective experience, understanding the higher nervous activity of man as a whole requires an objective, experimental study. It was one of the great merits of the Pavlovian school that it made the first steps towards such an exact scientific analysis. In this connection, Pavlov's idea of the second signalling system is especially important. It provides the possibility of distinguishing between those features of the higher nervous activity which are common in man and animals and those which are specific for the human being, and of comprehending their dialectical interrelations.

The Word as "Signal of Signals"

To the animal various environmental stimuli which are perceived by its receptors may become signals for each inborn, unconditioned reflex. As a rule, these conditioned reflexes are not formed to isolated, single stimuli, but rather to complex stimuli and to various stimulus relations. But in every case the influence of a concrete stimulus (complex stimulus or stimulus relation) must initiate the organism's reaction. The totality of all temporary connections which have developed during the whole individual life of the animal and which constitute a dynamic adaptation to the changing environment, were called by Pavlov the "signalling system" (the single signalling system of animals).

In man as well as in animals all concrete stimuli, complex stimuli, and stimulus relations, which are perceived by the receptors, can become conditioned signals. But in man, in addition, abstract signs for the objects and processes, expressed by spoken and written words, may also evoke conditioned responses. These spoken or written signals which are peculiar only for man, are called *verbal signals*. Pavlov called the totality of all signal relations of the verbal type peculiar to man the *second signalling system*.

A simple experiment may demonstrate the mentioned fact.

When in a child 9–10 years old the experimenter has applied a weak electric current to the middle finger of the right hand immediately after the spoken word "light" † and has repeated this combination several times, then after a fews combinations the child withdraws his hand already after the word "light" and before the electric current is turned on. The method of elaborating this conditioned reflex differs in no way from the elaboration of a conditioned reflex in animals. But an essential difference results. The child withdraws his hand likewise when after the formation of the conditioned reflex we project the written word "light" onto a screen in front of the child. The pronunciation of a word with a similar abstract meaning, i.e. "candle", by the experimenter also evokes the same conditioned reaction. This never occurs in any animal.

This simple example may demonstrate the fundamental difference between the immediate or concrete and the verbal signal. In animals, for instance in dogs, a spoken word acts only by its acoustic nature, including the manner of intonation. Therefore words with a similar acoustic sound evoke the same reaction if a special acoustic differentiation was not formerly elaborated. Thus a trained dog also sits down when his master, instead of the word "place", calls "brace", "race", "case", or similar words provided the intonation is the same. In animals, only the character of the immediate, acoustic stimulus determines the actual reaction.

But the situation is different in man. For man the spoken word is above all not an acoustic but an abstract, verbal signal displaying a definite abstract meaning. Therefore a conditioned reaction elaborated to a special word in man is not evoked by an acoustically similar word but by a word identical or similar in its semantic content. Not even signalling by the acoustic analyzer is necessary; the same reaction may be evoked when the same abstract signal meaning is mediated by another analyzer (i.e. in reading the respective word—by the optic analyzer, or in writing the respective word on the skin—by the tactile analyzer). This means that for man the abstract content of the verbal signal is decisive. It signalizes, as it were, the

† Verbal signals will be marked by quotation marks to distinguish them from concrete signals.

immediate, concrete object or process (in our case the immediate influence of the light), which itself may be the signal for a conditioned reaction. Therefore, Pavlov (1928, 1941) named the verbal signal the "signal of the signals" and the whole system of abstract signals the "second signalling system".

We must clearly distinguish between the "second signalling system" and the "conditioned reflexes of the second order". Conditioned reflexes of the second or higher order are elaborated on the basis of stable conditioned reflexes within the single signalling system of animals but without the conditioned stimuli receiving in this way the character of abstract signals. Conditioned reflexes of the second order can also be formed in children within the first signalling system. But later on we will show that after the complete development of the second signalling system in adults we can no longer speak about the formation of conditioned reflexes of higher order.

Considering again the above-mentioned example of the formation of a conditioned avoidance reflex to the word "light", we see that a conditioned reflex to the concrete light is not even elaborated before hand. On the contrary, the conditioned reflex to the verbal signal is formed immediately. Only in special cases is this process accompanied by the formation of a conditioned reflex to the immediate light signal without an additional elaboration.

Whereas the term "second signalling system" comprises all verbal environmental connections of man, his temporary connections to immediate signals are called the *first signalling system*. This is not identical with the single signalling system of animals, because the additional second signalling system in man also influences the connections of the first signalling system on a large scale. On the other hand, the development of the second signalling system is only possible on the basis of the first signalling system, and every verbal signal, even the most abstract, can be reduced finally (sometimes by a long chain of intermediate links) to immediate signals of the real world. Both the signalling systems of man must always be considered in their interconnection as factors of a uniform process (i.e. of the higher nervous activity of man). Analyzing their mechanisms, one must keep one's eyes on this fact.

Considering these facts it emerges that the second signalling system includes not only the spoken language but also the whole abstract thinking of man and all actions which are an expression of verbalized, abstract ideas. In fact, spoken language is only one, although an essential part of the second signalling system.

This phenomenon is better comprehensible when we consider the phylogenetic development of the ability to form abstractions, i.e. the development of the second signalling system.

The function of articulated language and the ability to form abstractions have developed gradually during phylogenesis in close dependence on the labour and social life of human society (Friedrich Engels). At the beginning of its development, in addition to the immediate motor reactions to concrete objects and events in the environment a motor reaction of the speech muscles was formed. Coinciding very often with immediate reactions to the respective object or event, these sounds became a signal for this object or event. In that way, in addition to the immediate reflection of the environment in the animal's behaviour, man obtained the possibility of reproducing within the kinesthetic analyzer of the speech muscles, stimulus traces separated ("abstracted") from the concrete objects and events of the environment, and of forming temporary connections between these stimulus traces. Simultaneously, other means of concrete, image-like reflection develop to a high perfection (figurative performances, e.g. gesture, cave-painting and so on). In this development the whole kinesthetic analyzer participates. In this stage of development, thinking may be characterized as concrete and objective (first stage of abstraction).

In connection with the progressive development of the larynx and mouth muscles and the respective parts of the kinesthetic analyzer in the cortex, differentiated sound formation (concrete verbal naming) develops more and more to a subtle means of transmitting information over distance. Simultaneously with social development in primitive society, the second stage of abstraction arises, consisting of the formation of abstract terms which no longer name only a definite, concrete object, but comprise groups of objects, according to determined characteristic signs.

The second stage of abstraction (the formation of abstract terms) includes the differentiated formation of words as well as abridged, symbolic, figurative reflection (hieroglyphs). The primary forms of thinking in abstract terms thus arise. In this stage the development of the kinesthetic–motor analyzer of the hand and speech muscles is especially important; but the other analyzers also undergo a progressive evolution. The progressive process of abstraction becomes evident in the transition from hieroglyphic to syllabic and phonetic characters as well as in the elaboration of intricate syntactic connections. The effector expression of abstract signals may be transposed into all parts of the somato-motor analyzer.

In connection with the successive formation of abstract terms and relatively constant temporary connections between them (associations) the effector acts (motor phonetic utterances) may be inhibited more and more. By this means, only sub-threshold impulses reach the speech and/or hand muscles, whereas connections of "abstracted" terms are formed within the brain. This process may be called the third stage of abstraction.

Therefore the physiological mechanism underlying the development of the second signalling system is characterized by the fact that the effector part of the connections to the environment is moved successively into the speech muscles, and that the motor reactions are simultaneously inhibited more and more. In a later stage of the evolution of the second signalling system this inhibition of the motor reactions spreads also to the motor activity of the speech muscles. Setchenov had already recognized this development, in his *Brain Reflexes* (1863) characterizing thinking as "reflexes with an inhibited terminal link". The progressive character of the inhibition of effector motor reactions during the development of the second signalling systems is shown, amongst other things by the fact that in older children, during the processing of verbal stimuli, one can observe small movements of the lips or at least record sub-threshold impulses going to the speech muscles. In adults, in most cases, this is no longer possible.

For the development of the second signalling system, the kinesthetic-motor analyzer, especially that of the speech muscles and of the muscles of the upper extremities, is of decisive importance. The morphological correlate of this development may be found in the cortex, in the very surroundings of the kinesthetic-motor analyzer of the hand and larynx muscles and in the intermediate regions between the kinesthetic-motor, acoustic, and optic analyzers.

There is no inborn preformation of the second signalling system in the cortex of man. The respective brain centres grow under the continuous influence of afferent impulses, originating from the developing connections to the environment. It is no mere chance that the motor speech centre is situated on that side of the brain to which run the afferent impulses from that hand which displays the greatest skill and exactness of movements (i.a. on the left side in right-handed people). Therefore, persons who have suffered a right-sided hemiparesis during earliest childhood, later on do not show any aphasic symptoms (Rubino and Scoppa, 1957).

Finally in man, with the increasing development of central closure mechanisms with inhibited terminal links more and more new verbal connections are formed—not by combination of verbal stimuli with the immediate influence of concrete objects and events of the environment, but by their combination with already elaborated verbal signals, which have fixed the previous influence of concrete objects and events. In this way the reflection of the environment in man's brain receives a qualitatively new character. The animal reflects the influences of the environment more or less passively in its immediate (unconditioned and conditioned) reactions, but by the inhibition of effector acts and the processing and storing of abstract signals, man has acquired the possibility of confronting himself with his environment, of understanding its laws, planning the future, and to managing nature and human society according to his concepts. But this is possible only if the newly formed abstract signals are controlled continuously, comparing them with human practice. Otherwise, phantastic abstract terms, not corresponding to reality, arise and retard the development of the human society, as superstition and religion do.

We wish to emphasize once more that animals have no second signalling system. The most highly developed animals do not dispose of abstract terms nor of reactions to verbal signals. Therefore it is no scientific procedure to use terms which characterize the psychic phenomena of man, like "thinking" or "consciousness", to describe processes of the higher nervous activity of animals. It is true that in higher animals we can find some elements of higher nervous activity, which subsequently, under the special conditions of the phylogenesis of man, developed finally to the higher nervous activity of man. But such elements as the conception of numbers (up to 7) in some birds, the formation of conditioned reflexes to stimulus relations, the elaboration of stable conditioned connections between indifferent stimuli and the formation of highly intricate combinations of reflex chains in anthropoids are not yet real types of abstract thinking which developed only in human society, representing a qualitatively new function.

From the philosophical point of view it is extremely important not to veil this dialectical sudden change from quantity (accumulation of more and more types of highly specialized analytic-synthetic activity) into a new quality (formation of abstract, verbal terms). Therefore it is incorrect to speak about "object-related or concrete thinking" of apes, because this formulation is a contradiction in itself. "Thinking" is a function of the second signalling system, bound to the existence of verbal signals, whereas the reactions of apes to the concrete stimuli of their environment are realized within their single signalling system. An ape, trained to a special stereotype sequence of two different reactions (RLRRLRRLLL), can not react immediately in the right way to the inverse sequence of the same reactions (RRRLLRLLRL); to do this, a completely new elaboration is necessary. The ape is unable to abstract this whole process (Cole, 1951).

Sometimes one comes across the objection that the specific functions of the higher nervous activity of man—language and thinking—may not be considered as conditioned reflexes only. This objection is justified when it is raised against a simplified transfer of the results of experimental investigations in animals to man. But it ignores the fact that the second signalling system is formed by means of the same principal laws which are valid for the higher nervous activity of animals. The fact that, corresponding to the special living conditions of man, qualitatively new laws, peculiar only to the second signalling system, develop, does not abolish the phylogenetically older laws which retain their (though restricted) validity as before.

Conditioned Reflexes in Man

Before dealing in more detail with the ontogenesis of the higher nervous activity of man and the formation of the second signalling system, we shall briefly review the most important conditioned reflexes in man and the methods applied to their experimental study.

As in animals, we can also elaborate conditioned reflexes in man on the basis of all inborn unconditioned reactions. Beginning in 1907, Krasnogorsky

(1954) performed the earliest investigations on conditioned reflexes in man. In those experiments he simultaneously recorded the motor reactions of the mouth muscles and the secretory reactions of the salivary glands (by means of salivary capsules, independently devised by Lashley and Krasnogorsky). As unconditioned stimuli, sweets, sweet cranberries, citric acid, or other stimulating substances were introduced into the mouth. The application of this method is very simple, and the discomfort for the subject is very small. Moreover, the method may be applied even during earliest childhood. In Figure 1 we show one example of a conditioned alimentary reflex recorded in a child. Here, after a short latency, the conditioned stimulus evokes a clear motor and salivary conditioned reflex. Normally in man, conditioned alimentary reflexes are formed after few combinations.

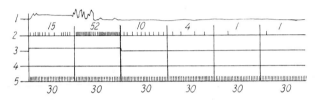

Fig. 1. Motor and secretory alimentary conditioned reflex in a child (Krasnogorsky, 1953). 1, actogram of mouth muscles; 2, salivary secretion (in drops); 3, conditioned stimulus; 4, reinforcement; 5, time in secounds

In 1918 Citovich applied the plethymographic method for the first time to study of the higher nervous activity of man. Extensive investigations on unconditioned and conditioned vasomotor reflexes in man were published later on by Rogov (1951) and Pshonik (1952). They all used arm plethysmographs. Compared with the alimentary method, the plethysmographic method used to study the conditioned reflexes in man involves much more difficulties, because very small, unknown, unconditioned or conditioned stimuli may evoke clear changes in the plethysmogram. Therefore many preparatory sessions are necessary before obtaining a rest plethysmogram, which is needed as a basis for the elaboration of conditioned reflexes.

In 1922 Cason elaborated conditioned pupillary reflexes for the first time. As an unconditioned stimulus he used light stimuli which produced a constriction of the pupils. At first, the changes in pupillary size were observed subjectively by the experimeter; later on they were recorded continuously by a photoelectric device.

Conditioned blink reflexes (avoidance reflexes of the eye-lid) were also elaborated for the first time by Cason in 1922. He used electric current, applied to the outer corner of the eye, as the unconditioned stimulus. Later investigators used a weak air-puff, directed against the cornea (Campbell and Hilgard, 1936). This method is nowadays applied in many laboratories, to

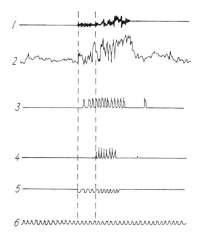

FIG. 2. Conditioned eyelid reflex to a tactile stimulus at the skin in a child 150 days old (Kasatkin 1952). 1, actogram; 2, pneumogram; 3, eyelid movement; 4, unconditioned stimulus; 5, conditioned stimulus; 6, time in seconds

children as well as in adults. In Figure 2 a conditioned eye-lid reflex in a child 150 days old is represented.

Many investigations were carried out to study the formation of conditioned reflexes on the basis of unconditioned changes in the functions of internal organs (respiration, circulation, kidney, alimentary tract, metabolism and so on). The orienting reflex, imcluding its various components (motor, cardiovascular, respiratory, electro-galvanic skin reflex) may also be conditioned. Among this group one can reckon also the conditioned depression of the alpha-rhythm in the electroencephalogram, which has proved to be a valuable method in studying the higher nervous activity of man. (Jus and Jus, 1957 a, 1957 b).

Spinal reflexes may also be conditioned. Schlosberg (1928) and Campbell (1938) elaborated conditioned patellar reflexes in man. Plantar reflexes were conditioned by Shipley (1932). The possibility of conditioning "pure" spinal reflexes demonstrates once more the fact that all responses of the organism are reactions of the organism as a whole. These three investigators all found, that the elaboration of these particular conditioned reflexes succeeded with certainty only if the unconditioned stimulus was very strong.

All these conditioned reflexes, elaborated on the basis of unconditioned vegetative reactions, have in common that they can be formed in children also and in the same manner as in adults. As in animals, they begin to appear after several combinations of the conditioned and the unconditioned stimulus, the necessary number of combinations depending on the ecological significance of the new stimulus combination. On the basis of the eyelid reflex, which is extremely important and easy to evoke, a conditioned reflex is already formed after a few combinations; but the conditioned patellar reflex appears only after a much greater number of combinations.

Besides these vegetative conditioned reflexes, somatic conditioned reflexes can also be elaborated. Since 1909 the method of conditioned avoidance reflexes to electric current, proposed by Protopopov, has been applied in man. With this method electrodes are fixed to one or more of the subject's fingers and a weak electric current is applied as the unconditioned reinforcement. The intensity of the current must be strong enough to induce the subject to draw back his hand. In this case, unlike the above-mentioned reactions, the subject performs a response of the somatic-motor apparatus, which in fact plays a very important role in the development of the second signalling system. This is the reason that the conditioning of such an avoidance reflex to electric current in adult humans takes a different course from that in children. Whereas in children the conditioned somato-motor reflex is formed, according to the usual scheme, after a few reinforcements and disappears again after several unreinforced applications of the conditioned stimulus, in addults a strange phenomenon is observed. Most healthy adult subjects respond in one of two extremely different ways. In the first group, after the first (or second) combination of the signal stimulus and the unconditioned reinforcement, a stable connection has already formed, which without further reinforcement does not disappear. In the second group, in spite of several hundred reinforcements, the conditioned reflex to the signal stimulus is not formed; the subject withdraws his hand only after the application of the electric current.

These results are surprising, and their physiological analysis is only possible when the total reaction of the subject is considered and not exclusively his motor reaction. In man, one part of his total reaction is the subject's report on his subjective experiences. Questioning the two groups of subjects, we find that the first group from the second combination of stimuli begins to respond permanently to the signals, because they assume that the experimenter is "expecting" this type of reaction. On the contrary, the second group "concentrates" on the application of the electric current. In this way, by questioning the subjects, we learn that immediately at the beginning of the experiment, a definite set is formed which determines all following reactions. We may call it a dominant within the second signalling system. Generally, it is formed very fast (practically at once), and without additional new influences from the second signalling system, it is very stable. By experiment one can show that in the first signalling system of the first group of subjects a conditioned connection was also formed, but that it was inhibited by the dominant in the second signalling system. This inhibition can be abolished, for instance, by a strong extrastimulus, operating as an external inhibitor and producing the conditioned avoidance reaction to the signal. Moreover, in most cases, by recording the electromyogram of the respective arm muscles, one can see a sub-threshold response during the first

stimulus combinations, which only disappears completely with further combinations, by stabilization of the dominant in the second signalling system.
These observations demonstrate that in man the conditioned reflexes of the
somato-motor system are much more intricate having very intimate connections with the second signalling systems.

The same can be shown when we condition the grasp reflex in man. We
can do it in a very simple form by giving the child a rubber balloon to take
into his hand and pressing his hand passively during the sounding of a
signal, at which moment an automatic apparatus delivers a candy. After
several repetitions, the child himself presses the balloon when the signal is
turned on.

The second method, applied more fully by Ivanov-Smolensky and his
collaborators, requires that the experimenter regulates the formation of the
conditioned reflexes by verbal stimuli. Ivanov-Smolensky has called this
method "elaboration of conditioned motor reflexes by verbal reinforcement
or speech reinforcement" (Ivanov-Smolensky, 1933; Povorinsky, 1954).
During this experiment the subject has a rubber balloon in his hand, or his
hand is laid upon a key. Then, without any previous instruction, the experimenter says the verbal signal "press" after every conditioned stimulus.
Each correct pressing is reinforced by the experimenter with the word
"correct". Differentiation can be formed when the experimenter accompanies
the respective signal with the word "no pressing".

This method has been criticized with respect to its applicability in healthy
adults. Also in this type of experiment it turns out that most subjects, either
beginning with the second or third combination, perform the reaction to
the signal stimulus continuously (first group) or only react to the verbal
reinforcement (second group). The subject's verbal reports show that in
these experiments also, the different reactions depend on the formation of
different dominants in the second signalling system. In most cases this
dominant is formed immediately. It consists either of the stable closure of a
connection between the signal stimulus and the verbal reinforcement
(preserved over a long time without any further reinforcement) or of the
inhibition of this reaction; in the second case, the subject presses the key
only after every verbal reinforcement. This inhibition, produced by the
second signalling system, can again be disinhibited by a special experimental
set (external inhibition). This method should therefore not be applied in
healthy adults and juveniles without special caution, because in spite of its
apparent simplicity, the interference with the second signalling system
leads to vague results.

Therefore, investigating human subjects in whom the formation of such
a dominant in the second signalling system must be assumed, it seems more
useful to give a special instruction at the very beginning of the experiment
(i.e. "Press the key after the red light, but do not press after the green
light"). In this way, from the beginning of the experiment, a known domi-

nant is produced within the second signalling system. However, in children, and in patients, where the normal relationship between the first and second signalling system is disturbed, this method of Ivanov-Smolensky can be used with success.

The observation is interesting that healthy, wakeful adults can be conditioned to sub-threshold stimuli, i.e. to stimuli which are not perceived by the subject consciously. Gershuni (1955) has performed such experiments, applying sub-threshold acoustic stimuli. As indicators, he used the galvanic skin reflex and the depression of the alpha rhythm in the electroencephalogram. The unconditioned reflex was evoked by applying an electric current to one finger of the left hand. In all four subjects clear conditioned galvanic skin responses and conditioned depressions of the alpha rhythm appeared to acoustic stimuli whose intensity was about 6 db below the threshold for verbal report on the stimulus. These conditioned reflexes to subthreshold stimuli displayed some differences compared with conditioned reflexes to acoustic stimuli of an intensity above the threshold for verbal report. The latency of the conditioned galvanic skin response was prolonged (nearly doubled), and the elaboration of a stable conditioned reflex took a longer time; the depression of the alpha rhythm was shorter than with conditioned stimuli above threshold. Conditioned motor avoidance reactions to subthreshold stimuli did not appear. Samsonova (1953) hat similar results, conditioning the galvanic skin response to sub-threshold optic stimuli. Jus and Jus (1957a) elaborated a conditioned depression of the alpha rhythm to a stimulus of intensity 20 db below the threshold for verbal report (Figure 3).

These results are not so astonishing as may seem at first glance. They are only examples of the numerous types of vegetative conditioned reflexes

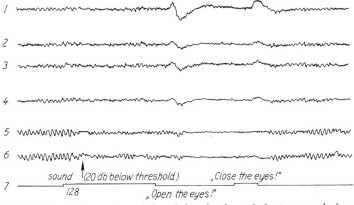

FIG. 3. Conditioned depression of the alpha rhythm of electroencephalogram to a stimulus 20 db below the threshold for the verbal report (Jus and Jus 1957). 1, left region of Rolando; 2, right region of Rolando; 3, left parietal region; 4, right parietal region; 5, left occipital region; 6, right occipital region; 7, conditioned and unconditioned stimulus

which are formed to very different environmental stimuli without the participation of the second signalling system. But they make it evident that for
each analyzer not only one, but several stimulus thresholds exist, depending
on the indicator used and the experimental conditions applied (Samsonova,
1953; Gershuni, 1957). When a conditioned reflex is formed to a stimulus
below the threshold for verbal report, the formation takes place within the
first signalling system. But when the conditioned stimulus is consciously
perceived by the subject, i.e. when it is verbalized, the second signalling
system participates in the formation of the conditioned reflex. Gershuni
shows that this different mechanism of formation results in a different
latency. Whereas the latency of conditioned reactions to stimuli above
threshold does not change from threshold values up to 70 db, the latency
undergoes an abrupt decrease when one proceeds from sub-threshold stimuli
(on an average 3,1 sec) to threshold stimuli (on an average 1,7 sec). Figure 4

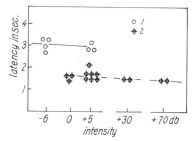

FIG. 4. Latency of the galvanic skin reflex elicited by acoustic signals of different intensity (related to the median threshold for verbal report) (Gershuni,
1955). 1, galvanic skin reflex in cases, in which the verbal report is lacking; 2,
galvanic skin reflex accompanied by a verbal report

represents the values of ten subjects (Gershuni, 1955). One can see that the
latencies of the galvanic skin responses which are accompanied by a verbal
report on the tone belong to one group, whereas the latencies of the conditioned reflexes to which no verbal report is given form another group.
Between the two groups no intermediate exists. The three reactions to a
stimulus intensity of + 5 db without verbal report were formed under
special experimental conditions (extra-stimuli, drowsiness), during which no
verbal report was given; they fit very well into the general picture.

Therefore, it is evident that the participation of the second signalling
system immediately induces a change of the reaction (in the present case, a
shortening of the latency). Gershuni supposes that this change arises because
using threshold stimuli a motor orienting reaction is evoked. We assume,
that it is more convenient to speak about an intervention of a dominant
belonging to the systematized functions of the second signalling system. In
the functional structure of this system motor-kinesthetic components play an

important role (as afferent-efferent-reafferent functional circuits on different levels). It gives rise to "directed attentiveness" and leads, among other things to a decrease in the threshold of the analyzer concerned. It also causes a refinement of the analyzing function of the different analyzers. Thus the differentiation threshold for optic stimuli is markedly diminished if the subject is instructed to give a verbal report compared with the same experiment in which, without any instruction, only the vegetative or motor reaction is recorded (Samsonova, 1956).

This influence of the second signalling system must be taken into consideration during all investigations on conditioned reflexes in man, especially in adult humans. Already the fact whether the subject has been instructed to give a verbal report after each experiment or not, may influence the course of the experiment. For instance Trofimov (1955) observed such an influence in conditioning eyelid reflexes in adults. Without any instruction, in healthy adults the conditioned eyelid reflexes were formed after 6–8 combinations, a differentiation after 5–7 unreinforced applications. But when the subject was instructed to give an exact report on the number, type and sequence of the stimuli after each experiment, conditioned reflexes were formed not at all or were very instable.

In the Pavlovian school the so-called *association experiment (or verbal experiment)* is used as a special method to investigate the function of the second signalling system. It was introduced by Ivanov-Smolensky and corresponds in some respect to the association experiment of C. Jung. Here, the subject is instructed to respond to a series of verbal stimuli by saying the first word that comes to mind. In addition, the latency of the verbal response is recorded.

In its simple form this method is not useful for investigating the higher nervous activity of healthy subjects. But in pathological cases, especially when conflict words are used, it can give important information on the subject's second signalling system. During recent years, some variants of the association experiment have been proposed. Thus Gakkel (1951) introduced the method of "directed verbal reactions", in which the average duration of latency, the latency prolongation of reactions to single words using extra-stimuli, and the number of word repetitions in a series of association experiments were evaluated. Pervov (1956), using the association experiment, gives words a positive or negative meaning by instruction and studies the changes by switching this meaning. Plotitcher (1955) excludes defined categories of verbal stimuli, or demands that the subject should answer with a word of contrary meaning. Furthermore, she changes the signal meaning of verbal stimuli and proves the connected motor and verbal reactions. Hrbek (1954) developed a method named "artificial laboratory language", combining definite objects with unknown disyllabic "words" and investigating the speed of formation and the stability of the newly formed connections.

An interesting variation of the association experiment was elaborated by Morávek (1954, 1957) who, by previous instruction, introduced inhibitions to optic stimuli. Among other things, he instructed the subject after an optic stimulus had been given during the association experiment without stereotype to inhibit the verbal response or not to react before the optic stimulus was switched on. In this way he could delay the verbal response as far as necessary from the verbal stimulus and investigate the inhibition of delay in the second signalling system. Such modifications of the methods are necessary and must be extended. In this connection methods of experimental psychology must also be used, but, of course, without uncritical acceptance of its theoretical ideas.

We have by no means mentioned all methods used to elaborate conditioned reflexes in man. But these examples show that an essential difference exists between conditioned reflexes in whose formation the second signalling system participates and those in which it does not. Generally, one can state that in adults conditioned reflexes in which the motor-kinesthetic analyzer is included, are performed in nearly all cases with the participation of the second signalling system. But in many vegetative conditioned reflexes, which are not merely accompaniments of simultaneously occurring motor-kinesthetic reactions, the second signalling system does not participate.

The Leading Role of the Second Signalling System

Beginning with the formation of the earliest environmental connections to immediate (unconditioned and conditioned) stimuli, the higher nervous activity of man develops in a specific manner. In man, the reactions within the first signalling system already display human character being the prerequisite and basis for the development of the second signalling system which later on makes full social contact and creative cooperation in human society possible. The formation of the second signalling system is a protracted process during which we cannot pick out any moment, from which the existence of the second signalling system may be assumed, just as we cannot state any moment in which the formation of the second signalling system has finished. But one can observe, how, during the ontogenesis of the human being, the behavioral acts are more and more guided by the systematized experiences of the second signalling system.

Here, some comments seem necessary on the so-called "relations" or "interrelations" between the first and second signalling systems. The use of these words seem to suggest that the first and the second signalling systems are two divided, or at least divisible processes, because only between those are "interrelations" possible. But this assumption would be wrong. Rather, the two signalling systems are a uniform function which may only be subdivided in abstract terms. During phylo- and ontogenesis their relationship develops in such a way that the second signalling system arises on the basis of the first one, simultaneously developing the first one and leading it to a higher level of performance.Therefore, it would be wrong to speak of a "reflection" of the processes of the first signalling system into the second. Only the objective processes of the environment may be reflected in the brain and its functional performance, which even in man consists of both the first and the second signalling systems. Whether and to what extent the neurodynamic functions of the second signalling system participate in a particular case, depends on the conditions and behavior of the whole organism towards the actual stimuli.

The first and second signalling systems are partial functions of the higher nervous activity of man. The first as the phylogenetically older function, is more stable and less disruptable, the second, on the contrary, is more mobile, plastic and capable of development almost without limit. When relations with the environment are disturbed, especially in the case of illness, the second signalling system, as a rule, is earlier and more greatly affected than the first one.

As the child approaches more and more to an adult age (during the years at school), its relations with the environment are more and more guided by the second signalling system. This may be demonstrated very clearly by elaborating motor conditioned reflexes with verbal reinforcement according to the method of Ivanov-Smolensky (a combination of a signal stimulus with the verbal stimulus "press"). As shown above, this reflex can be elaborated in the way described by Ivanov-Smolensky only during school-age (conditioned pressing to the conditioned signal after several combinations). In adults, as shown in our own experiments, this conditioned reflex is not performed in the same way. Here, with the first combinations, a dominant setting is already formed within the second signalling system, determining all the subject's later reactions (either pressing only to the verbal stimulus or an immediately constituted pressing to the conditioned stimulus which cannot be extinguished). Dmitrijev (1956) proved in a large series of experiments, that the number of subjects in whom the elaboration of a conditioned reflex with the classical method is impossible, increases with rising age. At the age of 7–8 years it amounts to 3,7 per cent, at the age of 12–13 years to 17 per cent, at the age of 16–18 years to 28,6 per cent and at the age of 19–22 years to 58,3 per cent (Figure 5). According to our own experiments, in the older age-groups most responses classified by Dmitrijev as motor conditioned reflexes are also formed by the existence of a dominant focus in the second signalling system ("pressing to the signal"). In the overwhelming number of cases, adult subjects give themselves a self–instruction from the beginning of the experiment, and the content of this cannot be influenced by the experimenter in the method of Ivanov-Smolensky. (The conclusions which follow for performing the experiment are mentioned above, p. 135.)

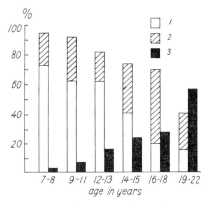

FIG. 5. Quantitative relationship between the subjects in whom a conditioned reflex according to the motor method with verbal reinforcement was formed, and those in whom it was not formed, related to different age groups (Dmitrijev, 1956). 1, subjects in whom a stable conditioned reflex was formed; 2, subjects in whom only an inconstant conditioned reflex was formed; 3, subjects in whom no conditioned reflex was formed at all

In healthy adult subjects, during the wakeful stage this participation of the second signalling system may be observed in most of the reponses in which the kinesthetic-motor analyzer is included. This participation of the second signalling system causes:

(a) The (positive and negative) conditioned connections to be formed essentially faster, in most cases instantaneously, i.e. after one or two combinations.

(b) Formed connections to be extremely stable, also without any further reinforcement, but they may be changed at any time, when changes in the dynamic structure of the second signalling system occur.

(c) The environmental influences to be analyzed and synthetized more subtly by utilization of all the previous, systematized experiences of the subject.

Because in these conditions complicated chains of intracentral verbal connections are included in the performance, which, having an "inhibited final link", are not directly accessible to the observer, the subject must be asked for his subjective experiences. Only in this way can the total response of the subject be comprehended. These subjective reports must be evaluated as additional objective indicators of the subject's total reaction (pp. 135, 137).

Animals can be conditioned not only on the basis of unconditioned, but also on the basis of formerly established conditioned reflexes. These reflexes are called conditioned reflexes of second, third or higher order depending on the number of conditioned reflexes which were included. Such conditioned reflexes of higher order can be formed also in humans, especially in children, within the first signalling system. But such a distinction loses its meaning when the second signalling system is included in the reaction. Within the second signalling system the signal meaning of a stimulus is no more determined by its nearer or further relation to the unconditioned reflex, but above all by the type of generalization of the very different signals according to a definite fundamental sign. The formation of conditioned inhibitory reflexes (of first, second, and third order) in adults was proved in experiments by Benua (1957).

The dominant influence of the second signalling system which leads to dominant settings during the elaboration of conditioned reflexes, can be demonstrated also in the electroencephalogram. During the elaboration of a conditioned grasp reflex to immediate non-verbal stimuli one can observe a conditioned blockade only of the contralateral Rolando rhythm which disappears again with frequent repetitions. But if the experimenter gives the instruction "press!" to the subject, a blockade of the ipsilateral Rolando rhythm occurs also by commissural pathways. This increased and more propagated blockade which indicates the participation of a new neurodynamic factor, the second signalling system, continues during the whole experiment, i.e. as long as the instruction is valid. This emphasizes again the close relationship between the second signalling system and the kinesthetic-motor analyzer, for the Rolando rhythm is recorded above the cortical end of the kinesthetic-motor analyzer.

Stressing the great importance of the kinesthetic-motor analyzer for the functioning of the second signalling system we must yet take care not to identify it with the second signalling system. The participation of the kinesthetic-motor analyzer in any reaction does not mean the same as the participation of the second signalling system. Samsonova (1956) demonstrated that the kinesthetic-motor analyzer as a function of the first signalling system can improve the functions of other analyzers by itself. Investigating the differentiation threshold for optic stimuli, she instructed the subject to perform graduated movements with his arm whose size corresponded to the perceived distance of an illuminated area. In this way, the precision of optic differentiation could be markedly improved. This improvement is caused by increase in the analytic-synthetic function of the cortex produced by the participation of graduated stimuli within the kinesthetic-motor analyzer (without participation by the second signalling system). The same may also hold true for the improvement of the acoustic and optic analysis of stimuli, which is observed, if the subject not only displays a vegetative or motor reaction, but gives a report on the respective stimulus as response. This effect may also be produced by the participation of the kinesthetic-motor analyzer of the speech muscles. But these very complex connections need further experimental analysis.

Having demonstrated the far—reaching influence of the second signalling system in man, we must examine the question how far this influence may also be extended to those vegetative functions which are not normally influenced.

But are there processes in the human organism which really proceed without any influence of the second signalling system? In collaboration with Mühlke (1958) we showed, that the functioning of the second signalling system influences salivary secretion. Investigations on adult subjects demonstrated that during "subvocal" reading a conditioned increase appears in the salivary secretion of the parotis glands. This conditioned connection is formed during the constantly repeating combination of the neurodynamic processes in the second signalling system during speaking and reading aloud, with the drying of the mouth cavity (the last being an unconditioned stimulus for salivary secretion). This is a non-specific influence of the second signalling system because the semantic meaning of the words which are read does not play any part. Certainly, all vegetative processes in the human organism are influenced in such a non-specific way, during the various voluntary motor acts.

But when we ask whether the influence of the second signalling system may also be extended to the vegetative functions of the organism, we do not mean this non-specific influence, but a deliberate change in the particular vegetative function in question. An excellent experimental contribution to this topic came from Hudgins (1933) who, in the course of a long and complicated conditioning experiment, succeeded in subjecting the pupillary reaction to voluntary influence.

It is known that under normal conditions the pupillary reflex, being a purely involuntary response, is not accessible to any voluntary influence. Conditioned reflexes, formed on the basis of the unconditioned pupillary reflex (with light on the eye), were elaborated by Cason (1922a). Using the same method, Hudgins conditioned the pupillary reflex to the sound of a bell in 14 adult, healthy subjects. After 100 combinations the first signs of the conditioned reflex were observed; then this reflex was stabilized by an additional 100 combinations. During the next stage of the experiment the subject received the instruction (in response to the command "contract") to squeeze the handle of a dynamometer with the right hand, thereby switching on the bell (conditioned stimulus) and the light (unconditioned stimulus). In the following experiments, the experimenter spoke the word "contract" after which the subject contracted his hand and turned on the stimuli. Four seconds later, the experimenter said "relax", after which the subject relaxed his hand, thereby turning off the light. With intervals of 10 sec, this experimental set was repeated 200 times. When the bell signal and the contractions of the hand were omitted as a control, the subject did not yet display a conditioned pupillary response to the verbal stimuli of the experimenter alone. During the third stage of the experiment, the bell was omitted. Instead of this, the subject received the additional instruction: "Whenever I give the command, repeat it for yourself subvocally." Now after the experimenter's first command, the subject contracted his hand, thereby turning on the light, and simultaneously repeated the command "contract" subvocally. Four seconds later, the experimenter gave the command "relax", after which the subject by relaxing his hand, turned off the light, simultaneously repeating the command subvocally again.

When Hudgins tested the command words alone after 200 additional combinations, without the subject moving his hand, the verbal stimuli elicited a clear conditioned pupillary reflex. Therefore one can conclude that this conditioned reflex was formed only after involvement of the subject's own speech with participation of the kinesthetic impulses of his speech apparatus. Additional control experiments showed that it was now sufficient that the subject himself spoke the words "contract" or "relax" or vividly imagined speaking these words, to evoke the respective conditioned pupillary reflex. Now through the participation of the second signalling system the subject had the possibility of contracting or relaxing his pupil "voluntarily", i.e. according to his own intention. In this connection, the conventional semantic content of the words "contract" and "relax" was naturally without significance; the application of any meaningless syllables during the conditioning process had the same effect. In this phenomenon the participation of the kinesthetic-motor analyzer and the introduction of the verbal stimuli into the neurodynamic functions of the second signalling system were decisive. Hudgins also states that the signal effect of the bell could be extinguished in the usual manner; but even after many repetitions without reinforcement, it was impossible to extinguish the conditioned reflex elaborated to the verbal stimuli, whether they were spoken by the experimenter or by the subject himself. This confirms the general experience that connections elaborated within the second signalling system are extremely stable, which is related to their high level of internal structure and their systematized interrelations.

These experiments of Hudgins show that the influence of the second signalling system may be extended to such vegetative functions as the pupillary reaction, which seems to be completely autonomic. It is very likely that on the basis of all vegetative reactions conditioned reflexes may not only be formed within the single signalling system of animals responding to the first signalling system of man, but that, under suitable conditions, they may also be influenced by the second signalling system. Pavlov had expressed this same opinion on February 24, 1932, saying that "after some training, the ability may be developed to perceive and to guide functions of the organism, which during the usual synthetic activity of cortex, are not accessible to perception and guidance." "When anybody feels inclined," he said, "to devote his life to this question, then probably, everybody will be able by training to change many involuntary processes and phenomena to voluntary ones."

An experimental proof of the possibility of influencing all somatic functions by the second signalling system is finally praised by experiences collected during hypnosis.

In the so-called "animal hypnosis" a very strong stimulus (instantaneous turning backwards, "fright situation" by seeing a snake etc.) induces a general inhibition of all connections with the environment. This "Totstell-reflex" spreads from subcortical structures and induces an inhibition of the whole cortex (Svorad, 1957). The animal may be "aroused" from this state (external stimuli evoke an arousal reaction in the electroencephalogram), but as long as the state exists no influence on the higher nervous activity is possible.

In its physiological mechanism human hypnosis is essentially a sleeping condition. During hypnosis the influx of afferent impulses by way of the non-specific activating system of the reticular formation is blocked. But in this special case blocking of the reticular formation is achieved and controlled by definite connections of the second signalling system. By a dominant rapport point in the second signalling system of the hypnotized subject the hypnotist can influence the most varied functions of the organism in a deliberate manner. This means the formation of new positive and negative temporary connections in the subject's cortex, and in this connection the word of the hypnotist acts as conditioned stimulus. During this process the hypnotist interferes with the functional connections of the verbal system, determines the direction of these connections, and elicits definite (motor and vegetative) effector acts.

Here, it is convenient to discuss so-called "free will". We consider our voluntary acts as free as long as we determine the design of our actions by ourselves, i.e. within the systematized experiences of our second signalling system. This means, that the "freedom of decision" is determined by the systematized store of our experiences and by the actual stimuli. When a hypnotist gives a posthypnotic order, then the hypnotized subject does not perceive these actions as compelled, but as voluntary acts. The hypnotist has interfered directly with the course of the functional connections in the verbal system, in which the design of the action is determined, without disturbing their orderly course. However, when we evoke body movements or the occurrence of a memory sequence in an awake human subject by stimulating the cortex, then the subject perceives these processes as "involuntary" or "compelled" because the orderly course of the functional connections in the second signalling system is disturbed.

Hypnosis may be a method of studying the neurodynamic processes of higher nervous activity in man, especially the physiological mechanisms, by which the second signalling system acts. As example one experiment of Korotkin and Suslova who are working in the laboratory of F. P. Majorov in Leningrad, may be mentioned (Korotkin and Suslova 1955a, 1955b).

These workers used the eyelid reflex evoked by three short air-puffs against the cornea, as the unconditioned reflex. As conditioned stimuli,

they applied two complex stimuli: buzzer (B) + metronom (M–120) and
light (L) + metronom (M–120), the second component following the first
after about 1–2 sec. Figure 6 a represents the well established conditioned
reflexes to the complex stimuli B + M–120 and L + M–120. By introducing hypnosis, these reflexes were not changed (Figure 6b). During hypnosis the suggestion was given: "Light and metronom is followed by an air-
puff, buzzer and metronom is not followed by an air-puff." The effect of
this suggestion is shown in Figure 6c. The conditioned reflex to the single

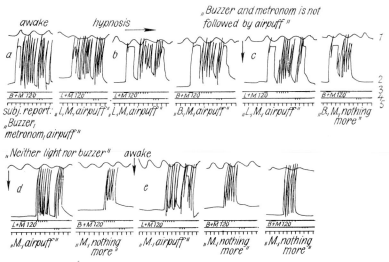

FIG. 6. Influence of "eliminations" of the conditioned and unconditioned eyelid
reflex suggested in hypnosis (Korotkin and Suslova 1955a). a, respiration; b,
eyelid movement; c, conditioned stimuli; d, unconditioned stimuli; e, time in
seconds

components of the two complex stimuli is present as before; but according
to the suggestion the unconditioned reflex is inhibited after B + M–120.
When questioned, the subject did not report having perceived an air-puff
after this complex stimulus. At this stage of the experiment the first components of the two complex stimuli were excluded by a new suggestion:
"Neither light nor buzzer will be used." As we see in Figure 6d the conditioned reflex to the first component of the two complex stimuli (L and B) is
now completely inhibited, but the second component (M–120) elicits the
conditioned reflex. In his verbal report, the subject mentions only the metronom stimulus. The unconditioned reflex, as before, appears only after
the complex L + M–120 and is inhibited after the complex B + M–120.

Therefore, as is shown by their different influences on the unconditioned
reflex, the two complex stimuli can be differentiated as before. However,

their first component is completely inhibited, in relation to both the reaction within the second (subjective report of the subject) and within the first signalling system (conditioned eyelid reflex). This result demonstrates that the inhibition produced by the hypnotic suggestion may not be an inhibition in the first analyzer link, because the "excluded" stimulus remains its signal meaning in respect to other functions. Rather, it must be assumed, that the hypnosis interferes with the analytic-synthetic function of the cortex in a very intricate way.

Hypnosis and the above mentioned example no doubt represent extreme cases, but they demonstrate the principal possibility of influencing all somatic processes in man by means of the second signalling system. This does not imply that all somatic processes are permanently guided by the second signalling system, nor even by the first. Rather, the basic functions of the organism are regulated by mechanisms operating in the lower parts of the central nervous system. However, the cortical regulatory mechanisms may be included and this happens when special influences of the environment require it to obtain a better adaptation to the environment. In highly organized animals, this takes place more often than in more primitive ones. For the human organism, these subtle adapting mechanisms are especially important.

REFERENCES

BENUA, N. N. (1957) Importance of the second signalling system for the differentiation in adults (Russian). *Zb. vyssh. nervn. dejat. Pavlova* **7**, pp. 391–400.

BYKOV, K. M. (1957) *Cerebral Cortex and Internal Organs* (ed. W. H. Gantt), Chemical Publ., New York.

CAMPBELL, A. A. (1938) The interrelations of two measures of conditioning in man, *J. Exp. Psychol.* **22**, pp. 225–43.

CAMPBELL, A. A., HILGARD, E. R. (1936) Individual differences in case of conditioning, *J. Exp. Psychol.* **19**, pp. 561–71.

CASON, H. (1922a) The conditioned pupillary reaction, *J. Exp. Psychol.* **5**, pp. 108–46.

CASON, H. (1922b) The conditioned eye lid reaction, *J. Exp. Psychol.* **5**, pp. 153–96.

CITOVICH, I. S. (1918) On the so-called vasomotor psycho-reflexes (Russian), *Russ. Fiziol. Zh.* **1**, pp. 113–27.

COLE, J. (1951) Study of discrimination reversal learning in Monkeys, *J. Comp. Physiol. Psychol.* **44**, pp. 467–72.

DMITRIJEV, A. S. (1956) On the methods to study the higher nervous activity in man, (Russian) *Zh. vyssh. nervn. dejat. Pavlova* **5**, pp. 501–9.

ENGELS, F. (1952) Anteil der Arbeit an der Menschwerdung des Affen, in *Dialektik der Natur*, Dietz-Verlag, Berlin, pp. 179–94.

GAKKEL, L. B. (1951) Method to investigate directed speech reactions, (Russian) *Fiziol. Zh. SSSR* **37**, pp. 547–52.

Gastaut, H., Jus, A. and K., Morrell, F., Storm van Leeuwen, W., Dongier, S., Naquet, R., Regis, H., Roger, A., Bekkering, D., Kamp, A., and Werre, J. (1957a) Étude topographique des réactions électroencéphalographiques conditionées chez l'homme (Essai d'interprétation neurophysiologique), *Electroenceph. clin. Neurophysiol.* **9**, pp. 1–34.

Gastaut, H., Jus, A. and K., Morrell, F., Bekkering, D., Kamp, A., and Werre, J. (1957b) Electroencephalographic characterization of the formation of conditioned reflexes in man (Russian), *Zh. vyssh. nervn. dejat. Pavlova* **7**, pp. 14–35.

Gershuni, G. V. (1955) Pecularities of conditioned galvanic skin reactions and depression of alpha rhythm evoked by sub-threshold and over-threshold acoustic stimuli (Russian), *Zh. vyssh. nervn. dejat. Pavlova* **5**, 390–404.

Hrbek, J. (1954) Study on the interrelations between the first and second signalling system with the method of artificial (experimental, laboratory) language, (Russian) *Zh. vyssh. nervn. dejat. Pavlova* **4**, pp. 457–64

Hudgins, C. V. (1933) Conditioning and the voluntary control of the pupillary light reflexes, *J. Gen. Psychol.* **8**, pp. 3–51.

Ivanov-Smolensky, A. G. (1933) *Methods to study conditioned reflexes in man* (Russian), Moscow.

Jus, A., and Jus, K. (1957a) L'Application des réactions électroencéphalographiques conditionées en neuro-psychiatrie, considérations physiopathologiques, *Premier Congr. Sci. Neurol., Rapports*, pp. 345–70.

Jus, A., and Jus, K. (1957b) Importance of electroencephalographic conditioned reactions for pathophysiological investigations in neurology and psychiatry (Russian), *Zh. nevropatol. psikhiatr.* **57**, pp. 1363–72.

Kasatkin, N. I. (1952) Early conditioned reflexes in child (Russian), *Zh. vyssh. nervn. dejat. Pavlova* **2**, pp. 757–68.

Korotkin, I. I., and Suslova, M. M. (1955a) Investigation on the nervous mechanism of a suggestion given during hypnosis (Russian). *Dokl. akad. nauk SSSR* **150** pp. 384–86.

Korotkin, I. I , and Suslova, M. M. (1955b) Some pecularities of the interrelations between the signalling systems during hypnosis and during the post-hypnotic conditions (Russian), *Zh. vyssh. nervn. dejat. Pavlova* **6**, pp. 298–308.

Krasnogorsky, N. I. (1953) On typological pecularities of the higher nervous activity of children (Russian), *Zh. vyssh. nervn. dejat. Pavlova* **3**, pp. 203–18.

Krasnogosky, N. I. (1954) *Investigations on the Higher Nervous Activity of Man and Animals*, Vol. 1 (Russian), Moscow.

Morávek, M. (1954) Contribution to the methods to investigate the interrelations between the signalling systems (Russian), *Physiologia bohemoslov.* **3**, pp. 437–43.

Morávek, M. (1957) *Contribution to the Idea of the Signalling Systems* (Czech), Prague.

Pavlov, I. P. (1928) *Lectures on Contidioned Reflexes* (ed. W. H. Gantt), Ed. International, New York.

Pavlov, I. P. (1941) *Conditioned Reflexes and Psychiatry* (ed. W. H. Gantt), Ed. International, New York.

Pervov, L. G. (1956) Verbal method to define the condition of the higher nervous activity of man (Russian), *Zh. vyssh. nervn. dejat. Pavlova* **6**, pp. 174–77.

Pickenhain, L., and Mühlke, H. (1958) Der Einfluß der Mundatmung, des Sprechens und des Lesens auf die Speichelsekretion des Menschen, *Acta biol. med. germ.* **1**, pp. 188–93.

PLOTITCHER, A. I. (1955) Methodical variants to study the conditioned verbal connections in psychopathological subjects (Russian), *Zh. vyssh. nervn. dejat. Pavlova* **5,** pp. 479–91.

POVORINSKI, J. A. (1954) *Methods to Study Motor Conditioned Reflexes with Verbal Reinforcement* (Russian), Leningrad.

PROTOPOPOV, V. P. (1950) *Investigations on the Higher Nervous Activity of Man in Natural Experiment* (Russian), Kiew.

PSHONIK, A. T. (1952) *The Cortex and the Receptor Function of the Organism* (Russian), Moscow.

ROGOV, A. A. (1951) *Conditioned and Unconditioned Vasomotor Reflexes in Man* (Russian), Moscow.

RUBINO, A., and SCOPPA, A. (1957) Considerations on the formation of the motor speech centre (Italian), *Acta neurol.* **10,** pp. 657–66.

SAMSONOVA, V. G. (1953) Some pecularities of the interrelation between first and second signalling system during the elaboration of conditioned reactions to optic stimuli with weak intensity (Russian), *Zh. vyssh. nervn. dejat. Pavlova* **3,** pp. 789–807.

SAMSONOVA, V. G. (1956) Importance of the kinesthetic stimuli accompanying the response, for the perception of optic stimuli (Russian), *Dokl. akad. nauk SSSR* **109,** pp. 1069–72.

SCHLOSBERG, H. (1928) A study of conditioned patellar reflex, *J. Exp. Psychol.* **11,** pp. 468–94.

SETCHENOV, I. M. (1952) *Brain Reflexes*, (Russian), ed. Koshtoyantc, Moscow.

SHIPLEY, W. (1932) Conditioning the human plantar reflex, *J. Exp. Psychol.* **15,** p. 42.

TROFIMOV, N. M. (1955) On the mechanism of the inductive interrelations between the signal systems (Russian), *Zh. vyssh. nervn. dejat. Pavlova* **5,** pp. 462–70.

SVORAD, S. (1957) "Animal hypnosis" (Totstellreflex) as experimental model for psychiatry, *Arch. Neurol. Psychiat.* **77,** pp. 533–9.

PART III

EXPERIMENTAL NEUROSES AND CLINICAL APPLICATIONS OF THE CONDITIONED REFLEX METHOD

ABNORMAL ANIMAL BEHAVIOUR†

P. L. BROADHURST

IF psychologists can point to one achievement of their infant science in which they can properly profess some pride, it is the development of modern learning theory, to which the contribution of animal studies does not need stressing. Here we are not primarily concerned with learning theory, but rather with animal studies which have been more influential in psychiatry than psychology. Since the earliest experiments involving experimental neurosis in Pavlov's laboratory before World War I, a body of work on this topic has accumulated, much of which purports to be relevant to human psychopathology. It is proposed to subject this literature to scrutiny in order to assess its worth and its relevance to the human field. In doing so, the status of the concept of experimental neurosis ‡ will inevitably be called into question.

The field to be covered is somewhat arbitrarily defined. Abnormalities of behaviour produced in infrahuman animals by psychological or functional means will be included. Disorders of behaviour resulting from the ingestion of drugs, or from physical methods causing tissue damage, e.g., cortical insult, and electroconvulsive shock, will be excluded. On the other hand, where such methods have been used in attempted therapy of abnormal behaviour, they will be considered. Discerning readers will find other omissions: thus, audiogenic seizure phenomena—the so-called "neurotic pattern" rediscovered and described by Maier (1939), the advent of which was hailed as an alkahest for the all-too-solid problems in this field—will not be dealt with. A wealth of studies—Finger (1947), and Bevan (1955) review some 200 papers—compels the conclusion that the convulsive phenomena observed are primarily a response to loud noise of high frequency,

---

† From: Handbook of Abnormal Psychology, edited by H. J. Eysenck, Pitman, London 1960

‡ The use of the term "experimental neurosis" is frequently avoided by authors who feel that its use, even when parenthetically protected, suggests acceptance of the implied identification of animal and human neuroses. They prefer circumlocutions such as "behaviour disorders"—seemingly innocuous, but in fact question–begging. Since much of this chapter is devoted to an attempt to examine the validity of the identification mentioned in cases where it is accepted, there is no special reason to avoid the term.

facilitated, in many cases, by middle–ear disease. Similarly no treatment will be found of "abnormal fixations" in learning situations. The evidence so far available (Wilcoxon, 1952) suggests that such "frustration instigated" behaviour (Maier, 1949) can be explained in terms of conventional Hullian learning theory, no new principle of the sort Maier (1956) advocates being necessary. Another omission is the neglect of the phenomena classed as "animal hypnosis". While our understanding of human hypnosis is still obscure, and it retains a flavour of the abnormal, there are no good grounds for regarding the immobility which may in some circumstances be induced in animals as examples of hypnosis. As Weitzenhoffer (1953) notes, the characteristic of hypnosis in humans is heightened suggestibility to verbal commands and statements. Even allowing for the absence of speech in lower animals, nothing remotely comparable has been reported. A fourth omission which may be detected is a lack of emphasis on those animal studies designed to confirm or refute some aspect of psychoanalytic theory. While some are superior to certain of the studies given prominence below, in that they are at least grounded in a theoretical position and so have greater heuristic potential, they are in general peripheral to the topic of this chapter. Usually they are concerned with an animal analogue of a psychoanalytic mechanism held to be operative in human development (Sears, 1943; Hilgard, 1956), and not with abnormal behaviour as such.

The Definition of Abnormal Behaviour in Animals

Fundamental to the topic of this chapter is the problem of the definition of abnormality in animals. One way of proceeding (Karn, 1940, 1940a) is to accept as experimental neurosis what the experimenter in question defines as experimental neurosis. This leads to the inclusion in other reviews of a paper by Carmichael (1938) which has absolutely no bearing on the topic, apparently because of the mention of the words "experimental neurosis". Some of the rats used as subjects in a maze learning study developed a resistance to running a new maze pattern: "In such cases, the animal's general behavior as indicated by head-turning, irregular movement, and the like, seemed typical of the behavior described by those who have set up so-called experimental neuroses in animals" (Carmichael, 1938, p. 162). That is all. If head–turning is to be the sole criterion of neurotic behaviour then centre-court spectators at Wimbledon would be ideal subjects for the investigation of neurosis in humans!

The alternative is to attempt to define criteria of abnormal behaviour applicable to animals, and then to apply them rigorously. This procedure is clearly superior to relying on the judgement of the individual investigatour. In the absence of anything comparable to human neurosis or psychosis in animals in their natural or domesticated states, the selection of such criteria and their definition must inevitably be based on human experience. This is not to deny that bizarre behaviour is not seen in domesticated animals (Croft, 1951), but rather to stress the absence of a body knowledge about such abnormalities, comparable with that available from human psychiatry (but *see* Melzack, 1952).

Fortunately, outstanding among studies of the problem (e.g. Hamilton, 1927; Foley, 1935; Lubin, 1943; Davis, 1954) Hebb's penetrating analysis (1947) has provided us with a set of criteria against which to evaluate behaviour thought to be indicative of experimental neurosis. For this purpose, he first defines human neurosis in behavioural terms which do not involve the use of the patient's verbal report of his subjective state, thus allowing the use of the definition at the animal level. To do so, he makes use of his concept of "associated signs" of emotion (Hebb, 1946), for the purpose of which a sharp distinction must be made between behaviour arising from a central state or event, and that central state itself—that is, between neurotic behaviour and neurosis, to which one can add *neuroticism*, the factorial definition of the constitutional predisposition to the central state itself. These latter two are, however, constructs designed to classify and to guide research; and it is the former, neurotic acts, which are the associated signs of the central state. Hebb makes it plain that he is not seeking to establish what this neurotic condition essentially is; it is merely a stage in the search for criteria "to test whether a given disturbance of animal behaviour should be called neurotic".

His analysis of human neurosis along these lines leads him to advance the following definition: "Neurosis is in practice an undesirable emotional condition which is generalized and persistent; it occours in a minority of the population and has no origin in a gross neural lesion" (Hebb, 1947, p. 11). This definition contains six elements which Hebb considers essential. Omit any one of them and the definition becomes too wide, thus:

Undesirable implies evaluationally abnormal—otherwise, e.g. exceptional love of sports is neurotic.

Emotional implies involving emotional activity—otherwise, e.g. laziness is neurotic.

Generalized implies shown in many ways, not solely in response to a specific excitant—otherwise, e.g. dislike of cats is neurotic.

Persistent implies chronic to some degree, especially persisting after the cessation of the specific excitant—otherwise e.g. transient irritability or depression is neurotic.

Occurs in a minority of the population implies statistically abnormal—otherwise, e.g. emotional prudery is neurotic.

No origin in a gross neural lesion implies the absence of such physical causation as cortical insult—otherwise, e.g. emotional changes caused by brain damage are neurotic.

Hebb notes that though the first four of these criteria are inescapable, they are of different kinds. The fifth, statistical abnormality, he regards as in a sense accidental, being in fact dependent upon the current *mores*. If emotional prudery, for example, were shown to have the same origin as other aspects of neurosis, then neurosis might be said to occur in a majority of the population. The sixth criterion (absence of physical causation) resembles the previous one in being of doubtful theoretical value in the definition, but must be included because of the part both have played in clinical diagnosis of neurotic disorders.

Hebb rejects as components for inclusion in his definition—

> *Neurosis has no known physiological base*—because, in his view, an aetiology dependent upon metabolic derangement does not change a diagnosis of neurosis *per se*.

> *Neurosis produces a marked change of behaviour from an earlier base-line* —because this concept, despite its profound influence on research, is not a necessary condition of neurosis; neither is

> *Neurosis follows from some "traumatic" experience like conflict or frustration*—because, though human neurosis can follow psychological strain it can also result from metabolic processes free from strain.

These three principles, Hebb feels, are not essentially true of human neurosis, though they have dominated much theorizing on the topic and have come to be accepted widely as intrinsically related to the neurotic central state. They will, nevertheless, be borne in mind so that the reader who disagrees with Hebb's estimate of their minor function will not feel cheated on that score. Another reason for the retention of these ancillary criteria is that the last two, at least, have occasionally so dominated animal research that positive evidence that the subject's behaviour has changed after a putatively traumatic experience, has, *ipso facto*, been taken as evidence of experimental neurosis. Examples of this may be noted later.

Enough has been said to indicate that Hebb's analysis provides us with a powerful instrument for evaluating abnormal animal behaviour, especially with respect to its relevance to human studies. It is clearly of little use to argue about human abnormality on the basis of animal findings if such data are themselves not related to abnormality in the animal subjects used. True, the criteria which Hebb offers and of which extensive use will be made, are themselves derived from the human field. But no other course is at present available, and a reasonable anthropomorphism must operate in both directions, that is, not only in employing animal data to illuminate human behaviour †, but also in using criteria derived from our more exten-

---

† This procedure implies a judicious anthropomorphism, which is inseparable from the use of animals as subjects for experimentation. It is frequently thought that the benefits deriving from such use—inevitable in, for example, selective mating, or experiments with large rewards or punishments—are only achieved at the cost of some clarity in the interpretation of the relevance of the findings

sive study of human behaviour to evaluate the animal data. In this way, it becomes possible to assess the suitability of such data for the constructions but upon them.

Early Russian Work on Experimental Neurosis

Priorities in science are rarely awarded accurately, and frequently what is stated to be "the first" later turns out to be "the second" or even "the third". This process appears to have started in connexion with the present topic, for, quite apart from the question of priority within Pavlov's own laboratory, discussed below, we find that the claims of Itard to be the first to have produced an experimental neurosis are advanced (Landis and Bolles, 1949). He used colour and form matching tasks in training Victor, the wild boy of Aveyron, but had to give up when the required discriminations were made so difficult that Victor failed to respond and showed violent anger instead.

But, as is generally known, the idea of experimental neurosis originated with Pavlov. Most accounts give the name of Shenger-Krestovnikova (1921) as the first to observe an experimental neurosis. Her experiment, begun in 1914, is one of the classics of experimental psychology. A dog, conditioned to salivate to the appearance of a circle, but not to an ellipse, was trained to make finer and finer discriminations as the ellipse was made more and more circular. The disturbed behaviour which eventuated when the animal was no longer able to make the required discrimination Pavlov (1927) named experimental neurosis. But Sen (1953) points out that such behaviour had been observed previously in Pavlov's laboratory by Yerofeeva (1912, 1916, 1953), as is clear from the accounts of this early work by Pavlov himself (1927) and by his pupil, Gantt (1944). Yerofeeva's own account, though only published in abstract (1916) is therefore the pioneer report † of behavioural disturbances due to conditioning techniques, though, as Pavlov puts it: "The investigation of the higher nervous activity under difficult conditions, carried out in the course of M. N. Yerofeeva's experiments, unexpectedly

to human psychology. But both Hull (1937) and Hebb (1947) have examined this problem, and conclude that cross-species identification of behaviour may properly be made if it can be shown that the principles or mechanisms governing the behaviour are the same. (See also Hebb and Thompson, 1954.)

† Available in the West, that is. For the study of much of this early Russian work on experimental neurosis, and on conditioning in general, we must rely on secondary sources and reviews—an unsatisfactory substitute for perusal of original research reports. This difficulty, which is not entirely a matter of a language barrier, has decreased recently with the publication of the English translation of Ivanov-Smolensky's important review (1954), of Liberson's review (1957), and of some further snippets of Pavlov's writings in the edition edited by Koshtoyants (1955). The writer, however, is sufficiently well aware of the difficulties preventing an adequate review of the interesting work going on in this field—see, for example, Zverev (1957) and Fonberg (1958)—to know that this chapter will certainly not do justice to it. He therefore apologizes for this omission and cautions the reader to bear it in mind.

11*

resulted in the development for the first time of a chronic pathological state which, however, did not attract proper attention" (1927, p. 290). One might add parenthetically that the reason may have been that Pavlov's theory construction was not sufficiently advanced at that time to handle Yerofeeva's facts. On the other hand we must respect his statement that: "Possibly on account of the special nature of the stimulus used in these experiments, all these facts did not attract sufficient attention on our part" (Pavlov, 1927, p. 290).

The stimulus in question was electric shock used as a conditioned stimulus for a salivary response to meat powder, and the facts were these: the original unconditioned defence reaction to this shock, which Yerofeeva characterized as "strong", was abolished by training so that the shock became recognized by the subject as the signal for food, and gave rise to salivation, but when she attempted to generalize the response to other parts of the body than that originally stimulated by the shock, the defence reaction was restored, whatever area was now stimulated. The finding was confirmed on two dogs: the stimulation of new areas with the conditioned shock gives rise to general excitement "qui rend impossible tout travail de canalisation, et détruit tout le travail déjà fait" (Yerofeeva, 1916, p. 240). Note here this early hint of the Pavlovian emphasis on the abolition of previously elaborated simple conditioned responses as a criterion of the abnormal. The original state was only restored in one dog after a period of 3 months, and not at all in the other (Pavlov, 1927).

And there the matter was left until the well-known experiment of Shenger-Krestovnikova. What appears to have impressed Pavlov is that disordered behaviour similar to that found by Yerofeeva using electric shock was also found in an experiment employing more usual procedures. The programme of work then initiated which absorbed Pavlov's last 15 years of life has been reported by him (1927, 1928, 1941) and by Ivanov-Smolensky (1954) on whose fuller account the following discussion is based.

The four phases in the study of experimental neurosis in Pavlov's laboratory comprise, firstly, the phase from 1922 to 1925, in which methods used and forms of breakdown were studied and the reaction shown to depend on the dog's nervous "type"; secondly, the next phase in which the concept of overstrain of excitatory and inhibitory processes was developed, the theory of types revised, and phasic states described; thirdly, the last phase before Pavlov's death (in 1936) saw emphasis on changes in complicated patterns of conditioned responses and their interrelationships; and, fourthly, since Pavlov's death, attention seems to have been concentrated more on the effect of experimental neurosis on other aspects of functioning—reaction to disease, or internal vegetative action—rather than on the neurotic behaviour itself.

After Shenger-Krestovnikova's experiment, the experimental work on neurosis was next taken up by Pavlov's distinguished colleague Petrova (1924, 1926), yet even her experiment appears to be only accidentally con-

cerned with the topic. She was investigating sleep in two dogs chosen as
extreme exemplars ("as judged by their general behaviour") of nervous
systems based on the dominance of excitation, or of inhibition. To delay sleep
on the stand, five diverse sensory conditioned stimuli were used, and delays
of up to 5 min between signal and reward were achieved with the inhibitable
dog. But with only 2 min delay the excitable dog showed "general
excitation", and with 3 min "became quite crazy, unceasingly and violently
moving all parts of its body, howling, barking and squealing intolerably"
(Pavlov, 1927, p. 294). Practice with only one stimulus at a time restored
normal responses and delays up to 3 min were achieved: "The differences
in the nervous system of the two dogs was thus made clear", and the main
object of the experiment altered to inducing abnormal behaviour by a
disturbance in the "normal relations between the two antagonistic nervous
processes". The technique of differentiation of positive and negative conditioned stimuli as used by Shenger-Krestovnikova, as well as others involving prolonged inhibition of the two dogs' responses, produced only
transient general excitation in the excitable one. Accordingly the painful
stimulus used in Yerofeeva's original work—electric shock—was employed.
Again the dogs differed in their response to the shock initially but when the
strenght of shock was increased, delayed reflexes were "disturbed", and
conditioned inhibition "incomplete". The consequent abandonment of the
use of shock is surprising, if the purpose was in fact to produce disturbed
behaviour: nevertheless, inhibition continued to weaken so that the excitable dog gave responses to all stimuli, negative as well as positive. The same
treatment led to the inhibitable dog developing responses to the shock quite
easily, but with practice it led to a decrease in the salivary response to this
as well as to all other stimuli. This process was repeated later, when the
"ultraparadoxical" phenomenon was observed. This is Pavlov's descriptive
term for the condition in which no response is made to positive stimuli, but
only to previously negative ones. He clearly always regards this as evidence
of abnormal cortical functioning.

Thus:

> ... in these two dogs with different type of nervous system, prolonged
> disturbances of the higher nervous activity which developed under pre-
> cisely identical injurious influences took quite different directions. In the
> excitable dog the inhibitory function of the cortical elements became ex-
> tremely weakened. In the quiet dog it was the excitation of the correspond-
> ing cells (since the stimuli were identical) which became extremely weak.
> In other words, two quite different types of neurosis were produced. (Pavlov,
> 1927, p. 299.)

Pavlov's ideas about the "type" of nervous system may be conveniently
summarized as shown in Table 1.

Ivanov-Smolensky (1954, p. 100) notes that:

> For some time after these experiments, the idea prevailed in the Pavlov
> laboratories that the character of the nervous breakdown as well as of the

Table 1. Pavlov's Temperamental Types in Dogs
(Adapted from Babkin, 1938)

"Type" of nervous system	Strength of nervous system		Balance of nervous system		Predominance in nervous system of		Susceptible to nervous breakdown	Type of experimental neurosis seems
	Strong	Weak	Balanced	Unbalanced	Excitation	Inhibition		
Sanguine	Yes		Yes				No	
Phlegmatic	Yes		Yes				No	
Choleric	Yes			Yes	Yes		Yes	Excitatory
Melancholic		Yes		Yes		Yes	Yes	Inhibitory

experimental neurosis evoked by it, depended mainly on the type of the animals' nervous system. However, as we shall see later, experimental facts obtained in the course of further investigations forced us considerably to revise this notion and to introduce substantial corrections.

About the same time Rosenthal (1926) precipitated in an inhibitable animal a disturbance of behaviour lasting several months and taking the form of extreme drowsiness. It followed when the inhibitory stimulus of a discrimination involving two tactile rhythms succeeded the excitatory one too closely. Kreps (1924) also produced an inhibitory breakdown by a tactile discrimination, as did Razenkov (1924) in a pioneer experiment on "phasic states" of the cerebral cortex—so called because of the display of phases of more, or less, disordered conditioned responses—by making a single transition from negative to positive conditioned stimulus. This disturbing combination was attenuated by repetition, so that by the fourth presentation no deleterious effect was observed. Siryatsky (1925) also found that discrimination of auditory stimuli occasioned the disappearance of established conditioned responses.

So far, the work in Pavlov's laboratory had been on disturbances produced by difficult discriminations or the temporal contrast of two sorts of stimulation. Rickman's work (1928) was novel because he used unusual or intense stimuli alone:

Experiments were carried out with an animal manifestly belonging to the inhibitory type of nervous system. The following stimuli were simultaneously applied to exert such unusual and intense functional influence upon the nervous system: (1) a loud rhythmic crackle produced by a rattle and resembling the crackle of gun-fire; (2) a sudden emergence in front of the dog of an unusual figure in a mask and fur coat turned inside out; (3) an explosion of powder near the stand; (4) a special swinging platform mounted on the stand and on which the dog was placed.

Clearly this dog did not like fireworks, hated swings, and did not believe in Santa Claus, because "At the very beginning the animal started, rushed forward, instantaneously rose on its hind legs, set its forelegs against the food receptacle which was before its muzzle and became rigid, its limbs extended, its head thrown back, its eyes wide open" (Ivanov-Smolensky, 1954 p. 102). A loud tone ended this posture and motor excitement followed for a fortnight, during which no conditioned or even unconditioned responses could be elicited. Re-introduction of the swinging platform caused excitement again: ". . . the neurosis was fully reproduced as if by the mechanism of conditioned reaction to one of the components of the initial pathogenic situation" (Ivanov-Smolensky, 1954, p. 103).

This animal was among those previously subjected to the well–known natural experiment of the Leningrad flood of 1924 so that its pre- and post-flood responses are known. The rescue from the flood exerted an inhibiting influence, judging from the animal's general behaviour (Pavlov, 1927), and this was confirmed by the performance of this particular dog in the conditioning situation. For 8 months thereafter whenever the previously learned negative conditioned response was elicited it abolished all other responses.

> The powerful and unusual stimuli arising from the flood increased the susceptibility of cortical elements to so great an extent that even a comparatively minute intensification of inhibition from the outside in the form of a conditioned inhibitory stimulus, rendered impossible for a long time any existence of positive conditioned reflexes under ordinary experimental conditions" (Pavlov, 1927, p. 318).

Speransky (1925) also profited by the flood. His dog, of the inhibitable type, appeared normal immediately after the flood, but a week later was restless and refused food. Though increasing the food deprivation had no effect, the presence of the experimenter had, and normal responses were restored after 2 months. Then, as in Rickman's experiment, a component of the traumatic situation was restored by allowing water to flow under the door of the experimental chamber. Pavlov writes vividly: "The animal jumps up quickly, gazes restlessly at the floor, tries to get off the stand and breathes heavily. The conditioned stimuli serve only to increase the general excitation, the animal declines the food" (1927, p. 315). Only several months further training restored conditioned responses to their former level. "Thus, the reproduction of a situation somewhat resembling the picture of the flood immediately evoked a new breakdown with the resulting pathological state; this convincingly proved that the first nervous breakdown in the given dog had been really caused by the flood" (Ivanov-Smolensky, 1954, p. 105). In one other dog, called "Brains" because of its facility in forming conditioned responses, Vishnevsky found disturbances of responses 4 months after the flood, though in this case they had also been seen before the flood (Pavlov, 1928).

Neither Pavlov, nor Frolov (1937), nor Ivanov-Smolensky review the Pavlovian work on experimental neuroses after its first phase in sufficient detail to permit independent evaluation. A further limitation is the current extension of the concept implied by the term experimental neurosis beyond Pavlov's original intention. Experimental neusrosis for Pavlov appears to mean a neurosis within the experiment, or even a neurosis of the experiment (cf. Konorski's use of the term "neurotic state of the alimentary centre" [1948, p. 209] to describe the inhibition of eating, frequently met with in classical experimental neurosis); and some writers of Pavlov's school caution against an extension beyond narrow limits. Thus: "Such states were described by Pavlov as *experimental neuroses*; however, it would not be quite correct to regard them as full analogues of human neuroses and stop at that. While some of them actually are what we may call simplified models of human neuroses, others are not" (Ivanov-Smolensky, 1954, pp. 81–82), and: "The designation of these disturbances by the name of 'neurosis' does not mean that they are always of the same type or that they are the same as may be observed in human beings" (Babkin, 1938, p. 616). Nevertheless, Pavlov clearly shows in his writings that he thought them related to human psychopathology.

How then can we evaluate the experiments reviewed above, limited by our dependence upon secondary sources? It is not unreasonable to apply Hebb's criteria for abnormality, bearing in mind that deficiencies revealed may be due to faulty communication. In Table 2 therefore, will be found summarized the main points of these experiments, as they relate to Hebb's criteria. To mitigate the inevitable arbitrariness in such a procedure the "benefit of the doubt" has usually been given to the Russian worker.

It is clear from the Table that a principal failing of this work in its putative relation to the abnormal is the lack of data about responses external to the experiment. Thus it is only by inference that we learn that the criterion of statistical abnormality of the responses of the dogs rescued from the flood may have been met. We are told that all the dogs were resuced from their kennels; if all had been equally affected we should no doubt have heard of it. Even more striking is the lack of information about the generalization of the abnormal behaviour—little being reported about the subject's behaviour outside the conditioning situation. This neglect throughout of the more purely behavioural aspects of the animals' response follows from Pavlov's conviction that his field of study was physiology and not psychology. For him the conditioned reflex method demonstrated the totality of the subject's higher nervous activity, hence the paucity of detail about other aspects of behaviour. But Hebb has argued that the concept of human neurosis as a behavioural abnormality implies a response which has generalized beyond the causal stimulus.

Without this, demonstrations of animal abnormality become less convincing, as they may, for example, be merely fear responses, and as such within the normal range. The available evidence suggests the verdict on this pioneer Russian work should be the Scottish one of "not proven".

American Work
on Experimental Neurosis: Liddell and the Cornell Group

Several reviews of literature on the topic of this chapter already exist; in addition to Hebb's important contribution (1947), those by Babkin (1938), Cook (1939), Karn (1940; 1940a), Gantt (1944), Freeman and Watts (1944). Liddell (1947), Russell (1950), Patton (1951), Kupalov (1952), Pilgrim and Patton (1953) and Beach (1953) may be cited. The justification for adding another lies perhaps in the greater rigour of the approach adopted here, as well as in the growing recognition of the limitations of the results achieved by traditional methods (Harlow, 1956; Chance, 1957). Furthermore, the output of work appears to have passed its peak. Three major American contributions to the literature appeared in the early 1940s (Anderson and Parmenter, 1941; Masserman, 1943; Gantt, 1944). This productivity, originating in Liddell's pioneer work on conditioning in sheep (1926) and the establishment in 1929 of the Pavlovian Laboratory at Johns Hopkins University under Gantt, a translator and former student of Pavlov, has not been equalled since. It is proposed, therefore, to organize our discussion of the readily available literature around these three contributions, and pride of place, because of its range, novelty and volume, must go to that of the Cornell group associated with Liddell.

The story is told (in Tanner and Inhelder, 1956) of how Liddell was studying thyroidectomy in sheep and goats and found no effects on maze learning (1925, 1925a; Liddell and Simpson, 1925). He therefore turned to conditioned reflex methods for a more precise measure (Liddell and Simpson, 1926; Liddell and Bayne, 1927). This quickly led to the incidental and unintentional production of experimental neurosis in a sheep (Liddell and Bayne, 1927a), and the field of study changed. The techniques routinely used resemble the Russian, but differ in that the salivary reflex—difficult, but not impossible (Denton, 1957), with ruminants like sheep—was avoided, and the motor response to an electric shock to the foreleg, which appears as a brisk muscular flexion, used instead. This unconditioned response becomes associated in the usual way with a conditioned stimulus which then evokes it before, or in the absence of, the shock. In a study (Liddell, James and Anderson, 1934) of this motor conditioned response in the sheep, and four other species (dog, goat, pig and rabbit), it is claimed as an advance on Pavlovian procedure, because it is a more discrete event than salivation, and is easily quantified using a work accumulator (see Anderson, 1941, and Liddell, 1942, p. 19!), though this device has not been consistently used. While physiological measures, such as respiration, heart rate and P. G. R., were recorded as well as movement of parts of the body other than that to

TABLE 2. EARLY RUSSIAN WORK ON

Experimenter	Date of work		Source of information	No, of cases	Techniques used	
	Done	Reported			General	Specific
Yerofeeva	1912	1916	Yerofeeva (1916), Pavlov (1927) and Ivanov-Smolensky (1954)	2, 3	Salivary conditioning to shock	Generalization of area used
Shenger-Krestovnikova	1914	1921	Pavlov (1927)	1	Salivary conditioning to visual stimulus	Differentiation
Petrova	1922–3	1924, 1926	Pavlov (1927)	2	Salivary conditioning to various stimuli, including shock later	Delayed reflexes principally
Rosenthal	1922–3	1926	Ivanov-Smolensky (1954)	1	Salivary conditioning to cutaneous stimulus and "clashing"	Differentiation
Kreps	1923	1924	Ivanov-Smolensky (1954)	1	As above	Differentiation
Razenkov	1923	1924	Pavlov (1927)	1	Salivary conditioning to various stimuli	"Clashing"
Siryatsky	1923	1925	Ivanov-Smolensky (1954)	?2	Salivary conditioning to auditory stimulus	Differentiation

Hebb's criteria

Evaluationally abnormal	Emotional	Generalized	Chronic	Statistically abnormal	Not due to neural lesion	No known physiological basis	Change from previous baseline	Followed trauma
1	1	?	1	?	1	?	1	1
1	1	?	?	?	1	1	1	1
1	1	?	?	?	1	1	1	1
1	0	?	1	?	1	1	1	1
0	0	?	?	?	1	1	?	1
?	0	?	0	?	1	1	1	1
?	0	?	?	?	?	?	?	1

Table 2 (cont.)

| Experi-menter | Date of work | | Source of information | No. of cases | Techniques used | |
	Done	Report-ed			General	Specific
Speransky	1924	1925	Pavlov (1927)	1	Salivary con-ditioning to various stimuli	Flood
Vishnevsky	1924	?	Pavlov (1927)	1	As above	Ditto
Rickman	1926	1928	Ivanov–Smolens-ky (1954)	1	?	Fright

1 means criterion apparently met
0 means criterion apparently not met
? means doubtful, or insufficient evidence to judge.

be conditioned, only a few subjects of species other than sheep were used, and the normative data presented are inadequate, no statistic more refined than a range being given. From observations of the stressful aspects of the conditioned motor reflex procedure it is concluded that nervous strain develops when negative conditioned stimuli are introduced, restraint thus being required of the animal.

This point is developed in a paper on four cases of experimental neurosis in sheep (Anderson and Liddell, 1935). The first, briefly reported before (Liddell and Bayne, 1927), showed persistent movement of the conditioned forelimb during intervals between the stimuli when they were increased from 10 to 20 during a period of 6 days. Moreover, contrary to its previous willing-ness to enter the laboratory, it now resisted and had to be forced in and on to the stand. Once there it was calm enough: "As soon, however, as the experimenter left the room, the sheep began its fidgeting tentative move-ments of the left foreleg" (Anderson and Liddell, 1935, p. 334). Neither this sheep's thyroidectomized twin, nor two other non-operates were disturbed by comparable increases in conditioning practice. These comparisons are vitiated, however, by the operation in the first case, and the use of somewhat different conditioning signals in the second. Short periods of rest did not

TABLE 2 (cont.)

Hebb's criteria

Evaluationally abnormal	Emotional	Generalized	Chronic	Statistically abnormal	Not due to neural lesion	No known physiological basis	Change from previous baseline	Followed trauma
1	1	?	1	?1	1	?	1	1
1	0	?	1	?1	1	0	1	1
1	1	?	?	?	1	1	1	1

restore the former precision of the sheep's responses, but $1\frac{1}{2}$ years away from the laboratory did. Resuming work with delayed responses precipitated further "interval activity" and resistance to experimentation in a second sheep, the introduction of non–reinforced conditioned signals to be discriminated from the positive ones caused similar symptoms, still apparent 5 years later. In a third, good discrimination between different metronome rates was achieved; only when the different rates were presented in the same experimental session did the disturbed behaviour appear, and was present 3 years later. Rhythmical patterning of a simple discrimination caused similar restless and unmanageable behaviour in a fourth sheep, although it did not affect another similarly treated. Thus each neurosis was of an excitatory nature in Pavlov's sense, though passing through a premonitory inhibitory phase in two cases.

An apparatus devised for measuring heart rate outside the conditioning chamber, as well as inside it, represents a methodological advance by this group (Anderson, Parmenter and Liddell, 1939). By strapping to the sheep thechest-piece of a stethoscope attached to a long, flexible tube at the end of which the hidden experimenter listened, counting the beats[†], records of

† In later work a cardiotachometer and a cardiograph were used.

heart rate of six sheep were obtained. Two of those whose experimental neurosis is described above are included in a group of four "neurotics", and there were two normals. The authors conclude: "Sheep in which an experi mental neurosis has been developed reveal, upon examination, a cardiac disorder which is characterized by a rapid and irregular pulse and by extreme sensitivity of the heart's action to conditioned and other stimulation" (Anderson, Parmenter and Liddell, 1939, p. 100). Evidence for rapidity of pulse comes from a systematic though unspecified number of observations as shown in Table 3, which may or may not indicate a statistically significant elevation of pulse rate. Evidence for irregularity and sensitivity comes from the experience of the observers in comparing the normal and neurotic sheep under different conditions, but since one of the "normals" became "neuro-tic" later (Anderson and Parmenter, 1941; Rose, Tainton-Pottberg and Anderson, 1938), the value of these comparisons is dubious. Thus recognition of the methodological advance is tempered by the absence of any satisfactory statistical treatment of the data collected. Unfortunately this criticism is also applicable to the major work of this group (Anderson and Parmenter, 1941)†. In this monograph the series of cases of experimental neurosis extended to ten (seven sheep, and three dogs) some of which had been report-ed before (Anderson and Liddell, 1935; Anderson, Parmenter and Liddell, 1939; Liddell, Sutherland, Parmenter and Bayne, 1936; Liddell, Sutherland, Parmenter, Curtis and Anderson, 1937; Anderson, 1939). All cases of ex-perimental neurosis except one in a dog with whom a salivary conditioning method was used, resulted from motor conditioned reflex procedures. Three main topics are dealt with: the signs of neurosis, the methods which initiate and maintain it, and therapeutic procedures. Reproduction of polygraph recordings to illustrate the points discussed does not prevent the presenta-tion from remaining anecdotal in flavour.

The signs of experimental neurosis are numerous. *Hyperirritability* showed as increased conditioned motor responses and startle responses. *Restlessness*, especially interval activity, is shown to be greater in a neurotic animal than in a normal, and in one sheep transferred from the reaction foreleg to the other ‡. The diurnal activity of the four sheep—two neurotic and two

† These strictures do not apply solely to the work of the Cornell group. Most of the work in this field is characterized by a poverty of experimental design, manifest in inadequate control, and the almost entire absence of quantitative data, appropriately analysed. Perhaps workers have been overinfluenced by Pavlov's manner of exposition as seen in translation. Typically, he makes a statement and then cites a detail of an experiment to support it. But not all investigators follow his manner of working, which involved scrupulously check-ing experimental findings (Babkin, 1951), and which to some extent renders statistical sophistication necessary.

‡ An identical occurrence in two dogs also undergoing motor conditioning to shock (Drabovitch and Weger, 1937) hardly deserves the appellation of experi-mental neurosis since the authors explicitly deny any generalization—the dogs otherwise remaining normal.

TABLE 3. THE PULSE RATE OF NORMAL AND NEUROTIC SHEEP UNDER NATURAL AND LABORATORY CONDITIONS
(From Anderson, Parmenter, and Liddell, 1939)

	In animal quarters				In laboratory			
	Hourly diurnal observation				Observations every minute for 30 min		Observations every minute for 15 min	
	Range of pulse		Average pulse rate		Range of pulse		Range of pulse	Average pulse rate in 15 min period
	Day	Night	Day	Night	Noon	Midnight		
Normal Sheep								
Sheep 1	68–84	64–84	72	72	68–76	68–76	80–88	85
Sheep 11	56–80	56–72	70	65	60–72		74–88	80
			—	—			—	—
	Average		71		compare with		Average	83
Neurotic Sheep								
Sheep 7	68–96	60–88	84	72	76–96	60–80	107–152	129
Sheep 8	80–104	72–120	87	89	76–88	80–112	88–136	111
Sheep "D"	60–100	60–88	78	71	60–80	60–80	76–92	83
			—				—	—
	Average		83		compare with		Average	107

normal—was measured by means of a large activity platform, or a leg pedo-
meter (Curtis, 1937a). The authors recognize that the resulting data are
insufficient for exact comparison, principally because different breeds of
sheep were used. Nevertheless, the figures suggest, not a greater total activity of the neurotics, but a decrease of the normal nocturnal rest: "The
neurotic animal, like the neurotic human, is apparently a frequent sufferer
from 'insomnia'" (Anderson and Parmenter, 1941, p. 37). *Postural changes*
were prominent, especially among cases of inhibitory neuroses—now noted
for the first time as occurring among sheep. In the conditioning situation
one regularly adopted an unusual posture with concavely flexed back, and
another extended the reaction limb instead of flexing it. One dog showed
"pseudo–decerebrate rigidity", which allowed passive moulding of limbs into
bizarre poses.

The records of *respiration* taken from many sheep suggest that the experimentally neurotic ones, as well as displaying a disordered rhythm, have
an increased breathing rate, and a long-range pneumograph technique confirmed that these differences persist in the animals' living quarters. Data
from systematic observation of respiration in twelve dogs suggest that the
three neurotic animals had a higher breathing rate, but these data are
inadequately presented for appropriate comparison. *Cardiac records* are
taken as confirming previous findings, and reveal conditioning of cardiac
responses. A curious inversion of the T-wave (Part of the P-Q-R-S-T car-
diogram complex) was observed in three sheep, but since only one was neurotic, the significance of this observation is not apparent. Another anomaly—
—the coupled heartbeat—seen in the cardiotachometer records of one neurotic sheep is probably an artefact to which this method of recording heart
rate is prone. Another example, in this case recognized as a double recording of two (instead of one) aspects of the complex, is noted by James (1943).
Elimination of urine and faeces in the laboratory was only observed among
neurotic animals, and their *social behaviour* changed in the direction of
greater solitariness, especially noticeable in the normally gregarious sheep.
Neurotic animals occasionally attacked the experimenter, normal ones never.
Maternal and sexual behaviour is briefly reported, but five of the seven sheep
were castrated males. In later accounts of work on sheep, Liddell (1953,
1956) notes this deficiency, and characterizes the conditioning procedure as
an essentially "castrating" one for the young ram, which is not tolerated by
adult ones, two of whom became aggressive with a defence reaction (butting)
to each stimulus (Liddell, 1951).

The conditioning procedure which gave rise to the signs of abnormal
behaviour were, in order of importance, discrimination between positive and
negative stimuli, experimental extinction of a positive conditioned response,
and training according to a rigid time schedule. Liddell claims (1947, 1950,
1951) that this method, employing the positive conditioned stimulus only,
is standard procedure for producing experimental neurosis, and even that

the type of neurosis may be determined by the interval between the stimuli, 5–7 min giving an excitatory and 2 min an inhibitory breakdown. Anderson and Parmenter only show that nervous behaviour was *maintained*—through for six years—by this method. Increasing the amount of practice as a method of producing breakdown is not now stressed.

Therapeutic procedures resemble Pavlov's, with emphasis on *rest* from experimentation and the use of *drugs*. "The periods of rest we have given our animals have ranged from one month to as long as three years. The result was somewhat beneficial. However, the improvement was of short duration, once testing of the animal was resumed. The degree of improvement did not seem to be a function of the duration of the period of rest" (Anderson and Parmenter, 1941, p. 74). The effect of sedatives (sodium bromide, sodium amytal and ethyl alcohol) on the excitatory neurosis of one sheep is unclear from the few data presented. In a somewhat more extensive test, phenobarbiton increased the magnitude of the conditioned motor responses, decreased the interval activity, and made the animal quieter in the barn. A similar effect had been found (Liddell, Anderson, Kotyuka and Hartman, 1935, 1935a) in earlier work on four neurotic sheep in which the hormone cortin was used and its effect contrasted with that of adrenalin which decreased the magnitude of the response, and increased interval activity. Thyroxin is said to have no effect. These suggestive findings do not appear to have been followed up (Liddell, 1952a). *Spontaneous remission* of the neurosis in one old sheep aged 12 years may have resulted from senile changes, though in another case disordered behaviour persisted until death some 13 years after it was first observed.

The admirable longitudinal approach of these authors is seen in the complete case histories of the subjects† which are appended to the monograph. The patient documentation of experimental and observational work over long periods—the shortest being 2 years in the dog, and 5 years in the sheep—is unfortunately marred by the absence of any standard experimental approach. Procedures vary between subjects, and with the same subject from time to time. Considering that the subjects were of different species, and different breeds within species, it is not surprising that no new principles emerge from the plethora of observations. The need for precise standardization on a sizeable number of subjects now appears to have been recognized (Liddell, 1950, 1950a). By means of central polygraph recording "... our arrangements for conditioning six to eight sheep or goats simultaneously by automatic controls will enable us to observe and compare enough animals subjected to standard stress situations to arrive at statistically valid conclusions" (Liddell, 1950a, p. 166). Its use with four sheep of, however, varying

---

† The seven sheep reported to have developed experimental neurosis represent a quarter of a total population of twenty–eight tested. For the dogs, the figures are three out of twenty-six.

ages and strains, led to another of the "accidental" experiments which
abound in the literature on experimental neurosis. A fault in the electrical
circuits caused a slight shock to be delivered to the foreleg with each click of
the conditioned metronome signal in advance of the reinforcing unconditioned
shock. Only after this was repaired and the "warning" shock no longer
received did experimental neurosis quickly supervene in all cases (Liddell,
1950a). But no further behavioural details are given, nor have any other
reports of the use of this ingenious procedure of simultaneously conditioning
many subjects come to hand.

The Cornell group have also done work on two additional species, and
further work on the dog. In these, strict Pavlovian techniques were not
always followed. James (1943) used a conditioned avoidance technique
(James, 1934) in his work on two dogs, and sought to introduce a conflict
into the situation by weighting down the foot which the dog had to withdraw
to avoid shock. Thus one Alsatian was attempting to lift over 30 lb on its
foreleg to avoid a shock of the maximum (unspecified) intensity. It does not
seem remarkable that ". . . total flight and escape behaviour was released,
signalled in the kennel by the entrance of the experimenter rather than a
specific signal in the laboratory" (1943, p. 117). After 6 months rest, the
first signal caused one dog to react so vigorously that it fell out of the harness
(James, 1953). No data on other aspects of the dogs' behaviour are presented
(Jensen, 1945).

The early work of this group on the pig is diffusely reported with few
experimental details (Liddell, 1936; Liddell, Sutherland, Parmenter and
Bayne, 1936; Curtis, 1937; Liddell, Sutherland Parmenter, Curtis and Anderson, 1937; Liddell, 1938; Sutherland, 1939; Altmann, 1941). Liddell's own
account (1942, 1944) relates how early attempts (Liddell, James and Anderson, 1934) to condition adult pigs required brute force to handle them, whereas training pigs when young succeeded. An instrumental conditioned
response was used, one pig learning to lift the lid of a food box at the positive
conditioned signal, and not to do so at the negative one, which was sometimes reinforced with shock to the foreleg. Only when the pig was punished
with shock for opening the box before the positive signal, was abnormal
behaviour precipitated. This finally took on an inhibitory nature; the pig
delayed responding to the positive food signals—during which time it was
unresponsive even to food on its snout (Liddell, 1938)—and finally ignored
them altogether. Respiration was slow and deep (Liddell, 1951), and the
pig's behaviour outside the conditioning situation ". . . showed a marked
change from friendliness to irascibility, so that it was no longer to be
trusted" (Liddell, 1942, p. 393).

Later Marcuse and Moore (1942, 1946; Moore and Marcuse, 1945) did
careful work at Cornell on several aspects of conditioning in pigs. In only
one case was abnormal behaviour observed (1944), but the authors doubt
that this "tantrum behaviour" deserved the name experimental neurosis,

since the pig still came to the laboratory willingly, and its heart rate during its vocal protests remained unchanged.

The interesting Cornell work on goats is even more diffusely reported than that on swine. In early work, positive and negative motor response were conditioned in adult goats (Goldman, 1939), using a rigid time schedule, usually with a 2-min interval between stimuli. Liddell (1947, 1949, 1950, 1951) notes that a "tonic immobility" was thus produced with rigid extension of the reaction foreleg. There was no cardiac conditioned response, and though respiration was disordered in the conditioning situation, it was normal outside it (Liddell, 1951). The condition persisted for 7 years in one case and 8 years in another (Liddell, 1952). More recent work has employed the technique for conditioning in freely moving animals (Parmenter, 1940), and has been concerned with the protective effect of the presence of the mother goat against the effects of a rigid time schedule of conditioning in the young kid. The use of flexible suspensions permitted the experimenter to record activity and respiration and to shock the foreleg. At first the method of conditioned avoidance of shock appears to have been used (Liddell, 1951), the experimenter being present in the room with the kid, and turning off the shock if the leg was flexed to the conditioned signal. Later, training was begun with eight young kids, four of whom had their respective mothers with them, while their twin siblings underwent the same conditioning schedule (of 10 sec of darkness followed by shock every 2 min) alone in an adjoining room. The results reported (Liddell, 1950, 1950a, 1952, 1954; Patton, 1951; Tanner and Inhelder, 1956) show that after relatively few trials, compared with the precipitation of experimental neurosis in adult animals, a restriction of movement of the isolated kids occurred. One of the experimental isolates ceased sucking and died. Comparable findings are reported in an experiment involving twin lambs and their mother (Liddell, 1955). Liddell reports (1954) that 2 years later experimental neurosis was precipitated in the now adult goats from the experimental group merely by restraining them in a conditioning harness for 2 hr a day for 20 days, and giving signals every 6 min, whereas the adult controls were not so affected. It is to be regretted that all these suggestive findings, which have aroused widespread interest (e.g. Bowlby, 1951), do not appear to have been reported in detail, especially since the method of co-twin control is a powerful tool for the isolation of environmental effects.

How do the Cornell findings stand in relation to Hebb's criteria of abnormality? It is plain that many examples of behaviour reported are abnormal in the sense of being *evaluationally undesirable*, not only from the point of view of the experimenter and of the individual subject, but also from a broader biological standpoint. An example is the reduction in gregariousness in one sheep which, it is claimed (Anderson and Parmenter, 1941), led to its death when the flock was attacked by dogs. The *emotional* quality of many reactions is confirmed by the disordered physiological

12*

measures, and there is no evidence that the behaviour reported may be attributed to a *gross neural lesion*. The *persistence* of the disorders is well established. On Hebb's ancillary criteria the Cornell casess stand up well: there is usually *marked change in behaviour* from an earlier base-line, though established solely in terms of conditioned response measure, the behaviour outside the laboratory being observed casually or not at all. The selection of cases is not always beyond reproach in this respect, e.g. the use of a sheep for a study of experimental neurosis ". . . because of its atypical reactions outside the laboratory" (Anderson, Parmenter and Liddell, 1939, p. 98). The occurrence of *trauma or conflict* in most cases can be agreed, especially if Liddell's view (1942a) of the conditioning procedure as an essentially traumatizing one is accepted. But some difficulties arise with the important criteria of *statistical abnormality* and *generalization,* despite this group's laudable efforts in this latter direction. Two sorts of generalization may be distinguished in this connexion. Firstly, what might be termed system generalization, the involvement in the disturbed activity of segments of behaviour not specifically manipulated by the experimental procedures. This category is admittedly somewhat artificial, since the whole animal goes into the experimental situation, so all aspects of its behaviour may be modified, but one can point to certain ones unlikely to be thus modified, such as innate responses to stimuli remote from those used experimentally. Nothing in the work of the Cornell group suggests such an effect as, for example, the involvement of the urino-genital system of Gantt's dog Nick (see later). The failure of gregariousness noted in some sheep hardly qualifies, since isolation from the flock is itself a component of conditioning†. The emergence, or re-emergence rather, of cardiac, respiratory and motor disturbances in the experimental situation is less impressive because they are clearly components of the initial unconditioned reaction to electric shock. The fact that they re-emerged after being suppressed by adaptation to the situation is probably not of significance—change from a previous base-line not being an adequate criterion of neurosis—and on some views is exactly what one might expect, as will be shown later. The second kind of generalization may be termed situational generalization, that is, the temporal spread of disturbed behaviour to situations outside the experimental one. This Liddell has called "the subject carrying its troubles into the barn". Despite the surmounting of the difficulties involved in obtaining quantitative measures of physiological variables in the free situation, the evidence collected on this point fails to convince. The data are fragmentary, inadequately controlled and open to two fundamental objections as Hebb noted (1947).

---

† The use of a "social sheep" during conditioning, mentioned in the early Cornell work, appears to have been dropped later, though Liddell's later work on maternal deprivation apparently begins systematic exploration of this rather obvious variable.

The apparatus used to measure respiration, heart rate, etc., were themselves components of the laboratory situation, and may themselves have initiated the disturbances they recorded by serving as conditioned stimuli for them. It may only seem that the sheep has carried its troubles to the barn because the experimenter has followed it there with part of the laboratory. This is a logical objection which can only be met by control data from longitudinal investigations of the measures in question *before* conditioning starts. It is not enough simply to compare neurotics with normals (Anderson, Parmenter and Liddell, 1939). The second objection is that the data in generalization were usually gathered during the period when the subjects were undergoing conditioning training and displaying signs of neurosis in the experimental situation. Regarding the neurotic animals' "insomnia": "Anxiety at night is not evidence of abnormal emotional functioning when the animal is exposed every morning to noxious stimuli" (Hebb, 1947, p. 13).

The evidence on the final criterion of statistical abnormality is even scantier, though it is allowed that it would be a large undertaking to establish the statistical abnormality of a behavioural response using animals larger than the rat. A reasonable quantitative expression of this criterion may be adopted from the human field: Fraser (1947) found that 10 per cent of an industrial population showed clinical signs of neurosis. Now, the evidence presented suggests that in the sheep—the species most studied—about 25 per cent developed experimental neurosis. Though the sample is still too small to allow anything less tentative, this figure seems more suggestive of a normal reaction to the stresses imposed, when the differences in its intensity and the almost certain differences in constitutional predisposition are considered. Thus, one sheep remained unaffected by conditioning procedures far more extensive and strenuous than those causing breakdown in others (Anderson and Parmenter, 1941). To sum up, it appears from the evidence reviewed that the Cornell group's efforts to establish the Pavlovian experimental neurosis on a firmer basis have produced equivocal results, and the reasons for this have been indicated. Liddell, however, believes that in some animals ". . . subjected to experimental procedures there is satisfactory evidence of a psychopathological state, i.e. a breakdown of the emotional mechanism" (1947, p. 571).

In considering Liddell's theoretical formulation of the causation of the disorders he and his colleagues have studied, it should be noted that he has consistently avoided the cross-species identification implicit in Pavlov's term experimental neurosis, which he regards as unfortunate (1950). Nevertheless, he does contend that the behaviour is abnormal, and further that is has relevance for human psychopathology: "It may be regarded as the anlage or prototype of the elaborately differentiated forms of human abnormality. Like them, however, it may be self–perpetuating and persist until death" (Liddell, 1947, p. 572). What, then, in Liddell's view, is the origin of this disorder? Its stems from the view he has developed of the conditioning procedure as in itself constituting a stress situation. "The conditioning procedure which we regarded as innocuous" (in 1927) "apparently meant murder to the sheep" (1956, p. 74) because "during the past 10 years we have become convinced that all conditioning procedures which are based upon the animal's self-imposed restraint will, if long enough continued, cause that animal to become experimentally neurotic" (1956, pp. 66–67). If *all* animals broke down, then that would, ipso facto, be the normal reaction, of course. But Liddell probably had in mind the view that, given sufficient stress, all humans would develop neuroses.

The self-restraint of the trained animal conceals a tense expectancy. For this, he uses Head's term "vigilance" which approximates to Pavlov's investigatory reflex. Vigilance, rather than the unconditioned stimuli of shock or food, . . .

> . . . supplies the power for both positive and negative conditioned reflex action. If this hypothesis proves to be sound, it will lead us to another. We may then suppose that when the capacity for maintaining intense and unremitting vigilance is exceeded (for example, during long-continued and difficult regimes of conditioning) the pent-up nervous tension thereby released will disrupt the operation of the complex and delicate conditioning machinery and lead to chronic states of diffuse or congealed vigilance—experimental neurosis (Liddell, 1950b, pp. 189–90).

Among the further stresses which the experimenter can add to this vigilance, Liddell identifies loneliness, monotony, confusion and overstimulation—examples of which have already been cited. The inhibitory type of neurosis—"tonic immobility"—was regarded ". . . as a state of congealed vigilance. The alarm reaction here appears to be frozen" (1951, p. 145). The excitatory type was regarded as a state of diffused vigilance, though in the most complete statements of Liddell's theory (1955, 1956) the former is now a precursor of the latter.

This brief outline probably does injustice to a theory based on a lifetime of experimental observation and experience, especially as our account of the work which nutured it has not stressed experiments which are regarded as confirmatory, such as the accidental circuit fault which gave subjects a preliminary shock. Disorders developed only *after* the restoration of the signal to its putative role of tension arouser, unrelieved by the inadvertent shocks. Similarly a rise in tension or vigilance can be seen in indicators such as respiration rate during long conditioning sessions, even in well-trained animals (Liddell, 1951). But it must be said that the theory is not formulated in precise enough terms to have heuristic value; few testable deductions flow from it. Only Parmenter (1940, 1940a) has made attempts. He showed that the absence of the restraining harness altered responses in a well-trained sheep. Among other omissions, however, he did not attempt to show whether it was more difficult to precipitate neurosis in untrained sheep by this method of no restraint. Apter (1952) claims to have done so on dogs, though Kaminsky's findings on monkeys (1939) apparently support Liddell. Secondly, Parmenter evolved a method of rapid rexperimental extinction in one sheep by stopping the conditioned stimulus when the response seemed imminent, thus ending the sheep's "uncertainty" sooner. But since other sheep extinguished without disturbance the support this gives to Liddell's theory is not clear.

The Work of Gantt

The work of the second major researcher in the field, Gantt, is Pavlovian, as might be expected from his training, yet, like Liddell, he is concerned with the problem of the generalization of conditioned neuroses. He, too, appears not to have been primarily concerned with abnormal behaviour at first, but in the course of his conditioning work on dogs accidentally provoked experimental neuroses which appeared to resemble those reported by Pavlov. The accumulation of data on novel aspects of the abnormal behaviour led him to organize his earlier and frequently brief reports (1936, 1938, 1940, 1940a, 1942; Gantt and Muncie, 1941) into his important monograph contribution (1944). This is his "monumental study of his experimentally neurotic dog, Nick (the most meticulous and complete case history of a single animal to be found in the conditioned reflex literature)" (Liddell, 1951, p. 127).

Using dogs as subjects for salivary conditioning with food or acid injected into the mouth as the unconditioned stimuli, Gantt reports on the effect of natural emotional shocks. *Parturition* in bitches disturbs differentiated conditioned reponses temporarily. An *accidental disturbance*, comparable to the Leningrad flood, occurred one week-end when some fifteen dogs escaped from their quarters and roamed the building, barking and fighting. One young collie, judged of an inhibitory labile type, showed subdued behaviour and disturbed conditioned responses for a week; in two other dogs studied, the changes were short-lived. Further *fighting*, both accidental and experimentally provoked, caused temporarily altered behaviour. *Restriction* of freedom in a cage eight feet square caused a severe diminution of activity in one young bitch, who died after four months.

Experimental procedures which may give rise to disturbed conditioned responses were next considered. *Conflict of drives* was studied by observing the deleterious effect of a female in oestrus on the alimentary conditioned responses of two male dogs. *Conflict of excitatory and inhibitory* conditioned stimuli is a potent source of disturbance. Unlike Liddell, Gantt does not think the restraint involved important. *Changes in conditioning routine*, e.g. the temporal patterning of stimuli (Gantt, 1940), or during experimental extinction, may cause agitated behaviour. But the major part of the work

is devoted to the case histories of three dogs who reacted to approximately
the same experimental procedures with different degrees of disturbance.

Fritz, a male Alsatian, was a stable, somewhat aggressive animal who
developed conditioned differentiation to tones of different pitch. When the
discrimination was made more difficult 2 years later, he showed some disturbance, barking and panting, and a loss of the conditioned responses. More
radical measures, such as putting him in a swing and causing explosions,
brought only temporary disturbance. After another 2 years a tactile differentiation was easily achieved, and the response to auditory stimuli well
retained. He died of old age in 1938, after 7 years work in the laboratory. At
no time did Fritz shun the experimenter or the experimental room, always
ate food offered there, and displayed normal sexual activity. The second
dog, Peter, was a male beagle, active and playful. In 1931, though he formed
rather unstable salivary responses to the same tones as Fritz quite quickly,
he barked somewhat. The initial stages of the same discrimination were
successfully accomplished; when made more difficult, however, he howled,
refused food in the experimental room, and had to be coaxed to enter it.
Next year all conditioned responses disappeared and he and to be forced
into the room. He became quieter later, resumed eating, and while the use of
the swing and explosions produced disturbances, short rests from work
restored normal behaviour. After a further rest of $1\frac{1}{2}$ years, he was quiet and
gave conditioned responses. He was killed in a fight in 1936.

The case history of the celebrated Nick is longer—he was studied for
12 years—and shows even more severe disturbance of behaviour. He was a
male mongrel about 3 years old, and active and playful when work began in
1932. "Nothing was noted that impressed one as remarkable; in fact he was
selected with Fritz and Peter for laboratory work, as being, according to
general appearances, normal" (Gantt, 1953a, p. 77). He was more restless
than most dogs during adaptation to feeding in the experimental room, and
slow in showing the conditioned salivary response, with restlessness and
whining. When the auditory differentiation was introduced he refused food
and showed defence reactions. A rest restored food acceptance, but with an
increase in the difficulty of the discrimination, he refused it again (October,
1932) and he ". . . continued to refuse it practically during his whole laboratory life . . . in spite of over 10,000 presentations of (the conditioned stimulus) and food" (Gantt, 1944, p. 53). His negativism in this respect contrasts with Fritz's behaviour, and persisted despite an increase in hunger
drive. The added restraint of a Pavlov harness did not affect him.

In the following year all conditioned responses failed, and a definite physical progression in the inhibitory effect of the experimental room was
observed; Nick would eat the more readily the farther he was away. In the
room he showed a stereotyped restlessness, frequently seen afterwards,
whenever he was released from the apparatus. It consisted of rushing

around, jumping up on the table and off it again, and barking at, fumbling in his mouth, and dropping, the uneaten food. The additional strain of the swing and the explosions did not exacerbate the behaviour, but neither did injections of cortin nor a 3 weeks' rest from experimentation improve it. A further rest of 2 years (1934–6) caused only a slight restoration of improvement as judged by his eating and the temporary restoration of conditioned responses. To ameliorate his condition, Nick was fed the whole of his meat ration in the experimental room every day for 7 months in 1936. This attempt at therapy failed; indeed, Nick showed fresh abnormalities, involving other physiological systems. Disturbed respiration took the form of "loud, forced breathing", which was heard whenever he was excited, especially when approaching the experimental room or people connected with the experiment. The disturbance in social behaviour thus demonstrated is characteristic of Nick; Gantt repeatedly noted that he was friendlier towards strangers than towards anyone associated with the experimentation on him. Other disturbances became apparent at the end of 1936; Nick would start urinating when being brought to the experimental room where the frequency was as much as twenty-five times in 30 min. This exaggeration of a male canine habit was unaffected by punishment. Concurrently, abnormal sexual excitation—as judged by penile erection—was observed during conditioned stimulation, or even occasioned, apparently, by the experimental setting itself. These persistent sexual erections contrasted with the occasional short erection seen in young male dogs, especially in spring or when excited†. A further piece of unusual behaviour, noted around this time and which persisted for at least 6 years, was Nick's habit of reacting—with defence movements, gazing, etc.—towards the place where the auditory signal *previously* came from, after its location had been changed. Pavlov (1941) mentions a similar occurrence in an experiment by Filaretov.

The rest of Nick's history—he died in a fight in 1944—was devoted to a study of his abnormalities, which did not proliferate further but fluctuated in intensity. New methods of investigation and therapy were tried. Generalization within the experimental situation was demonstrated by the prompt conditioning of Nick's responses when a new stimulus, a visual one, was given in association with the tone. Wide generalization outside the situation was observed, especially on Gantt's farm in the country, where Nick was kept for periods of 2 and 17 months during 1937 and 1939–41 respectively. In this respect, the particular food given as reinforcement in the experimental situation was consistently refused there, and sexual excitation, pollakuria, disturbed respiration, and a marked increase in heart rate were sometimes observed at the approach of people previously associated with the experimentation, or even members of their families.

† Both the urinary and sexual abnormalities occurred after a bitch in oestrus had been used in the experimental situation in order to test the effect of normal sexual excitation upon Nick's other abnormal signs.

The rests in the country were therapeutic to the extent that afterwards the anxiety and stereotyped responses in the experimental room were lessened, though after the longer one this may have been part of a general improvement due to advancing age or to a change in method. In 1942 a motor conditioned response, using shock to the paw as the unconditioned stimulus was developed, to see if altering the response involved would prove beneficial. Unfortunately, the experimental room was also altered. The change was striking: the positive conditioned response to a tone (though not the same one as originally used) was developed readily, and some progress towards differentiation was even made. Moreover, Nick was quieter and without the sexual and respiratory disturbances which could, however, be reinstated on visits to the old experimental room. The new routine had, therefore, "... extinguished the pathological anxiety reactions to the specific auditory signals but it had not abolished the effect of the total environment of (the former room)" (Gantt, 1944, p. 99), which latter is hardly to be expected in view of the change in location.

The therapeutic effect of normal sexual activity outside the experimental situation was investigated by caging Nick with a female in oestrus. Less anxiety was displayed and measurement of cage activity showed a decrease. Sexual activity inside the experimental situation, however, showed a reciprocal relation with the anxiety reactions. In the presence of an oestrous female or during artificial sexual stimulation by means of electric stimulation of the external genitalia, the conditioned signal produced no reactions and its effect was diminished for some time afterwards if ejaculation had occurred. On the other hand, the experimental environment affected the sexual reflex itself. In an attempt to quantify this effect on the latency and duration of Nicks' sexual response to the artificial stimulation, control measures were taken outside the experimental situation and also upon two normal dogs in both situations. The data, though inadequate for satisfactory analysis, suggest that the experimental room decreased Nick's latent period for ejaculation and duration of erection, whereas there were no marked changes in the control dogs. The effect of alcohol on Nick's disturbed behaviour was also observed (Gantt, 1940, 1952) and appeared to abolish the anxiety responses to the tone temporarily. Nick showed a greatly diminished sensitivity to the effects of adrenalin (Gantt and Freile, 1944).

In further contributions (1953; Gantt and Dykman, 1957) Gantt briefly describes another dog, V_3—"the most persistently neurotic of any dog we have had" (Gantt, 1953, p. 154). This male French poodle, born in the laboratory, had always been shy and fearful (Gantt, 1953a) and showed a stereotyped pattern of activity in rushing in and out of the experimental room, but a passivity on the experimental stand when limbs were retained in unusual positions in which they were placed, and the dog was apparently insensitive to pain. Since this occurred without any conditioning procedure beyond the use of restraint, it suggests a spontaneous, as opposed to an experimental, neurosis (see Fuller, 1947). The only experimental work reported was a study of the effects of alcohol on V_3's sexual reflexes, which, atypically, could only be elicited under the influence of this drug. His frightened behaviour was also thereby alleviated.

Gantt, though he does attempt to quantify certain behaviour, shares with the Cornell group a tendency to present inadequate data which have not been subjected to proper analysis, making unequivocal conclusions impossible. Thus most of the work reviewed here is oberservational or even anecdotal in character. He has a distressing technique which may be termed "evidence by appeal to the bystander". One example will suffice: he deems it worthy of report that ". . . two boys aged 7 said apropos of his [Nick's] raucous breathing, 'Gee that dog certainly does breathe funny'." (Gantt, 1944, p. 102). Moreover, the design of the experiments undertaken is not beyond criticism, as been indicated. Gantt's use of the longitudinal approach with Fritz, Peter and Nick is a praiseworthy contribution but would have been more informative if all subjects had been from the same litter, or at least from the same breed. Again, one has the impression of an experiment turning into a study of neurosis by accident, since Nick was originally selected for his apparent normality. Having shown disturbance, he was used, one has the further impression, mainly for demonstration purposes, and the therapeutic aspects perhaps not explored as thoroughly as otherwise might have been the case. On the other hand, Gantt in his Foreword (1944) doubts if the understanding of conditioning in physiological terms, despite the important contributions which he has made and continues to make (1957), is sufficiently advanced to evaluate abnormal behaviour in such terms. Hence his recourse to description in "behavioral terms". But there are, and indeed were in 1944, grounds for believing that behavioural measures, especially in the laboratory, may be objectified and quantified.

Hebb's criteria are easily applied to Gantt's work. Thus, Nick's behaviour was frequently *evaluationally undesirable*, e.g. his refusal of food when hungry, and was markedly *emotional*, judging by overt signs. We know from the autopsy report Gantt gives (1944) that he had *no gross neural lesion*. The persistence of disorders is strikingly well established in Nick's case, as is their *generalization* to situations other than the experimental. Their generalization to systems other than those especially concerned in the original conditioning appears as confirmation of their abnormal character, but there are dubious features about this as will be shown later. Considering two of Hebb's ancillary criteria, the *change from a previous base-line* is well seen in Nick, though less well in V_3, just as is the presence of *trauma or conflict* in their history. It is in connection with the criterion of *statistical abnormality* that reservation must be made. Gantt does not say from what total these two cases came; it is clear it must have been a substantial number, thus yielding a figure probably less than the 33 per cent implied by his presentation of the three cases of Fritz, Peter and Nick, only one of whom became neurotic. On the other hand the selection of these three for their apparent normality originally may have depressed this figure, and we are thus left in doubt. Nevertheless, we may say that Gantt's work, while not entirely satisfactory on all counts, comes closest of those so far reviewed in this chapter to meeting Hebb's criteria of abnormality which can probably be related to human neurosis.

Gantt's theoretical views (1953) employ two fundamental concepts: "schizokinesis" and "autokinesis". The former, originally called "dysfunction", implies a cleavage in response between the emotional and visceral systems and the skeletal musculature, and has its origins in obersvations, especially of cardiac function, suggesting that cardiac conditioned responses are formed more quickly than motor ones, are of comparatively greater intensity, and are more resistant to extinction (Gantt, 1924a, 1946, 1948; Gantt and Hoffman, 1940; Gantt and Muncie, 1941; Gantt and Traugott, 1949; Gantt and Dykman, 1952, 1957; Gantt, Hoffman and Dworkin, 1947; Gantt, Gakenheimer and Stunkard, 1951; Robinson and Gantt, 1946, 1947; Owens and Gantt, 1950). Consequently large emotional and endocrine responses may persist after the need for the appropriate accompanying motor response has passed. "Autokinesis" refers to the internal development of responses on the basis of old excitations, as seen in the spontaneous restoration of extinguished conditioned responses and the appearance of signs of experimental neurosis long after the causal conflict has been removed.

Gantt's theoretical formulation has some of the same characteristics as Liddell's. It is too imprecise to provide testable deductions, and some of the facts it endeavours to subsume are insecure. This especially applies to schizokinesis as is seen in a well-designed study with proper statistical procedures by Dykman, Gantt and Whitehorn (1956), previously reported in brief (Dykman and Gantt, 1951, 1951a). Four dogs were each given motor conditioning (leg flexion) to three intensities of shock as the unconditioned stimulus. In addition to measures of latency and amplitude of the motor response, cardiac and respiratory records were taken, though only the analysis of the former is reported. The results clearly show the development of a differential motor response—larger and swifter, usually at a satisfactory level of significance, the greater the shock stimulus, and a differential cardiac conditioned response was also detected. However, the cardiac conditioned responses did not develop more quickly than the motor ones, and the differentiation observed did not proceed faster in the cardiac than in the skeletal system. Unfortunately, no systematic study of the extinction of the conditioning was reported. The authors do say, however, that after a month two subjects showed unimpaired differentiation, presumably of both motor and cardiac responses. These findings from a well-designed and adequately analysed experiment run counter, therefore, to expectations based on the schizokinetic principle, itself elaborated from data from experiments, which (as judged by the brief reports cited above) were less well controlled. This suggests that the concept of schizokinesis itself may need revision.

The Work of Masserman

The contribution of the third major American worker in the field of abnormal animal behaviour, Masserman, is based on a psychoanalytic interpretation of behaviour, and so differs markedly from that of Gantt and Liddell, both of whom began as Pavlovians. An example of the lengths to which Masserman is prepared to go is his interpretation of Yerofeeva's experiment, in which shock was used as a conditioned stimulus (see p. 157), as a demonstration of animal "masochism" (Masserman, 1943, pp. 176–7; Masserman and Jacques, 1948). This approach is one to which the writer is unsympathetic: the reader is, therefore, cautioned against this bias. Moreover, Masserman is avowedly anthropomorphic (1942, pp. 345–346) in a way which is rightly eschewed nowadays.

Masserman's research is presented in numerous articles, but especially in his book *Behavior and Neurosis* (1943), which also reports on his work in experimental neurophysiology which will not be discussed here. For his experiments on neuroses in cats, less fully reported earlier (1942), he used a learned motor response to a warning stimulus. This response, the lifting of the lid of a food trough to secure food, had been employed by Sutherland and others in work on the pig (*see* page 172), but more extensively by Dworkin and his associates, including Sutherland, at McGill University in Montreal, in a series of experiments on the auditory capacities of the dog and the cat (Dworkin, 1935, 1935a; Dworkin, Seymour and Sutherland, 1934; Dworkin, Katzman, Hutchinson and McCabe, 1940; Davis, Dworkin, Lurie and Katzman, 1937; Dworkin, Baxt and Gross, 1942). As several cases of experimental neurosis eventuated from the use of this method, some account of Dworkin's work—itself almost a major contribution to the field—will serve as an introduction to that of Masserman.

The cats were restrained in a cage (large enough to allow free movement) in which there was a food box into which a piece of food was automatically delivered by a rotary feeder, after an auditory signal has sounded. The arrangements for dogs were similar except that they were confined in a Pavlov harness before the food box. The lifting of the lid of the food box was regarded as the response in the trained animal, and in studies of auditory thresholds indicated that the subject had heard the tone. In discrimination studies, opening the lid indicated that the subject had recognized the positive signal—the negative one not being followed by food. Both these procedures gave rise to disturbances in both species (Dworkin, 1938, 1939). Tests of pitch discrimination involved increasingly difficult judgements as the positive and negative tones were made more alike, and in two dogs caused a progressive inhibition of the alimentary response, failure to eat the food offered, even when very hungry, and restlessness, barking and whining in the experimental situation. One dog developed a marked flexion of the left foreleg, obviously thinking it was at Cornell, not McGill! Periods of rest did not restore responses, but no unusual behaviour was observed outside the experimental situation. In cats disinhibition was observed; they responded to the negative signals as well as the positive. However, they never refused food nor showed any other sign of disturbance.

The tests of auditory acuity involved presenting the subjects with very weak tones; four out of seven dogs showed progressive inhibition of response, first to the weak tones, but later to all stimuli, so that after 4–6 months two of them remained stock still in their harness, not asleep, but insensitive to all but unusual stimuli. Rest had little effect, but drugs (including alcohol, sodium amytal, avertin and nembutal) had beneficial effects in certain cases (Dworkin, Bourne and Raginsky, 1937, 1937a; Dworkin, Raginsky and Bourne, 1937). In the reactions of thirty-four cats to the same procedures, Dworkin distinguished three groups. Firstly, nine animals went through the whole experiment with no disturbances. Secondly, a group of four cats who developed inhibition to superthreshold tones after being exposed to faint ones, and showed stereotyped movements and attempts to escape. The third group, the remaining 21 cats, displayed a lack of restraint so that they opened the lid not only to all stimuli but constantly in between stimuli as well ("interval activity"). Rest restored the trained responses, at least temporarily. Three cases of more profound disturbances in cats are reported separately by Dworkin, Baxt and Dworkin (1942). In one cat, which had been subject to cochlear damage, the onset of the interval activity was preceded over a period of 2 years by restlessness and vomiting in the experimental box on at least five occasions. The absence of gastrointestinal disorder was confirmed by necropsy, and the cat ate well elsewhere. Two further cats urinated in the box, one of them alternating with periods of interval activity, and also displaying changed behaviour outside the experimental situation. He became aggressive, and resisted coming for testing. Rest helped little, but a different experimental room and the restoration of superthreshold stimuli were beneficial. In each case bromide therapy afforded little relief. Only these last cases evidence any generalization, and so approach Hebb's criteria for abnormal behaviour. Dworkin, however, believes the disturbances of behaviour to have been more serious in dog than cat, and suggests that this supports Liddell's emphasis on the importance of restraint in the production of neurosis, since the dogs were confined in a harness whereas the cats were not. The confounding of the species difference with this variable clearly vitiates any such conclusion.

A study using the same alimentary motor reaction specifically for the production of neurosis in cats is reported by Dimmick, Ludlow and Whiteman (1939). After six cats had been trained to lift the lid of the food box on signal, they were shocked whenever they lifted it *between* the signals. They stopped feeding altogether, whereupon the presentation of the signal itself was associated with a "punishing shock". It is not clear how often this was done nor whether all subjects were treated alike or not, but the descriptive results presented show that the anxiety responses thus established generalized to the experimenters and to the cats' living quarters, and persisted despite increased motivation and a rest of 10 days.

Masserman's technique (1939) is very similar, except that he also used as an aversive stimulus a blast of air to the side of the animal's head, sometimes in combination with shock, sometimes alone. It was physically harmless but made a "rather loud, sudden noise" (Wikler and Masserman, 1943), elsewhere described as "explosive" (Masserman and Jacques, 1948). Masserman's work suffers from the defects of insufficient control and inadequate quantitative analysis which it has been so frequently necessary to mention in this review, but has an ingenuity about it which compels attention. Nevertheless his description of it in his monograph (1943) is usually unsatisfactory. There is no standard experimental procedure; the intensity of the stimuli used is not specified, and the results are described in the form of a "typical" subject's reaction. Even these are sometimes internally self–inconsistent, larded with alliterative anthropomorphisms (the cat ". . . came up to the food box and muzzled it meditatively . . ." (1943, p. 69), and contain statements for which no evidence is offered (". . . many of these animals showed chronic disturbances of pulse and respiration . . ." (1943, p. 67)). Background data—age, past experience, even sex—are lacking, and there is confusion over the number of subjects and experiments, eighty-two being mentioned in one place as to the total number of cats used, though other figures relating to the number given shock, blast, or both suggest a total of 106. The blast was favoured as a traumatic stimulus on the grounds that it was "psychologically more significant". Certain control observations were made which suggest that hungry cats trained to lid lifting on signal did not become neurotic if their path to the box was blocked, or the lid locked, or, what Masserman picturesquely calls "fractional frustration" (partial reinforcement) instituted. As might be expected, the feeding response was extinguished in the first two cases and very persistent in the third (Jenkins and Stanley, 1950). More crucial are the observations that the conditioned light and bell signals, alone or in combination with the air blast, were not disturbing, and it is claimed that the blast, after such a combination, could be used even when a cat was feeding, without ill effect, but the procedure used is unclear from the description. Even more important, in view of the criticisms of this works to be discussed, is that no such control observations involving the use of the shock are reported.

The behavioural responses to the imposition of an air blast across the food box, or the electrification of the floor or both, just as the animal opened the lid, showed individual differences. Usually there was a marked fear response, failure to feed from the box any more, and evidence of conditioned fear reactions to the signals for the delivery of food. These manifestations could be increased by pushing the cat towards the food box and persisted for months, but were, Masserman claims, at their height after 3 days, a time he identifies (though without supporting evidence) as coinciding with maximal hunger in the cat. The use of air blast with two dogs in a larger box gave essentially congruent results.

Evidence for the generalization of these reponses is adduced from the changed "personalities" of some cats and from the fact that both dogs developed resistance to entering the apparatus. In addition, Masserman and Siever (1944) showed that the dominance order in groups of four cats— established by allowing them to compete at the food box—was disrupted by the fear conditioning. The least dominant cat could be transmogrified by successively affecting animals higher in the hierarchy. The emergence of aggression towards the competing cat is said to depend on previous experience of dominance, but this does not seem to follow from the carefully documented report on, however, only one of the groups of four.

Masserman is especially concerned with possible therapies of experimental neuroses and their relative efficacy. This enterprise is doomed to failure in any objective sense, of course, by the absence of quantification of the intensity of the disturbances induced, and of an untreated control group to assess spontaneous recovery. The techniques he applied were rest from experimentation, which had little effect, and others designed to abolish the "motivational conflicts" (between hunger and fear) which Masserman believed he had set up in his cats, thus reducing "their aberrant behavioural expression". Specifically, they included: reducing the hunger drive by feeding before an experimental trial, increasing it to starvation point, reassuring and petting the cat, and forcing it towards the food box. Interestingly, it seems from Masserman's description that the movement of the barrier by which this was done developed into a conditioned signal for feeding in several animals. The technique of imitation—allowing a well-trained non-traumatized cat in the cage with the neurotic one—was ineffective as therapy, but what Masserman calls "working through", more so. This involved prior training so that the cat itself initiated the feeding signals by pressing a switch. After the fear had been induced, such cats began feeding again sooner than ones not so trained.

Masserman completes his monograph on experimental neurosis with a comprehensive, if polemical, review of the pertinent literature. It is bewildering to find familiar studies cited in support of psychoanalytic notions completely at variance with their authors intensions. Fears tend to become "phobias", repetition is always "compulsive" and the reappearance of an earlier habit, "regression". He is critical of conditioned reflex concepts, preferring a theoretical position akin to McDougall's "hormic psychology". Thus, Anderson and Parmenter's (1941) observations: ". . . all but beg for more dynamic and meaningful interpretations" (1943, p. 120). His own position is expressed in four "principles of behavior", basic to his "bio-dynamic system". They are very general statements, some of which are widely acceptable, and comparably devoid of heuristic value. Behaviour is motivated (first principle), adaptive (second principle), symbolic (third principle) and fourthly, subject to vicissitudes: ". . . when the meanings of the perceptive field become confused or the motivations conflictful". Then behaviour becomes "hesitant, vacillating, inefficient, inappropriate, or excessively symbolic or substitutive", that is, neurotic. To the extent that the above adjectives fit the observed behaviour of his animals, Masserman regards that behaviour as neurotic, and the principle itself, by some naive logic, validated. Beach's (1953, p. 376) comment applies:

> We do not intend to deny the possibility of a close relationship between the psychological mechanisms involved in human neurosis and the behavioral deviations which have been described in some animals. But it is very important to hold in mind the fact that this problem is unsolved and until the solution is available egregious extrapolations are unwarranted and dangerous.

The extent to which the behaviour Masserman reports can be described as abnormal can be judged as before by reference to Hebb's criteria. It was not *statistically abnormal*, and neither its *persistence* nor its *generalization*, in terms of situations or systems has been satisfactorily demonstrated. It is not even clear that it was *evaluationally abnormal* from the cats' point of view. The absence of *gross neural lesions* may be presumed, and the ancillary criteria of *change from a previous base-line*, and the presence of *trauma or conflict* certainly met. Indeed, the last two provide the rationale for the whole experimentation. But of all the major studies noted so far, it must be said that Masserman's least approaches the criteria adopted. The true nature of the behaviour described will be suggested, after some subsidiary work has been reviewed, and some repititions described.

In a series of studies Masserman has investigated the therapeutic effects of various drugs, of electroconvulsive shock and of brain lesions on the disturbed behaviour. Some of the techniques used are an advance on his earlier purely observational methods. Thus, in a study of the effects of alcohol (Massermann, Yum, Nicholson and Lee, 1944; Masserman, Jacques, and Nicholson, 1945; Masserman and Yum, 1946) six-point rating scales covering seventeen aspects of behaviour (e.g. reactions to experimenter, to other animals, to a caged mouse; autonomic changes; activity, etc), were developed and applied to 21 cats to arrive at an "index of neurosis", said to reflect changed behaviour after air blast or shock. The use of statistical techniques such as correlation, regression, and significance tests on these data cannot be unreservedly welcomed in the absence of indications of the reliability and validity of the scales. The results suggest that if given before the introduction of the aversive stimulus, alcohol prevents the development of disturbed behaviour, though the cats developed a dislike for its taste, presumably because of a conditioned association with the fear stimuli which always followed its ingestion (cf. the rationale of conditioning pharmaco-therapies of alcoholism [Franks, 1958]). This contrasts with experiments where the drug was given *after* the fear responses had developed and afforded relief from feeding inhibitions, etc., in proportion to the dosage given. In this case the development of a preference for milk and alcohol as opposed to the plain milk previously preferred could be demonstrated. No "addition" developed†. The preference was thus ". . . a learned adaptation, contingent upon intercurrent neurotic stress, and reversible when these stresses were resolved" (Masserman and Yum, 1946, p. 51). Macleod (1953) has criticized Masserman's interpretation, and Conger's careful work (1951) on the effect of alcohol on rats in an approach-avoidance conflict situation (Miller, 1944, 1951), which showed that the specific effect of alcohol is to reduce the avoidance response to shock, leads him to question Masserman's formulation also. However, Miller (1956) has been able to repeat neither Masserman and Yum's nor Conger's findings.

An earlier study on the effects of morphine and one not using the Masserman-Yum scales (Wikler and Masserman, 1943) gave results comparable to those found with alcohol. Four cats showed relief from anxiety and one of them did not display it again. A fifth, however, was not relieved by large, and finally fatal, doses. In studies of electroconvulsive shock using sine wave (Masserman and Jacques, 1947) and square wave (Masserman, Arieff, Pechtel and Klehr, 1950) currents, it was shown that electroconvulsive shock abolished the neurotic response as rated, but also disorganized the normal feeding responses thus restored. Further work on the effect of brain lesions used 23 cats (Masserman and Pechtel, 1956), but a fuller report by Pechtel, Masserman, Schreiner and Levitt (1955), on the effects of lesions on nine animals operated on before being subjected to shock compared with eight operate controls not traumatized, shows that the former group had greatly diminished in their fear reactions to stimuli, including odours (Masserman, Pechtel and Schreiner, 1953), which had served as signals for shock. In most cases, however, residual muscular tension was still detectable, and the cats were rated as having become significantly more aggressive to others. For this work, the experimental box had been modified to include two upper compartments containing the switches for initiating the feeding signals, thus permitting a series of problems which, from the curves given, can be graded in difficulty. All animals had forgotten these routines post-operatively, and had to relearn them.

Thus, Masserman has energetically applied the technique he had adopted to study a series of agents which might be expected to modify the disturb-

† See Stainton (1943) for a review of the literature (mostly anecdotal reports) on addiction in animals.

ances in behaviour produced. Despite the slightly greater sophistication of the experimental methods used, the results have not been especially precise, though in most cases it has been shown that the disturbances have been attenuated (Masserman, 1951, 1953). The value these investigations have to topics other than neurosis, i.e. electroconvulsive shock, and psychosurgery, has not been stressed here.

Masserman's interpretation of his basic work has been challenged by Watson and by Wolpe. Watson (1954) trained 17 cats to press a switch to activate feeding signals. Air blast or shock was applied at the moment of feeding, and the learned response was disorganized. However, one of two stable behaviour patterns soon emerged; either the cat resumed feeding or withdrew from the food altogether. No changes in behaviour in the home cages were observed. The effects of exposing ten control subjects to the aversive stimuli gave "a different acute reaction", which soon wore off, so that the stimuli were tolerated later. While noting that his work does not repeat Masserman's exactly—in particular, the cats lived in spacious group cages—Watson suggests that the behaviour observed could not be considered abnormal as it was neither chronic, nor maladaptive (Hebb's criterion of evaluationally abnormal). The two distinct patterns of behaviour which evolved are both considered adaptive—the resumption of feeding to avoid starvation, and the refusal to do so to avoid injury, which for all the cat knew may have resulted in death. Unfortunately, the value of this contribution is lessened by the serious deficiencies in the presentation of even the observational data it offers, brief descriptive statements alone being given.

Wolpe starts from a more seriously critical standpoint than is implied by Watson's simple repetition. He notes (1952) that both Masserman and Dimmick, Ludlow, and Whiteman, in using the learned alimentary response, fail to control for the effects of the noxious stimuli apart from its effects on that response, and so couch their explanations of the changed behaviour in terms of irrelevant motivational conflicts. His own experimentation is designed to remedy this deficiency.

He used twelve cats in an apparatus like Masserman's; six were trained to feed on hearing a signal and then given a shock (air blast was not used) when attempting to do so. The control group of six was not trained to feed, but given only shocks, preceded by the signal, in the same box as the others. The number of shocks given was not, however, equal—the control group receiving more.

The results are presented descriptively. All animals showed resistance to being placed in the cage, and signs of anxiety especially muscular tension and mydriasis, when inside; all refused to eat there even after 1–3 days starvation. On occasion howling and rapid respiration were observed, and all these signs of fear were intensified by the auditory signal. One cat developed a tic reminiscent of abortive jumping which may have had its origin in

13*

his leap out of the top of the cage, left open inadvertently, when first he was shocked. An ingenious attempt was made to observe the generalization of the responses to the shock by the use of different rooms—a method used by Liddell (1944, 1956) and by Gantt (1944). Wolpe used three rooms which ". . . seemed, to the human eye and ear, to have decreasing degrees of resemblance to" the experimental room. The signs of anxiety to the conditioning signal were weaker in these rooms to the extent to which they differed from the experimental room.

In attempting therapy for five of his subjects' anxiety responses, Wolpe also used this series of rooms. A room was found in which the hungry cat's anxiety was sufficiently attenuated to allow it to feed at all. After feeding in this room, a move was made to the one next higher in the scale of resemblance to the experimental room, and so on, until the cat was feeding in the latter room itself, and finally, in the box. Other therapies achieving the same result involved feeding the cats from the hand (four subjects), or forcing them to the food box (three subjects). Elimination of anxiety to the auditory signal was then effected in two cats by reducing the intensity of the signal to the point where it was ignored, and then gradually increasing its strength. With another seven subjects, a brief sounding of the signal was used to herald the presentation of a meat pellet. It was thus converted into a condtitioned alimentary signal—for the second time in the case of the group originally trained in this way. After these procedures the auditory signal had no effect whatsoever.

Despite the lack of adequate quantification of the phenomena observed, Wolpe's experiment is superior to Masserman's because of the careful control of the variable relating to the effect of the aversive stimulus, independently of its effect on learned responses and he has replied sharply (1954) to Masserman's failure (1954; Masserman, Gross and Pechtel, 1954) to recognize this fact. He bases himself on a rational theory of learning and seeks to utilize it to devise therapies for animal and human anxiety (Wolpe, 1958) and to account for some aspects of experimental neurosis, as will be shown later. But his interpretation of the changes in behaviour produced in his cats as experimental neurosis is less satisfactory. His definition of experimental neurosis as ". . . unadaptive responses that are characterized by anxiety, that are persistent, and that have been produced by behavioural means . . ." (Wolpe, 1952, p. 243) is reminiscent of, though less comprehensive, than Hebb's. His criterion of unadaptiveness he considers to be met because the cats refused to feed even when no further shocks were to be given. But how were the subjects to know this? As Watson notes in connexion with the same problem: "It does not seem possible to regard the cats' behaviour as maladaptive without presupposing capacities to evaluate danger which cats may not possess" (1954, p. 345).

Scheflen (1957) has also studied the extinction of a fear response in cats, using air-blast as the noxious stimulus to break up a previously learned alimentary response. She used two different boxes, and showed that extinction of the fear response in one occurred sooner if the original training and aversive stimulus had occurred in the other. No suggestion that the fear responses observed are abnormal is made by this author nor by Lichtenstein (1950). He produced an inhibition of feeding in hungry dogs, who had been trained to eat in a Pavlov harness. He found that a group of ten dogs, shocked when actually eating the food, ceased feeding sooner than three dogs, shocked on the majority of occasions when only presented with it. Lichtenstein also observed catalepsy, tremors and tics (cf. Wolpe's cat)†, and autonomic signs of fear. Some dogs always struggled and fought in the apparatus, and two dogs refused the food used in the experiment when it was offered in their home cages, one of them persistently. Excited or aggressive behaviour in their living quarters was also observed. The feeding inhibitions were relieved in most cases by prefrontal leucotomy, while a control group subjected to sham operation maintained theirs for one to three weeks (1950a).

Lichtenstein identifies the complex of behaviour observed in his experiments, of which the actual feeding inhibition is only a part, as one of fear or anxiety, and develops a closely reasoned argument against calling it experimental neurosis (1950). Despite differences in the details of the results obtained by these workers studying feeding inhibitions‡, it seems clear that what the investigators using alimentary responses in dogs and cats in the experiments discussed above have been observing is the conditioned emotional response or C.E.R. (Watson and Rayner, 1920; Brady and Hunt, 1955). Masserman would almost certainly disagree with this appraisal, as he has specifically denied that the responses he has elicited are conditioned fear responses (1950; Masserman and Siever, 1944), basing himself partly on the argument that "... the reactions of anxiety and patterned defense began to spread to other situations, only remotely or 'symbolically' associated with the neurotigenic one—a process of 'irrational generalisation' that every clinician will recognize as characteristic of human neuroses" (1950, p. 56). Masserman's lack of confidence in the often demonstrated normal generalization of conditioned fear receives melodramatic expression in his claim that, in the absence of dynamic, motivational conflict, "... human neuroses would quite literally be confined to people who had either been caught in an

---

† Meige and Feindel (1907) cite other examples of tics in animals.

‡ In all likelihood, many of these differences are attributable to differences in techniques used. Thus, in the experiments using shock as the aversive stimulus, its strength, nowhere precisely specified, was probably weakest in Watsons's case, since many of his cats resumed feeding, the next strongest in Masserman's since he does note that five cats were at first unaffected by it, and the strongest in Wolpe's and Lichtenstein's, since all animals were affected by it and the disorders were persistent. Two further repetitions of Masserman's work using cats have been reported in abstract, Yacorzynski (1946, 1948) reaching conclusions at variance with Masserman's, while Cain and Extremet (1957) do not.,

electrical short-circuit or struck by lightning at the moment they were pushing an accustomed button to secure food from an automat" (1954, p. 222).

It is not possible, of course, to accept Masserman's assertions regarding the nature of the behaviour he has studied, couched as they are in subjective terms, without the backing of quantification, control and appropriate analysis. Furthermore, the appellation of experimental neurosis is especially inapposite here, since, as we have seen, there is no satisfactory evidence that the responses are abnormal, even at the level of the species in question. The application of this conceptual framework to the field of psychopharmacology (Jacobsen and Skaarup, 1955) is therefore unfortunate, especially now that the parameters of conditioned fear are more fully understood and and better methods of quantification available.

Masserman's further work has been on primates. It will not be reviewed in detail, not only because a promised monograph has not yet appeared, but also because the methods used and the results reported parallel those for cats. The apparatus used is a larger and more complicated version of that previously described, and the aversive stimuli used with monkeys included electric shock, a water jet, ". . . or, more significantly, the sudden appearance of a toy rubber snake in the food box" (Masserman and Pechtel, 1956). The reactions claimed as a direct and exclusive reaction to the sight of this snake as compared with other moving toy or mechanical objects (Masserman and Pechtel, 1953, 1953a) are almost incredible. They include, as well as the feeding inhibitions met with in the cat, muscular and gastro-intestinal dysfunctions, sexual deviations, and behaviour boldly identified as "hallucinatory" in two monkeys who appeared to eat "imaginary" pieces of food. The evidence presented is neither sufficiently detailed nor well-controlled to be convincing, and the unsubstantiated claims of a psychoanalyst to have discovered in so obvious a phallic "symbol" the one object to cause persistent experimental neurosis is necessarily subject to a pardonable scepticism. This is reinforced by lack of experimental evidence for the generality of this finding. Thus, Jones and Jones (1928) showed there is no innate fear of snakes in human infant, and Rand (1941, 1942) found that fear of a dummy snake is soon extinguished in certain species of birds. Moreover, in monkeys the conditioned avoidance response based on shock is subject to the usual—if slow—experimental extinction (Waterhouse, 1957).

Masserman has made some use of that neglected sensory modality, smell, and has demonstrated (Masserman, Pechtel and Schreiner, 1953; Pechtel and Masserman, 1954; Masserman and Pechtel, 1956b) that odours are not so readily learned as conditioned signals for food as lights or sounds, but when associated with fear stimuli they become potent, and generalize widely to other smells. The effect of brain lesions and drugs on the monkeys' behaviour has also been reported. Again using rating scales, now said to have high reliability. Masserman and Pechtel (1956) have shown that lesions in the amygdaloid nucleus appear to have a large effect on the disturbed behaviour. The large number of variables liable to affect these findings is rightly stressed. No marked effects of drugs were found (Masserman and Pechtel, 1956a), and, indeed, this paper is more notable for the careful attempts to analyse some parameters of the behaviour observed. Thus age is shown to be important, younger monkeys being more susceptible to disturbance than older ones. The largest correlation, however, is that between "number of traumata to produce neurosis" and "spacing of traumata", which is negative and about 0·8. Confirmation of one of the fundamentals of learning theory—the greater efficiency of spaced, as compared with massed, practice—is unexpected from such a quarter.

While the extension of Masserman's work to another species is to be welcomed, many of the criticisms made of his earlier work on cats are unfortunately still applicable. Penrose's comment that "the implications of Masserman's work do not seem to be clear at present" (1953, p. 77), still holds.

While Masserman is alone in having deliberately attempted to produce experimental neurosis in primates, several reports of the accidental or spontaneous occurrence of neurosis are found. The most celebrated of these is that of Jacobsen and his co-workers, the early reports of which (Jacobsen, 1935; Fulton and Jacobsen, 1935) inspired Moniz to initiate the technique of prefrontal leucotomy (Crawford, Fulton, Jacobsen and Wolfe, 1947). One of two chimpanzees frequently had a temper tantrum when it made a mistake on a test of delayed reaction, in which the animals were trained to choose between one of two cups under which they had seen food hidden, but which had been out of their sight in the interim. As the task was made more difficult, this behaviour became more frequent, no responses were made and the subject had to be forced into the experimental cage. "It was as complete an 'experimental neurosis' as those obtained by Pavlov's conditioned reflex procedures" (Jacobsen, Wolfe, and Jackson, 1935, p. 9). Be that as it may, the disturbance was cured by feeding, petting and simplifying the problem. After one frontal area of the cortex had been removed, the same events occurred on retraining and were treated in the same way. But after the second frontal area was removed a marked change was noted. The animal no longer became upset over errors, and willingly came to the experiment despite them: "It was as if the animal had joined the 'happiness cult of Elder Micheaux', and had placed its burdens on the Lord!" (1935, p. 10). Hence the interest of psychiatrists.

Wendt (1934) also reports "blow-ups' (Pavlov's 'experimental neurosis')" in one baboon during training to delay an alimentary reaction, but since they did not occur when she had been fully trained, they were probably examples of the upsets likely to disturb the smooth progress of conditioning. According to Dworkin (1939) it is difficult to distinguish such disturbances from "border-line neurosis" except by their duration. Yerkes (1943) relies heavily on this distinction: he identifies the disturbance in behaviour of a chimpanzee which bit him when she failed in a difficult problem-solving task and never applied herself to it again as a neurosis, because it was "relatively permanent". Galt (1939) found a similar change in behaviour lasting 2 months in a *cebus* monkey after it had been presented with an especially difficult discrimination problem, and Firsov (1952, in Liberson, 1957) reports that during operant conditioning (squeezing a bulb) to visual and auditory signals in monkeys, one broke down and became neurotic for a month when discrimination of signals was required.

Apparently spontaneous cases of neurosis in primates are also reported. Leavitt and Riggs (1942) recount the case of a young monkey who exhibited a "change of personality" after living for $2\frac{1}{2}$ years with a policeman, but better authenticated are Hebb's cases of two adult chimpanzees who both showed disturbed behaviour not traceable to any discoverable trauma (1947). The first had been reared in the laboratory since birth, the second since 9 months of age, so that their histories are well documented. The first showed a recurrent food phobia, occasionally associated with fear of an attendant; the second, recurrent fits of depression. In neither case was it possible to find any specific experiential cause. For example, Hebb examines and rejects the possibility that a hurtful object may have occasioned the food phobia. He considers that the disorders mentioned meet all the criteria he has laid down for animal neurosis, "as far as this can ever be possible in the absence of the verbal examination of the patient" (1947, p. 11). An apparently spontaneous case of gross self-mutilation which appears to have been associated with depression and the relationship with an attendant, is reported by Tinkelpaugh (1928), but the possibilty of chronic disseminated, encephalitis must be suspected in such cases (Hutyra, Marek and Manninger, 1946). Apparently abnormal motor behaviour in caged wild animals, such as stereotyped pacing movements may be attributed (Hediger, 1950) to the interaction of the shape and size of the cage and the animal's "flight distance". Little appears to be known about abnormal behaviour in wild animals in their natural state. The apparently purposeless mass migrations occasionally reported are probably the result of ecological factors.

Later Studies, especially on the Rat

Turning to the last major section of work to be included in this review, we encounter a somewhat more rigorous methodological climate. This is perhaps because the investigators were usually trained psychologists, and frequently worked with the rat as subject. The early work of Liddell and Gantt aroused interest in the topic of experimental neuroses in the late 1930s, as may be seen by the numerous reviews of the field which appeared (Murray, 1937; Miles, 1938; Cook, 1939, 1939a; Witkin, 1939; Karn, 1940, 1940a). Interested workers tried to study the phenomena described by using the standard laboratory animal—the rat. Advantage lay in the greater accessibility and convenience of this subject over the more esoteric species previously used, and the·possibility of using larger numbers was also clearly attractive, thus avoiding the defects of lack of control and of statistical criteria, which it has been unfortunately necessary to stress time and again in this chapter. There seem to be two reasons, however, why research along these lines did not develop. Firstly, the problem proved intractable, as, looking back on it, one might have expected in view of the nature of the evidence produced. Secondly, the investigation of audiogenic seizures claimed the attention of many workers. Effort was needed to establish that the convulsive phenomena observed were not rodent parallels of the classical experimental neurosis, and they were thereafter studied for their own interest. The more basic research on the rat has never been resumed on the same scale. After reading this chapter, it may be conceded that this, perhaps, is not a bad thing.

This is not to say that early references to experimental neurosis in rats are not be found. Some writers identify any slight deviation from what they consider to be normal performance as "neurotic" (Fields, 1931; Hall, 1933; Carmichael, 1938)†, though others are more restrained (Miller and Stevenson, 1936; Sampson and Schneirla, 1941). However: "During the period from 1937 to 1940 there was a rather widespread effort to establish experimental neuroses in the rat with conflict as the precipitating factor. Very few of the published studies reported success, however, and it is reasonable to assume that many failures never reached print" (Finger, 1944, p. 413). Among those reported, Cook's are notable for his thoughful analysis of the problems involved (1939, 1939a) and his painstaking attempts to overcome them (1939b). Defining experimental neurosis in terms involving Hebb's criteria of chronicity, evaluational abnormality and departure from a previous base-line, he reviews the literature to date and identifies four major factors common to the situations yielding experimental neurosis. They are: the use of restraint, the development of learned responses by Pavlovian conditioning, the discrimination of similar stimuli giving rise to antagonistic responses, and the inhibition of responses during excitatory stimulation. In preliminary work he used three situations in which the first two of these elements were lacking before turning to a method of conditioning in the rat, developed by Schlosberg and his associates (1934, 1934a, 1934b; 1936, 1936a; Schlosberg and Kappauf, 1935; Kappauf and Schlosberg, 1937; Hughes and Schlosberg, 1938).

The rat is immobilized by strapping it down in a miniature harness to a stand, and attaching an electrode to one foreleg, the withdrawal of which is automatically recorded. Cook's technique was to associate foreleg retrac-

† This tendency persists; examples range from cattle (Fraser, 1957), through rodents (Green, 1958; Hansen, 1956), to the amoeba (Goldacre, 1958)!

tion first to the appearance of food in a cup near the rat's head, then to limit the movement's effectiveness in producing the food reward to the period when a bright light—the positive conditioned stimulus—shone. Next came training to inhibit the foreleg response in the presence of a dim light—the negative stimulus—by punishing such responses with shock, before the intensity of this light was increased to make the discrimination more difficult. All the six rats put through this procedure showed their dislike of it by squealing, tenseness, etc., and there were transient disturbances of the learned response, but only three rats showed some other change in behaviour such as avoiding being handled by the experimenter or becoming unresponsive to stimuli—changes which Cook thinks meet his definition of experimental neurosis: "chronic, abnormal behaviour, experimentally produced." He notes that the effectiveness of the situation involving restraint supports Liddell's view on the importance of this factor in the aetiology of experimental neurosis.

An even more thoroughgoing attempt to adapt the Pavlovian conditioning procedure to the study of experimental neurosis in the rat is due to Bijou (1942, 1943, 1947, 1951). In preliminary work (1942) he found that quicker learning was achieved by using head movement rather than leg retraction, and greater discrimination by varying the position of the stimulus lights rather than the brightness of a single panel. In a further study of eight rats differential conditioning was developed, after many trials, in five of them to the point where they were discriminating lights about 1 in. apart. Activity, measured before each training session, the degree of restraint used, and the subjects' emotionality, defined by defecation scores in Hall's open-field test (1934), were apparently unrelated to the speed of learning, but the use of shock to punish wrong responses "markedly increased excitable behaviour". No abnormalities other than this latter were found. Later modifications to this apparatus and procedure (Bijou, 1951) and work using it to investigate other aspects of learning (Rohrer, 1947; Rigby, 1954) have been published without further attempts to precipitate experimental neurosis.

Using a more strictly Pavlovian procedure, but still employing movement as the response to be conditioned, Kawamura and Yoshii (1951) restrained thirty-six rats in a cloth holder (Cowles and Pennington, 1943) and applied an electric shock to the hind leg, preceded by an acoustic stimulus. In the absence of quantitative data it is not clear how the conditioning developed. Tremors and tics of the hind legs are reported in five subjects, trained over 2 months, as well as resistance to being placed in the conditioning box and hypersensitivity to stimuli in their home cages. It is not, of course, possible to agree with the authors' identification of such behaviour as experimental neurosis, nor is their definition of phases of rats' behaviour involving hyperactivity as "acute experimental neurosis" helpful. Their use of stimulant and depressant drugs, of surgical intervention including prefrontal leucotomy, and of electroencephalography is of greater interest. Only the last is reported in any detail: Yoshii and Kawamura (1951) implanted electrodes in five rats. No abnormal wave forms were observed, and, though there is some evidence that two "neurotic" rats showed faster waves, the absence of normative data does not permit firm conclusions.

Another attempt to use Pavlovian conditioning techniques in the rat arose out of the report (Jamison, 1951) of the conditioning of a heart rate decrement which reflexly follows the inhalation of ammonia gas. A preliminary report (Broadhurst, 1954) failed to confirm the existence of this conditioned response, though a small, albeit statistically significant, conditioned cardiac response based on shock, rather than on ammonia gas, as the unconditioned stimulus was found, as well as unstable squeak and respiratory conditioning, also based on the shock. No responses, however, were sufficiently definite to form the basis for differential conditioning.

It may, therefore, he said that the application of conditioning methods to the rat for the production of experimental neurosis has failed in its object. Not only have there been no reports of disturbances comparable to those reported with the use of higher animals, but the conditioning technique itself has not produced unequivocal results. It has proved just as time-consuming as with higher animals, thus frustrating the aim of employing large numbers of cheap and readily available subjects for control and statistical purposes. It is not surprising that other methods have been frequently tried.

Hunt and Schlosberg (1950) belatedly report work done in 1938–40 on the use of a "continuous conflict" situation. Of ten rats kept in stabilimeter cages to record activity, six had their water supply electrified so that every time they took a drink they received a shock from the nozzle of the water bottle, and the other four served as controls. The data presented on activity suggest that the experimental animals became more active throughout the whole day instead of sleeping principally during the day and becoming livelier at night—the rat being a nocturnal animal:

> The writers interpreted this difference to mean that continued thirst kept the animals active during the normal hours of diminished activity, but did not increase the total amount of time spent in resting or sleep. Since the relatively meager results seemed to have little to do with conflict, *per se*, no further study was made of general activity (1950, p. 150).

This view reflects the search for the overt signs of abnormal behaviour in animals, which are probably not to be found. It is especially unfortunate in this case, since this same finding of increased activity during the animal's "night" is one of the few reported in other species, as mentioned in discussing the Cornell work on sheep, where thirst could not be invoked as an explanation. Hunt and Schlosberg, however, are more impressed by some incidental observations. Rats bit the nozzle of an unelectrified water bottle, apparently trying to get it into the cage; they would suddenly cease drinking from it as if shocked, and finally showed "tantrums" in which they threw food about and breathed noisily. But the latter behaviour may be observed in naïve rats never subjected to experimentation, and water-deprived ones will display the apparently aggressive behaviour towards a water nozzle with no experience of shock whatsoever. Finally, the "hallucinatory" behaviour towards the previously electrified spout may be the result of a conditioned anxiety response to it.

Only Finger (1941) appears to have taken up the suggestive findings relating to changes in activity. In a carefully controlled study, he measured general cage activity during an extended period while the subjects were also exposed to difficult discrimination problems in a Lashley jumping stand. He found a significant decrease in activity in the 24-hr period following jumping sessions in which four or more errors had been made, as well as a significant increase during the following day—the rat's night. Non-jumping controls showed no change. To what extent these changes are attributable to the conflict caused by the difficult discriminations is not clear since an alternative possibility, that the incorrect jumpers were simply more tired than the others, and so slept more during the next rodent "day", is not excluded. Some data showing that the effect dissipates within 24 hr are not inconsistent with this explanation, though others militate against it.

King and Mavromatis (1956) used Hunt and Schlosberg's technique to study the disruptive effect on the re-learning of a conditioned avoidance response to shock of intermittently electrifying the water supply of two strains of mice. While there was a significant decrement in saving scores, as compared with appropriate control groups, the authors rightly conclude: "... it is impossible to assign this interference to emotional 'disturbance' experienced by the mice in the conflict situation or to a physiological adaptation to shock" (1956, p. 468). The further use of the continuous conflict technique in the production of gastrointestinal disorders in animals will be noted later. Cook's use of it (1939b) in his search for a method of producing abnormal behaviour in the rat yielded no positive findings; neither did his use of a Miller-Mowrer type shuttle box in which the rats had to learn a brightness discrimination to avoid shock. Gentry and Dunlap (1942), however, forced the rat to escape from a strong shock only to meet a weak one. None of these workers found disturbed behaviour, though Gentry and Dunlap claim to have shown "atypical" learning among their twelve subjects after exposure to the shock situation and Eränkö and Muittari (1957) report changes in thyroid structure as a result of extinguishing a jumping response.

An apparatus designed to enforce wakefulness in rats might be thought provocative of disordered behaviour. Licklider and Bunch (1946) kept each subject in a cell, the floor of which was a roller surrounded by water. For control groups, the roller was locked stationary, whereas for experimental groups it was free moving, thus forming a treadmill on which animals had to move every 10–15 sec in order to avoid falling off into the water. While the sleepless animals which survived became highly irritable and aggressive by the thirtieth day, no more profound disorders were reported. This was also the case in a report of enforced lack of sleep in dogs (Okazaki, 1925).

Humphrey and Marcuse's (1939, 1941) claim to have produced "neurotic behaviour" in rats by dragging the bottomless goal box of a maze across the floor after the rat had entered it cannot be entertained seriously, if only because the behaviour in question consisted principally in hesitation in entering the same goal box on subsequent trials. A very different situation has been reported to produce "psychotic" behaviour in wild rats. During toxicity tests, Richter (1950) found that wild Norway rats developed "refusal" responses after a sublethal dose of one poison, ANTU (alpha-naphthyl thiourea), presumably because they had associated its taste and smell with the respiratory distress caused. Typically, Richter used two food cups and switched the poison from one to the other. Just after this had been done, one animal developed a pseudo-catatonia, maintaining an awkward posture on its hind feet despite interruptions, including the opening ot the cage. This is most unusual for wild rats, which are always eager to escape. This "straphanging" behaviour lasted for 2 months before the rat was finally poisoned. Other rats showed similar behaviour which Richter interprets as "an ever–present fear of being poisoned". But this promising lead has petered out, as further work on over a hundred subjects has proved negative (Richter, 1953) and it is now thought that the upright posture may have resulted from the earlier experience of huddling closely, when many were confined together in one cage. Moreover, wild rats sometimes show their intense fearfulness after capture by remaining motionless, even starving to death in the process, by dying of fright when handled, as Richter himself has shown (1957), or when fighting, even when uninjured (Barnett, 1955). The domesticated rats in Richter's experiments never showed comparable behaviour, and this fact alone robs the original finding of its relevance in the present connection, since the wild rat, which needs special techniques in handling and testing (Broadhurst, 1958a), cannot be regarded as a standard laboratory animal. At this point the reader may be disposed to agree with Hebb's comment of over 10 years ago: "I have seen nothing in the literature which remotely justifies calling rat behaviour neurotic" (1947, p. 14).

While examples of abnormal behaviour in animals other than the rat, or as a result of using techniques other than those discussed are worthy of mention, none of them approach the definition of neurosis adopted here. Karn (1938, 1938a; Karn and Malamud, 1939) used the double-alternation problem in a temporal maze. This is a difficult problem, the animal being required to go through the same passages of a rectangular maze four times, making different turns on the last two trials from those made on the first two. Two cases of behaviour disturbance are reported, one in a cat and one in a dog. Another animal of each species was not affected. In each case the affected animal halted at the choice-point, and cried; the cat showed a reluctance to enter the maze. Both animals failed to reach their previous performance, which fact in particular led Karn to describe the behaviour as "neurotic". However, subsequent workers using this type of problem with a larger number of cats specifically note the absence of behaviour comparable to that reported by Karn (Willoughby and Andrews, 1940; Stewart and Warren, 1957).

Cameron (1936) encased the rear legs of eighteen guinea pigs hoping to produce experimental depression by frustration of movement. This treatment did reduce the rate of respiration, but since it caused physical damage to the legs in almost all cases, the finding is on these grounds alone uninterpretable.

Despite the widespread use of birds as experimental animals, and their tendency to "superstitious behaviour" (Skinner, 1948; Morse and Skinner, 1957), there are few reports of abnormal behaviour among them. Bajandurov (1933) developed a Pavlovian conditioning procedure in doves that were restrained in a holder with an electrode attached to one foot. The response of the leg to a shock was recorded by an attached thread, and was conditioned to the appearance of illuminated shapes before the bird. The classic method of developing a positive response to a circle, a negative one to an ellipse, and then making the ellipse progressively more circular, had the expected result. The discrimination broke down, and the previously quiet bird struggled against the restraint. A second subject became agitated with interval activity of the reaction limb, though retaining the discrimination. Brückner (1933) induced disordered behaviour in four hens by isolating them in a closed box for the first 7 weeks of life. On restoration to the flock, two of them were distinguishable by their unusual behaviour for 3 days in one case and 12 days in another. But the deprivation of visual stimulation during what probably was a "critical period" of development (see Thorpe, 1956) may be at least as important a factor as the isolation. Many studies (see Beach and Jaynes' review, 1954) indicate the importance of the effect of early experience on adult behaviour. Examples of observational accounts of abnormal behaviour in birds are Lorenz's description (1940) of depression in a grey goose after one wing was clipped, and Räber's report (1948) of the abnormal development of courting behaviour in a turkey. It would display before a mackintosh hanging on a post, which it never did before a hen bird.

These contributions have clearly not advanced a solution of the problems raised by experimental neurosis as reported by early workers. The problem has indeed proved intractable so long as it continued to be posed in terms demanding a solution by the production of overt abnormalities which would serve as convincing analogies of those seen in human neurosis to be regarded as a discrete disease entity, instead of the extreme of a continuum of learned, and probably overgeneralized, responses, some of which are in fact amenable to rational therapy based on learning theory (Wolpe, 1952, 1952a, 1958; Jones, 1956; Yates, 1958). This view makes the study of disorders of emotional responses in animals by approaches other than that of experimental neurosis directly relevant to human problems. This is particularly true if the view is taken that cross-species identification of behaviour is permissible when it can be shown that the mechanisms giving rise to the behaviour are the same in the two cases. No attempt is made here to review all the pertinent literature, but mention of some papers will indicate the range of the possible approaches.

An interesting early attempt by Higginson (1930) sought to quantify the effect of emotional stress—a naturalistic one, the fear of cats (Curti, 1935)—on a series of measures of rats' performance in a maze. Turner (1941) amplified this approach by observing the effect of a difficult size discrimination on rats' behaviour in other situations. He confirmed Finger's finding (1941) of a depression in activity and showed a similar effect on respiration, with no effect on startle responses. Scott (1947; Scott and Marston, 1953) has also used a naturalistic stress—in this case defeats in fights—to study emotional behaviour in mice. McCleary (1954) gives a good-humoured account of a quest for cardiac measures of stress in rats. After solving the not inconsiderable difficulties associated with obtaining such records from a freely moving animal, thus avoiding the objections, both practical and theoretical (see p. 173), to attaching electrodes he succeeded in getting clear records of increase in heart rate when the rat heard a tone associated with shock. But control tests showed a similar increase in simple movements which apparently involved no anxiety. He doubts the value of cardiac measures of anxiety: "Maybe one would rather conclude that the rat is simply 'anxious' about everything he does. It's a moot point. Operationally one ends up at the same place" (1954, p. 107).

The approach–avoidance model of behaviour developed by Miller (1944, 1951) offers a fruitful approach to the study of conflict between tendencies. An example is Winnick's success (1956) in giving quantitative expression to the fluctuation in anxiety, postulated as occurring in such conflict situations (Schoenfeld, 1950). She recorded the intensity with which hungry rats pushed against a panel, the release of which in order to feed would switch on a bright light—an aversive stimulus. The measurement in a readily quantified form of the conditioned emotional response or C.E.R., referred to earlier as the probable basis for feeding inhibitions, has given rise to a number of studies in which the effect on it of other variables has been examined (see Brady and Hunt, 1955; Brady, 1957). Another, somewhat more direct, measure of autonomic arousal in the rat—the defecation score in Hall's open-field test (1934)—has been used in the analysis of the determinants of emotionality (Broadhurst, 1957, 1958, 1958a) as well as providing the basis for the investigation of inherited emotional characteristics (1959a, 1960) and of their effect on learning (1957a, 1957b, 1958b). This work suggests that emotionality may be a rodent analogue of neuroticism in humans; the analogue of the orthogonal dimension of introversion–extraversion has also been tentatively identified (Sinha, Franks, and Broadhurst, 1958). Factor analysis is another promising approach (Royce, 1950). Examples are seen in Royce's work on the dog (1955), Sen's on the rat (1953), and Willingham's on the mouse (1956).

The effect of psychological stress on physiological function, as seen in Pilgrim and Patton's study (1953) of growth in rats, which yielded negative results, and Ullman's (1951, 1952) on "compulsive eating", which was positive, has received new impetus with the report of the experimental production of gastric ulcers in the rat by Sawrey and Weisz (1956). A continuous-conflict technique like that used by Hunt and Schlosberg opposed severe hunger and thirst drives against fear induced by shock as the animals tried to approach food or water. Both authors have published apparently independent analyses of the variables involved (Sawrey, Conger, and Turrell, 1956; Weisz, 1957) which agree in assigning an important role in ulcer formation to the conflict involved, as opposed to the effect of shock or of deprivation alone. No overt behavioural changes were observed. The influence of some social factors has been demonstrated (Conger, Sawrey, and Turrell, 1958), and other works showing that ulceration may be induced by direct brain stimulation (French, Porter, Cavanaugh, and Longmire, 1957) suggests the possibility of identification of the cerebral mechanism involved, especially in view of the extension of the technique to primates (Porter, Brady, Conrad, Mason, Galambos and Rioch, 1958).

The approach of comparative ethologists† to the problems of abnormal behaviour is based on their concept of "displacement activity", the manifestation of an innate behaviour pattern in circumstances which are judged biologically inappropriate for its emergence (Tinbergen, 1952; Barnett, 1955a). Careful analysis of the determinants of such behaviour have been made (see Thorpe, 1956). Displacement activities are viewed as the basis of the phenomena of experimental neurosis (Bastock, Morris, and Moynihan, 1953), as well as being related to those seen in human neurosis (Armstrong, 1950) especially psychosomatic disorders, which Barnett (1955a) suggests may be analogous to displacement activities in lower animals. The difficulty that the responses in lower animals are usually motor ones, whereas in man they tend, especially when pathological, to be visceral, is now less cogent in view of the work on gastric ulcers mentioned above and the development of

† Many ethological concepts can be criticized on various scores (Schneirla, 1952; Kennedy, 1954), and the ethologists' models may repel those accustomed to the greater sophistication of modern learning theory, which covers part of the same ground: "The gulfs between psychiatry, psychology, ethology, and physiology are both deep and wide, and the attempt to bridge them is liable to bring on fits of dizziness" (Barnett, 1955a, p. 1207). Such attempts are not encouraged by some ethologists' definition of their area of work as the scientific study of behaviour, thus pre-empting a field long studied by psychologists, the relevant contributions of whom many ethologists in their writings, though with certain significant exceptions, e.g. Thorpe (1956), appear to ignore.

methods for the study of asthma in lower animals (Ottenberg, Stein, Lewis, and Hamilton, 1958).

This, then concludes the review of the factual evidence which is to be found in the experimental literature and which goes to make up our knowledge about experimental neurosis. As has been indicated, there seems very little justification for the view that the phenomena observed can, in all but a very few cases, be regarded as at all analogous to the phenomena observable in human neurosis. Nevertheless, it has frequently been accepted that they are so related, probably because of the lack of a theoretical framework which links them to the main body of findings in the field of animal studies. This reinforces the view, as Lichtenstein has noted (1950), that one is dealing with examples of behaviour which are strange, and thus "abnormal"; it is then but a short step to defining them as "neurotic".

Theoretical Formulations of Experimental Neurosis

Two attempts have been made to describe the disturbances of behaviour experimentally produced in terms of a coherent theoretical system. These are the "vigilance" theory of Liddell, and Gantt's principles of "auto-" and "schizokinesis". Both of them, however, are *sui generis*, in that they account only for the facts of experimental neurosis as observed by their authors, and there has been very little success in demonstrating that they have any relevance beyond the situation which they were designed to illuminate. Moreover, as has been indicated in discussing them, they are not couched in terms sufficiently precise to allow testable predictions to be made from them.

To achieve the desired theoretical integration in this field, then it seems necessary to go back to the originator of the area of study. Pavlov viewed experimental neurosis as behaviour resulting from a "clash" between cortical excitation and inhibition. This explanation, in terms of a theory of brain physiology which is not widely accepted by physiologists (Liddell, 1949) in fact adds little to our understanding of the nature of the behaviour involved, and it is natural that, in seeking to encompass the problem, recourse should be had to the modern successor to Pavlovian reflex theory, that is the learning theory of Hull whose debt to Pavlov is insufficiently recognized. While recognizing the system's imperfections, it seems true to say that many, perhaps a majority, of psychologists, would acknowledge that learning theory as developed by Hull and elaborated by his pupil Spence, and by Mowrer, Miller, and Eysenck, is at present the only coherent and consistent explanation of numerous widely differing phenomena which range from the behaviour of *paramecia* (Grosslight and Tickner, 1953) to the development of social attitudes (Eysenck, 1954). Two attempts within this general framework may be noted. Hebb's (1947) is in the nature of a series of general suggestions which might adumbrate a fuller treatment. For example, he stresses the importance of generalization in the development of disturbed behaviour outside the precipitating situation, and regards the emotional responses displayed within it as being the result of "normal emotional conditioning". A more elaborate attempt is that of Wolpe (1952); indeed, Wolpe's whole thesis is that experimental neuroses are in fact learned behaviour, irrespective of whether one regards them as abnormal or not. To this end, he categorizes the precipitating situations into those employing severe shock, those employing mild shock, and those employing ambivalent stimulation. The behaviour resulting from the first he regards as straight-forward fear conditioning in which the stimuli associated with the punishing shock become conditioned stimuli for the arousal of intense conditioned fear, that is anxiety. With regard to the second situation in which mild shock only is used, "it is necessary to explain how a severe anxiety reaction could arise from what is apparently nothing more than the repeated conditioning of a mildly disturbing stimulus" (Wolpe, 1952, p. 265). His solution is to postu-late that fear and anxiety have additive properties. To the slight amount of fear evoked by the conditioned stimulus must be added the even smaller anxiety conditioned to it by the previous occasion on which it was used. This, however, allows a slightly larger amount of the complex of fear and anxiety to be conditioned to the stimulus, which, in turn, means a greater amount of anxiety to be added to the fear on the next occasion—and so it goes on. In this way, Wolpe suggests, anxiety can mount, so that, in time, the responses to it overwhelm other learned behaviour. With respect to the third situation, that of ambiguous stimulation, Wolpe (1952, p. 266) offers this hypothesis:

> However slight and transient the anxiety produced by this conflict of tendencies may be at first, the drive reduction associated with its cessation results in the anxiety responses becoming reinforced to whatever stimuli are contiguous, and among these is the ambivalent stimulation itself. In the same way as suggested above for the case of mild noxious stimuli, the strength of the anxiety response is conceived to be gradually stepped up at each presentation of the ambivalent stimulus situation while drive-reduc-tion potential correspondingly grows. Eventually very powerful anxiety re-sponses are evoked, and strong avoidance behaviour entirely replaces the approach responses to the experimental situation which were previously established by repeated feeding (1952, p. 266).

Thus, two authorities appear to support the view taken earlier in this chapter that the responses observed in the situations in which strong shock or other noxious stimuli are used (e.g. Masserman's) may be subsumed under the category of conditioned emotional reponses. Hebb also appears to think that all phenomena of experimental neurosis can be so explained. Signifi-cantly, the only exception he apparently makes is the phenomenon of dimin-ished capacity for making simple discriminations of conditioned stimuli after the application of difficult ones has caused a breakdown. It is this latter situation also which causes Wolpe most difficulty. To be sure, it is easy to see that once intense anxiety has been produced in the difficult discrimination situation, a conditioned emotional response to the stimuli used, and to the whole situation, will develop and generalize in the usual way. What is more difficult to see, is how this anxiety developed in the first place, in the absence of primary fear-producing stimuli. Wolpe's explanation, though ingenious, does not appear to the writer to be wholly satisfactory. Firstly, his assumption that fear and anxiety are additive may not be tenable. Secondly, that they do interact in the way suggested is equally hypothetical. Thirdly, even if these points are conceded, then in the discrimination situation, his explanation rests on the assumption that ambiguous stimulation gives rise to anxiety, directly. He claims that: ". . . it is a matter of everyday experience that in human subjects ambivalent stimuli arouse feelings of tension" (Wolpe, 1952, p. 266). Admittedly, there is a body of evidence which suggests that this may be in fact true, but Wolpe does not indicate how this occurs in animals. An explanation in terms of changes in difficulty level may be of assistance here; such an explanation is available in terms of the operation of the principle known as the Yerkes–Dodson law.

In 1908 Yerkes and Dodson published the results of a study of learning in mice in a brightness discrimination situation. They found that as the motivation—in this case a combination of hunger drive and electric shock punishment for wrong responses—increased, an optimum motivation was reached beyond which increases in intensity gave poorer rather than better learning. But in addition they investigated the effect of variations in the *difficulty* of the task. They discovered that the more difficult the task, the sooner the optimum motivation was reached, that is, as task difficulty increases, so the optimum motivation approaches threshold. The curvilinear relationship between performance and motivation has been confirmed in many different situations subsequently, but the relationship between it and the level of difficulty appears to have been lost sight of until recently, when the law was invoked (Eysenck, 1955) to explain the differences in performance between neurotics and normals in their accomplishment of simple tasks like conditioning, and more complex ones like maze learning (Taylor, 1956). Broadhurst (1957a) has demonstrated the action of the law itself in a factorial experiment in which it appeared as a significant interaction effect between intensity of motivation and level of task difficulty. This confirmation is thought to gain weight because a different situation, different motivation, and even a different species of subjects from those of Yerkes and Dodson (1908) were used. In addition, the phenomena designated by the law may be explained in terms of Hullian learning theory. Thus, increasing drive level may increase the functional difficulty of a discrimination, so that objective increases in difficulty are in fact rendered more severe than the circumstances otherwise warrant. Once the optimum motivation is reached, then the decrease in task performance may be viewed as an energization of incorrect responses which are lower in the habit–family–hierarchy

14*

than the correct ones (Broadhurst, 1959). The application of this reformu-
lation of the Yerkes–Dodson law has been shown to have relevance to such
diverse fields as perceptual defence and avoidance learning, as well as experimental neuroses.

The application to the problem of how to account for the disturbed behaviour seen in experimental neurosis precipitated by difficult discriminations derives from the nature of the task imposed in this type of situation.
After preliminary training in restraint, during which time the subject's
fear reactions to the restraint and to the experimental situation generally
are gradually inhibited and replaced by food–seeking responses, the task
proper begins. A feature of it is that the task becomes progressively more
and more difficult—as soon as the animal masters one discrimination a
start is made on the next and so on. Now from a consideration of the action
of the Yerkes–Dodson law, it is clear that the optimum performance will be
achieved by the subject in this situation with a progressive lowering of
motivation. That is to say, the optimum motivation for each new level of
difficulty will be lower than that for the preceding, easier one. But it seems
unlikely that experimental animals will have encountered situations before
in which this principle operates, that is in which greater reinforcement
follows lower rather than higher motivation, and so will not have had the
opportunity for learning which particular level of motivation will secure a
desired goal. On the contrary, most of the situations they are likely to have
encountered previously are simple ones in which higher drive levels have in
general been more efficacious than lower ones. It is postulated, therefore,
that the result of failure in the discrimination situation to receive the anticipated reinforcement when the subject responds wrongly to a negative conditioned stimulus will result in an increase of motivation, by virtue of the
previously learned responses referred to above. Subjectively speaking, the
natural result of failure is to try harder. Thus a conditioned increase of
drive (Brown and Farber, 1951; Marx, 1956) may be added to that already
existing. This, in turn, will lead to further failure to make the discrimination,
and additional slight increments in drive may be expected because of the
added delay in anticipated reinforcement which may occur, and because of
the drive arousal cues now associated with both positive and negative stimuli
which, typically, are now both responded to equally. At this stage, it is
further suggested, the increased drive level energizes incorrect responses in
competition with the correct ones—responses, especially fear ones, which
were suppressed early in the training. So it is that struggling, howling,
and agitated behaviour in general, which were previously characteristic of
the subject's initial reactions to the situation are reinstated anew.

This formulation serves to reconcile certain phenomena frequently reported in conditioning work which do not seem to have been adequately explained hitherto. Several experimenters have mentioned the failure of the
method of improving the subject's discrimination performance by increasing

the hunger drive; if the above analysis is correct, the prediction might be made that reducing the hunger drive, rather than increasing it, would be more beneficial. In the same way, the observation of some workers that making the discrimination problem simpler has therapeutic value fits in with our formulation. On the other hand, the more common finding is that after the breakdown of discrimination at extreme levels of difficulty, even simple discriminations are no longer made and have to be re-learned. It seems probable that this characteristic failure of simple discrimination can be accounted for if it is recalled that even relatively simple tasks have an optimum motivation, which may well be surpassed if anxiety is added to the motivational complex.

One ubiquitous finding—Pavlov and Gantt, as well as Liddell and Masserman all mention it—is that the presence of the experimenter in the conditioning chamber with the subject appears to have a quieting effect on neurotic animals. Anderson and Liddell (1935) came nearest to a rational explanation of this fact when they observed that conditioned signals are not given when the experimenter is in the room. Now, the task this poses the animal is to distinguish between "experimenter present" and "experimenter absent"—an extremely simple perceptual discrimination. The simplicity of this task is such that it seems likely that it will be very well learned, even under the extremely high drive postulated as eventuating from the previous breakdown. Also this high drive level may be responsible fo rthe rapid learning of any other novel feature in the experimental situation, especially if it has any drive–reducing properties. Herein may lie the clue to the so-called pathological generalization of the disorder of Gantt's dog Nick who, it will be recalled, developed genito-urinary signs long after the original precipitating cause of the experimental neurosis had passed. They did not, however, arise spontaneously. They followed the introduction of a bitch in oestrus into the experimental situation for therapeutic purposes. It is suggested that the pollakiuria and sexual erections noted in this dog thereafter may in fact have been conditioned responses to the experimental situation, the female acting as the original unconditioned stimulus. It should be noted that the transient abnormalities of sexual function noted in another dog (Gantt, 1944) followed attempts to develop sexual conditioned responses in the experimental situation. Two further facts about Nick seem to support our view: the dog learned a new association to light as a conditioned stimulus without any reward, which suggests a continuing high drive level; as does the observation that he persisted in looking towards the location of the original auditory conditioned stimulus, many years after it had been altered.

While this attempt to account for some of the facts of experimental neurosis in learning theory terms is doubtless deficient in many respects, it serves to indicate that it is likely that the phenomena observed can be brought under the rubric of conventional learning theory in a general way. More can hardly be expected at this time in view of the deficiencies in the evidence available. Significant advance in the future probably lies in the use of more strictly controlled situations for the study of the development of emotional responses—the conditioned emotional response (C.E.R.), for example—which permit detailed analysis of the stimuli and responses involved, such as that, for example, of Schoenfeld (1950, p. 95). He writes:

> The distance from rat to man is a long one, yet it may turn out to be filled with differences in detail rather than in principle. Most, or all, experimental psychologists are as vitally interested as the clinician in understanding man, but use the laboratory as their route to that goal in the belief that through it may be achieved a sound theory of behavior leading to widened practical successes in the field.

REFERENCES

Altmann, M. (1941) A study of activity and neighbourly relations in swine, *J. Comp. Psychol.* **31**, pp. 473–80.

Anderson, O. D. (1939) Two cases of experimental neurosis in dogs of known genetic constitution, *Am J. Physiol.* **126**, pp. 421–22 [abstract].

Anderson, O. D. (1941) The role of the glands of internal secretion in the production of behavioral types in the dog, in *The Genetic and Endocrinic Basis for Differences in Form and Behavior* (ed. C. R. Stockard), Philadelphia, Wistar Inst., pp. 647–747.

Anderson, O. D., and Liddell, H. S. (1935) Observations on experimental neurosis in sheep, *Arch. Neurol. Psychiat. Chicago*, **34**, pp. 330–54.

Anderson, O. D., and Parmenter, R. (1941) A long-term study of the experimental neurosis in the sheep and dog, *Psychosom. Med. Monogr.* **2**, pp. 1–150

Anderson, O. D., Parmenter, R., and Liddell. H. S. (1939) Some cardiovascular manifestations of the experimental neurosis in the sheep, *Psychosom. Med.* **1**, pp. 93–100.

Apter, I. M. (1952) A contribution to the problem of the formation of experimental disruption of higher nervous activity in dogs under conditions of natural experiment, *Zh. Vyssh. Nervn. Deiatel.* **2**, pp. 104–12. (Psychol. Abstr. **27** (2), p. 143, 1953).

Armstrong, E. A. (1950) The nature and function of displacement activities, in *Physiological Mechanisms in Animal Behaviour* (eds. J. F. Danielli and R. Brown), *Sympos. Soc. Exp. Biol.* **4**, pp. 361–84.

Babkin, B. P. (1938) Experimental neuroses in animals and their treatment with bromides, *Edinb. Med. J.* **45**, pp. 605–19.

Babkin, B. P. (1951) *Pavlov: A Biography*, London, Gollancz.

Bajandurov, B. I. (1933) Zur Physiologie des Sehanalysators bei Vögeln, *Z. Vergl. Physiol.* **18**, pp. 298–306.

Barnett, S. A. (1955) Competition among wild rats, *Nature, London* **75**, pp. 126–7.

Barnett, S. A. (1955a) "Displacement" behaviour and "psychosomatic" disorder, *Lancet* **2**, pp. 1203–8.

Bastock, M., Morris, D., and Moynihan, M. (1953) Some comments on conflict and thwarting in animals, *Behaviour* **6**, pp. 66–84.

BEACH, F. A. (1953) Animal research and psychiatric theory. *Psychosom. Med.* **15**, pp. 374–89.

BEACH, F. A., and JAYNES, J. (1954) Effects of early experience upon the behaviour of animals, *Psychol. Bull.* **51**, pp. 230–63.

BEVAN, W. (1955) Sound-precipitated convulsions: 1947–1954, *Psychol. Bull.* **52**, pp. 473–504.

BIJOU, S. W. (1942) The development of conditioning methodology for studying experimental neurosis in the rat, *J. Comp. Psychol.* **34**, pp. 91–106.

BIJOU, S. W., (1943) A study of "experimental neurosis" in the rat by the conditioned response technique, *J. Comp. Psychol.* **36**, pp. 1–20.

BIJOU, S. W. (1947) A new conditioned response technique to investigate "experimental neurosis" in the rat, *Am. Psychologist* **2**, p. 319 [abstract].

BIJOU, S. W. (1951) A conditioned response technique to investigate "experimental neurosis" in the rat, *J. Comp. Physiol. Psychol.* **44**, pp. 84–87.

BOWLBY, J. (1951) *Maternal Care and Mental Health*, World Health Organization Monogr. Ser. **2**, Geneva.

BRADY, J. V. (1957) A comparative approach to the experimental analysis of emotional behavior, in *Experimental Psychopathology* (ed. P. H. Hoch and J. Zubin), New York, Grune and Stratton, pp. 20–33.

BRADY, J. V., and HUNT, H. F. (1955) An experimental approach to the analysis of emotional behavior, *J. Psychol.* **40**, pp. 313–24.

BROADHURST, P. L. (1955) Cardiac, respiratory and squeak conditioning in the rat, *Bull. Brit. Psychol. Soc.* **23** (Inset), p. 3 [abstract].

BROADHURST, P. L. (1957) Determinants of emotionality in the rat. I. Situational factors, *Brit. J. Psychol.* **48**, pp. 1–12.

BROADHURST, P. L. (1957a) Emotionality and the Yerkes-Dodson Law, *J. Exp. Psychol.* **54**, pp. 345–52.

BROADHURST, P. L. (1957b) Air deprivation as a motivational technique in the rat, and its application to the problem of emotionality as a determinant of drive, *Bull. Brit. Psychol. Soc.* **32** (Inset), p. 23 [abstract].

BROADHURST, P. L. (1958) Determinants of emotionality in the rat: II. Antecedent factors, *Brit. J. Psychol.* **49**, pp. 12–20.

BROADHURST, P. L. (1958a) Determinants of emonality in the rat: III. Strain differences, *J. Comp. Physiol. Psychol.* **51**, pp. 55–59.

BROADHURST, P. L. (1958b) A "Crespi effect" in the analysis of emotionality as a drive in rats, *Brit. J. Psychol.* **49**, pp. 56–58.

BROADHURST, P. L. (1959) The interaction of task difficulty and motivation: the Yerkes-Dodson Law revived, *Acta Psychol.* **16**, pp. 321–38.

BROADHURST, P. L. (1959a) Application of biometrical genetics to behaviour in rats, *Nature, London*, **184**, pp. 1517–18.

BROADHURST, P. L. (1960) Studies in psychogenetics applications of biometrical genetics to the inheritance of behaviour, in *Experiments in Personality*, Vol. I, *Psychogenetics and Psychopharmacology* (ed. H. J. Eysenck), London, Routledge and Kegan Paul.

BROWN, J. S., and FARBER, I. E. (1951) Emotions conceptualized as intervening variables with suggestions toward a theory of frustration, *Psychol. Bull.* **48**, pp. 465–95.

BRÜCKNER, G. H. (1933) Untersuchungen zur Tiersoziologie, insbesondere zur Auflösung der Familie, *Z. Psychol.* **128**, pp. 1–110.

CAIN, J., and EXTREMET, J. (1957) Étude comparative des procédés de création de la névrose expérimentale chez l'animal, *Proc. XV Int. Congr. Psychol.*, *Brussels*, p. 599 [abstract].

CAMERON, D. E. (1936) Studies in depression, *J. Ment. Sci.* **82**, pp. 148–61.

Carmichael, L. (1938) Learning which modifies an animal's subsequent capacity for learning, *J. Genet. Psychol.* **52,** pp. 159–63.

Chance, M. R. H. (1957) Mammalian behaviour studies in medical research, *Lancet* **2,** pp. 687–90.

Conger, J. J. (1951) The effects of alcohol on conflict behavior in the albino rat, *Quart. J. Stud. Alc.* **12,** pp. 1–29.

Conger, J. J., Sawrey, W. L., and Turrell, E. S. (1958) The role of social experience in the production of gastric ulcers in hooded rats, *J. Abnorm. (Soc.) Psychol.* **52,** pp. 214–20.

Cook, S. W. (1939) A survey of methods used to produce "experimental neurosis", *Am. J. Psychiat.* **95,** pp. 1259–76.

Cook, S. W. (1939a). Some theoretical considerations relating to "experimental neurosis", Psychol. Bull. **36,** p. 516 [abstract].

Cook, S. W. (1939b) The production of "experimental neurosis" in the white rat, *Psychosom. Med.* **1,** pp. 293–308.

Cowles, J. T., and Pennington, L. A. (1943) An improved conditioning technique for determining auditory acuity of the rat, *J. Psychol.* **15,** pp. 41–47.

Crawford, M. P., Fulton, J. F., Jacobsen, C. F., and Wolfe, J. B. (1947) Frontal lobe ablation in chimpanzee; a résumé of Becky" and "Lucy", in "The Frontal Lobes" (ed. J. F. Fulton, C. D. Aring, and S. B. Wortis), *Assoc. Res. Nerv. Ment. Dis.* **27,** pp. 3–58.

Croft, P. G. (1951) Some observations on neurosis in farm animals, *J. Ment. Sci.* **97,** pp. 584–88.

Curti, M. W. (1935) Native fear responses of white rats in the presence of cats, in "Studies in Psychology from Smith College" (ed. J. J. Gibson), *Psychol. Monogr.* **46,** Whole No. 210, pp. 78–98.

Curtis, Q. F. (1937) Experimental neurosis in the pig, *Psychol. Bull.* **34,** p. 723 [abstract].

Curtis, Q. F. (1937a) Diurnal variation in the free activity of sheep and pig, *Proc. Soc. Exp. Biol.,* N. Y., **35,** pp. 566–67.

Davis, D. R. (1954) Some applications of behaviour theory in psychopathology, *Brit. J. Med. Psychol.* **27,** pp. 216–23.

Davis, H., Dworkin, S., Lurie, H. M., and Katzman, J. (1937) Symposium on the neural mechanism of hearing: III. Animal investigations (a) Behavioral, electrical and anatomical studies of abnormal ears, *Larygoscope* **47,** pp. 415–47.

Denton, D. A. (1957) A gregarious factor in the natural conditioned salivary reflexes of sheep, *Nature, London,* **179,** pp. 341–44.

Dimmick, F. L., Ludlow, N., and Whiteman, A. (1939) A study of "experimental neurosis" in cats, *J. Comp. Psychol.* **28,** pp. 39–43.

Drabovitch, W., and Weger, P. (1937) Deux cas de névrose expérimentale chez le chien, *C. R. Acad. Sci.* **204,** pp. 902–5.

Dworkin, S. (1935) Pitch and intensity discriminations by cats, *Am. J. Physiol.* **112,** pp. 1–4.

Dworkin, S. (1935a) Alimentary motor conditioning and pitch discrimination in dogs, *Am. J. Physiol.* **112,** pp. 323–8.

Dworkin, S. (1938) Conditioning neurosis in the dog and cat, *Am. J. Physiol.* **123,** p. 57 [abstract].

Dworkin, S. (1939) Conditioning neurosis in dogs and cats, *Psychosom. Med.* **1,** pp. 388–96.

Dworkin, S., Baxt, J. O., and Dworkin, E. (1942) Behavioral disturbances of vomiting and micturition in conditioned cats, *Psychosom. Med.* **4,** pp. 75–81.

Dworkin, S., Baxt, J. O., and Gross, J. (1942). Deafness neurosis in the cat as a special form of disinhibition, *Fed. Proc.* **1,** p. 23.

DWORKIN, S., BOURNE, W., and RAGINSKY, B. B. (1937) Changes in conditioned responses brought about by anaesthetics and sedatives, *Canad. Med. Ass.* **37**, pp. 136–39.

DWORKIN, S., BOURNE, W., and RAGINSKY, B. B. (1937a) Action des anesthésiques, sédatifs, hypnotiques sur les centres nerveux supérieurs, *Anésth. Analgés.* **3**, pp. 335–49.

DWORKIN, S., KATZMAN, J., HUTCHINSON, G. A., and MC. CABE, J. R. (1940) Hearing acuity of animals as measured by conditioning methods, *J. Exp. Psychol.* **26**, pp. 281–98.

DWORKIN, S., RAGINSKY, B. B., and BOURNE, W. (1937) Action of anaesthetics and sedatives upon the inhibited nervous system, *Curr. Res. Anesth.* **16**, pp. 238–40.

DWORKIN, S., SEYMOUR, S. L., and SUTHERLAND, G. (1934) A conditioned reflex method of testing hearing in cats, *Quart. J. Exp. Physiol.* **24**, pp. 23–30.

DYKMAN, R. A., and GANTT, W. H. (1951) A comparative study of cardiac and motor conditioned responses, *Am. J. Physiol.* **167**, p. 780 [abstract].

DYKMAN, R. A., and GANTT, W. H. (1951a) A comparative study of cardiac conditioned responses and motor conditioned responses in controlled "stress" situation, *Am. Psychologist* **6**, pp. 263–64 [abstract].

DYKMAN, R. A., GANTT, W. H., and WHITEHORN, J. C. (1956) Conditioning as emotional sensitization and differentiation, *Psychol. Monogr.* **70**, 422.

ERÄNKÖ, M., and MUITTARI, A. (1957) Effects of experimental neurosis on the thyroid and adrenal gland of the rat, *Acta Endocrinol. Copenhagen* **26**, pp. 109–116.

EYSENCK, H. J. (1954) *The Psychol. of Pol.*, London, Routledge and Kegan Paul.

EYSENCK, H. J. (1955) A dynamic theory of anxiety and hysteria, *J. Ment. Sci.* **101**, pp. 28–51.

FIELDS, P. E. (1931) Contributions to visual discrimination in the white rat: II, *J. Comp. Psychol.* **11**, pp. 349–66.

FINGER, F. W. (1941) Quantit. stud. of "conflict": II. The effect of "conflict" upon the general activity of the white rat, *J. Comp. Psychol.* **32**, pp. 139–52.

FINGER, F. W. (1944) Experimental behavior disorder in the rat, in *Personality and the Behavior Disorders* (ed. J. McV. Hunt), New York, Ronald Press, pp. 413–30.

FINGER, F. W. (1947) Convuls. behav. in the rat, *Psych. Bull.* **44**, pp. 201–48.

FOLEY, J. P., JNR. (1935) The criterion of abnormality, *J. Abnorm. (Soc.) Psychol.* **30**, pp. 279–91.

FONBERG, E. (1958) The manifestation of the defensive reactions in neurotic states, *Acta Biol. Exp.* **18**, pp. 89–112.

FRANKS, C. M. (1958) Alcohol, alcoholism and conditioning: a review of the literature and some theoretical considerations, *J. Ment. Sci.* **104**, pp. 14–33.

FRASER, A. F. (1957) The disposition of the bull, *Brit. J. Anim. Behav.* **5**, pp. 110–15.

FRASER, R. (1947) *The Incidence of Neurosis among Factory Workers*, London, H. M. S. O.

FREEMAN, W., and WATTS, I. W. (1944) Physiological psychology, *Annu. Rev. Physiol.* **6**, pp. 517–42.

FRENCH, J. D., PORTER, R. W., CAVANAUGH, E. B., and LONGMIRE, R. L. (1957) Experimental gastroduodenal lesions induced by stimulation of the brain, *Psychosom. Med.* **19**, pp. 209–20.

FROLOV, Y. P. (1937) *Pavlov and his School*, London, Kegan Paul.

FULLER, J. L. (1947) Individual differences in the emotional level of dogs, *Anat. Rec.* **99**, p. 621 [abstract].

Fulton, J. F., and Jacobsen, C. F. (1935) The functions of the frontal lobes: a comparative study in monkeys, chimpanzee and man, *Proc. II Int. Congr. Neurol., London.*

Galt, W. E. (1939) The capacity of the rhesus and cebus monkey and the gibbon to acquire differential response to complex visual stimuli, *Genet. Psychol. Monogr.* **21,** pp. 387–457.

Gantt, W. H. (1936) An experimental approach to psychiatry, *Am. J. Psychiat.* **92,** pp. 1007–21.

Gantt, W. H. (1938) Extension of a conflict based on food to other physiological systems and its reciprocal relations with sexual function, *Am. J. Physiol.* **123,** pp. 73–74 [abstract].

Gantt, W. H. (1940) Effect of alcohol on sexual reflexes in dogs, *Am. J. Physiol.* **129,** p. 360 [abstract].

Gantt, W. H. (1940a) The role of the isolated conditioned stimulus in the integrated pattern response, and the relation of the pattern changes to psychopathology, *J. Gen. Psychol.* **23,** pp. 3–16.

Gantt, W. H. (1942) The origin and development of nervous disturbances experimentally produced, *Am. J. Psychiat.* **98,** pp. 475–81.

Gantt, W. H. (1942a) Cardiac conditioned reflexes to painful stimuli, *Fed. Proc.* **1,** p. 28 [abstract].

Gantt, W. H. (1944) *Experimental Basis for Neurotic Behavior: Origin and Development of Artificially Produced Disturbances of Behavior in Dogs,* New York, Hoeber. (also Psychosom. Med. Monogr. 3, Nos. 3 and 4).

Gantt, W. H. (1946) Cardiac conditional reflexes to time, *Trans. Am. Neurol. Assoc.* **72,** p. 166 [abstract].

Gantt, W. H. (1948) Physiological psychology, *Annu. Rev. Physiol.* **10,** pp. pp. 453–78.

Gantt, W. H. (1952) Effect of alcohol on the sexual reflexes of normal and neurotic male dogs, *Psychosom. Med.* **14,** pp. 174–81.

Gantt, W. H. (1953) Principles of nervous breakdown in schizokinesis and autokinesis, in *Comparative Conditioned Neuroses* (ed. E. J. Kempf), *Ann. N. Y. Acad. Sci.* **56,** pp. 141–65.

Gantt, W. H. (1953a) The physiological basis of psychiatry: the conditional reflex, in *Basic Problems in Psychiatry* (ed. J. Wortis), New York, Grune and Stratton, pp. 52–89.

Gantt, W. H. (1957) *Physiological Basis of Psychiatry* (ed.), Springfield, Ill., Thomas.

Gantt, W. H., and Dykman, R. A. (1952) Experimental psychogenic tachycardia, *Am. J. Physiol.* **171,** pp. 725–26 [abstract].

Gantt, W. H., and Dykman, R. A. (1957) Experimental psychogenic tachycardia, in *Experimental Psychopathology* (eds. P. H. Hoch and J. Zubin), New York, Grune and Stratton, pp. 12–19.

Gantt, W. H., and Freile, M. (1944) Effect of adrenalin and acetylcholin on excitation, inhibition and neuroses, *Trans. Am. Neurol. Assoc.* **69,** pp. pp. 180–81 [abstract].

Gantt, W. H., Gakenheimer, W. A., and Stunkard, A. (1951) Development of cardiac reflex to time intervals, *Fed. Proc.* **10,** pp. 47–48 [abstract].

Gantt, W. H., and Hoffman, W. C. (1940) Conditioned cardio–respiratory changes accompanying conditioned food reflexes, *Am. J. Physiol.* **129,** pp. 360–361 [abstract].

Gantt, W. H., Hoffman, W. C., and Dworkin, S. (1947) The cardiac conditional reflex, *Abstr. Comm. XVII Int. Congr. Physiol.,* Oxford, p. 15.

Gantt, W. H., and Muncie, W. (1941) Rhythmic variations of muscular activity in normal and neurotic dogs correlated with secretion and with conditioned reflexes, *Am. J. Physiol.* **133**, p. 287 [abstract].

GANTT, W. H., and TRAUGOTT, U. (1949) Retention of cardiac, salivary and motor conditional reflexes, *Am. J. Physiol.* **159**, p. 569 [abstract].

GENTRY, E. and DUNLAP, K. (1942) An attempt to produce neurotic behavior in rats, *J. Comp. Psychol.* **33**, pp. 107–12.

GOLDACRE, R. J. (1958) Polar locomotion and experimental "neurosis" in the amoeba, *Anim. Behav.* **6**, p. 242 [abstract].

GOLDMAN, M. M. (1939) Motor conditioning in the goat, *Am. J. Physiol.* **126**, pp. 504–5 [abstract].

GREEN, R. T. (1958) Threshold for electric shock of the laboratory rat, *Anim. Behav.* **6**, pp. 72–76.

GROSSLIGHT, J. H., and TICKNER, W. (1953) Variability and reactive inhibition in the mealworm as a function of determined turning sequences, *J. Comp. Physiol. Psychol.* **46**, pp. 35–38.

HALL, C. S. (1933) A comparative psychologist's approach to problems in abnormal psychology, *J. Abnorm. (Soc.) Psychol.* **28**, pp. 1–5.

HALL, C. S. (1934) Emotional behavior in the rat: I. Defecation and urination as measures of individual differences in emotionality, *J. Comp. Psychol.* **18**, pp. 385–403.

HAMILTON, G. V. (1927) Comparative psychology and psychopathology, *Am. J. Psychol.* **39**, pp. 200–11.

HANSEN, K. H. (1956) *After-effects in the Behaviour of Mice*, Copenhagen, Munksgaard.

HARLOW, H. F. (1956) Current and future advances in physiological and comparative psychology, *Am. Psychologists* **2**, pp. 273–77.

HEBB, D. O. (1946) Emotion in man and animal: an analysis of the intuitive process of recognition, *Psychol. Rev.* **53**, pp. 88–106.

HEBB, D. O. (1947) Spontaneous neurosis in chimpanzees: theoretical relations with clinical and experimental phenomena, *Psychosom. Med.* **9**, pp. 3–16.

HEBB, D. O., and THOMPSON, W. R. (1954) The social significance of animal studies, in *Handbook of Social Psychology*, Vol. I, *Theory and Method* (ed. G. Lindzey), Cambridge, Mass., Addison-Wesley, pp. 532–61.

HEDIGER, H. (1950) *Wild Animals in Captivity*, London, Butterworth.

HIGGINSON, G. D. (1930) The after-effects of certain emotional situations upon maze learning among white rats, *J. Comp. Psychol.* **10**, pp. 1–10.

HILGARD, E. R. (1956) *Theories of Learning*, 2nd ed., New York, Appleton-Century-Crofts.

HUGHES, B., and SCHLOSBERG, H. (1938) Conditioning in the white rat: IV. The conditioned lid reflex, *J. Exp. Psychol.* **23**, pp. 641–50.

HULL, C. L. (1937) A projected integration of the conditioned–reflex and the psychoanalytic approaches to the study of psychogenic disorders, *Proc. Conference Exp. Neuroses and Allied Problems*, Washington, National Research Council.

HUMPHREY, G., and MARCUSE, F. (1939) New methods of obtaining neurotic behavior in rats, *Am. J. Psychol.* **52**, pp. 616–19.

HUMPHREY, G., and MARCUSE, F. (1941) Factors influencing the susceptibility of albino rats to convulsive attacks under intense auditory stimulation, *J. Comp. Psychol.* **32**, pp. 285–306.

HUNT, J. McV., and SCHLOSBERG, H. (1950) Rats in continuous conflict, *J. Comp. Physiol. Psychol.* **43**, pp. 351–57.

HUTYRA, F., MAREK, J., and MANNINGER, R. (1946) *Special Pathology and Therapeutics of the Diseases of Domestic Animals*, 5th Engl. ed. London, Baillière, Tindall and Cox.

Ivanov-Smolensky, A. G. (1954) *Essays on the Pathophysiology of the Higher Nervous Activity: according to I. P. Pavlov and his School*, Moscow, Foreign Languages Publishing House.

Jacobsen, C. F. (1935) Experimental analysis of the functions of the frontal association areas in primates, *J. Nerv. Ment. Dis.* **81**, pp. 437–42.

Jacobsen, C. F., Wolfe, J. B., and Jackson, T. A. (1935) An experimental analysis of the functions of the frontal association areas in primates, *J. Nerv. Ment. Dis.* **82**, pp. 1–14.

Jacobsen, E., and Skaarup, Y. (1955) Experimental induction of conflict behaviour in cats: its use in pharmacological investigations, *Acta Pharm. Tox., Kbh.* **11**, pp. 117–24.

James, W. T. (1934) A conditioned avoiding posture of the dog, *Psychol. Bull.*, **31**, p. 730 [abstract].

James, W. T. (1943) The formation of neurosis in dogs by increasing the energy requirements of a conditioned avoiding response, *J. Comp. Psychol.* **36**, pp. 109–24.

James, W. T. (1953) Morphological and constitutional factors in conditioning, in *Comparative Conditioned Neuroses* (ed. E. J. Kempf), *Ann. N. Y. Acad. Sci.* **56**, pp. 171–83.

Jamison, J. H. (1951) Measurement of auditory intensity thresholds in the rat by conditioning of an autonomic response, *J. Comp. Physiol. Psychol.* **44**, pp. 118–25.

Jenkins, W. O., and Stanley, J. C., Jnr. (1950) Partial reinforcement: a review and critique, *Psychol. Bull.* **47**, pp. 193–234.

Jensen, A. V. (1945) Identification of gun-shyness with experimental neurosis in dogs, *Fed. Proc.* **4**, p. 36 [abstract].

Jones, H. E., and Jones, M. C. (1928) A study of fear, *Childhood Educ.* **5**, pp. 136–43.

Jones, H. G. (1956) The application of conditioning and learning techniques to the treatment of a psychiatric patient, *J. Abnorm. (Soc.) Psychol.* **52**, pp. 414–19.

Kaminsky, S. D. (1939) Problem of experimental neurosis: the active adaptation of monkeyst o difficult experimental conditions, *Arkh. Biol. Nauk* **53**, pp. 69–88. (Psychol. Abstr. **13**, No. 5711, 1939).

Kappauf, W. E., and Schlosberg, H. (1937) Conditioned responses in the white rat: III. Conditioning as a function of the length of the period of delay, *J. Genet. Psychol.* **50**, pp. 27–45.

Karn, H. W. (1938) The behavior of cats on the double alternation problem in the temporal maze, *J. Comp. Psychol.* **26**, pp. 201–208.

Karn, H. W. (1938a) A case of experimentally induced neurosis in the cat. *J. Exp. Psychol.* **22**, pp. 589–92.

Karn, H. W. (1940) The experimental study of neurotic behavior in infrahuman animals, *J. Gen. Psychol.* **22**, pp. 431–36.

Karn, H. W. (1940a) Experimental neurosis in infrahuman animals – a bibliography, *Psychol. Rev.* **4**, pp. 35–39.

Karn, H. W., and Malamud, H. R. (1939) The behavior of dogs on the double alternation problem in the temporal maze, *J. Comp. Psychol.* **27**, pp. 46to 66.

Kawamura, Y, and Yoshii, N. (1951) A study on the experimental neurosis of rats: behavior patterns, *Med. J. Osaka Univ.* **2**, pp. 133–48.

Kennedy, J. S. (1954) Is modern ethology objective? *Brit. J. Anim. Behav.* **2**, pp. 12–19.

King, J. A., and Mavromatis, A. (1956) The effect of a conflict situation on the learning ability in two strains of inbred mice, *J. Comp. Physiol. Psychol.* **49**, pp. 465–68.

KONORSKI, J. (1948) *Conditioned Reflexes and Neuron Organization*, London, Cambridge Univ. Press.

KREPS, E. M. (1924) An attempt to establish a classification of experimental animals according to type, *Coll. Papers Physiol. Lab. I. P. Pavlov* **1,** pp. 118–40.

KUPALOV, P. S. (1952) On experimental neuroses in animals, *Zh. vyssh. Nervn. Deiatel.* **2,** pp. 457–73. (Psychol. Abstr., **28,** no. 8907, 1954).

LANDIS, C., and BOLLES, M., MARJORIE. (1949) *Textbook of Abnormal Psychology*, New York, Macmillan.

LEAVITT, F. H., and RIGGS, H. E. (1942) Pathologic study of a monkey exhibiting behavior disorder, *Arch. Neurol. Psychiat, Chicago*, **47,** pp. 186–88.

LIBERSON, W. T. (1957) Recent advances in Russian neurophysiology, *Annu. Rev. Physiol.* **19,** pp. 557–88.

LICHTENSTEIN, P. E. (1950) Studies of anxiety: I. The production of a feeding inhibition in dogs, *J. Comp. Physiol. Psychol.* **43,** pp. 16–29.

LICHTENSTEIN, P. E. (1950a) Studies of anxiety: II. The effect of lobotomy on a feeding inhibition in dogs, *J. Comp. Physiol. Psychol.* **43,** pp. 419–27.

LICKLIDER, J. C. R., and BUNCH, M. E. (1946) Effects of enforced wakefulness upon growth and the maze-learning performance of white rats, *J. Comp. Psychol.* **39,** pp. 339–50.

LIDDELL, H. S. (1925) The behavior of sheep and goats in learning a simple maze, *Am. J. Psychol.* **36,** pp. 544–52.

LIDDELL, H. S. (1925a) The relation between maze learning and spontaneous activity in the sheep, *J. Comp. Psychol.* **5,** pp. 475–84.

LIDDELL, H. S. (1926) A laboratory for the study of conditioned motor reflexes, *Am. J. Psychol.* **37,** pp. 418–19.

LIDDELL, H. S. (1936) Nervous strain in domesticated animals and man, *Cornell Vet.* **26,** pp. 107–12.

LIDDELL, H. S. (1938) The experimental neurosis and the problem of mental disorder, *Am. J. Psychiat.* **94,** pp. 1035–43.

LIDDELL, H. S. (1942) The conditioned reflex, in *Comparative Psychology*, 2nd ed. (ed. F. A. Moss), New York, Prentice-Hall, pp. 178–216.

LIDDELL, H. S. (1942a) The alteration of the instinctual processes through the influence of conditioned reflexes, *Psychosom. Med.* **4,** pp. 390–95.

LIDDELL, H. S. (1944) Conditioned reflex method and experimental neurosis, in *Personality and the Behavior Disorders* (ed. J. McV. Hunt), New York, Ronald Press, pp. 389–412.

LIDDELL, H. S. (1947) The experimental neurosis, *Annu. Rev. Physiol.* **9,** pp. 569–80.

LIDDELL, H. S. (1949) The nervous system as a whole: the conditioned reflex, in *Physiology of the Nervous System*, 3rd ed. (ed. J. F. Fulton), New York, Oxford Univ. Press, pp. 537–68.

LIDDELL, H. S. (1950) Animal origins of anxiety, in *Feelings and Emotions* (ed. M. L. Reymert) New York, McGraw-Hill, pp. 181–88.

LIDDELL, H. S. (1950a) Some specific factors that modify tolerance for environmental stress, in *Life Stress and Bodily Disease* (eds. H. H. Wolff, S. G. Wolf, and C. C. Hare), *Assoc. Res. Nerv. Ment. Dis.* **29,** pp. 155–71.

LIDDELL, H. S. (1950b) The role of vigilance in the development of animal neurosis, in *Anxiety* (eds. P. Hoch and J. Zubin), New York, Grune and Stratton, pp. 183–96.

LIDDELL, H. S. (1951) The influence of experimental neuroses on the respiratory function, in *Somatic and Psychiatric Treatment of Asthma* (ed. H. A. Abramson). Baltimore, Williams and Wilkins, pp. 126–47.

LIDDELL, H. S. (1952) Experimental induction of psychoneuroses by conditioned reflex with stress, in *The Biology of Mental Health and Disease*, Millbank Memorial Fund, New York, Hoeber, pp. 498–507.

Liddell, H. S. (1952a) Effect of corticosteroids in experimental psychoneurosis, in *The Biology of Mental Health and Disease*, Millbank Memorial Fund, New York, Hoeber, pp. 591–94.

Liddell, H. S. (1953) A comparative approach to the dynamics of experimental neuroses, in *Comparative Conditioned Neuroses* (ed. E. J. Kempf), *Ann. N. Y. Acad. Sci.* **56,** pp. 164–70.

Liddell, H. S. (1954) Conditioning and emotions, *Sci. Am.* **190,** pp. 48–57.

Liddell, H. S. (1955) The natural history of neurotic behavior, in *Society and Medicine: Lectures to the Laity* (ed. I. Galdston), No. **17,** New York, Int. Univ. Press, pp. 46–69.

Liddell, H. S. (1956) *Emotional Hazards in Animals and Man*, Springfield, Ill., C. C. Thomas.

Liddell, H. S., Anderson, O. D., Kotyuka, E., and Hartman, F. A. (1935) The effect of cortin on the experimental neurosis in sheep, *Am. J. Physiol.* **113,** pp. 87–88 [abstract].

Liddell, H. S., Anderson, O. D., Kotyuka, E., and Hartman, F. A. (1935a) Effect of extract of adrenal cortex on experimental neurosis in sheep, *Arch. Neurol. Psychiat. Chicago*, **34,** pp. 973–93.

Liddell, H. S., and Bayne, T. L. (1927) Auditory conditioned reflexes in the thryoidectomized sheep and goat, *Proc. Soc. Exp. Biol. N. Y.* **24,** pp. 289 to 91.

Liddell, H. S., and Bayne, T. L. (1927a) The development of "experimental neurasthenia" in the sheep during the formation of difficult conditioned reflexes, *Am. J. Physiol.* **81,** p. 494 [abstract].

Liddell, H. S., James, W. T., and Anderson, O. D. (1934) The comparative physiology of the conditioned motor reflex based on experiments with the pig, dog, sheep, goat and rabbit, *Comp. Psychol. Monogr.* **11,** No. 51, pp. 1–89.

Liddell, H. S., and Simpson, E. D. (1926) A preliminary study of motor conditioned reflexes in thyroidectomized sheep, *Proc. Soc. Exp. Biol. N. Y.* **23,** pp. 720–22.

Liddell, H. S., and Simpson, S. (1925) The effects of thyroid therapy on the neuromuscular activity of cretin sheep, *Am. J. Physiol.* **72,** pp. 63–68.

Liddell, H. S., Sutherland, G. F., Parmenter, R., and Bayne, T. L. (1936) A study of the conditioned reflex method for producing experimental neurosis, *Am. J. Physiol.* **116,** pp. 95–96 [abstract].

Liddell, H. S., Sutherland, G. F., Parmenter, R., Curtis, Q. F., and Anderson, O. D. (1937) Further analysis of the conditioned reflex method in relation to the experimental neurosis, *Am. J. Physiol.* **119,** p. 361 [abstract].

Lorenz, K. (1940) Durch Domestikation verursachte Störungen arteigenen Verhaltens, *Z. Angew. Psychol. Charakterk.* **59.**

Lubin, A. J. (1943) The experimental neurosis in animal and man, *Am. J. Med. Sci.* **205,** pp. 269–77.

Macleod, L. D. (1935) "A monthly bulletin" research report, *Brit. J. Addict.* **50,** pp. 89–135.

Maier, N. R. F. (1939) *Studies of Abnormal Behavior in the Rat: The Neurotic Pattern and an Analysis of the Situation which Produces it*, New York, Harper and Bros.

Maier, N. R. F. (1949) *Frustration: the Study of Behavior Without a Goal*, New York, McGraw-Hill.

Maier, N. R. F. (1956) Frustration theory: restatement and extension, *Psychol. Rev.* **63,** pp. 370–88.

MARCUSE, F., and MOORE, A. U. (1942) Conditioned reflexes in the pig. *Bull. Canad. Psychol. Assoc.* **2**, pp. 13–14.

MARCUSE, F., and MOORE, A. U. (1944) Tantrum behavior in the pig, *J. Comp. Psychol.* **37,** pp. 235–47.

MARCUSE, F., and MOORE, A. U. (1946) Motor criteria of discrimination, *J. Comp. Psychol.* **39,** pp. 25–27.

MARX, M. H. (1956) Some relations between frustration and drive, in *Nebraska Symposium on Motivation* (ed. M. R. Jones), Lincoln, Univ. of Nebraska Press, pp. 92–130.

MASSERMAN, J. H. (1939) An automatic apparatus for the central conditioning of small animals, *J. Comp. Psychol.* **28,** pp. 201–5.

MASSERMAN, J. H. (1942) Psychobiologic dynamisms in behaviour: an experimental study of neuroses and therapy, *Psychiatry* **5**, pp. 341–47.

MASSERMAN, J. H. (1943) *Behavior and Neurosis: an Emperimental Psychoanalytic Approach to Psychobiologic Principles*, Chicago, Univ. of Chicago Press.

MASSERMAN, J. H. (1950) A biodynamic psychoanalytic approach to the problems of feeling and emotions, in *Feelings and Emotions* (ed. M. L. Reymert) New York, McGraw-Hill, pp. 49–75.

MASSERMAN, J. H. (1951) La création des névroses expérimentales, *Psyché*, Paris, **6,** pp. 799–808.

MASSERMAN, J. H. (1953) Psycho-analysis and biodynamics — an integration, *Int. J. Psycho-Anal.* **34**, (Suppl.) pp. 13–42.

MASSERMAN, J. H. (1954) Letter to the editor, *Brit. J. Psychol.* **45,** pp. 221–22.

MASSERMAN, J. H., ARIEFF, A., PECHTEL, C., and KLEHR, H. (1950) Effects of direct interrupted electroshock on experimental neuroses, *J. Nerv. Ment. Dis.* **112**, pp. 384–92.

MASSERMAN, J. H., GROSS, Z., and PECHTEL, C. (1954) Abnormalities of behavior, *Annu. Rev. Psychol.* **5,** pp. 263–80.

MASSERMAN, J. H., and JACQUES, M. G. (1947) Effects of cerebral electroshock on experimental neurosis, *Am. J. Psychiat.* **104,** pp. 92–99.

MASSERMAN, J. H., and JACQUES, M. G. (1948) Experimental masochism, *Arch. Neurol. Psychiat. Chicago* **60,** pp. 402–4.

MASSERMAN, J. H., JACQUES, M. G., and NICHOLSON, M. R. (1945) Alcohol as preventive of experimental neuroses, *Quart. J. Stud. Alc.* **6,** pp. 281–99.

MASSERMAN, J. H., and PECHTEL, C. (1953) Neuroses in monkeys: a preliminary report of experimental observations, in *Comparative Conditioned Neuroses* (ed. E. J. Kempf), *Ann. N. Y. Acad. Sci.* **56,** pp. 253–65.

MASSERMAN, J. H., and PECHTEL, C. (1953a) Conflict-engendered neurotic and psychotic behavior in monkeys, *J. Nerv. Ment. Dis.* **118,** pp. 408–11.

MASSERMAN, J. H., and PECHTEL, C. (1956) How brain lesions affect normal and neurotic behavior: an experimental approach, *Am. J. Psychiat.* **112,** pp. 865–72.

MASSERMAN, J. H., and PECHTEL, C. (1956a) Neurophysiologic and pharmacologic influences on experimental neuroses, *Am. J. Psychiat.* **113,** pp. 510–14.

MASSERMAN, J. H., and PECHTEL, C. (1956b) Normal and neurotic olfactory behavior in monkeys: a motion picture, *J. Nerv. Ment. Dis.* **124,** pp. 518–19.

MASSERMANN, J. H., PECHTEL, C., and SCHREINER, L. (1953) The role of olfaction in normal and neurotic behavior in animals: preliminary report, *Psychosom. Med.* **15,** pp. 396–404.

MASSERMAN, H. J., and SIEVER, P. W. (1944) Dominance, neurosis, and aggression: an experimental study, *Psychosom. Med.* **6,** pp. 7–16.

MASSERMAN, J. H., and YUM, K. S. (1946) An analysis of the influence of alcohol on experimental neuroses in cats, *Psychosom. Med.* **8,** pp. 36–52.

MASSERMAN, J. H., YUM, K. S., NICHOLSON, M. R., and LEE, S. (1944) Neurosis and alcohol: an experimental study, *Am. J. Psychiat.* **101,** pp. 389–95.

McCLEARY, R. A. (1954) Measurement of experimental anxiety in the rat: an attempt, *J. Genet. Psychol.* **84,** pp. 95–108.

MEIGE, H., and FEINDEL, E. (1907) *Tics and their Treatment,* London, Appleton.

MELZACK, R. (1952) Irrational fears in the dog, Canad. *J. Psychol.* **6,** pp. 141–47.

MILES, W. R. (ed.) (1938) *Problems of Neurotic Behavior; the Experimental Production and Treatment of Behavior Derangement,* Washington, National Research Council.

MILLER, N. E. (1944) Experimental studies of conflict, in *Personality and the Behavior Disorders* (ed. J. McV. Hunt), New York, Ronald Press, pp. 431 to 65.

MILLER, N. E. (1951) Learnable drives and rewards, in *Handbook of Experimental Psychology* (ed. S. S. Stevens), New York, John Wiley and Sons, Inc., pp. 435–73.

MILLER, N. E. (1956) Effects of drugs on motivation: the value of using a variety of measures, in *Techniques for the Behavioral Study of Drugs* (ed. P. B. Dews), *Ann. N. Y. Acad. Sci.* **65,** pp. 318–33.

MILLER, N. E., and STEVENSON, S. S. (1936) Agitated behavior of rats during experimental extinction and a curve of spontaneous recovery, *J. Comp. Psychol.* **21,** pp. 205–31.

MOORE, A. U., and MARCUSE, F. L. (1945) Salivary, cardiac and motor indices of conditioning in two sows, *J. Comp. Psychol.* **38,** pp. 1–16.

MORSE, W. H., and SKINNER, B. F. (1957) A second type of superstition in the pigeon, *Am. J. Psychol.* **70,** pp. 308–11.

MURRAY, H. A., JNR. (1937) The available procedures for the production of neurotic-like phenomena, *Proc. Conference Exp. Neuroses and Allied Problems,* Washington, National Research Council.

OKAZAKI, S. (1925) An experimental study of the lack of sleep, *Shinsei Gaku Zatshi* **25,** Psychol. Abstr. **2,** No. 2773, 1928).

OTTENBERG, P., STEIN, M., LEWIS, J., and HAMILTON, C. (1958) Learned asthma in the guinea pig, *Psychosom. Med.* **20,** pp. 395–400.

OWENS, O., and GANTT, W. H. (1950) Does the presence of a person act on the cardiac rate of the dog as an unconditional stimulus? *Am. J. Physiol.* **163,** p. 740 [abstract].

PARMENTER, R. (1940) The influence of degrees of freedom upon stereotyped conditioned motor reflexes in the sheep, *J. Gen. Psychol.* **23,** pp. 47–54.

PARMENTER, R. (1940a) Avoidance of nervous strain in experimental extinction of the conditioned motor reflex, *J. Gen. Psychol.* **23,** pp. 55–63.

PATTON, R. A. (1951) Abnormal behavior in animals, in *Comparative Psychology,* 3rd ed. (ed. C. P. Stone), New York, Prentice-Hall, pp. 458–513.

PAVLOV, I. P. (1927) *Conditioned Reflexes: an Investigation of the Physiological Activity of the Cerebral Cortex,* London, Oxford Univ. Press.

PAVLOV, I. P., (1928) *Lectures on Conditioned Reflexes: Twenty–five Years of Objective Study of the Higher Nervous Activity (Behavior) of Animals,* Vol. I., New York, Int. Publishers.

PAVLOV, I. P. (1941) *Lectures on Conditioned Reflexes,* Vol. II, *Conditioned Reflexes and Psychiatry,* London, Lawrence and Wishart.

PAVLOV, I. P. (1955) *Selected Works* (ed. Kh. S. Koshtoyants), Moscow, Foreign Languages Publishing House.

PECHTEL, C. and MASSERMAN, J. H. (1954) The osmotic responses of normal and neurotic monkeys, *Ann. N. Y. Acad. Sci.* **58,** pp. 256–60.

PECHTEL, C., MASSERMAN, J. H., SCHREINER, L. and LEVITT, M. (1955) Differential effects of lesions of the mediodorsal nuclei of the thalamus on normal and neurotic behavior in the cat, *J. Nerv. Ment. Dis.* **121,** pp. 26–33.

PENROSE, L. S. (1953) Psycho-analysis and experimental science, *Int. J. Psychol. Anal.* **34,** (Suppl.), pp. 74–82.

PETROVA, M. K. (1924) Different kinds of internal inhibition under a particularly difficult situation, *Coll. Papers Physiol. Lab. I. P. Pavlov,* **1,** pp. 61–70.

PETROVA, M. K. (1926) Pathological deviations of the inhibitory and excitatory process in a case of their clashing, *Coll. Papers Physiol. Lab. I. P. Pavlov* **1,** pp. 199–211.

PILGRIM, F. J., and PATTON, R. A. (1953) Food consumption and growth of the rat as a measure of motivational stress, *J. Genet. Psychol.* **83,** pp. 89–119.

PORTER, R. W., BRADY, J. V., CONRAD, D., MASON, J. W., GALAMBOS, R., and RIOCH, D. McK. (1958) Some experimental observations on gastro-intestinal lesions in behaviorally conditioned monkeys, *Psychosom. Med.* **20,** pp. 379–94.

RÄBER, H. (1948) Analyse des Balzverhaltens eines domestizierten Truthahns (Melagris), *Behaviour* **1,** pp. 237–66.

RAND, A. (1941) Development and enemy recognition of curve-billed thrasher Toxostoma curvirostre, *Bull. Am. Mus. Nat. Hist.* **78,** pp. 213–42.

RAND, A. (1942) Some notes on bird behavior, *Bull. Am. Mus. Nat. Hist.* **79,** pp. 517–24.

RAZENKOV, I. P. (1924) Modifications of the excitatory process in the cortex under some complex conditions, *Coll. Papers Physiol. Lab. I. P. Pavlov* **1,** pp. 103–17.

RICHTER, C. P. (1950) Psychotic behavior produced in wild Norway and Alexandrine rats apparently by the fear of food poisoning, in *Feelings and Emotions* (ed. M. K. Reymert), New York, McGraw-Hill, pp. 189–202.

RICHTER, C. P. (1953) Experimentally produced behavior reactions to food poisoning in wild and domesticated rats, in *Comparative Conditioned Neuroses* (ed. E. J. Kempf), Ann. N. Y. Acad. Sci. **56,** pp. 225–39.

RICHTER, C. P. (1957) On the phenomenon of sudden death in animals and man, *Psychosom. Med.* **19,** pp. 191–98.

RICKMAN, V. V. (1928) Disturbance of the normal nervous activity in the dog, effected by powerful extraneous stimuli, *Coll. Papers Physiol. Lab. I. P. Pavlov* **3,** pp. 19-34.

RIGBY, W. K. (1954) Approach and avoidance gradients and conflict behavior in a predominantly temporal situation, *J. Comp. Physiol. Psychol.* **47,** pp. 83–89.

ROBINSON, J., and GANTT, W. H. (1946) The cardiac component of the orienting reflex, *Fed. Proc.* **5,** pp. 87–88 [abstract].

ROBINSON, J., and GANTT, W. H. (1947) The orienting reflex (questioning reaction): cardiac, respiratory, salivary and motor components, *Johns Hopkins Hosp. Bull.* **80,** pp. 231–53.

ROHRER, J. H. (1947) Experimental extinction as a function of the distribution of extinction trials and response strength, *J. Exp. Psychol.* **37,** pp. 473–93.

ROSE, J. A., TAINTON-POTTBERG, A., and ANDERSON, O. D. (1938) Effects of insulin shock on behavior and conditioned reflex action in the well-trained sheep, *Proc. Soc. Exp. Biol. N. Y.* **38,** pp. 653–55.

ROSENTHAL, O. S. (1926) The mutual interactions of the excitatory and inhibitory processes (a new type of differentiation of tactile conditioned stimuli), *Coll. Papers Physiol. Lab. I. P. Pavlov* **1,** pp. 141–60.

ROYCE, J. R. (1950) The factorial analysis of animal behavior, *Psychol. Bull.* **47,** pp. 235–59.

ROYCE, J. R. (1955) *A Factorial Study of Emotionality in the Dog,* Psychol. Monogr. **69,** Whole No. 407.

220   P. L. Broadhurst

Russell, R. W. (1950) The comparative study of "conflict" and "experimental neurosis", *Brit. J. Psychol.* **41**, pp. 95–108.

Sampson, B. H., and Schneirla, T. C. (1941) The appearance of nail–biting in a rat: a fixation in a frustrating problem situation, *J. Comp. Psychol.* **32**, pp. pp. 437–510.

Sawrey, W. L., Conger, J. J., and Turrell, E. S. (1956) An experimental investigation of the role of psychological factors in the production of gastric ulcers in rats, *J. Comp. Physiol.* Psychol. **49**, pp. 457–61.

Sawrey, W. L., and Weisz, J. D. (1956) An experimental method of producing gastric ulcers, *J. Comp. Physiol. Psychol.* **49**, pp. 269–70.

Scheflen, N. (1957) Generalization and extinction of experimentally induced fear in cats, in *Experimental Psychopathology* (eds. P. H. Hoch and J. Zubin), New York, Grune and Stratton, pp. 1–11.

Schlosberg, H. (1934) A preliminary description of the behavior of the white rat in a simple conditioned response situation, *Psychol. Bull.* **31**, pp. 615–16 [abstract].

Schlosberg, H. (1934a) A quantitative study of certain factors influencing the rate and depth of conditioning in the white rat, *Psychol. Bull.* **31**, p. 732 [abstract].

Schlosberg, H. (1934b) Conditioned responses in the white rat, *J. Genet. Psychol.* **45**, pp. 303–35.

Schlosberg, H. (1936) Conditioned responses in the white rat, II. Conditioned responses based on shock to the foreleg, *J. Genet. Psychol.* **49**, pp. 107–38.

Schlosberg, H. (1936a) Comparison of the conditioned and unconditioned responses based on foreleg shock in the rat, *Psychol. Bull.* **33**, p. 782 [abstract].

Schlosberg, H., and Kappauf, W. E. (1935) The role of "effect" in conditioned leg withdrawal, *Psychol. Bull.* **32**, p. 562 [abstract].

Schneirla, T. C. (1952) A consideration of some conceptual trends in comparative psychology, *Psychol. Bull.* **49**, pp. 559–97.

Schoenfeld, W. N. (1950) An experimental approach to anxiety, escape and avoidance behavior, in *Anxiety* (eds. P. H. Hoch and J. Zubin), New York, Grune and Stratton, pp. 70–99.

Scott, J. P. (1947) "Emotional" behavior of fighting mice caused by conflict between stimulatory and weak inhibitory training, *J. Comp. Physiol. Psychol.* **40**, pp. 275–82.

Scott, J. P., and Marston, Mary-Vesta (1953) Nonadaptive behavior resulting from a series of defeats in fighting mice, *J. Abnorm. (Soc.) Psychol.* **48**, pp. 417–28.

Sears, R. R. (1943) Survey of objective studies of psychoanalytic concepts, *Soc. Sci. Res. Council Bull.* No. 51.

Sen, N. N. (1953) Behavioural traits associated with experimental neurosis in rats, Unpubl. *Doctor's Dissertation*, Univ. of London Lib.

Shenger-Krestovnikova, N. R. (1921) Contributions to the question of differentiation of visual stimuli and the limits of differentiation by the visual analyser of the dog, *Bull. Lesgaft Inst. Petrograd* **3**, pp. 1–43.

Sinha, S. H., Franks, C. M., and Broadhurst, P. L. (1958) The effect of a stimulant and a depressant drug on a measure of reactive inhibition, *J. Exp. Psychol.* **56**, pp. 349–54.

Siryatsky, V. V. (1925) Pathological deviations in the activity of the central nervous system in the case of clashing of excitation and inhibition, *Russ. J. Physiol.* **8**.

Skinner, B. F. (1948) "Superstition" in the pigeon, *J. Exp. Psychol.* **38**, pp. 168–72.

SPERANSKY, A. D. (1925) Modifications of the interrelations between the excitatory and inhibitory processes in a dog after a flood, *Russ. J. Physiol.* **8.**

STAINTON, H. (1943) Addiction in animals, *Brit. J. Inebr.* **41,** pp. 24–31.

STEWART, C. N., and WARREN, J. M. (1957) The behavior of cats on the double-alternation problem, *J. Comp. Physiol. Psychol.* **50,** pp. 26–28.

SUTHERLAND, G. F. (1939) Salivary conditioned reflexes in swine, *Am. J. Physiol.* **126,** pp. 640–41 [abstract].

TANNER, J. M., and INHELDER, B. (eds.) (1956) *Discussions on Child Development,* Vol. II, London, Tavistock Publ.

TAYLOR, J. A. (1956) Drive theory and manifest anxiety, *Psychol. Bull.* **53,** pp. 303–20.

THORPE, W. H. (1956) *Learning and Instinct in Animals,* Cambridge, Mass., Harvard Univ. Press.

TINBERGEN, N. (1952) "Derived" activities: their causation, biological significance, origin, and emancipation during evolution, *Quart. Rev. Biol.* **27,** pp. 1–32.

TINKELPAUGH, O. L. (1928) The self-mutilation of a male macacus rhesus monkey, *J. Mammal.* **9,** pp. 293–300.

TURNER, R. H. (1941) An approach to the problem of neurosis through the study of respiration, activity, and startle in the rat as influenced by the difficulty of visual size discrimination, *J. Comp. Psychol.* **32,** pp. 389–405.

ULLMAN, A. D. (1951) The experimental production and analysis of a "compulsive eating symptom" in rats, *J. Comp. Physiol. Psychol* **44,** pp. 575–81.

ULLMAN, A. D. (1952) Three factors involved in producing compulsive eating in rats, *J. Comp. Physiol. Psychol.* **45,** pp. 490–96.

WATERHOUSE, I. K. (1957) Effects of prefrontal lobotomy on conditioned fear and food responses in monkey, *J. Comp. Physiol. Psychol.* **50,** pp. 81–88.

WATSON, J. B., and RAYNER, R. (1920) Conditioned emotional responses, *J. Exp. Psychol.* **3,** pp. 1–14.

WATSON, R. E. (1954) Experimentally induced conflict in cats, *Psychosom. Med.* **16,** pp. 340–47.

WEISZ, J. D. (1957) The etiology of experimental gastric ulceration, *Psychosom. Med.* **19,** pp. 61–73.

WEITZENHOFFER, A. M. (1953) *Hypnotism: an Objective Study in Suggestibility,* New York, John Wiley and Sons, Inc.

WENDT, G. R. (1934) Auditory Acuity of Monkeys, *Comp. Psychol. Monogr.* **10,** No. 3.

WIKLER, A., and MASSERMAN, J. H. (1943) Effects of morphine on learned adaptive responses and experimental neurosis in cats, *Arch. Neurol. Psychiat. Chicago* **50,** pp. 401–04.

WILCOXON, H. C. (1952) "Abnormal fixation" and learning, *J. Exp. Psychol.* **44,** pp. 324–31.

WILLINGHAM, W. W. (1956) The organization of emotional behavior in mice, *J. Comp. Physiol. Psychol.* **49,** pp. 345–48.

WILLOUGHBY, R. R., and ANDREWS, R. C. (1940) Stimulation interval as a possible psychopathogenic factor, *J. Comp. Psychol.* **30,** p. 137.

WINNICK, W. A. (1956) Anxiety indicators in an avoidance response during conflict and non-conflict, *J. Comp. Physiol. Psychol.* **49,** pp. 52–59.

WITKIN, H. A. (1939) Abnormal behavior in animals, *Psychol. League J.* **3,** pp. 75–83.

WOLPE, J. (1952) Experimental neuroses as learned behaviour, *Brit. J. Psychol.* **43,** pp. 243–68.

WOLPE, J. (1952a) Objective psychotherapy of the neuroses, *S. Afr. Med. J.* **26,** pp. 825–29.

WOLPE, J. (1954) Letter to the editor, *Brit. J. Psychol.* **45,** pp. 220–21.

WOLPE, J. (1958) *Psychotherapy by Reciprocal Inhibition,* Stanford, Stanford Univ. Press.

YACORZYNSKI, G. K. (1946) Necessary and facilitating conditions in producing experimental neurosis in cats, *Am. Psychologist* **1,** p. 245 [abstract].

YACORZYNSKI, G. K. (1948) Etiologic factors in experimental neurosis from the standpoint of behavior, *Arch. Neurol. Psychiat. Chicago* **60,** pp. 323–24 [abstract].

YATES, A. J. (1958) The application of learning theory to the treatment of tics, *J. Abnorm. (Soc.) Psychol.* **56,** pp. 175–82.

YERKES, R. M. (1943) *Chimpanzees: a Laboratory Colony,* New Haven, Yale Univ. Press.

YERKES, R. M., and DODSON, J. D. (1908) The relation of strength of stimulus to rapidity of habit-formation, *J. Comp. Neurol. Psychol.* **18,** pp. 459–82.

YEROFEEVA, M. N. (1912) Electrical stimulation of the skin of the dog as a conditioned salivary stimulus, Thesis, St. Petersburg. (Also Moscow: *Akad. Med. Nauk S.S.S.R.,* 1953) (Psychol. Abstr. **29,** No. 443, 1955).

YEROFEEVA, M. N. (1916) Contribution à l'étude des réflexes conditionnels distructifs, *C. R. Soc. Biol.* **79,** pp. 239–40 [abstract].

YOSHII, N., and KAWAMURA, Y. (1951) A study on experimental neurosis of rats: II. Electroencephalography of experimentally induced neurotic rats, *Jap. J. Physiol.* **2,** pp. 125–29.

ZVEREV, A. T. (1957) On the mechanism of some experimental neuroses in dogs, *Zh. Vyssh. Nervn. Deiatel.* **7,** pp. 434–41. (Psychol. Abstr. **32,** No. 4427, 1958).

THE FORMATION AND EXTINCTION OF CONDITIONED REFLEXES IN "BRAIN-DAMAGED" AND MONGOLOID CHILDREN†

Herbert G. Birch, and Howard Demb

THE terms "brain-damaged" or "brain-injured" when applied to children refer to a combination of psychologic functions that are presumed to originate in prenatal, perinatal, or infantile insults to the cerebrum. The category is entirely behavioral [4, 5] and implies that any of a number of kinds of cerebral damage will result in a common pattern of behavioral disturbance. Locus of injury, nature of the lesion and the temporal course in the designation, and the non-behavioral, neurologic confirmation of the fact of anatomic insult has been conspicuous by its absence. These considerations make it clear that the term brain-damaged refers to a behavior syndrome and not to the fact of brain damage as such.

The identification of a pathological pattern of behavior, characterized by difficulties in figure-ground perception, abnormal distractibility, perseverative tendencies, conceptual rigidity, emotional lability, and hyperactivity, by Strauss and Werner [4–16] was an important contribution to the more refined differential diagnosis and treatment of psychologically disturbed children. However, the unfortunate characterization of the pattern as *the* brain-damaged child has led to confusion in two directions. First, Strauss [5] has declared that the syndrome is pathognomonic of brain damage and has assumed behavior problems to have such an etiology even in the absence of any clearly substantiating neurologic or historical data. Second, it has come to be widely assumed that the behavior sydrome described is the typical consequence of organic brain damage in childhood. Neither of these extensions appears to be warranted by experience. In earlier discussions [1, 2] one of us has pointed to a variety of patterns of behavioral alternation that may occour as the consequence of organic brain damage in infancy and childhood and has argued that the syndrome described by Strauss and his colleagues represents only one of many different types of behavioral alternation that may be associated with cerebral lesions in children. However, to

† By permission of *J. Nerv. Ment. Dis.*, 1959

define the numerous distinct behavioral syndromes which may occur as consequences of infantile cerebral damage is beyond the scope of the present report. It is concerned, rather, with a more limited and specific inquiry into the behavioral sequellae of brain damage. Basic to the present study is the view that a population of children who are known to have cerebral injury may, at the very least, be divided into two groups, one of which contains children who exhibit hyperactivity and/or distractibility and a second whose members do not show either of these characteristics. Possible underlying differences in the central nervous system organization in each of the groups can then be analyzed through the use of both psychologic and physiologic techniques.

The use of conditioned reflex methods for such analysis seems especially desirable since conditioned reflex theory [3] permits the formulation of some quite specific hypotheses concerning the nature of the functional alterations in central nervous system activity that may underlie hyperactivity and distractibility features of the behavior occurring in some of the children who have sustained cerebral damage. From the point of view of Pavlovian theory the behavioral phenomena of distractibility, hyperactivity and even of perseveration can be conceptualized as manifestations of defective equilibration between the processes of cortical excitation and inhibition. If this conceptualization is correct one should find differences in the character of the processes of cortical excitatory and inhibitory activity in normal and hyperactive groups. For this reason the present study is concerned with a comparative examination of the conditioning and extinction process in hyperactive and/or distractible brain-damaged children and in brain-damaged children who exhibit neither hyperactivity nor distractibility. It includes as well an analysis of the functioning of a sample of mongoloid children and of a small number of normal children.

Method

Subjects

In examining the records of children in a pediatric psychiatric installation, it was possible to obtain records of eighteen children who showed unequivocal evidence of central nervous system trauma acquired either perinatally or as a consequence of meningitis or encephalitis in infancy. Supportive evidence included the presence of seizures, and/or of neurological signs such as pathologic reflexes and abnormal EEG. The presence or absence of stereotyped behavioral characteristics was not used as a variable in the selection. The sex, I.Q., and age of the subjects are presented in Table 1.

Behavioral analysis of these 18 children showed that ten of them were hyperactive and/or distractible, whereas the remaining 8 included 6 normoactive and 2 hypoactive children. For comparative purposes 8 mongoloid

Table 1. Classification, Sex, Age and I.Q. of Subjects

Brain-damaged								Mongoloid			
Non-H and Non-D				Hyperactive and/or Distractible							
Subj.	Sex.	Age	I.Q.	Subj.	Sex.	Age	I.Q.	Subj.	Sex.	Age	I.Q.
J.E.	M	8–5	85	S.P.	F	10–5	85	E.P.	F	6–2	68
J.o.	M	10–2	68	L.G.	F	8–6	80	L.L.	M	6–2	67
S.B.	M	15–1	60	A.M.	F.	13–2	63	A.S.	F	9–8	54
S.S.	M	12–2	55	C.H.	F	12–10	60	L.D.	F	8–5	48
J.S.	F	16–9	51	M.S.	F	10–6	60	L.C.	M	6–9	38
B.W.	M	17–5	50	C.C.	M	12–4	57	C.K.	F	15–0	36
J.M.	M	12–10	48	V.M.	M	13–1	54	B.H.	F	13–0	35
R.A.	M	15–1	42	S.H.	M	10–8	54	G.H.	F	11–7	33
				W.B.	M	15–11	49				
				W.W.	F	14–0	30				
Mean I.Q.†		57.4		59.2				47.4			
	S.D.	12·8		15·3				13·4			

† There is no statistically significant difference between the mean I.Q.'s of these groups.

children with no history of central nervous system trauma, and 4 normal children who were convalescing from non-neurologic illness were studied.

Apparatus and Procedures

The unconditioned stimulus used was a mild electric shock adjusted by means of a Variac supplied by a 120 volt, 60 cycle a.c. source. The shock was administered through two polished copper electrodes which were taped to the inside of each forearm. A 7 $\frac{1}{2}$ watt white frosted bulb served as the conditioned stimulus. It was placed on the wall 5 ft in front of the subject, who was seated in a cushioned chair provided with broad wooden arm rests. Continuous recordings of the skin resistance were taken by means of a C.E.M. Research Laboratories Physiological Galvanometer, model No. 650. Extraneous visual stimuli were minimized, but no control over auditory stimuli was maintained.

Since a new stimulus can affect the GSR, at the beginning of each child's first session the light was presented alone for approximately 1 $\frac{1}{2}$ sec once every 30 sec. This was done until there was no measurable response to three consecutive presentation of the light. Then the intensity of the shock was built up to a level which resulted in a decrease in skin resistance equivalent to an increased current flow of at least 0.039 mA. This amplitude was chosen because it was of greater magnitude than 90 per cent of the observed random fluctuations in skin resistance. After the desired level of shock was attained,

the light alone was again presented every 30 sec to the criterion of three consecutive zero responses, in order to eliminate the possibility of "pseudo-
conditioning", i.e. the creation by shock alone of a hypersensitive nervous
system which could produce a high level of response to any subsequent
neutral stimulus. In no case were the responses to the light alone following
the determination of the proper shock level of sufficient duration and amplitude to warrant the possibility that the criterion for conditioning could be
reached without true conditioning taking place.

Following a second extinction of the skin response to the light the conditioning series itself was started. This consisted of alternate presentations of
the light and shock in combination and then light alone. The interval between
each step in the sequence was 90 sec so that any two successive presentations
of either light alone or of the light shock combination occurred at 3 min
intervals. When the stimuli were paired, the onset of the light would precede
the shock by $\frac{1}{2}$ sec and would be present for a total time of $1\frac{1}{2}$ sec.

The alternate presentations of light paired with shock and light alone continued until there were three successive responses to the light alone which
were either equal to, or greater than 0·039 mA in amplitude. The extinction
series began 90 sec after the third consecutive CR. For the extinction
series, the light alone was presented every 90 sec until three consecutive
zero responses to this stimulus were produced.

In the majority of cases the entire process could not comfortably be completed in a single session. Therefore, each experimental period was limited
to one hour. The only exception to this rule occurred after the conditioning
criterion had been reached and the extinction series was initiated. Since extinction was sometimes prolonged, the final session lasted for between one
and two hours.

Results

Quantitative Features of the CR Formation

When the course of conditioning is examined, it is found (Table 2) that the
hyperactive and/or distractible group of brain–damaged children required a
significantly greater number of trials ($p = 0·02$) to reach the criterion of
conditioning than did the non-hyperactive and non-distractible brain damaged group. The mean number of trials required was 31·2 for the hyperactive and 10·6 for the non-hyperactive children. In only one case is there any
overlap between the number of trials required to reach conditioning by the
individuals in the two groups. It is of further interest to note that whereas it
was possible to complete the conditioning of all the non-hyperactive children,
40 per cent of the hyperactive children could not achieve criterion levels of
conditioning despite prolonged training periods.

The mongoloid group performs significantly more poorly than does the
non-hyperactive and non-distractible brain-damaged group ($p = 0.05$). The

Table 2. Number of Presentations of Light Paired with Shock Necessary to Reach Criterion for Conditioning

Brain-damaged			Mongoloid		Normal	
Non-H and non-D	Hyperactive and/or distractible Completed Inc.					
Subj. No. of Trials	Subj. No. of Trials	Subj. No. of trials	Subj. No. of trials		Subj. No. of trials	
J.J. 4	A.M. 13	S.P. 31+	C.K. 4		D.T. 4	
J.M. 7	W.B. 19	C.H. 37+	G.H. 4		S.S. 5	
S.S. 8	W.W. 21	M.S. 40+	L.D. 19		B.A. 6	
J.E. 9	V.M. 30	L.G. 78+	A.S. 25		E.R. 10	
J.S. 9	C.C. 48		B.H. 36			
B.W. 14	S.H. 56		L.L. 40			
R.A. 17			E.P. 45			
S.B. 17			L.C. 91			
Mean 10·6	31·2		33·0		6·3	
S.D. 4·5	15·5		26·5		2·3	

The scores of the subjects who did not reach the criterion for conditioning are indicated by a + and were not included in the calculation of the means.

t-Scores and Corresponding Probability Values that the Null Hypothesis Regarding the Differences between the Mean Number of Presentations of Light Paired with Shock Necessary to Reach Criterion for Conditioning Can be Rejected

	H and/or D		Mongoloid		Normal	
	t-score	p-value	t-score	p-value	t-score	p-value
Non-H and Non-D	2·87	2 %	2·20	5 %	2·03	10 %
H and/or D			0·15	50 %	3·53	1 %
Mongoloid					2·64	5 %

The p-values were calculated by using Fisher's t for small samples.

mongoloid children require approximately the same number of trials to achieve the conditioning criterion as do those of the hyperactice and/or distractible subjects who could be conditioned. It is possible that this elevation in number of trials required by the mongoloid children is largely the contribution made by the three youngest children of the group, all of whom were under 7 years of age. If these young children are eliminated from consideration the conditioning of the remaining mongoloid children tends to become significantly more efficient than that of the hyperactive and/or distractible children, who were conditionable.

When the performances of the four normal children are analyzed it is found that they required significantly fewer trials to reach the criterion for adequate conditioning than either the hyperactive and/or distractible ($p = 0.01$) or mongoloid group ($p = 0.05$). However, they do not condition at a level which is significantly different from the performances of the non-hyperactive and nondistractible subjects ($p = 0.10$).

In order to determine whether the differences among the retarded children with respect to conditioning rate is in any way a reflection of differences among these children with respect to intellectual capacity as measured by I.Q. a correlation was made between these two variables. The product-moment correlation was $r = -0.07$, which suggests that for the children in this study the I.Q. and the formation of the conditioned reflex are independent measures. Thus, for the children in this study the measure of the number of reinforced trials necessary for conditioning is not merely another means of demonstrating those consequences of brain damage which may be reflected in a modified I.Q.

Qualitative Features of the CR Formation

There were marked differences in the behavior of the children of the different groups during the conditioning series. The two groups of brain-damaged children showed the most extreme differences in behavior. The group of hyperactive and/or distractible children could only cooperate for a short time. Their capacities to sit still, to concentrate on one stimulus, to refrain from talking, and to ignore the temptation to manipulate the electrodes were all limited. Moreover, as the session wore on this behavior became pronounced and occurred more and more frequently. The type of increased activity varied from child to child. Some chose to talk to the experimenter. According to the level of functioning of the child the talking ranged from coherent statements and questions in an attempt to engage the experimenter in conversation to apparently incoherent and disconnected verbalizations. Two children chose to sing and whistle during the sessions.

Other of the hyperactive children resorted to an increase in gross motor activity, either of the entire body or of parts, such as slapping their hands against the arm rests or kicking their feet against the floor. Still others would try to manipulate objects within reach, such as the door latch or the wire leading to the bulb. Additional distractions were auditory stimuli from outside of the experimental situation, many of which were of such low intensity that the experimenter was not aware of them until the child would call his attention to them by asking "What's that?" These children tended to resort to several activities, but each seemed to have his or her characteristic preferred activity which increased progressively during a given training session.

The non-hyperactive and non-distractible group of brain-damaged children provided a distinct contrast to the hyperactive and/or distractible group. Although they were not entirely at ease in the experimental situation, a small amount of restlessness was all that was exhibited. In no case did this restlessness tend to increase during the initial session or to recur in the second session when more than one training period was required.

The mongoloid group varied slightly in the amount of motor activity and distractibility exhibited. With only one of the children however, was there any excessive restlessness, talking, increase in activity, or distractibility. This one mongoloid child (L.C.) was restless and extremely distractible and required an unusually long series of reinforcements before the criterion for conditioning was reached. L.C. was perhaps the most distractible subject used in this experiment in that he would respond to all extraneous auditory stimuli (including some that were almost inaudible to the experimenter) by asking what it was. This type of behavior was very similar to that encountered in the group of hyperactive and/or distractible brain-damaged children and gives one the impression that L.C. may have been such a child.

Of the four normal patients tested, none exhibited excessive motor activity.

Extinction of the Conditioned Reflex

When the quantitative features of extinction are explored (Table 3) it is found that no significant difference in mean number of trials required to achieve extinction exists among the three retarded groups. However, a qualitative consideration of the course of events during the extincton serves to distinguish the groups of children from each other.

Extinction in the hyperactive group was characterized by a progressive increase in extraneous activity of the children and appeared to be the result of a displacement of the conditioned reflex by external extinction through the development of adventitious movements. In the group of non-hyperactive brain-damaged children extinction pursued a classical course, with no progressive increase in restlessness occurring. In the mongoloid group and in the normal children the extinction series resulted in the progressive increase in inhibition, with four of the eight mongoloid children and two of the four normal children falling sound asleep during this session (Table 3). One of the mongoloid children slept for such a long period of time (more than 3 min) during the series that the extinction criterion was met by the sleep itself. Among the normal children, one child fell asleep for brief periods at five distinct points in the extinction sequence.

When sleep occurred there was a slow, steady, increase in skin resistance which persisted until the subject awoke. Upon awakening, there was a sharp decrease, of variable magnitude, in skin resistance. This course of events was peculiar to the sleeping children. In every case the experimenter observed the subjects while they were asleep in order to further verify that sleep had occurred. In all instances the subject could be seen in the completely relaxed posture characteristic of one who is asleep, with closed eyes and head resting on his or her chest or arm.

TABLE 3. NUMBER OF PRESENTATIONS OF LIGHT ALONE NECESSARY TO REACH CRITERION FOR EXTINCTION

	Brain-damaged				Mongoloid			Normal		
	Non-H and non-D		Hyperactive and/or distractible							
Subj.	No. of trials	Subj.	No. of trials	No. of trials to sleep	Subj.	No. of trials	No. of trials to sleep	Subj.	No. of trials	No. of trials to sleep
J.J.	33	A.M.	32+	12	C.K.	35		D.T.	41+	32
J.M.	36	W.B.	20		G.H.	13+	5	S.S.	43++	15
S.S.	8	W.W.	31		L.D.	27		B.A.	48+	
J.E.	27	V.M.	28		A.S.	14		E.R.	22	
J.S.	31+	C.C.	4		B.H.	29+	29			
B.W.	26	S.H.	20		L.L.	61++	5			
R.A.	9	S.P.	—		E.P.	22+	21			
S.B.	12	C.H.	—		L.C.	21+				
		M.S.	—							
		L.G.	—							
Mean	21·6		22·5			23·5	15·0		25·0	23·5
S.D.	10·8		9·6			9·9	10·3		11·5	8·5

+ Indicates that sleep occurred during the extinction period.
The scores of the subjects who did not reach the criterion for extinction are indicated by a + and were not included in the calculation of the means.

t-SCORES AND CORRESPONDING PROBABILITY VALUES THAT THE NULL HYPOTHESIS REGARDING THE DIFFERENCES BETWEEN THE MEAN NUMBER OF PRESENTATINOS OF LIGHT ALONE NECESSARY TO REACH FOR EXTINCTION CAN BE REJECTED

	H and/or D		Mongoloid	
	t-score	p-value	t-score	p-value
Non-H and Non-D	0·152	50 %	0·160	50 %
H and/or D			0·314	50 %

The p–values were calculated by using Fisher's t for small samples.

In contrast to the pattern just described the extinction series behavior of the hyperactive and/or distractible children was unmarked by any diminution of activity levels. The pattern of restlessness and high level mobility was sustained throughout the course of the extinction series.

Discussion

The results of the present study are best understood if the acquisition and the extinction of the conditioned reflex are considered separately. This is especially true since some of the findings concerning the formation or failure of formation of the conditioned galvanic skin response are illuminated by an independent consideration of the events that occurred during the subsequent extinction series.

The formation of a conditioned reflex involves the establishment of functional equivalence between two stimuli, one of which is initially neutral and the other initially effective in producing the response. In normal children the neutral stimulus rapidly becomes a focus of attention and, after a variable number of presentations which overlap in time with the administration of the effective stimulus, conditioning results. This classical course of events does not occur in our hyperactive-distractible children, in 40 per cent of whom we were unable to establish a definite conditioned reflex. Attention was rarely focused and responses were made to a miscellany of situational aspects. This lack of selectivity in attention may be interpreted as a manifestation of a defective process of inhibition, with the relevant stimulus incapable of achieving dominance and so reducing the effectiveness of explicit sensory arousals. Children in the non-hyperactive brain-damaged, mongoloid, and normal groups do not exhibit this type of difficulty.

The data on the extinction of the conditioned reflex support the view that a defective equilibrium between excitatory and inhibitory relations characterizes the hyperactive and distractible brain–damaged group. A brief statement of general conditioning theory is necessary in discussing the extinction data. Pavlov has advanced two concepts to account for the disapperance of a conditioned reflex—internal inhibition and external inhibition. Internal inhibition refers to the progressive development of inhibitory activity at a cortical locus which occurs in response to the continued unreinforced presentation of the conditioned stimulus. External inhibition refers to the process whereby the presentation of extraneous stimuli may have an interference function to make the conditioned stimulus ineffective. The first of these postulated mechanisms appears to be an analogue of adaptation, and the second of displacement. Among the subjects in the present investigation the hyperactive-distractible group appear to lose the conditioned reflex by external inhibition or displacement, whereas, the other groups appear to achieve conditioned reflex extinction by internal inhibition. Thus the hyperactive brain–damaged group approaches the extinction of the conditioned reflex through an ever–increasing degree of generalized motor activity. The children in the remaining groups appear to achieve conditioned reflex extinction through the development of internal inhibition, a process which is distinguished by a diminution of general motor activity level. In the normal children and in the mongoloid children this inhibitory phenomenon is generalized into sleep which Pavlov [3] viewed as "an inhibition which has spread over a great section of the cerebrum, over the entire hemispheres and even into the lower lying midbrain".

It is apparent that the obtained differences in both establishment of conditioning and the extinction of the conditioned reflex found are independent of the scores made on tests of intelligence, and have independent implications for the management and training of hyperactive and non-hyperactive brain-injured retarded children. Thus, the children who are in the hyperactive group may function most effectively in an environment which promotes inhibition by being repetitive and limited in the number and kinds of extraneous stimuli presented. However, such a situation would not be desirable for the non-hyperactive brain-injured group and could result in generalized inhibition.

Summary

The conditionability and rate of extinction of conditioned galvanic skin reflex of two groups of brain-injured children—a group of mongoloid, and a small group of normal children—was studied. It was found that the group of brain-injured children who were characterized as being hyperactive and/or distractible required a significantly larger number of paired presentations of light and shock to reach the criterion for conditioning than did a group of brain-injured children who were not so characterized. It was found that the group of mongoloid children required a longer conditioning period than did the group of non-hyperactive and/or distractible brain-injured children.

While there was no significant difference in the number of extinction trials required by the groups studied, there were major differences in the extinction process. The most striking difference was that the hyperactive and/or distractible group of brain–injured children gave little evidence of a buildup of internal inhibition and maintained and sometimes increased their activity level as the extinction series wore on. On the other hand, half of the children in both the mongoloid and normal groups demonstrated that internal inhibition was building up by falling asleep at some point during the extinction series.

The results are discussed from the standpoint of conditioned reflex theory and suggest that the population of brain-injured children is not a homogeneous one. The various kinds of behavior displayed by brain-injured children may be understood as the result of disturbances in normal cerebral functioning which modify the effective equilibration of excitation and inhibition.

REFERENCES

1. Birch, H. G. (1956) Problems in the differential diagnosis of mental retardation, in *The Evaluation and Treatment of the Mentally Retarded Child in Clinics*, National Association for Retarded Children, New York, pp. 40–49.
2. Birch, H. G. (1956) Theoretical aspects of psychological behavior in the brain damaged, in *Psychological Services for the Cerebral Palsied*, United Cerebral Palsy Associations, New York, pp. 28–51.
3. Pavlov, I. P. (1927) *Conditioned Reflexes*, Oxford Univ. Press. New York.
4. Strauss, A. A. (1947) *Psychopathology and Education of the Brain-injured Child*, Vol. 1, Grune and Stratton, New York.
5. Strauss, A. A. (1955) *Psychopathology and Education of the Brain-injured Child*, Vol. 2, Grune and Stratton, New York.
6. Strauss, A. A. (1944) Ways of thinking in brain-crippled deficient children, *Am. J. Psychiat.* **100,** pp. 639–47.
7. Strauss, A. A., and Kephart, N. C. (1940) Behavior differences in mentally retarded children measured by a new behavior rating scale, *Am.J. Psychiat.* **19,** pp. 1117–24.
8. Strauss, A. A., and Werner, H. (1942) Disorders of conceptual thinking in the brain-injured child, *J. Nerv. and Ment. Dis.* **96,** pp. 153–72.
9. Strauss, A. A., and Werner, H. (1942) Experimental analysis of the clinical symptom "perseveration" in mentally retarded children, *Am. J. Ment. Deficiency* **47,** pp. 185–88.
10. Werner, H. (1944) Development of visuo-motor performance on the marble-board test in mentally retarded children, *J. Genetic Psychol.* **64,** pp. 269–79.
11. Werner, H. (1946) Abnormal and subnormal rigidity, *J. Abnorm. and Social Psychol.* **41,** pp. 15–24.
12. Werner, H., and Bowers, M. (1941) Auditory-motor organization in two clinical types of mentally deficient children, *J. Genetic Psychol.* **59,** pp. 85 to 99.
13. Werner, H., and Carrison, D. (1944) Animistic thinking in brain-injured, mentally retarded children, *J. Abnorm. and Social Psychol.* **39,** pp. 43–62.

14. WERNER, H., and STRAUSS, A. A. (1940) Causal factors in low performance, *Am. J. Ment. Deficiency* **45,** pp. 213–18.
15. WERNER, H., and STRAUSS, A. A. (1941) Pathology of figure–background relation in the brain-injured child, *J. Abnorm. and Social Psychol.* **36,** pp. 236–48.
16. WERNER, H., and THUMA, B. D. (1942) A deficiency in the perception of apparent motion in children with brain–injury, *Am. J. Psychol.* **55,** pp. 58–67.

14

DIFFERENTIAL DIAGNOSIS BETWEEN PSYCHOGENIC AND PHYSICAL PAIN

THE CONDITIONAL PSYCHOGALVANIC REFLEX AS AN AID†

Leo Alexander

Obervations of skin resistance were made on a test group of twenty patients whose chief complaint was pain and on a contrast group of fourtenn consecutive patients free from pain. The results indicated that in psychgenic pain the spontaneous fluctuations (expressed in ohms per minute) were smaller than the responses to electrical stimulation of a finger (unconditional psychogalvanic reflex) and smaller than the responses to a tone annoucing the electrical stimulus (the conditional psychogalvanic reflex). In physical pain, with demonstradet pathological basis, the spontaneous fluctuatios were greater than the responses tn the electrical stimulus and to the tone annouuncing the stimulus.

THE differential diagnosis between physical and psychogenic pain states is often difficult. This difficulty is essentially due to the fact that these conditions may not be encountered or remain for long in their pure and pristine states. Thus, certain patients actually suffering from physical pain of unidentified causation may in the course of prolonged and inconclusive diagnostic studies develop an overlay of dejection, concern, and preoccupation that may make these patients clinically resemble those suffering from psychogenic pain.

Severe and excruciating physical pain inevitably becomes associated with emotional suffering which in predisposed individuals may evoke regressive emotional disturbances sufficiently severe to mask the entire clinical picture and to simulate mental disturbance. Psychogenic pain, on the other hand, often evokes peripheral, reflex-like reverberations in the target area, which may be so prominent as to suggest that these peripheral effects actually summon the pain or are evidence of psychosomatically induced or primarily physical disease.

† By permission of *American Journal of Psychiatry*, 1943

The erroneous impression of physical illness is especially convincing when the successful displacement and projection of conflict or anguish in the form of pain prevents the overt eruption of anxiety or depression for a long time, thus masking the entire clinical picture as one of physical disease. This is particularly true for somatization reactions in the form of one specific localized pain (psychalgia), which occur not uncommonly as somatic equivalents of depression that often and for long periods may be mistaken for states of physical pain. Thus, we are frequently faced with a clinically vexing picture and often an actual admixture of mental suffering to physical pain and of, physical reverberation to psychogenic pain.

Nevertheless, the clinical diagnostician (and the consulting psychiatrist from whom he requests assistance) is continually faced with the necessity of making a differential diagnosis for cogent reasons, regardless of an overlay of emotional and mental anguish or disturbance. He must find the severe life-threatening illness of which the pain may be the first signal before it is too late to alter the course of the disease; and he must recognize the psychogenic nature of a pain in spite of a contracted neck or a twisted pelvis, in order to be able to rehabilitate the patient.

A test that may be useful as an objective measure or marker in this often difficult task should be able to reflect both the qualitative and quantitative aspects of pain as well as of mental disturbance. Such a test should faithfully record the response of the nervous system to pain signals arising from physical noxious stimulation of peripheral tissues, unobscured by superimposed emotional or mental disturbance, and should reveal the presence of mental disorder, unobscured by the peripheral muscular or circulatory effects of psychogenic pain. The psychogalvanic reflex appears to be adaptable to this task.

The psychogalvanic reflex consists of a sharply defined fall in skin resistance in response to painful stimuli, startling noises, mental challenges (such as mathematical tasks), or acutely disturbing thoughts. This reflex occurs after a latency of $1\frac{1}{2}$–$2\frac{1}{2}$ sec in response to such unconditional stimuli, while the latency of the reflex in response to conditional stimuli is longer (2–3 sec).

In a study of the conditional and unconditional psychogalvanic reflex in patients suffering from a variety of nervous and mental disorders, carried out with the aim of establishing an objective parameter of psychiatric diagnosis, prognosis, and evaluation of treatment effects, [1-4] a number of patients were encountered whose chief complaint was pain. It soon became apparent from our polygraphic recordings that the galvanic skin responses in patients suffering from physical pain were strikingly different from those suffering from psychogenic pain when the spontaneous fluctuations of the skin resistance were compared with the evoked responses, especially the conditional ones [4, 5].

Case Material

The present study is based on twenty consecutive patients whose chief complaint was pain, in whom it has so far been possible to ascertain its nature unequivocally, as either physical or psychogenic (Tables 1 and 2). For the purposes of this study, the two pain states are defined as physical pain—pain that originates in the body of the patient from noxious stimulation of peripheral tissues by disease or injury, with demonstrable pathology, and that is perceived and reacted to by the mind in varying degrees; and psychogenic pain—pain that originates in the mind of the patient from tension or anguish, and that is projected upon a bodily target area, with or without physiologic effects upon the target area.

The physical cause (eight cases, Table 2), was demonstrated in cases 13–19, by operation or biopsy, and by cardiologic study in case 20. The diagnosis of psychogenic pain (twelve cases, Table 1) was regarded as validated when no organic cause was found after appropriate search and sustained relief was afforded by means of psychiatric treatment (cases 1–7 and 9–12; Table 1). In one case of paranoid schizophrenia, the patient's pain was identified as a somatic delusion by prolonged psychiatric observation (case 8).

For purposes of control, a group of fourteen consecutive patients free from pain who showed spontaneous fluctuation of skin resistance were compared with the two pain groups—the psychogenic and the physical.

The entire group of twenty patients had been referred either as depressive or anxiety reactions with somatization in the form of pain, or for the purpose of differential diagnosis between such reactions and a physical illness. It is of interest that in approximately one-half of the group (8 out of 20), a definite physical cause of the pain was found by careful diagnostic search. This is consistent with the general proportion found by others [6] among such diagnostic problems which are a distinct and often difficult diagnostic task of the clinical psychiatrist (Figure 1).

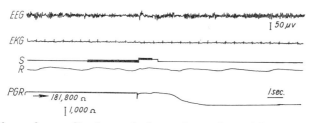

FIG. 1. Polygraph recording in manic-depressive patient with psychalgia (case 2) Channels are EEG, EKG, S (signals); R (respiration); and PGR (psychogalvanic reflex). Reading for skin resistance is shown lower left. Thick line on signal channel marks sounding of tone, elevated thick line, reinforcing shock. Note absence of conditional psychogalvanic reflex to tone and adequate but delayed unconditional response of patient to shock stimulus

TABLE 1. Psychogenic Pain States

Case No.	Sex	Age	Diagnosis	SP	CR−	CR+	Ratio	UR	GTR
1	F	58	Psychalgic reaction (abdominal) with agitated involutional psychotic depression (issue: loss)	550	767	350	0·40	5,500	0
2	F	38	Psychalgic reaction (a typical right facial neuralgia) with psychotic manic-depressive hypochondriac depression	150	17	50	2·94	1,567	50
3	F	75	Psychalgic reaction (cephalgia with bilateral facial pain), with neurotic reactive depression of psychasthenic-anhedonic type (issue: loss)	100	17	808	47·53	9,227	317
4	M	48	Psychalgic reaction (abdominal, left-sided) with neurotic psychasthenic-anhedonic depression (issue: power)	293	242	742	3·07	1,825	25
5	F	55	Psychalgic reaction (a typical facial neuralgia) with neurotic hypochondriac depressive reaction (issue: loss)	1,606	5,000	9,042	1·81	5,729	333
6	F	36	Psychalgic reaction (pseudoanginal chest pain) with neurotic hypochondriac depression (issue: loss and guilt)	128	317	1,262	3·90	2,395	0
7	F	62	Psychalgic reaction (headaches occipital, radiating down left side of body and extremities), with depressive reaction, involutional, psychotic borderline, of psychasthenic-anhedonic type (issue: loss)	0	562	2,568	4·57	12,500	41
8	M	34	Psychalgic reaction (facial and occipital myalgia, right) with paranoid schizophrenia	0	2,333	6,495	2·80	6,272	812

Case No.	Sex	Age	Diagnosis	SP	CR−	CR+	Ratio	UR	GTR
9	F	62	Psychalgic reaction (cephalgia with aural and facial neuralgia, bilateral), with anxiety tension reaction, involutional, neurotic	1,944	4,364	13,167	3·02	10,813	182
10	F	50	Psychalgic reaction (back pain, at cervico-dorsal junction, radiating into left extremities), with anxiety-hysteric reaction, neurotic	1,944	5,729	8,562	1·49	4,817	427
11	M	43	Psychalgic reaction (cephalgia, right-sided), with anxiety tension reaction, chronic, neurotic	8,500	12,955	15,636	1·21	3,500	1·125
12	M	43	Psychalgic reaction (right upper chest pain), with anxiety reaction with depressive features (issue: loss)	500	1,145	1,750	1·50	9,062	62

Abbreviations used in this and following tables and figures:

SP = Average spontaneous fluctuations of skin resistance per minute, in ohms,

CR − = Average psychogalvanic reflex response to inhibitory (nonreinforced) tone, in ohms.

CR + = Average psychogalvanic reflex response to excitatory (reinforced) tone, in ohms.

Ratio = Average response to CR+ divided by average response to CR− differential ratio between psychogalvanic responses to excitatory and inhibitory signals

UR = Average response to unconditional stimulus (electric shock to finger), in ohms

CTR = Average generalized time reflex to fifth second of inhibitory tone, in ohms.

TABLE 2. PHYSICAL PAIN STATES

Case No.	Sex	Age	Diagnosis	SP	CR−	CR+	Ratio	UR	GTR
13	F	53	Adenocarcinoma of pancreas	11,097	4,150	3,500	0·84	6,200	100
14	F	39	Endometriosis	10,300	1,042	2,000	1·92	7,625	807
15	F	64	Cervical arthritis with root sleeve fibrosis, C7—T1, left	8,500	2,908	4,500	1·60	2,340	1,827
16	F	29	Salpingitis, acute, left	8,600	1,550	5,900	3·81	4,300	700
17	F	46	Vasculitis, left leg	4,027	288	741	2·60	4,108	108
18	M	54	Hygroma, subdural, left frontal	1,338	45	641	14·20	3,800	16
19	F	52	Volvulus	5,222	1,687	2,458	1·40	5,520	291
20	F	81	Angina pectoris	1,572	336	177	0·52	631	281

Method

The method of the test is the Pavlovian conditional reflex technique used in Dr. W. Horsley Gantt's laboratory [7, 8] with his method of spacing and alternation of differential stimuli. The stimuli and the responses, as well as any responses occurring during the intervals between stimuli, were recorded continuously on a five–channel polygraph. [1] For the purposes of quantitative study, only the psychogalvanic responses were utilized because they could be easily and accurately measured and, hence, readily be subjected to quantitative analysis.

After the orienting responses were abolished, a conditional reflex was established according to the classical Pavlovian method by pairing one of two tones with an electric shock to the tip of a finger during the fifth second the tone was sounded, while another tone, which was never so reinforced, was presented in regular alternation with the reinforced tone at 1-min intervals. The reinforced (excitatory) tone was one of 512 c/s, while the non-reinforced (inhibitory) tone was one of 256 c/s. The reinforcing electric shock was selected by the patient according to his tolerance limit, varying from 0.7 to 2.5 mA, average 1.5 mA.

Whenever an evoked psychogalvanic reflex response occurred, it was sharply defined and came within about 1.5–2.5 sec after the beginning of the unconditional stimuli and within 2–3 sec after the onset of the conditional stimuli. It consisted of an easily distinguishable drop in skin resistance, measured in ohms. Thus, the reaction to the excitatory tone and its overlapping shock stimulus consisted usually of two deflections: the first to the tone, classified as the excitatory or positive conditional response (CR+); the other to the shock, classified as the unconditional response (UR). The response to the never-reinforced, that is the inhibitory tone, was called the inhibitory conditional response (CR—). In cases of perfect differentiation, such a response was absent and counted as zero. When response to the inhibitory tone occurred, this was usually a response to the on–effect, that is, to the first second of the sounding of the tone, appearing about 2 sec after the start of the sounding of the tone, classified as CR—. This was sometimes followed by an additional response to the fifth second after termination of the tone, and was classified as a generalized time reflex (GTR), since it was obviously a generalization effect by means of a time reflex patterned after the excitatory tone and its overlapping unconditional stimulus [1-4].

These four psychogalvanic reflex responses (CR—, CR+, UR, GTR) were measured as ohms drop in skin resistance for each pair of presentations of the stimuli in all patients. Averages for the responses in each of the four categories were calculated in ohms for each conditioning session, which uniformly consisted of 12 pairs of presentations. Conditionability, that is, the capacity to differentiate between the excitatory and the inhibitory signals, was calculated by dividing the average response to the excitatory tone (CR+) by the average responses to the inhibitory tone (CR—), and termed differentiation ratio. All spontaneous fluctuations of the skin resistance were measured in ohms during the intervals between the stimuli, beginning 5 sec after and ending 5 sec before each stimulus. Thus, any confusion of spontaneous responses with time reflexes was avoided. The spontaneous fluctuations were calculated in ohms per minute for the entire period of observation, comprising usually 18 min of interval time between stimuli which, as defined above, consisted of the presentation of twenty-four signals (twelve pairs of presentations) for each conditioning session (Figure 2).

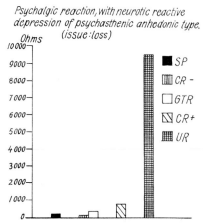

Fig. 2. Galvanic skin responses measured during pretreatment conditioning session (case 3). Note low spontaneous and conditional responses, but with CR+ greater than SP, CR—, and GTR; and adequate unconditional response (UR)

Results

Of the twelve patients suffering from psychogenic pain states, seven were psychalgic states incidental to depressive illnesses. Six of them achieved complete or social recovery, either after electro-convulsive treatment (case 1), or after drug therapy and psychotherapy (cases 3–7). One achieved marked improvement close to social recovery (case 2) by means of the latter form of treatment. Case 8, the schizophrenic patient in the group, did not recover after a brief period of drug therapy. Four patients suffered from psychalgic states incidental to anxiety reactions. Cases 9, 10, and 12 achieved complete or social recovery by means of psychotherapy added by drug therapy, while case 11 achieved improvement close to social recovery in the course of such therapy.

In five of the seven patients with depressive psychalgic states, the conditional response pattern was inhibitory, in that the positive conditional psychogalvanic reflex (CR+) measured less than 2000 ohms (Table 1), such as is characteristic of depressive states in general. [1, 4, 5, 9] In patients who showed such profound inhibition as in case 2, for example, the excitatory signal often evoked no response (Figure 1). This finding was representative of the responses to seven of the twelve excitatory signals administered, while only a small response of 100 ohms each was obtained to four of the twelve signals, and one of 200 ohms to one signal. The spontaneous fluctuations were of a similar low order in these cases (Table 1 and Figures 2). In one patient (case 7), the positive conditional psychogalvanic reflex fell into the average range; in case 5, into the excitatory range; the spontaneous fluctuations in case 5 were comparatively low (Table 1), in case 7, they were absent (Table 1).

Of the four psychalgic states secondary to anxiety reactions, including anxiety hysteria, three were characterized by markedly enhanced conditional PGR responses (Table 1, cases 9–11), and one of them (in whom depressive features were quite prominent) by inhibitory responses (case 12). In all of them the conditional PGR responses greatly exceeded the spontaneous fluctuations of skin resistance (Table 1 and Figure 3), as in anxiety states without pain.

In psychogenic pain states, the spontaneous fluctuations of the skin resistance fell into a category similar to or below the amplitude of the conditional responses and were generally very much below the level of the uncon-

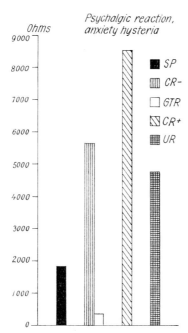

FIG. 3. Barograph that illustrates galvanic skin responses measured during pretreatment conditioning session (case 10). All evoked responses, especially CR+, greatly exceed spontaneous fluctuations per minute

ditional responses. The sole exception in this latter respect is case 11, in which the unconditional responses (averaging 3500 ohms) have not been accurately measurable because of the shift in the baseline engendered by the preceding high positive conditional responses that averaged 15,636 ohms.

Patients who suffered from physical pain showed marked spontaneous fluctuations of skin resistance that corresponded to the waxing and waning of the physical pain (Figure 4), while the responses to the positive conditional stimuli remained uninhibited (Figure 5). A particularly severe wave

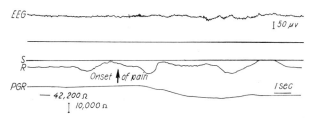

Fig. 4. Adenocarcinoma of the pancreas, with abdominal pain (case 13). Note spontaneous fluctuation of skin resistance (PGR) that correspond to the waxing and waning of patient's physical pain

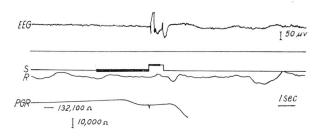

Fig. 5. Same patient as Fig. 4. Second presentation of the reinforced tone. Note good conditional PGR response (9,000 ohms) to tone 2 sec after onset of tone and prompt and marked unconditional PGR response (in excess of 25,000 ohms) to shock beginning 1·8 sec after onset. Note responses to conditional stimuli

of pain was occasionally accompanied and followed by temporary inhibition of the next two or three pairs of conditional responses, after which conditional responses were resumed. In fact, the pain seemed, at times, to improve responses to the conditional signals, probably because it produced an excitatory state that irradiated and thus facilitated conditional responsiveness. This may account for the fact that of the eight cases in this group (Table 2), five fell into the average or excitatory response groups, with the positive conditional reflex averaging 2000–4000 ohms or more respectively, while only three showed inhibitory response patterns, with the CR+ averaging less than 2000 ohms.[3]

In spite of the fact that in the majority of the patients in this group the positive conditional psychogalvanic responses fell into the average of excitatory group, in all of the patients suffering from physical pain states, the average spontaneous fluctuations per minute greatly exceeded the conditional responses, being of an order similar to or greater than the unconditional responses (Table 2, and Figure 6).

Statistical Comparison of Psychogalvanic Responses

In the psychogenic pain group, the average unconditional response exceeded the spontaneous fluctuations per minute in eleven of the twelve cases (Table 3), and the average positive conditional reflex exceeded the spontaneous fluctuation in ten of the twelve cases (Table 4). By contrast, in the patients suffering from physical pain, the spontaneous fluctuations per minute exceeded the average positive conditional reflex in all eight cases (Table 4), and exceeded the average unconditional response in five of the eight cases (Table 3).

TABLE 3. COMPARISON IN PHYSICAL AND PSYCHOGENIC PAIN OF SPONTANEOUS FLUCTUATIONS OF SKIN RESISTANCE PER MINUTE (SP) WITH AVERAGE UNCONDITIONAL EVOKED RESPONSES (UR)

Types	SP > UR	SP < UR	Total
Physical Pain	5	3	8
Psychogenic Pain	1	11	12
χ^2 (with Yates' correction) = 4·37)		$P < 0.05$	

TABLE 4. COMPARISON IN PHYSICAL AND PSYCHOGENIC PAIN OF SPONTANEOUS FLUCTUATIONS OF SKIN RESISTANCE PER MINUTE (SP) WITH AVERAGE PSYCHOGALVANIC REFLEX RESPONSES TO EXCITATORY TONE (CR+)

Types	SP > CR+	SP < CR+	Total
Physical Pain	8	0	8
Psychogenic Pain	2	10	12
χ^2 (with Yates' correction) = 10·2		$P < 0.01$	

Comparison of the spontaneous fluctuations per minute with the unconditional response differentiated between the physical and the psychogenic pain group at better than the 0·05 level of significance (Table 3), while comparison of the spontaneous fluctuations per minute with the positive conditional reflex differentiated between the physical and psychogenic pain groups at better than the 0·01 level of significance (Table 4).

Another differentiation between the 2 groups may be noted by comparing the amount of spontaneous fluctuations per minute in the two groups. The median for the psychogenic group (Table 1) is between 500 and 550 ohms, while that for the organic pain group is between 5200 and 8500 ohms (Table 2). This difference is significant at better than the 0.01 level by Mann-Whitney U test (U = 10·5).

For comparison with the two pain groups, fourteen consecutive patients who did not complain of pain, but who showed spontaneous fluctuations of the skin resistance, were selected at random (Table 5 and Figure 6). In some

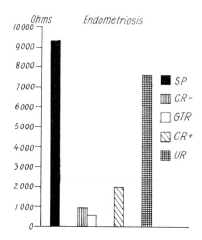

FIG. 6. Galvanic skin responses during conditioning session at diagnostic intake (case 14). Note spontaneous fluctuations (SP) of the skin resistance per minute greatly exceed evoked conditional responses (CR—, GTR, CR+) and are similar in magnitude to but slightly greater than the unconditional response (UR) evoked by electric shock to the index finger

of these cases, the patients related these fluctuations to disturbing thoughts, for example, an obsessive patient who had a buying compulsion (case 21) became disturbed by the thought that the store might be closed, while the patient suffering from a schizo-affective reaction wanted to ruin the test to prove the doctor wrong, by thinking of incidents of humiliation (case 22). The median for spontaneous fluctuations per minute in this group (Table 5) was between 900 and 1200 ohms. This measure did not differ from the psychogenic pain group (U = 55·5; P > 0·05), but was significantly different from the organic pain group (U = 10; P < 0·01).

Comment

In states of physical pain, the spontaneous fluctuations of the skin resistance per minute exceeded the evoked conditional response and were of an order similar to or greater than the unconditional responses. This suggests

TABLE 5. SPONTANEOUS FLUCTUATIONS OF SKIN RESISTANCE IN PATIENTS NOT COMPLAINING OF PAIN

Case No.	Sex	Age	Diagnosis	SP	CR−	CR+	Ratio	UR	GTR
21	F	36	Psychoneurosis, obsessive-compulsive reaction, chronic, severe	763	1,937	1,416	0·70	8,812	1,437
22	M	21	Schizo-affective reaction with depressive features	2,222	770	541	0·70	5,354	479
23	F	49	Schizophrenia, paranoid, with depressive features	2,222	308	541	1·75	2,133	100
24	M	25	Schizophrenic reaction, catatonic	1,233	283	112	0·30	1,983	291
25	M	29	Undiagnosed neurological syndrome with cerebral dysrhythmia and super-imposed anxiety reaction						
26	M	47	Depressive reaction, psychotic, involutional, with reactive triggering (issue: guilt)	761	137	208	1·50	737	179
27	M	36	Depressive reaction, with anxiety, neurotic (issue: loss, uprooting)	194	50	50	1·00	754	0
28	M	62	Depressive reaction, neurotic (issue: loss)	500	629	545	0·80	2,220	125
29	F	31	Depressive reaction with anxiety, neurotic, chronic, psychasthenic-anhedonic (issue: power, envy)	1,433	1,000	1,083	1·08	1,383	445
30	M	33	Depressive reaction, neurotic, psychasthenic-anhedonic (issue: power)	833	3,458	4,666	1·30	4,479	646
31	F	18	Schizo-affective reaction with depressive and hysterical features	1,666	1,750	1,937	1·10	4,604	791
32	M	21	Schizo-affective reaction with depressive features	916	2,375	8,333	3·51	12,607	125
33	F	60	Malignant melanoma, metastatic to liver. Symptomatic depressive reaction	367	1,300	1,171	0·90	8,538	75
34	F	26	Schizophrenic reaction, paranoid. History of spastic colitis, and of right ovarian cystectomy	1,431	1,855	1,745	0·94	5,545	109
				2,500	2,900	3,400	1·17	4,500	1,000

that physical pain impinges upon the nervous system in a manner comparable to that of any other external or unconditional stimulus.

In states of psychogenic pain, the spontaneous fluctuations of the skin resistance per minute were almost always much smaller than the evoked unconditional responses and were of an order smaller than or similar to that of the conditional responses. Furthermore, in psychogenic pain, the spontaneous fluctuations of the skin resistance per minute resembled the responses to the inhibitory signals more than those to the excitatory signals. This suggests that psychogenic pain may represent a conditional state of the nervous system, and that, like depression itself, it may represent an inhibitory state. The low rate of spontaneous fluctuations in these cases, as well as the low level of the evoked conditional responses, also suggest a provocative relationship between depressive psychalgic states and Yoga trance states. In the latter, the spontaneous and evoked psychogalvanic responses have also been found to be greatly reduced. [10]

An alternative explanation may be that physical pain states tend to be intermittent and varying, hence evoking apparently spontaneous psychogalvanic responses, while psychogenic pain states tend to be continuous and unvarying, [11] hence evoking less frequent and less marked psychogalvanic responses.

A surprising finding was that headaches with occipital myalgia (cases 7 and 8), or atypical facial neuralgia (case 9), in which peripheral physiologic effects in the form of muscle contractions are not only associated with, but also have been thought to cause the pain, did not differ from purely psychogenic pain by our test procedure. Both purely psychogenic pain and psychogenic pain with peripheral effects gave distinctly different test findings from physical pain with demonstrated pathology. This may be due to one of several reasons:

(1) That the muscular contractions of the neck and scalp muscles do not actually cause the pain.

(2) That since these muscular contractions are initiated by the nervous system, they lack the startling and alerting quality necessary to elicit a psychogalvanic reflex response, in contrast to pain arising from noxious stimulation of peripheral tissues, which, impinging upon the nervous system *de novo*, exerts such a startling and alerting effect.

(3) That physical pain, tending to be intermittent and varying, evokes frequent and distinct psychogalvanic reflex responses with each crescendo, while psychogenic pain, tending to be constant and unvarying, lacks the capacity of evoking comparable psychogalvanic reflex responses. This explanation is in line with the views of White and Sweet. [11]

Summary

The comparison of the spontaneous fluctuations of the skin resistance per minute with the conditional and unconditional evoked responses, especially with the positive conditional psychogalvanic reflex, offers a helpful test for the often difficult differential diagnosis between physical and psychogenic pain states. This test, like any other test, is not intended to replace a thorough clinical examination and good clinical judgement, but merely to supplement them and to be useful as a helpful marker on the road to diagnosis. It is hoped that the test described will be useful to clinicians in pointing the diagnostic search in the right direction.

REFERENCES

1. ALEXANDER, L. (1958) Apparatus and method for study of conditional reflexes in man. Preliminary results in normal control subjects, in mental disorders and as result of drug action, *Arch. Neurol.* **80,** pp. 629–49.
2. ALEXANDER, L. (1959) Objective approach to psychiatric diagnosis and evaluation of drug effects by means of conditional reflex technic, in *Biological Psychiatry* (ed. J. G. Masserman), New York, Grune and Stratton, pp. 154–81.
3. ALEXANDER, L., and HORNER, S. R. (1961) Effect of drugs on conditional psychogalvanic reflex in man, *J. Neuropsychiat.* **2,** pp. 246–61.
4. ALEXANDER, L. (1961) Effects of psychotropic drugs on conditional responses in man, *Neuro-Psychopharmacology*, Vol. 2, Amsterdam, Elsevier, pp. 93 to 122.
5. ALEXANDER, L. (1960) New diagnostic and therapeutic aspects of depression, in Rogers, D. M. (ed.): *Depression and Antidepressant drugs* (ed. D. M. Rogers), Waltham, Mass., Metropolitan State Hospital, Division of Massachusetts Department of Mental Health, pp. 23–33.
6. WRETMARK, G. (1961) Personal communication to the author.
7. GANTT, W. H. (1952) Conditional Reflex Function as Aid in Study of Psychiatric Patient, in: *Relation of Psychological Tests to Psychiatry*, eds. P. H. Hoch and J. Zubin, New York, Grune and Stratton, pp. 165–88.
8. GANTT, W. H. (ed.) (1958) *Physiological Bases of Psychiatry*, Springfield, Ill., Charles C. Thomas, pp. 1–344.
9. ALEXANDER, L. (1961) Objective evaluation of anti-depressant therapy by conditional reflex technique, *Dis. Nerv. Syst.* **22,** (Sec. 2, Suppl.) pp. 14–22.
10. BAGCHI, B. K., and WENGER. M. A. (1957) *Electro-physiological Correlates of Some Yogi Exercises*, First International Congress of Neurological Sciences, Brussels, July 21–28, 1957. London, Pergamon Press, Vol. 3, pp. 132–49.
11. WHITE, J. C., and SWEET, W. H. (1955) *Pain: Its Mechanisms and Neurosurgical Control*, Springfield, Ill., Charles C. Thomas, pp. 1–736.

15

CHARACTERISTICS OF THE BEHAVIOR OF CHRONIC PSYCHOTICS AS REVEALED BY FREE-OPERANT CONDITIONING METHODS

O. R. Lindsley

During the last 60 years experimental psychology has made great progress in objective behavioral measurement. The most sensitive, objective, and sophisticated of these methodological developments are those of B. F. Skinner and his associates. [3, 12, 15] These methods are generally described under the term "free-operant conditioning". The purpose of this research is to attempt to modify and make clinically relevant the methods of free-operant conditioning in order to produce medically useful, objective laboratory measures of the psychoses.

Behavioristic Approach to Psychosis

The general approach to the analysis of psychosis that we are using is behavioristic. Naturalistic or behavioristic approaches to mental illness are rare in psychiatry today, even though the word "behavioral" occurs in many titles and programs. The behaviorist uses behavior as the final criterion of behavior and does not resort to mentalism or physiologism as his final criterion of knowledge or relevance.

At earlier times naturalistic approaches [2] were briefly tried by men like Kraepelin, [5] Pavlov, [10] and even earlier by our own Benjamin Rush. [11] It is my conviction that early attempts at a behavioristic approach to psychiatry suffered from a lack of popular appeal and sound laboratory techniques of behavioral measurement. I am also convinced that today, even though the approach still suffers from popular appeal, methods which demonstrate its superiority over introspective approaches are available.

Skinner [13, 14] and Ferster [4] have discussed some of the implications of a behavioral approach to psychiatric problems. However, without objective data such discussions are at best scientific extrapolations, plans, or philosophies. The proof of the pudding is not the logical nature of the plans, but the knowledge and control of behavioral deviation produced by research based upon such plans.

To a behaviorist a psychotic is a person in a mental hospital. If psychosis is what makes, or has made this person psychotic, then psychosis is the behavioral deviation that caused this person to be hospitalized, or that is keeping him hospitalized. Looked at from this point of view, very few psychotics are at this moment behaving psychotically. Neither is there any assurance that they will behave psychotically when we wish to evaluate or to sample their behavior in a brief test conducted at irregular intervals. In fact psychosis, defined in terms of the behavior that hospitalizes a person, is most often highly infrequent.

Most patients are hospitalized because the time of occurrence of their infrequent psychotic episodes cannot be predicted. Since the occurrence of these episodes cannot be predicted, the patient must be continuously hospitalized to insure that such episodes do not occur outside of the hospital. Also, many currently hospitalized patients behave psychotically only when they go home. Even though relatively normal in the hospital, they continue to be hospitalized because there is no safe place to send them. There are other patients who once behaved psychotically, but have become institutionalized and do not wish to leave the hospital, and still others who have no home to return to. For these reasons we should not expect all the patients in a mental hospital to exhibit psychotic behavior at any given moment.

Therefore, a few patients should behave relatively normally on all behavioral tasks. In fact, any behavioral measure that clearly separates all hospitalized psychotics from all unhospitalized individuals is merely a correlate of hospitalization and no better a measure of psychosis than the absence of hospital keys, neckties, or some other side effect of the way we care for psychotics.

If we wish to maximize our chances of measuring psychosis, we should evaluate the behavior of patients at the time they are actually doing what they are hospitalized for occasionally doing. This means that we should study our patients long enough to capture a psychotic episode in one of our experimental observation sessions. For, at that moment we would be surely measuring the behavior of a psychotic at the time he is behaving psychotically. This demands that our experimental rooms and recording devices must be indestructible, so that they will not be rendered inoperative by the bizarre behavior of any patient when he has a psychotic episode. Very few of the previously used measurement devices are capable of measuring the behavior of patients while they are behaving maximally psychotic. In this sense the earlier devices are extremely limited.

Selection of Patients and Habitat

If we wish to investigate a new phenomenon we should select the idear conditions for observing it. We should maximize its amplitude and frequency of occurrence and minimize any changes in these properties, whether spontaneous or caused by agents other than those we can manipulate for investigational purposes. This means that the acutely ill psychotic is a poor research risk. For there is a high probability that his psychosis will change in degree or type while we are endeavoring to analyze it. Also, the natural habitat of the acute psychotic is a dynamic environment in which therapy is maximized and research design usually destroyed. The admissions unit is a model of confounded rather than isolated and controlled behavioral variables.

However, the chronic psychotic has a maximized form of psychosis and the lowest probability of spontaneously changing during the course of study. Also, the chronic psychotic's natural habitat (the back wards of large state hospitals), although far from the research ideal of full experimental control, more closely approximates this research ideal of full control than does an admissions ward. Moving chronic patients to admissions units or research wards, takes them from their natural habitat which reduces the probability that their psychosis will remain stable, and places them in an environment full of uncontrolled behavioral variables.

Therefore, in order to maximize our phenomenon and its stability we selected a group of approximately fifty chronic psychotics for intensive investigation, who would continue to live on the back wards in their natural habitat. They were hospitalized a median of 18 years, insuring that their behavioral deviations were maximum and stable. Males were selected to eliminate any behavioral fluctuations that might be correlated with menstrual cycles. Patients were selected independently of psychiatric diagnosis in order to eliminate any theoretical bias, and to approach our subject matter with a maximized degree of freedom, limited only by our methods of observation and creative ability in adopting the methods to the measurement of clinically relevant behaviors. The clinical relevance was sought in clinical practice and experience, rather than in formal theory or diagnosis.

Research Design

The research design is frankly Darwinian rather than Newtonian. It is our feeling that there is not enough experimental data on the behavior of psychotics in finely controlled situations to draw exact and meaningful generalizations at this time. Since the behavioral properties of psychosis are highly individual, each experiment must be conducted in such a fashion that each patient serves as his own control. We must not have to resort to the behavior of any other individual in order to determine the significance of the effects of any agent upon the behavior of our experimental subject.

The experimental observations are conducted in continuous experimental sessions of one or more hours duration each week-day, until we have exhausted our ability to obtain further important experimental information concerning the behavioral abilities and symptoms in a given patient. Although psychosis is clinically known as an oscillating, dynamic process, and patients are clinically known to be timid, afraid and nervous in novel situations, the majority of previous experimental studies of psychosis have investigated psychotics in novel situations. It is important to remember that we often evaluate a psychotic in 15 min, a secretary in 1 month, and an executive in one year. It seems to me that we might do better by reversing this order—at least until we develop reliable and exact methods of evaluation.

In our own research, we have found that the behavior of many psychotics is modifiable by manipulating properties of the immediate physical environment. However, their behavior is so slowly modified that experimental manipulation and observation must be continued over a period of years in order to disclose such slowly developing laws of psychotic behavior. Shorter periods of observation would show no lawful modification in the patient's behavior, and lead us to conclude that it was not modifiable, and the law of psychotic behavior would remain hidden.

Intensive investigation of single psychotics is the only way that a number of different behavioral deficits may be catalogued with respect to individual psychotics in attempts to locate and define syndromes of behavioral deficits which could define sub-types of psychosis.

Then again the currently used therapeutic variables (tranquilizing drugs, insulin, and psychotherapy), appear to take weeks, months, and even years to reach their maximum effect. Experiments must be conducted over a period of years in order to provide a continuous measure of the effects of such variables on the behavior of individual patients. This intensive and continuous study of single individuals also permits a comparison of the effects of several different therapeutic agents upon the same individual as the experimental case history grows. I know of no other way adequately to control for placebo effects without confounding the results with individual variability in reaction.

Apparatus and Techniques

The theoretical and historical background and the modifications of the method of free-operant conditioning for use with chronic psychotics, including its advantages and disadvantages have been discussed elsewhere. [6, 16] In brief, a volunteer patient is conducted, or conditioned to approach a small 6-foot square experimental room. In this room is only a chair and a manipulandum panel on one wall. On the panel is a plunger that can be pulled and a small aperture through which small objects can be automatically presented. Such a controlled environment can be used to measure the simplest operant or "volitional" behavior known—pulling a plunger for an unconditioned reinforcement or reward.

However, by manipulating the objects or events used as reinforcers, a wide variety of different motivations or "interests" can be studied. By manipulating the contingencies of these reinforcers upon the plunger-pulling responses, a wide variety of discriminations and other behavioral processes can be studied. For example, with such a simple experimental environment, motivations ranging from food to social altruism, and discriminations ranging from simple visual to time estimation and complicated concept formation can be studied.[8]

By permitting visual communication between such rooms, social interaction from the most primitive facilitation and imitation to complicated leader-follower relationships in cooperation and competition teams can be controlled and objectively measured. [1]

By changing the form of the manipulandum or plunger, a wide variety of different response topographies ranging from simple manual to complex vocal responses can be studied. If the manipulandum is carefully designed, peripheral response properties (fatigue, frequency limitation, etc.) can be overcome and will not confound the interpretation of the data.

By making intelligent and creative changes of the types described above, and making these one at a time so that variables are not confounded, the method of free-operant conditioning can be modified to the objective and exact measurement of behaviors as clinically relevant as vocal hallucinatory symptoms in chronic psychotics.

Behavioral Records

Since the response recorded by the operation of the manipulandum is free to occur at any moment during the experimental session, maximum information is obtained if responses are recorded as they occur in time. Graphs of the distribution of the responses in time are automatically made on cumulative response recorders. The operation of such a recorder is schematically shown in Figure 1. The paper is driven under the pen at a constant rate. The pen makes one small movement up the paper when each response is made. In this way a graph of cumulated responses plotted against time is automatically produced. The slope of the pen tracing gives an index of the rate

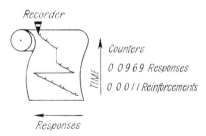

FIG. 1. Schematic diagram of operation of a cumulative response recorder. Described in text

of response. If the slope is almost vertical, the rate is high and even. If the slope is horizontal, no responses were made. Events, such as the presentation of reinforcements can be marked on the record by a downward deflection of the pen. After 500 responses have been made, the pen is automatically reset from the top to the bottom of the paper where it is ready to draw another segment of a cumulative response record.

Clinical records of the patient's behavior on the wards and in psychiatric and psychological evaluations are periodically made in the usual manner. Also the patients can be observed within the experimental rooms through a hidden periscopic system.

Important changes in their symptoms and other demeanor are written down and used for correlation with the operant response records. The non-operant records are useful in making plans for developing new manipulanda to bring clinically relevant response topographies out on an electrical switch for automatic recording and programming. The non-operant records are also useful for correlation with the operant records in demonstrations of the validity and meaning of the operant data.

Characteristics of the Operant Behavior of Chronics Psychotic

The first and most striking characteristic of the free-operant behavior of chronic psychotics is the extreme degree of behavioral debilitation found in the majority of patients. For example, approximately 90 per cent of the patients are unable to respond normally in the simple situation described above. Also surprising is the unpredictability of the patients' operant ability from observations of the patient's ward behavior and general appearance. Remember, that we are talking here of dynamic behavioral ability—the ability to develop and to maintain new behavioral repertoires, as distinguished from the behavioral repertoire that a patient may have acquired before he became ill.

For example, patient No. 48 has a much greater current behavioral repertoire, but much lower current behavioral modifiability than patient No. 46. The first patient was an acute depressive and now is a chronic schizophrenic with an operant response rate (candy reinforcement on a 1'VI schedule) of zero responses per hour. The second patient has always been a psychotic idiot, but he now has an operant response rate of over 1000 responses per hour and he can form primitive counting discriminations. Both patients are currently untestable by psychometric procedures.

I. Low, Erratic Operant Response Rates

Normal humans and lower organisms respond at moderately high (above 800 responses per hour) and remarkably even rates of response on variable-

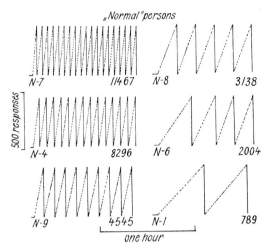

FIG. 2. Cumulative response records for six unhospitalized normal adults, responding on a 1-min variable-interval schedule of intermittent reinforcement with 5-cent coins. Each record is of the fifth hour of responding on this schedule. Under each record is printed the number of the subject on the left, and on the right the number of responses made during the hour

interval schedules of reinforcement. Figure 2 shows six records of normal humans respondig on that schedule for 5-cent coins as reinforcers. Note that although reliable individual differences in rate response exist, all the rates are above 800 responses per hour and are relatively even. These reliable individual differences in rate response have not been extensively studied, and could probably be related to personality differences in preferences for certain work tempos. Perhaps they might even be related to accident proneness, with the high rate person going through doors before he opened them, and the low rate person going through doors after he had closed them.

Figure 3 shows six records of chronic psychotics responding on the variable-interval schedule for candy reinforcement. Note that the majority of the patients respond intermittently. Approximately 50 per cent of those patients with a normally high number of responses per hour show an abnormally high number of pauses in responding greater than 10 sec. During these pauses patients that have readily observable psychotic symptoms can be observed displaying these symptoms.

Summarizing the debilities in simple operant responding on a one-minute variable interval schedule of intermittent reinforcement with candy, we find that only 20 per cent of our unselected group of fifty chronic psychotics are capable of responding at the normal rates above 800 responses per hour; 50 per cent of these, or only 10 per cent of the total group of patients responded at normally high and even rates of response, with no pauses in their responding greater than 10 sec in duration.

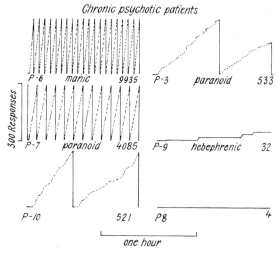

FIG. 3. Cumulative response records for six hospitalized adult chronic psychotics, responding on a 1-min variable-interval schedule of intermittent reinforcement for small assorted pieces of candy. Each record is of the fifth hour of responding on this schedule. Under each record is printed the number of each patient to the left, the most recent psychiatric diagnosis, and to the right the number of responses made during the hour

II. Psychotic Incidents

We have termed these small pauses in responding on a schedule of reinforcement which produces even responding in normals, "psychotic incidents." They have been successfully quantified by using, (1) automatic counters which record the total number of inter-response times greater than 10 sec that occur in each experimental session, and (2) automatic time indicators which record the total amount of time spent in interresponse times greater than 10 sec. These two quantities give a record of the number and total duration of psychotic incidents within a given experimental session. The average duration can be computed from the two. These measures correlate highly with clinical measures of ward behavior, and ward assignment, and with the ability to work in hospital industry. [9] However, they do not correlate with psychiatric diagnosis nor with years of hospitalization. Therefore they indicate the general degree of psychosis or psychotic debilitation rather than the presence of a particular form of psychosis from which a given patient suffers. In other words, these measures have the disadvantage of being non-specific measures of the different types of psychosis, but the distinct advantage of permitting a direct comparison of the effects of a given therapy on the severity of psychosis in several different patients with different types of psychosis. Therefore, the measures are useful in the evaluation of therapies on patients with different types of psychosis, once non-psychotic causes of intermittent responding have been ruled out.

Since low, erratic rates of response on variable-interval schedules occur in non-psychotic individuals under certain unusual conditions, erratic response rates do not indicate psychosis unless these other potential causes are ruled out. Low, erratic response rates occur in normal individuals when: (1) inappropriate reinforcement is used, (2) before the response is fully acquired and the experimental situation is still novel, (3) when a competing response system is present, and (4) in acute physiological illness or under the action of certain drugs. These are a difficult, but not impossible, set of variables to rule out in order to make our measures specific to the psychoses.

In order to further investigate and to rule out the *possibility of inappropriate reinforcement*, several different reinforcing stimuli were tried with a large number of patients. [7] Reinforcers used were: money, food, candy, cigarettes, male and female nude pictures, bursts of music, tokens, escape from loud noise, and escape from a dark room. Although significant differences in rate of response for these different reinforcers were found in most of the patients, no patient was restored to a normal rate of responding by any of these reinforcers. The different reinforcers could be used to develop motivation profiles for diagnostic use, but were not useful on providing high, even rates of response for the maintenance of behavior for further investigation. Therefore, the low rates of response did not appear to be due to inappropriate reinforcement.

To investigate the *possibility of slow acquisition* causing the low, erratic rates of response, patients with extremely low rates were held on the variable–interval schedule with candy reinforcement for over a year of one hour experimental sessions each week-day. Only three of these patients (approximately 10 per cent) showed a gradual increase in rate of response. The experimental history of one of these patients is shown in Figure 4. Responses per hour are plotted in thousands (10–day medians) against experimental sessions on the abscissa. The rate of response gradually increases from less than 10 responses per hour to over 6000 responses per hour in 260 hr, or 14 months. When the response was no longer reinforced (extinguished), it slowly declined in rate to less than ten responses per hour within 140 experimental hours, or 8 months of calendar time. This decrease in rate during extinction shows that the rate increase during reinforcement was produced and maintained by the candy reinforcement, and not by the patient's activation, visits to the laboratory, or personal attention in the waiting room and during the daily physical examination. When the responses were again reinforced, the rate immediately increased to over 4000 responses per hour. This immediate re-acquisistion showed that a permanent change had been made in the patient's behavior, and that he did not have to go through another long drawn-out re–acquisition process.

However, the patients that showed this slow acquisition did not develop completely normal rates of response. Even though their rates of response were well above the lowest normal rate of 800 responses per hour, their

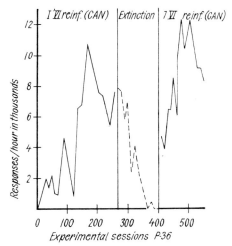

FIG. 4. Slow acquisition, slow extinction, and immediate re–acquisition of a high rate of plunger-pulling reinforced with candy on a 1'VI schedule in a chronic psychotic. Patient No. 36

responding was still erratic with an abnormally high number of pauses greater than 10 sec in duration. These three patients differed from the majority of the patients that did not show acquisition because the manual plunger-pulling response mechanically competed with their psychotic symptoms which were primarily manual in nature. These data suggest, that slow acquisition of a high rate of response is possible in some patients with candy reinforcement if a non-symptomatic response is reinforced which *mechanically* competes with the patient's most characteristic motor symptom.

Since slow acquisition only occurs with a very small number of patients, it is more probably a form of restricted occupational therapy, rather than a general property of the behavior of chronic psychotics. Therefore, the possibility that the low rates of response of the majority of the patients were due to slow acquisition was ruled out.

Since each patient was in a finely controlled environment during each experimental session, the *possibility of a competing response system* as normally conceived can be ruled out as a cause of the pause in responding or psychotic incidents. The records of the non-psychotic individuals shown in Fig. 5, attest to the fact that no stimuli were present in the rooms which would produce competing responses in non-psychotic individuals. However, our more recent analyses strongly suggest that many forms of psychosis act as a competing response system does on the free-operant behavior of non-psychotics. In other words, many psychotics behave similarly to non-psychotics who are being intermittently bombarded with behavioral stimuli.

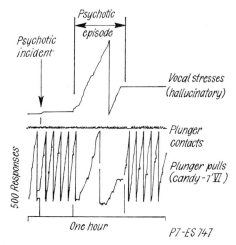

FIG. 5. A psychotic incident and episode appearing in simultaneous cumulative response records of vocal stresses with psychotic or hallucinatory origin and manual plunger-pulls reinforced with candy on a 1'VI schedule. Manual contacts with the plunger are recorded on the event marker between the cumulative records.

Our physiological controls (the daily physical and weekly laboratory examinations) and therapeutic controls adequately rule out the *possibility that acute physiological illness and drug action* caused the pauses in responding. It is important to note that in careful behaviora linvestigation such physiological controls are absolutely necessary in order to attribute any recorded behavioral deviations to other causes.

III. Psychotic Episodes

Occasionally certain patients who usually respond at higher, more even rates of response, will have a period of very low, erratic responding which lasts for a period of 20 or 30 min up to several hours. During these periods of lowered response rate, they can be observed displaying hallucinatory, disturbed, destructive, or other more extremely psychotic symptoms than they usually display. Psychiatric aides usually say a patient "went high" when such episodes occur on the wards. It is the unpredictable occurrence of such episodes that keeps many chronic patients in the hospital, off parole, or on the disturbed ward.

Such periods of temporarily lowered response rate, and increased duration and/or frequency of psychotic incidents, we have termed *psychotic episodes*. Cumulative response records of a single psychotic incident, and a psychotic episode in the behavior of patient No. 7 are shown in Figure 5. This figure will be described in more detail in a later section of this paper. Here, we wish only to point out that such psychotic episodes occur, and that they are the truly psychotic behavior which keeps many patients hospitalized, and that they can be automatically and objectively recorded. Some drugs, for example Benactyzine at high dosages, increase the frequency and duration of psychotic incidents and produce one of these psychotic epidoses in many patients.

IV. Psychotic Phases

In the intensive, longitudinal studies several of the patients showed marked rhythms in their rate of response. These rhythms characteristically occur over relatively long periods of time. For a few weeks the rate of response will be consistently high. Then, for a few weeks or months the rate will be consistently low. Then the rhythm will repeat. We have called these periods of low response rate *psychotic phases*. They are not related to temperature, humidity, phases of the moon, home visits, or changes in ward assignments or hospital social environment. They are related to ratings of the patients ward behavior until the behavior rating scales lose their sensitivity as a result of repeated administration.

An example of these psychotic phases is shown in Figure 6. At the start of the experiment the patient was hospitalized for 20 years and was 52 years old. Aged 18 he was first hospitalized and diagnosed as a manic-depressive. The diagnosis at admission for his current period of hospitalization was dementia praecox, hebephrenic type. His last hospital diagnosis (in 1951) was schizophrenia, paranoid type. A current "blind" diagnosis was organic psychosis.

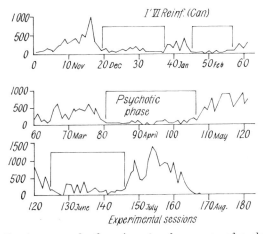

FIG. 6. Psychotic phases or rhythms in rate of response of a chronic psychotic responding on a 1'VI schedule of candy reinforcement. Each experimental session lasted 1 hr and was conducted on successive week–days. The months of the years are printed below the experimental session closest to the first of each month to indicate calendar time. Patient No. 52. Ordinates: responses per hour.

It is easy to see how long-term hospitalization and the loss of social rein-forcement could suppress the socially observable behavior of a patient to such a low level that such behavioral rhythms, which were originally easily observed without instrumentation and used to diagnose a manic-depressive psychosis, could later only be recorded by sensitive, and highly quantified behavioral recording devices.

It is important to note the havoc than can be wrought by including such a patient in a drug evaluation study of the type that would run a 30–day placebo control while the patient happened to be in a psychotic phase, and a 30–day drug run when the patient was in his following more normal phase. The drug would be interpreted as therapeutic. It is also important to note that such patients could be of great values in attempts to show physiolog-ical or biochemical correlates of psychosis. For, here in a single physiolog-ical system we have a naturally oscillating amount of psychosis, which could be correlated with samples of biochemical materials in order to deter-mine correlations without confounding the data with inter-patient dif-ferences in behavior or chemical quantity.

Practical Use of Free-Operant Rate of Response in Therapeutic Evaluations

Although the simple free-operant rate of response on a variable-interval schedule is a non-specific laboratory measure of the degree of psychotic disability, nevertheless, it is more reliable and more sensitive to most thera-peutic variables than other existing evaluative techniques. Here I shall present only a few examples of therapeutic evaluation. We have collected a large number of similar evaluations, which clearly demonstrate the practical utility of the method in its current form in this application.

Since we are methodologists, we will continue to refine and to develop more complicated and more exact measures of the psychoses. It is more efficient if large scale therapeutic evaluations using our currently available measures are undertaken by those trained and equipped for therapeutic evaluation. Like the lens maker in microscopy, we wish to hand our latest lens over to the histologist, and get back to our business of designing and polishing more powerful lenses.

I. Electroshock and Insulin Coma

In Figure 7, the rates of response on a 1-minute variable-interval schedule of reinforcement with candy (solid line) and feeding a kitten, or succor (dashed line) reinforcement are plotted against experimental sessions. The patient was in an acute psychotic depression and undergoing electroshock and insulin coma therapy. At the top of the graph the crosses mark the days in which EST was given in the morning before the afternoon experimental

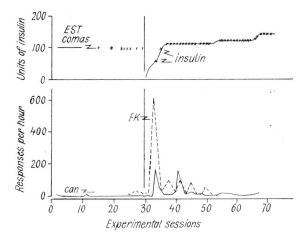

FIG. 7. Effect of electroshock and insulin comas on rate of response of an acute psychotic responding on a variable-interval schedule for candy (solid line) and for succor (feeding milk to a hungry kitten—(dashed line). The electroshocks had no effect and the insulin produced increases in the rate of response at the time of the first insulin reactions and comas. Patient No. PF–3

session. Note that the extremely low rate of response was not increased during the EST series.

At the vertical line, on the 32nd experimental session, the insulin treatment was begun. The number of units of crystalline insulin that were injected each day are plotted in the black curve at the top of the graph. Note that there was no increase in the operant response rate until the first coma occurred when the therapist levelled off the dosage of insulin. Note also, that the rate of response reinforced by feeding the kitten was increased much more than the rate reinforced with candy. This shows that the rate increase was not caused by a need for sugar increased by hypoglycemia, unless succor is also increased by hypoglycemia. The major therapeutic effect was produced by the first coma. The rate was also increased after the next ten insulin comas, but returned to the pretherapy level for the remainder of the treatment.

Monitoring courses of insulin therapy with operant response rates might prove to be useful in individualizing insulin treatment by providing an exact measure of the degree of therapy produced by each coma. The therapist would then have the information necessary to give the comas at intervals designed to produce the maximum therapeutic effect in each patient.

II. Iproniazid

In Figure 8, the rates of response on a one-minute variable-interval schedule of reinforcement are plotted against experimental sessions for a regressed

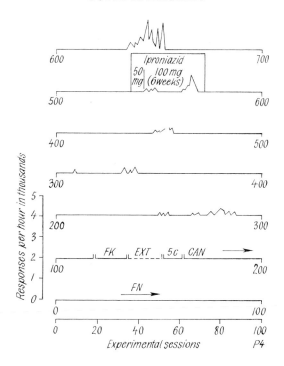

FIG. 8. Experimental history of a chronic psychotic responding on a variable-interval schedule for various reinforcers (FN – female nude pictures, FK – feeding a hungry kitten, EXT – Extinction, 5c – five-cent coins, and CAN – penny pieces of candy). The history covers a period of 5 years and 7 months of almost daily experimentation and reveals severely depressed operant behavior with several "spontaneous" recovery phases of extremely low magnitude in addition to an inital, but not sustained, therapeutic effect of iproniazid medication. Patient No. P–4

chronic psychotic, patient No. 4; 700 daily hour-long experimental sessions are shown in the graph. During the first 200 sessions, female nude pictures, feeding a kitten, 5-cent coins, and candy were used in attempts to determine the most appropriate reinforcer for this patient. From the 200th session on, candy was used as the reinforcer. Note periods of "spontaneous" increases in rate of response around the 250th, 280th, 310th, 340th and 460th sessions.

On the 535th session 50 mg t.i.d. of iproniazid (marsilid) was administered for 4 weeks with no therapeutic effect. On the 545th session, the dosage was increased to 100 mg t.i.d. and a slight rate increase was produced and sustained for a few days. However this increase was of no greater amplitude than the previously recorded "spontaneous" increases. About 3 weeks after the rate had declined, there was another temporary rate increase of a much greater magnitude than was found in any previous "spontaneous" increase. After 6 weeks of 100 mg t.i.d. iproniazid administration liver damage began to develop and the medication was terminated.

From about the 640th to the 660th session another "spontaneous" rate increase occured in which the rate went up to 1500 responses per hour.

In summary, the iproniazid given in the heaviest dosages that were medically feasible, appeared to produce only two "recovery cycles" in this chronic patient. The recovery cycles are only significant because of their timing with respect to the change in dosage of the drug. In terms of therapeutic significance, the "recovery" is not significant, for it was not maintained during or after the drug administration, and it was of no greater magnitude than the several "spontaneous" improvement periods in the patient's experimental history.

III. Student-Nurse Psychotherapy

In Fig. 9, the experimental case history of patient No. 4 is continued. At the first arrow, psychotherapy sessions with a student nurse were begun. Psychotherapy sessions lasted 1 hr and they were held on Mondays, Wednesdays and Fridays. At the second arrow, the patient stopped swearing during the therapy sessions. The nurse became a little irritated because the patient was inattentive and mumbled a lot during the therapy sessions.

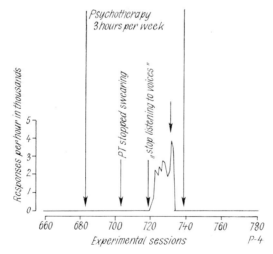

FIG. 9. Effect of psychotherapy sessions on operant rate of response of a chronic psychotic. The graph is a continuation of experimental history shown in Fig. 8 using same size ordinate and abscissa scales. A student nurse conducted the 1-hour therapy sessions three times a week. The effect of the psychotherapy was six times greater than that produced by 100 mg t.i.d. iproniazid given for 6 weeks, and three times greater than the highest "spontaneous" improvement cycle in the patient's six–year experimental history. Patient No. P–4

At the third arrow she told the patient to stop listening to his voices. "They are only part of your illness and you should not pay attention to them". By the third experimental session immediately following this therapeutic session the rate of response had climbed to over 2000 responses per hour. Responding was maintained at this high rate, even on the 2 days of each week that the nurse did not see the patient.

At the fourth arrow, the nurse told the patient that after 2 weeks she could no longer see him. The rate of response jumped up about another 2000 responses per hour immediately after this information was given the patient, and then abruptly fell to zero responses per hour. At the fifth arrow the nurse left the hospital and the therapy was terminated.

The rate increase which occurred during the psychotherapy was abrupt in onset and termination, in contrast to the gradually onsetting rate increases which were "spontaneously" and drug produced. This fact taken together with the close timing of the recovery with relevant psychotherapeutic variables, leaves little doubt that the recovery was produced by the nurse's visits. This was the highest rate of response emitted by the patient in over 4 years of daily experimental observation. Therefore, the effect has high statistical significance and cannot be attributed to chance. However, since the patient was by no means "normalized", and since the recovery was not maintained after termination of the therapy, the psychotherapeutic sessions had only a relatively weak and supportive effect. In this respect their therapeutic significance was relatively low, even though greater than that produced by iproniazid.

Nevertheless, quantified, objective measures of the effect of single psychotherapeutic sessions on the behavior of chronic psychotics are scarce and this effect is highly significant from that point of view. In cooperation with Dr. Jack R. Ewalt we have plans to continue the investigations of psychotherapeutic effects using other highly trained therapists. The method shows promise as a device for accurately calibrating the effect of single therapeutic sessions. Such sensitive calibrations of the effects of single therapeutic sessions will permit the therapist to determine by single manipulation which variables in the sessions were active. In this way a true experimental analysis of psychotherapy can be undertaken, and the functional aspects of psychotherapy can be proven by the methods of natural science in the laboratory.

In summary, 3 hr per week of psychotherapy conducted by a student nurse produced an increase in the rate of operant responding of this chronic psychotic that was three times that of any "spontaneous" improvement recorded in over 3 years of daily behavioral measurement, and that was six times the improvement produced by 100 mg t.i.d. of iproniazid administered for 6 weeks.

Specific Characteristics of Psychotic Behavior

More complicated behavioral processes are debilitated by fewer agents than the rate of a simple operant response. For this reason debilities in these more complicated behaviors more specifically indicate the presence of psychosis and the type of psychosis than do debilities in the simple rate of response. However, in order to determine debilities in more complicated behavior, the scientist needs enough behavior to study. Only about 50 per cent of the chronic patients have useful rates of response above 100 responses per hour, so specific debilities cannot be determined in the other 50 per cent of the patients who are extremely debilitated.

Due to our lack of time, I will only briefly summarize the more complicated, and hence more specific behavioral characteristics of the psychoses that we have located to date. The majority of the patients have extremely slow extinction processes. We have located one patient in which there appears to be a complete lack of extinction. In counting discriminations as measured on fixed–ratio schedules of reinforcement, approximately 50 per cent of the patients have deficits. In more complicated discriminations based upon differential responding to two manipulanda and two lights, 90 per cent of the patients show deficits. These discriminatory deficits have diagnostic utility in separating seniles and true mental defectives from the social mental defectives.

Simultaneous Recording of Vocal Symptoms and Non-Symptomatic Responses

Visual observation of patients through the hidden periscopic viewing system has shown that most patients with abnormally long pauses in their operant responding engage in their particular individualistic symptoms during these pauses. The development of keys or switches to record automatically and electrically the occurrence of these symptoms would facilitate their further analysis.

Simultaneously recorded cumulative records of both the psychotic symptoms and the reinforced operant responses would permit an exact and objective analysis of their competition. Such simultaneous records would also permit an objective search for symptom–specific drugs which should decrease the frequency of symptoms without decreasing the frequency of reinforced operant, normal, or non-symptomatic behavior.

Also, the symptom key could be used automatically to schedule the presentation of environmental stimuli contingent upon the psychotic symptoms. The differential reinforcement of symptomatic responses would show whether they are or are not affected by environmental changes in the same way as are non-symptomatic responses.

In Figure 5 simultaneously recorded cumulative records of vocal stresses and manual plunger-pulls are shown for the 747th experimental session with a chronic psychotic patient. The vocal responses were never experimentally reinforced and can be considered to have a psychotic origin. Their content was identical with that in the vocal behavior of the patient whenever he "went high" on the wards.

Patient No. 7 is male, 58 years old and he has been continuously hospitalized for 29 years. His experimental behavior has been under study for 5 years. Admitted in 1930, at the age of 29, he was diagnosed dementia praecox, paranoid type. The recent "blind" diagnoses were simple schizophrenia (by the clinical psychologist), and schizophrenia, mixed (by the psychiatrist). His recent Wechsler-Bellevue I.Q. was 60 and he scored in the third percentile on the Hospital Adjustment Scale and lives on a locked ward. His personality picture is "that of a withdrawn, colorless patient who shows little evidence of acting–out and whose general defense is that of compulsivity in terms of wanting a fixed routine, his own things, and to be left alone."

He is very untidy, but not incontinent. He collects worthless objects and eats cigarette butts. He cleans the hospital basement floors but needs almost constant supervision. He is a good worker unless provoked, when he has tantrums and runs about, yelling, biting his fists, and pounding the walls. He behaved in this fashion during the psychotic episode shown in Fig. 5, and it is this behavior which keeps him on a locked ward.

Consider Fig. 5 and note the exact nature of the functional competition between the patient's vocal symptoms and his manual operant responses. The manual responses were reinforced on a 1'VI schedule with candy. The rate of reinforced manual non–symptomatic responses was reduced about 75 per cent for two periods by competition from a moderate rate of never-reinforced vocal symptomatic responses.

The first period of symptom display and reduced rate of normal or non-symptomatic behavior lasted only about 1 min and might be properly called a "psychotic incident". The second period lasted about 20 min and appears to be composed of a long series of psychotic incidents. Such sustained periods of psychotic display are often called "psychotic episodes."

Note that in the psychotic episode the vocal symptoms began about 2 min before the manual response rate dropped. This delay in the reduction of the non-symptomatic responding by the symptomatic responding shows that the competitive effect of the symptoms takes a minute or two to build up. The delay also demonstrates the physical independence of the two responses and their recording systems.

Note also that at the end of the episode there was a period of about 2 min with no vocal responding before the non-symptomatic responses returned to their pre-incident rate. This delay in the recovery of the non-symptomatic responding shows that the competitive effect of the symptoms lasts longer than their display. These delays in onset and recovery of the competitive effect of the symptoms suggest that the competition is a higher-order behavioral effect than the symptom. The delays also show that symptoms can occur without the competition.

Note also that a relatively even rate of vocal symptoms and manual responses was maintained throughout the episode. These even episodic rates indicated that the severity of the psychotic episode and its competition with the normal behavior was maintained at about the same intensity throughout.

Also shown in Figure 5 is a record of the time that the patient's hand was in contact with the manipulandum (plunger contacts). The contacts were recorded by a capacitative relay circuit. The event pen on one recorder was in the "up" position whenever the patient's hand was on the manipulandum. Note that the patient usually took his hand off the manipulandum when a reinforcement was delivered. At this time he placed the candy in a paper bag that he carried. But also note that his hand was off the manipulandum during the psychotic incident and much of the time during the psychotic episode. This record of contacts shows that the symptomatic vocalizations not only compete with the recorded manual responding, but also compete with non-recorded responses necessary to the performance of the recorded responses.

In summary, a voice key to automatically record the competition between symptomatic vocalizations and the normal non-symptomatic behavior of patients within an experimental setting was developed. Its use has clearly shown that the pauses in the operant responding of patients with vocal hallucinatory symptoms are due to functional competition from these symptoms. The opportunity to record the exact nature of this competition will be useful in further research into the basic nature of psychosis. Objective recording of these vocal symptoms and their competitive effect will also be useful in the evaluation of therapeutic agents. Such a high degree of exactitude in the observation of the competition between the psychotic symptoms and normal behavior of a patient can be obtained by no other currently available psychiatric research device.

Functional Definition of a Psychosis

In order to show that Darwinian, naturalistic observations can lead to what might be called theories, lastly I shall present a way of defining a certain type of psychosis. This definition is functional because it describes the psychosis in terms of its effects on and interaction with non-psychotic behavior.

This notion is a direct outgrowth of the simultaneous measurement of symptomatic and non-symptomatic behavior described in the last section. When normal individuals are placed in this two-channel recording situation the only vocal responses they emit, when alone and being reinforced for their manual responses, are occasional bursts of singing and whistling. This singing and whistling can be readily separated from most psychotic hallu-

18*

cinating by the pattern of response emission which is regular for singing and whistling, and irregular for one-sided conversations with no one. Also, the singing and whistling does not compete with, but rather seems to "pace" along with the plunger-pulling responses.

However, if non-psychotic individuals are given an hallucinogenic drug (i.e. denactyzine in high dosages) and their name is called over a hidden microphone, they will carry on a "psychotic-like" one–sided conversation with no one. When questioned afterwards they report having had auditory hallucinations. The interesting fact is that the drug-induced vocal hallucinatory symptoms in the non-psychotic do not compete with their plunger-pulling responses. The non-psychotics pull the plunger for nickels without reduction in rate through their hallucinatory episode.

Also, the non-psychotics do not hallucinate for as long a period after their name is called over the hidden speaker as do the psychotics. The after-discharge of the drug-induced and experimentally stimulated hallucinatory episodes in the non-psychotic is much shorter than the after-discharge of the "spontaneous", or experimentally stimulated hallucinatory episodes in the psychotic.

To date we have run very few psychotic and non-psychotic subjects under these conditions, but the data collected are amazingly uniform. Therefore we tentatively venture the hypothesis that one property of one form of psychosis is discharge and an abnormally high degree of competition with strongly reinforced non-symptomatic behavior. In other words' it is not the symptom (talking to no one) that defines this form of psychosis. Neither is it the stimulus that produced the symptom ("hearing" your name called when no one is there) that defines the psychosis. Rather, it is having the symptomatic response (talking to no one) last long after a non-psychotic would stop, and more importantly being unable to do anything else demanded of him while this talking is going on, that defines the psychotic.

I think this definition of psychotic symptoms has a lot of clinical relevance. We are all familiar with the old lady walking down the street, obeying traffic signals, nodding and occasionally speaking to friends along the way. She is not hospitalized as a psychotic, because she is walking down the street and only talks to no one when there is nothing else to do with her mouth. She just "talks to herself".

And again, if a person goes to a psychiatrist and says, "I worry all the time, I think I am going to die, please help me." The psychiatrist will probably ask, "Do you sleep well? Do you eat well? Are you getting your work done?" If the answers to all of these questions are honestly in the affirmative, the patient is not diagnosed as psychotic and hospitalized. Rather he is classified as an interesting and compensated neurotic. On the other hand, if a man is located who has been talking to no one in a closet for three days, and has done nothing else, he stands a high probability of being immediately hospitalized if he won't even stop talking to his "friend" for the police.

Summary

Much of what we have learned from our carefully controlled experiments appears in retrospect to be composed of things that skilled, experienced clinicians "knew" all the time. But, that is as it should be, for the business of science is to separate the wisdom of casual and field observation from its superstition, and then to quantify and to make this wisdom practically useful. For the first time we have brought a few facts of psychosis into the body of natural science. In so doing much of what we have brought in looks just as the clinicians always said it did. But remember that we now have the advantage of measuring these things automatically in the laboratory. And also remember that we have left many things that clinicians say in the clinic.

REFERENCES

1. AZRIN, N. H., and LINDSLEY, O. R. (1956) *J. Abn. Soc. Psychol.* **52,** pp. 100-2.
2. BERNARD, C. (1865) *An Introduction to the Study of Experimental Medicine*, reprinted, Henry Schuman, 1949.
3. FERSTER, C. B., and SKINNER, B. F. (1957) *Schedules of Reinforcement*, New York, Appleton-Century-Crofts.
4. FERSTER, C. B. (1958) *Psychiat. Res. Reports* **10**, pp. 101–18.
5. KRAEPELIN, E. (1896) *The Psychological Experiment in Psychiatry, Psychol. Arbeit*, Leipzig, Engelmann.
6. LINDSLEY, O. R. (1956) Psych. Res. Repts, **5,** pp. 118–93, 140–53.
7. LINDSLEY, O. R., SKINNER, B. F., and SOLOMON, H. C. (1953–1956) *Periodic Project Reports*, Metropolitan State Hospital, Waltham, Mass., Microcard No. FO-57-524-527, L. C. No. MicP 57-30.
8. LINDSLEY, O. R. (1959) *Symposium on Cerebral Dysfunction and Mental Disturbance*, Chicago, Ill., to be published in Am. Psychiat. Assoc. Monogr.
9. MEDNICK, M. T., and LINDSLEY, O. R. (1958) *J. Abn. Soc. Psychol.* **57,** pp. 13–16.
10. PAVLOV, I. P. (1941) *Lectures on Conditioned Reflexes*, Volume II, *Conditioned Reflexes and Psychiatry*, translated by W. Horsley Gantt, New York, International.
11. RUSH, B. (1835) *Medical Inquiries and Observations on the Diseases of the Mind*.
12. SKINNER, B. F. (1938) *The Behavior of Organisms*, New York, Appleton-Century.
13. SKINNER, B. F. (1953) *Science and Human Behavior*, New York, Macmillan.
14. SKINNER, B. F. (1956) *Theory and Treatment of the Psychoses*, St. Louis: Washington University Studies.
15. SKINNER, B. F. (1957) *Amer. Scientist* **45,** pp. 343–71.
16. SKINNER, B. F., SOLOMON, H. C., and LINDSLEY, O. R. (1954) *J. Nerv. Ment. Dis.* **120,** pp. 403–6.

MEASURES OF SUSCEPTIBILITY
TO NERVOUS BREAKDOWN†

W. Horsley Gantt

I

An urgent problem in modern psychiatry is the prevention as well as the cure of nervous diseases. For this purpose it is necessary first to assay the vulnerability of the individual, by placing him in a test environment which will not impose too great a burden upon his nervous system.

Our present methods have been inadequate for this detection; treatment has proceeded much further than prevention. It is true that we obtain important information from the biographical (both family and individual) data, but this is difficult to get and often more difficult to evaluate; no careful records are available concerning the majority of individuals outside of a hospital. Furthermore, this type of information does not come from controlled situations. The methods of psychiatric examination, in contrast to those of physical examination, have been based mainly upon verbal reactions. The I.Q. and mental status often bear little or no relation to what interests us chiefly about the patient. The EEG, thought objective, is poorly understood at present and probably measures metabolic factors which may or may not be related to the elements of vulnerability to nervous breakdown.

A method is required which is (1) *objective* (therefore varying minimally with the examiner); (2) capable of being *recorded* (and thus available for comparison by day to day and from one individual to another); (3) *quantitative* to a certain degree; (4) concerned with *significant* items, having a high correlation with the characteristics of the patient that are essential, viz., those that determine his susceptibility to break under stress.

The method proposed here for detecting vulnerability actively imposes a certain task upon the nervous system comparable to the various functional tests used in medicine for the heart, kidneys, liver, etc. In this new method it is necessary first to establish the normal record for the given individual, i.e. his simple performance in an ordinary situation not too difficult; second, to place the individual under a graduated stress; and third, to detect the point at which subject begins to deviate from the normal. It is important

† By permission of *American Journal of Psychiatry* 1943

to note that the normal must be determined for that particular individual because what is normal for one is not normal for another; "one man's meat is another man's poison".

1. The Establishment of the Norm

In spite of the general recognition now among psychiatrists of psychosomatic relations, I wish to ascribe proper credit to Pavlov for having first irrefutably demonstrated experimentally the truth of "no psychosis without neurosis," viz. that the psychical can be objectively recorded in a somatic reaction. For this he used the salivary secretion as a measure of psychic excitation or inhibition. The conditional reflex is the measure of this somatic reaction.

That psychic phenomena are as subject to laws as the so-called physiological has been clearly demonstrated. In this laboratory it has not only been shown that there is as little daily variation (in a rigidly controlled situation) of the conditioned reflex (cr) as of the unconditioned (UR), but the cr can be expressed in an equation as readily as can the UR. Thus for the salivary cr the formula is cr $= a + b\ (1{-}e^{-cQ})$,[2,5] an exponential relationship, while for the UR (secretion of salivation) the formula, UR $= a + bQ$, shows a linear relationship.

These formulae simply mean that as the intensity of the stimulus is increased the cr at first increases but soon stops increasing or increases very slowly with added stimulation; while within the same limits the UR increases equally with each unit of added stimulus whether the unit is added to the basic large or small stimulus. Individual variations are accounted for by the constants (for a given individual) a, b, c.

We have extended the work of Pavlov to other autonomic functions. The sensitiveness of the heart rate in human subjects has been demonstrated by Whitehorn, and the cardiac conditioned reflex in dogs is one of the most interesting to show a quantitative relationship to the stimulus. For each individual there is a certain change in the heart rate accompanying each type and intensity of excitatory cr, and another change in the heart rate accompanying inhibition. That the cardiac cr is a more delicate measure of activity is convincingly shown by its persistence in dogs after a long period of rest when the other components (motor and secretory) have disappeared (experiments of Tunick in this laboratory). Thus the heart rate is a reliable quantitative measure of the intensity of conditioned excitation and inhibition. This seems the more remarkable when we consider that these measures of heart rate are made for very short periods, viz. 3 to 10 sec, while the conditioned stimulus is acting.

The following chart (Figure 1) shows that there is a change in heart rate during the cr which is practically equal to the change in heart rate during the UR and that there is a smaller change in heart rate during inhibition.

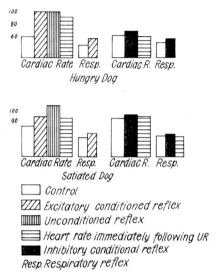

Fig. 1. Excitatory and inhibitory crs before and after satiation.

That the increase in heart rate accompanying the cr represents a measure of the conditional reflex or emotional tension, or in other words the conditional excitation is shown by that fact that in a satiated dog there is no conditional secretion nor a cardiac cr during the signal for food, and the animal also refuses to take the food.

Changes in respiration accompanying the crs have been frequently noted (Bechterev, Watson, Kellogg, Gantt, Liddell).

2. The Production of Strain

Some physiological conditions, as well as pathological, produce internal states, which lower the threshold at which the breakdown occurs, make the animal highly susceptible. Thus during the postpartum period in the dog, simply subjecting the animal to the routine conditional stimuli results in an imbalance. This was first noted in a dog (Kompa) in 1930 and it has been seen subsequently in others. The following chart (Figure 2) shows the drop in the salivary cr in Kompa on the first few days post–partum. In another dog (Zee) no change was observable in the motor crs, but by taking a more delicate measure, viz., the cardiac cr, it is evident soon after the birth of the puppies that there is a deviation of activity recorded in the cardiac crs, (Figure 2). A similar disturbance occurs in male dogs confined near a dog in estrus.

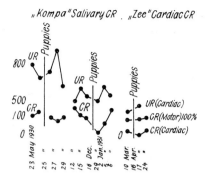

Fig. 2. Effect of parturition on CR

Natural emotional shocks also produce marked disturbances in the cr activity, although these cannot always be observed by the usual means of examination. Two examples follow. In April 1931 the dogs in the laboratory escaped from the paddocks, got into strange surroundings, and had to be forcibly returned; they fought among themselves and were whipped by the night watchman. Figure 3 shows the change produced in the cr activity in

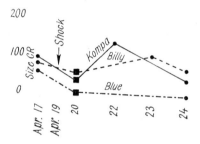

Fig. 3. Effect of natural emotional shock (escape from paddock) on CR in three types of dogs—excitatory labile (Kompa), stable (Billy) and inhibitory labile (Blue)

various individuals; the stable animal (Billy) was only slightly affected while an excitatory one (Kompa) was severely disturbed as was the inhibitory animal (Blue). After this event there were parallel changes in the ordinary observable behavior, Billy being affected very little and only for 1 day, while Kompa was much subdued for 3 days; and Blue slunk into the corner and kept his tail tucked though he was usually friendly and playful, and was inactive for a week. However the change in the crs outlasted any disturbance of behavior that could be detected by ordinary observation.[6]

Another instance occurred in 1932, involving the labile dog Kompa and the stable Billy—showing that the stable one was again stable and the labile one (Kompa) disturbed for a long time. These animals were seen fighting on

March 18, 1942. They had been fighting for about 24 hours, and appeared equally exhausted and wounded they could barely walk and had to be carried to the experimental camera. The salivary cr record revealed the much greater deviation in the labile Kompa than in the stable Billy; similar to the change seen in Figure 3.

In the above instances it was only by establishing previously a normal base line that we were able to see the pathological state reflected in the cr; for the criterion is *a change from the normal for that particular individual.*

Let us next consider artificial strain—produced deliberately and under controlled conditions in the laboratory, and the way in which dogs of different temperament behave under this imposed stress.

It is necessary to emphasize that by no ordinary method of observation was it possible in these dogs to distinguish the susceptible and labile from the stable. I have asked many psychiatrists and physicians and I have tried myself to predict from ordinary contacts with the dogs or from knowledge of their breed, etc., which ones will break down first. Even after long periods of ordinary observation gained by playing with and feeding the animal, accurate prediction is not possible. The individual must be placed under a definite stress and deviation from his normal measured. Photographs of these dogs did not reveal which are susceptible, although the following test situations do.

In dogs C and D the establishment of crs was started at the same time. But our results made evident that C quickly made a differentiation between the inhibitory and excitatory metronoms, giving the proper response to each, while D is hyper-reactive, continually reacting to the inhibitory as well as to the excitatory stimuli. D also showed more disturbance of the overt behavior in the test situation—e.g. whining, restlessness, and barking. The same occurred in respect to the respiration. Even at the time that C could not make the differentiation there was little disturbance in the respiration, but in D there were marked changes evident though only when the differentiation became difficult.

The cardiac crs showed a parallel disturbance. Normally both dogs give changes in the heart rate during the action of the conditioned reflex; but in C the changes were not so marked as in D. The difference in the two is brought out much more clearly in the cardiac crs where the situation is made more difficult. Thus on November 28, 1940, in D the cardiac rates increased from 100 per minute with the normal cr to about 200 with the cr when the differentiation was difficult (Figure 4). Actually C showed a decrease in heart rate to the normal cr but a greater decrease to the difficult differentiation, while D had an accelerated heart rate to the normal cr but a more marked acceleration with the difficult differentiation. Whether the the heart rate is decreased or increased depends upon the individual.

The salivary secretion is an autonomic function that has been made the conventional measure of the Pavlovian cr. Fluctuation from the normal

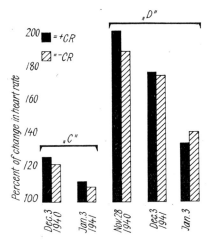

F IG. 4. Conditioned cardiac rates in stable dog (C) and labile dog (D) during strain (Nov. 28—Dec. 3) and during good differentiation (Jan. 3). Control represented as base line, 100 per cent

behavior may begin with a disturbance too slight to be detected by present methods in any other way than by the measure of the autonomic cr. If the conflict is prolonged the deviation may continue until not only all the artificial laboratory crs are abolished in the situation of conflict, but also even all crs to the old strong stimuli (sight and smell of food). An example of the acute disturbance is seen in the chart of Kompa; the introduction of an inhibitory metronom depressed the old well-established crs but for a period of only 5–10 min after the disturbing metronom. Each time the inhibitory metronom was given (for 30 sec) the effect of subsequent positive conditional stimuli was diminished or reduced to zero. Recovery occurred within a few minutes. However in another dog, Nick, all the positive food crs (motor and secretory, natural and artificial) were abolished when the animal was simply brought into the old environment—even as long as 9 years after the original conflict—but the unconditional reflex secretion was unchanged. Thus, on March 2, 1932, before the conflict the cr salivary secretion was 0.4 cc in 10 sec but on June 27, 1932, after the conflict and even to 1942, the cr secretion remained zero. In contrast to the labile dog, Nick, in the stable dog, Fritz, subjected to the same environment of conflict there was only a slight disturbance in ordinary behavior and in the salivary crs which lasted for a few days instead of years.

The external behavior of the two dogs under strain—in the laboratory situation of conflict—is often significant, but seeing the two animals under ordinary circumstances would not give a clue as to which one would break down. To the same tone that was used several years previously in a difficult differentation connected with food, Nick tugs to get away from the source of the tone, panting, tense, with a marked sexual erection, while Fritz pays no attention to the tone but calmly looks toward the experimenter.

Although we are not concerned here with chronic changes except as evidence of the labileness, Nick had a pronounced gastric hyperacidity (experiments in collaboration with Arnold Rich) in the environment of conflict.

The sexual reflexes are a delicate barometer of the strain to which the animal is subjected. There may be with a slight conflict only a temporary change in sexual reflexes; there are in the environment of conflict on the one hand, abnormal sexual erections, and, on the other hand, a decrease in sexual activity resembling impotence.

Besides the actual drop in the conditioned reflexes, the *degree of fluctuation* of both conditioned reflexes and other functions is an important evidence of pathology. This is reflected in chemical metabolic changes, e. g., in the blood sugar tolerance after a glucose test meal. Diethelm [1], Bridger and others have shown that the curve of blood sugar bears a relation to the acute emotional state of the organism. In three dogs of varying susceptibility who had repeated glucose test meals it was found that the most labile (Nick) had the greatest fluctuations from day to day, that the most stable (Fritz) had the least fluctuation and that Peter, whose disturbance of behavior was intermediate between Nick and Fritz, had fluctuation of blood sugar intermediate between Nick and Fritz. After standard deviations are made between all the zero hours on successive tests, all the half-hour readings on successive test–days, etc., Nick again shows the widest range of fluctuations; e.g., that (σ) for Fritz = 8·6, for Peter = 10 3, for Nick = 18·0.

In another function, the day's 24–hour running activity, it also appears that not the absolute activity but the change in this activity [7] is the important factor of susceptibility. For example, Nick and Brenda were the two dogs with the most pronounced neurotic disturbances, but Nick was the most active and Brenda the most inactive of all in the laboratory. Nick's activity fluctuated widely after he became neurotic; Brenda, who was formerly a pet in my home, had a remarkable drop to almost complete inactivity for several weeks, every time she was brought into the laboratory. This was parallel to her pathological behavior; she gave the signs of a marked depression, standing motionless with tail tucked, head hung for long periods, hardly moving from one spot during the 24 hr. The inactivity recurred every time she was brought into the laboratory. She finally died in the laboratory, apparently in a depressed condition.

II

The above records on dogs convince one that susceptibility to breakdown can be detected in a variety of objective measures when the animal is placed under a definite stress. Though the method has not been so thoroughly worked out for the human subject, I have considerable data in both the normal

and psychotic indicating that a similar procedure may be used. A sligth artificial conflict is produced by the conditioned response technic [3, 4]; the
problem is made gradually more difficult, at the same time carefully recording the reactions. In a normal subject the response is seen to be regular and
undisturbed by the test situation and the differentiation, and the movements
(positive conditioned reflexes) are regular and accurately related to the
stimuli†.

Contrast this record (Figure 5) with two abnormal ones. The first is an
hyperactive schizophrenic with anxiety (Figure 6). Here it is seen that the
respiration is markedly disturbed, revealing the anxiety; subsequently as
the patient developed the ability to differentiate there was less disturbance.

The second patient (S.R.) is a catatonic whose conditioned reflexes and
unconditioned reflexes were followed during various degrees of catalepsy. On
October 24, 1938, the patient was able to converse but showed some rigidity;
there is conditioned reflex in the hand making the purposeful movements
(lower line, Figure 7) which spreads to involve the other hand (upper line,
Figure 7). On October 31, 1938, there was increased tension with ineffective
conditioned reflexes—present in both hands—and mutism; the patient had
to be brought in a wheel chair (Figure 8). On January 30, 1939, the patient

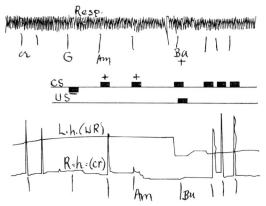

FIG. 5. Pt. O., January 11, 1939. Normal cr formation without marked disturbance in respiration. Upper line=respiration, middle two lines mark cs and US,
next to bottom line is L.h. showing chiefly URs, and bottom line is R.h. showing
integrated crs.

† The following abbreviations are used: cr(s) = conditioned reflex(es);
cs = conditioned stimulus; US = unconditioned stimulus; UR(s) = unconditioned reflexe(es); l.h. = left hand, i.e., the hand receiving the US and whose
recorded movements are chiefly URs, though sometimes also primary (spontaneous) crs; r.h. = right hand, i.e., the hand marking the purposeful movements to avoid shock, whose record shows chiefly the secondary (integrated)
crs; positive (excitatory) cs marked above the line; negative (inhibitory) below
the line.

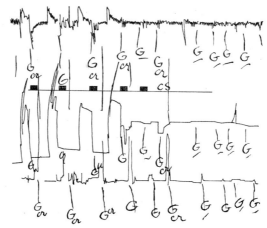

Fig. 6. Pt. Eg., January 14, 1939. Hyperactive schizophrenic with anxiety. Note disturbance in respiration and constant irregular movements in both hands connected with inability to differentiate positive from negative signals. Upper line=respiration, middle line=cs, next to bottom line=L.h. showing cr and UR activity, and lower line is R.h. with integrated crs.

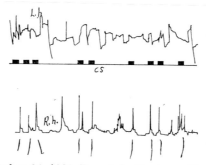

Fig. 7. Pt. S.R., October 24, 1938. Precataleptic stage. There is successful elaboration of crs but not differentiation (bottom line), tremors indicating tension in the hand receiving the unconditioned stimulus (top line)

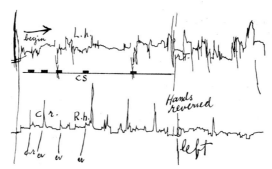

Fig. 8. Pt. S.R. October 31, 1938. Increased intensity but ineffectual crs

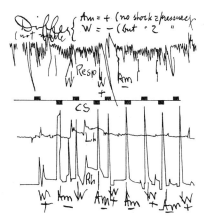

FIG. 9. Pt. S.R. January 30, 1939. Adequate cr formation in patient during improvement, but no differentiation

was able to converse rationally; he formed adequate conditioned reflexes (lower line, Figure 9), there was little spread to the other hand (middle line), and the respiration was only moderately disturbed (upper line). However there was no differentiation between the positive amber light and the negative white light. On March 6 the patient was again cataleptic, very rigid, mute, unable to walk. In Figure 10 there are no purposeful conditioned reflexes (low erline) but some primitive conditioned reflexes of a non–purposeful character and marked unconditioned reflexes—these occurred only to strong unconditioned stimuli (70 volts faradic current). These changes are seen in the middle line of Figure 10. The respiration is suppressed and distorted, chiefly abdominal (upper line Figure 10).

(In the figures the upper line represents the respiration, the middle line both the crs and the URs in the hand receiving the US, and the lower line the purposeful, integrated cr movements.)

The records for the three above mentioned patients are sufficient to demonstrate the fact that the changes in the character of the crs bear a close relationship to the clinical condition as well as to the individual patient. First, in the schizophrenic the respiration was less disturbed as he was able to make the differentiation and give the appropriate reactions to the conditional stimuli. Second, it is observable that the cr record is parallel in the catatonic to his clinical condition—when he was able to converse and showed rapport the cr record was nearer normal. Third, the patterns of the three subjects are characteristic. Owing to the limited scope of this paper it is not possible to give a more detailed discussion of the anomalies in the various psychiatric and neurological diseases (see Gantt and Gantt and Muncie [7]).

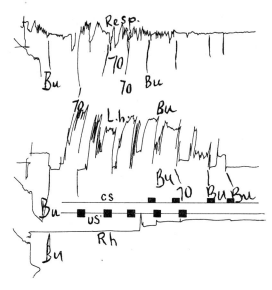

Fig. 10. Pt. S.R. March 6, 1939. Patient in cataleptic state. Note absence of all cr formation (bottom line), marked tension and irregular movements in hand receiving shock (middle line) (L.h.) and marked irregularity and suppression of respiration (top line)

III

The above observations reveal a marked difference in many types of measures between stable dogs and humans and certain proven susceptible (labile) dogs and humans.

The method is a functional test that can be readily applied without the aid of language and in the face of only a fair degree of cooperativeness, e.g., in catatonics. A measured strain can be introduced so that the degree of susceptibility may be registered for each individual.

The significance of this type of data—the examination of function—is an argument for the direct measurement of function rather than prediction of function from structure, for it is function that we are ultimately concerned with and structure only as it determines or modifies function.

First, are we recording chiefly individual patterns of reactivity or actual susceptibility to the imposed strain? Second, are we measuring only susceptibility of certain physiological systems in the given individuals or of the whole personality? For example it is known that one person will breakdown with a gastric ulcer, another with arteriosclerosis, another with hysterical paralysis under stress and conflict. Third, is the conflict (situation of stress) that we introduce concerned with items that are significant for the human subject or too trivial to be related with the important life experiences?

A satisfactory answer cannot be given to all these objections until further work has been completed. It is undoubtedly true that our tests do concern susceptibility of certain systems dependent upon the type of individual, giving us evidence not only of the susceptibility to breakdown but of the functional type of the individual and the relative susceptibility of the various systems. The question of system susceptibility vs. susceptibility of the whole personality, requires careful amalysis. It should be met by taking several measures that show a high correlation with the personality rather than by using a single measure.

The question of the significance of the test for the dog can be answered by the fact that many animals show a permanent disturbance lasting for years as a result of the stress of the laboratory procedure and that the symptoms are definitely related to the artificial conflict. Though the test is incomparably less significant for the human subject than his painful life experiences, it nevertheless gives us important information concerning the pattern of reactivity and the susceptibility to an acute temporary disturbance even though the stress is an artificial one. The fact that it is a slight rather than a severe conflict warrants its use in the human being as a direct test of function related to the stability of the nervous system, i.e. bearing a direct and close relation to the things about the individual with which we as psychiatrists are most concerned.

REFERENCES

1. Diethelm, O. (1936) Influence of emotions on dextrose tolerance, *Arch. Neur. Psychiat.* **36,** pp. 342–61.
2. Gantt, W. H. (1938) The nervous secretion of saliva: the relation of the conditioned reflex to the intensity of the unconditioned stimulus, *Am. J. Physiol.* **123,** p. 74.
3. Gantt, W. H. (1938) *Arch. Neurol. Psychiat,* **40,** pp. 79–85.
4. Gantt, W. H. (1938) *South Med. J.* **31,** pp. 12, 1219–25.
5. Gantt, W. H. (1942) The origin and development of nervous disturbances experimentally produced, Am. J. Psychiat., **98,** p. 4.
6. Gantt, W. H. (1943) The Experimental Basis of Neurotic Behavior, Harper Bros., N. Y.
7. Gantt, W. H., and Muncie, W. (1942) Analysis of the mental defect in chronic Korsakov's psychosis by means of the conditioned reflex method, *Bull. Johns Hopkins Hosp.* **70,** pp. 467–87.

17

THE EXPERIMENTAL FOUNDATIONS OF SOME NEW PSYCHOTHERAPEUTIC METHODS†

Joseph Wolpe

Psychiatric thought with regard to the neuroses and their treatment continues to be dominated by psychoanalytic theory, even though such basic propositions of psychoanalysis as repression, castration anxiety, and resistance are still without scientific validation. In the practical matter of treatment of neurosis, psychoanalytic *therapy* is increasingly under fire. The evidence (e.g. Eysenck, 1952) shows that its results have been no better than those obtained by relatively simple traditional methods that consist mainly of reassurance, explanation, persuasion, and suggestion, either separately or in combinations. The claim of the psychoanalysts (e.g., Fenichel, 1945; Hendrick, 1958) that their methods alone can achieve recoveries that may with assurance be expected to endure, is in conflict with the facts revealed in a survey of follow-up studies (Wolpe, 1961a).

More research, therefore, is being directed toward the exploration of other approaches to the explication and control of neuroses. In keeping with what has been done in other fields of medicine, it has seemed appropriate to try to understand the "abnormal" in terms of the "normal." Understanding of the factors determining the acquisition and elimination of "normal" behavior might have application to our understanding of neurotic behavior.

We know three kinds of processes that can lead to lasting (i.e. habitual) changes of response to specified stimulus conditions: growth, lesions‡, and learning. Because human neurotic habits of reaction can often be dated from particular experiences that involve stimuli to which the patient has come to react with anxiety, and because these habits can be altered through the techniques of psychotherapeutic interviews, there is a *prima facie* pre-

---

† The experimental foundations of some new psychotherapeutic methods," by J. Wolpe, M. D., Chapter 16 of *Experimental Foundations of Clinical Psychology*, edited by Arthur J. Bachrach, c 1962 byBasic Books, Inc., Publishers, New York

‡ This term is used here to mean either deviations from the normal physiological state in particular parts of the nervous system, or else generalized biochemical deviations such as may be produced by endocrine abnormalities.

sumption that neurotic reactions owe their existence to the learning process.

Some years ago, investigations were initiated to examine this presumption, partly for its own sake, but mainly because of the practical possibility that we might develop more effective methods for treating neuroses. These investigations, which have been reported in detail in several communications (Wolpe, 1948, 1952a, 1952b, 1954, 1958, 1959), led to the conclusion that neurotic behavior consists of *persistent habits of learned (conditioned) unadaptive behavior acquired in anxiety-generating situations*, and that therapy depends upon the unlearning of this behavior.

In the great majority of instances, the core of neurotic behavior lies, not in any particular motor activity, but in anxiety. Anxiety refers specifically to those responses, *predominantly of the autonomic nervous system, with which the individual characteristically* reacts to noxious (painful) stimuli. Its commonest manifestations are rapid respiration (sometimes irregular), rapid pulse, raised blood pressure, increased palmar sweating, and more or less generalized elevation of muscle tension. Not all anxiety is neurotic. Anxiety in response to an objective threat, such as being held up by a gunman or faced by the loss of one's livelihood, is entirely appropriate. Anxiety is unadaptive when it is evoked where there is no real danger—for example, in an elevator, driving past a cemetery, or on entering a room full of people†.

Observations by early workers with experimental neuroses suggested that neurotic behavior in the human being differs from that induced in laboratory animals only in such details as may be expected in an organism that is more complex and somewhat differently organized. Therefore, and because animal experiments offer far easier control of variables than is possible with human subjects (especially where illness is involved), it was logical first to explore in animals the applicability of principles of learning to neuroses and their treatment. The subsequent successful application to the human clinical situation of the lessons that were learned from the animal experiments vindicated the operational assumption that the most highly organized behavior of men and cats might conform to the same general laws no less than does the behavior of their respective digestive tracts.

Experimental Neuroses‡

Previous Experiments

The first reports of neuroses induced in experimental animals came from Pavlov's laboratories (1927). The earliest venture was the famous "circle

† In certain circles, it has become customary to refer to anxiety as "fear" when it is appropriate to the evoking situation, and "anxiety" when it is not. Since the physiological response patterns are the same in both contexts, the words "fear" and "anxiety" are here used synonymously.

‡ For a fuller discussion of this topic, see Wolpe (1952, 1958).

19*

and ellipse" experiment, which depended upon subjecting the animal to "difficult discrimination." A luminous circle was projected on to a screen placed in front of a dog held by a harness on the laboratory table. Each projection was succeeded by the dropping of a piece of food within easy reach of the animal. This cycle—appearance of circle, appearance of food—was repeated until a food-seeking response to the circle was firmly established. Then presentations of a luminous ellipse with semi-axes in the ratio of 2: 1 began to be interspersed among the presentations of the circle. The ellipse was never followed by food, so that it became a "negative alimentary stimulus"—that is, salivation and other "anticipatory" responses associated with feeding were inhibited. Quite soon, the difference of response to the two shapes became "complete and constant".

> The shape of the ellipse was now approximated by stages to that of the circle (ratios of semi-axes of 3 : 2, 4 : 3 and so on) and the development of differentiation continued . . . with some fluctuation, progressing at first more and more quickly, and then again slower, until an ellipse with ratio of semi-axes 9 : 8 was reached. In this case, although a considerable degree of discrimination did develop, it was far from being complete. After three weeks of work upon this differentiation, not only did the discrimination fail to improve but it became considerably worse and finally disappeared altogether. At the same time, the whole behavior of the animal underwent an abrupt change. The hitherto quiet dog, began to squeal in its stand, kept wriggling about, tore off with its teeth the apparatus for mechanical stimulation of the skin, and bit through the tubes connecting the animal's room with the observer, a behavior which never happened before. On being taken into the experimental room, the dog now barked violently.

Apparently, the close resemblance of the 9: 8 ellipse to the circle resulted in what may be called "a state of conflict," the strong simultaneous activation of opposite action tendencies—the activation of *both* the evocation and the inhibition of the alimentary response. Evidently this conflict engendered high–intensity autonomic responses of the anxiety pattern which came to be conditioned to the environmental stimuli that made impact on the animal at that time. (The similarity of the autonomic reaction pattern accompanying conflict to that associated with noxious [electrical] stimulation has been demonstrated by Fonberg [1956].)

In subsequent years, many experimental neuroses were induced by methods that involved the use of conflict in variations of the above experiment. Jacobsen, Wolfe, and Jackson (1935), working with chimpanzees, used difficult discriminations based on the distance between two identical cups, under one of which food was hidden. Dworkin, Raginsky, and Bourne (1937), and Gantt (1944) produced neuroses in dogs by conflict-producing use of auditory stimuli. Krasnogorsky (1925) did the same in children. An interesting and successful modification was the use of stimuli at, and just below, threshold (Dworkin, 1939; Dworkin, Baxt, and Dworkin, 1942). In addition, Karn (1938) reported a method in which the difficulty of discrimination depended on *internal* cues.

Another group of techniques for inducing experimental neuroses makes use of noxious stimulation, usually in the form of electric shock, to evoke the "unconditioned" anxiety responses to which "neutral" stimuli are conditioned. This method, too, had its inception in Pavlov's laboratories (Pavlov, 1927, pp. 289–90). A mild electric current to a spot on the animal's skin was made a conditioned stimulus to food-seeking by delivering food immediately after each application of it. The current was then gradually intensified until it became "extremely powerful." Although frequently applied during many months, it did not evoke a defense reaction until it was systematically applied to a different spot daily. This eventually produced "a most violent defense reaction," and the animal was thereafter disturbed whenever exposed to stimuli related to the experiment. The fact that each of the original stages of training built up an inhibition of the defense reaction evidently distracted Pavlov's attention from the crucial role of the noxious stimulus and led him to conclude that the neuroses were due to "a clash between excitation and inhibition." This conclusion seems erroneous because, during the long period in which defense reaction was inhibited, while inhibition counterbalanced excitation, no disturbance appeared. The neurotic state was induced only when the electric current was applied in a way that outran the initial scope of the conditioned inhibition. Since, as will be seen below with respect to certain experiments on cats, shock alone can produce such neuroses, there is no need to compound the etiology. Similar comments apply to the neuroses produced by the Cornell group (e.g., Anderson and Parmenter, 1941; Liddell, 1944) using weak electric shocks, and Cook's rat neuroses (1939). It is only necessary to say here, that there is much evidence to indicate that all the effects for which complex explanations have been advanced can be produced by direct conditioning to "neutral" stimuli of the responses elicited by electric shock.

In another group of experimental neuroses, the effects were ascribed to motivational conflict between approach to food and avoidance of shock. This explanation was given by Dimmick, Ludlow, and Whiteman (1939) for the neuroses they produced in cats. Subsequently, Masserman (1943) advanced the same theory in respect to his much more extensive and elaborate series. The explanation was a consequence of the fact that the experiments of these workers were so set up that avoidance of shock did, in fact, interrupt approaches to food. However, it does not explain why much the same effects result when an animal is shocked in a confined space, even when there is an apparent absence of any other major motivation (see below).

Experimental Neuroses as Learned Habits

The first experiment to indicate the learned basis of a persistent habit of unadaptive anxiety was Watson and Rayner's (1920) famous case of Little Albert. Finding that the child responded fearfully to the loud sound made by striking an iron bar behind him, the experimenters repeatedly struck the bar just as the child's hand touched a white rat. A fear reaction was conditioned to the rat and was found to have generalized to similar stimuli—a rabbit, a beaver fur, and a dog.

During the years 1947–48, I conditioned neurotic behavior in cats (Wolpe, 1948, 1952) using an experimental cage similar to that of Masserman (1943) —40 inches long, 20 inches wide, and 20 inches high, with an electrifiable grid on its floor. I demonstrated that the neurotic behavior developed even when the animal had not had previous experience with food in the cage. It was sufficient merely to subject him to several high-voltage, low-amperage shocks soon after his first introduction to the experimental cage. The shocks evoked a variety of motor responses (e.g., crouching, clawing at the sides of the cage, howling) and autonomic responses (e.g. pupillary dilatation, erection of hairs, and rapid respiration). It was subsequently found that the autonomic responses (and certain of the motor responses) had become conditioned to the visual stimuli of the experimental situation and to an auditory stimulus (e.g. a buzzer) that had preceded each shock. This anxious behavior was consistently evocable at high intensity in the experimental cage, but some anxiety was also noted on the floor of the experimental laboratory; smaller measures were noted in other rooms that had features of similarity to the experimental laboratory. In several of these places, *anxiety was severe enough to prevent the animal from eating attractive food placed before him*, even though he had been starved for 24 hours, or longer.

Neurotic reactivity was extremely persistent, although the animal was never again shocked. This was the case whether the animal was kept away from the experimental cage for months, or was replaced in it again and again, sometimes for hours. *The core of this persistent reactivity was always the autonomic complex of reactions*. For reasons given below, motor responses were far less likely to be so persistent: usually they diminished in strength and eventually disappeared.†

Two factors apparently contribute to the resistance to extinction of the autonomic response of anxiety. First, a relatively low level of muscle action is involved in autonomic responses, so that there is little generation of the fatigue-associated process known as reactive inhibition (RI) upon which extinction seems to depend (Hull, 1943; Wolpe, 1952c). (It would appear to be for the same reason that conditioned eyelid responses, involving very limited musculature, are unusually resistant to extinction.) Second, each time an organism is removed from an anxiety-evoking situation, there is a

---

† The central role of autonomic responses is also apparent in most human neuroses. While by such means as hypnotic suggestion particular motor responses may be eliminated, the neuroses continue as long as neurotic *anxiety response* habits persist. It may be predicted for the same reason that fundamental therapeutic effects would not as a rule result from therapist behavior that encourages at the interview certain classes of statements made by the patient and not others.

sharp reduction of an internal state of excitation that is conveniently termed anxiety drive. The reinforcing effect that this drive reduction has upon the anxiety response habit counteracts any fatigue-associated tendency toward extinction. That the mere cessation of an anxiety-evoking stimulus has a reinforcing effect upon antecedent anxiety responses appears from an experiment (Wolpe, 1958, p. 59) in which an auditory stimulus conditioned to anxiety was presented to a cat approaching a piece of food dropped in a corner of a room. The animal recoiled, hair erect, pupils dilated; and hesitated before again advancing. Repeating the procedure several times resulted in the establishment of anxiety and avoidance reactions to that corner and also to the sight of food dropped on any floor. The immediate response to the auditory stimulus was anxiety and reversal of forward movement. The only reinforcing state of affairs of which the situation contained evidence was the reduction of anxiety following cessation of the stimulus. Similar findings have been reported by other workers (e.g. Farber, 1948; Miller, 1948a).

Since autonomic responses are present continuously while the animal is in the experimental cage, they are inevitably reinforced at each reduction of anxiety drive that follows removal of the animal from the cage. Motor responses that happen sufficiently often to occur shortly before drive reduction are also reinforced. Motor responses that are repeated infrequently are likely to occur only occasionally just before drive reduction, and therefore tend to undergo gradual extinction. That is why, in our experiments, infrequent motor responses were quite soon extinguished from neurotic constellations.

Basic Therapeutic Experiments

Only a few of the experimenters working with animal neuroses have concerned themselves with therapeutic measures. Pavlov (1927), Petrova (1938), and Dworkin, Raginsky, and Bourne (1937) explored the use of drugs, regarding which we shall have more to say in a later section. Masserman (1943) was the first to employ behavioral methods for overcoming experimental neuroses. His interpretations were in the psychoanalytic framework, however, and he did not analyze his experimental results in terms of the processes of learning with regard to either neurotic change or its reversal.

Some light was thrown on the role of learning in the therapy of experimental neuroses in the course of therapeutic experiments conducted by the present writer (Wolpe, 1948, 1952a, 1958). The resistance of neurotic anxiety responses to the ordinary process of extinction has already been noted. The fact that anxiety could prevent experimental animals from feeding despite prolonged deprivation of food suggested that, reciprocally, feeding might inhibit anxiety in conditions where the anxiety reaction was weak; and that thus to inhibit it might result in a weakening of the anxiety response habit.

To test this possibility, we made use of the fact, mentioned above, that when the experimental animals were placed in other rooms, according to each room's degree of resemblance to the experimental laboratory, lesser degrees of anxiety were evoked. Each animal was offered food, first in the laboratory itself. If he refused to eat there, we proceeded on subsequent days to rooms successively more *unlike* the laboratory. When at last a room was found in which anxiety responses were so weak that feeding was not inhibited, the animal was presented with a succession of meat pellets. The feedings were accompanied by a gradual disappearance of all evidence of anxiety in the particular room. Tested the next day, the animal appeared free from anxiety in that room; and in the room next closest in resemblance to the experimental room showed relative little anxiety and no longer refused food. Here, too, repeated feedings led to complete elimination of anxiety. Proceeding thus by stages, the animal was eventually induced to eat in the experimental cage, which also, in the same way, was finally deprived of all power to elicit anxiety.

However, the auditory stimulus that had regularly preceded the electric shocks in the original conditioning *could still evoke anxiety*. This was an important observation, for it indicated that neurotic responses are *stimulus-specific*. Similar specificity was subsequently noted in the treatment of human neuroses (Wolpe, 1961b). For example, the overcoming of a fear of the accoutrements of death did not, in a particular patient, ameliorate a claustrophobia. Further, clinical observation seems to confirm the expectation that, if all stimulus "triggers" to neurotic responses are "deconditioned" from the responses, the responses cease permanently (Wolpe, 1961b). They do not reappear spontaneously, as they would if there were a focus of irritation or of "dammed-up forces". Only relearning can be expected to reestablish responses to particular stimuli.

To overcome the residual neurotic habit of responding with anxiety to the auditory stimulus, we applied methods parallel to those used in the case of the visual stimuli. Theoretically, it would have been possible to work along several dimensions of generalization—time, distance, intensity, pitch. In fact, the first two of these were both applied with success. The distance dimension was used as follows:

The animal was offered food at increasing distances from the sound of the buzzer until eating occurred. One animal responded to the buzzer with anxiety so great that even at the distance of 30 ft the sound could inhibit him from taking food, although he had not eaten for 20 hr. However, at 40 ft he hurriedly snapped up a pellet of meat. Pellets of meat were given repeatedly during the sounding of the buzzer, and overt anxiety at 40 ft gradually decreased to zero. When then tested at 30 ft, the animal had less anxiety than previously and accepted a pellet of meat, and after repeated feedings lost all signs of anxiety at that distance too. Increasingly close approaches were made by similar steps, with the eventual result that the animal had no anxiety with the buzzer sounding continuously only a few feet away—in fact, responded to the sound by looking around for food.

At this stage, we had to ask whether the anxiety response habit had been eliminated or was merely being suppressed by a more strongly conditioned feeding response. The matter was easily put to the test. The feeding response was extinguished by repeatedly presenting the buzzer without any further feeding. If the anxiety had been suppressed by the occurrence of feeding, the removal of the feeding reaction should have been followed by resurgence of anxiety to the sound of the buzzer. In no animal, as it turned out, was there any recurrence of anxiety to the sound of the buzzer upon the extinction of food seeking. This seemed to establish that the strength of the anxiety-response habit had been reduced to zero, and a basic method for overcoming neurotic reactions had become available.

A Psychotherapeutic Principle
and its Applications

The above therapeutic experiments led to the framing of a general hypothesis: *If a response inhibitory to anxiety can be made to occur in the presence of anxiety-evoking stimuli, it will weaken the connection between these stimuli and the anxiety responses.* This presumes the occurrence at a complex level of neural organization of the phenomenon of *reciprocal inhibition* first described by Sherrington (1906) in the context of spinal reflexes. A simple example of reciprocal inhibitions is the reflex relaxation of the extensor muscles of the arm that accompanies contraction of the flexor muscles flexing the elbow, and the reciprocal relaxation of the flexors when the extensors contract. Modern neurophysiological research (e.g. Lloyd, 1946) has shown that such relaxation is brought about by impulses that directly block the synaptic transmission of excitatory impulses to the antagonists of actively contracting muscles.

At higher levels of organization, the performance of a given response often leads to the inhibition of all other responses that involve the same functional units. An obvious example is the articulation of a word. Ordinarily, this inhibits all simultaneous tendencies to articulate other words. Again, an attempt to do two mental tasks at the same time results in some degree of inhibition of the performance of each (Messerschmidt, 1927).

In certain circumstances, the intercurrent arousal of a relatively strong response incompatible with an ongoing response will inhibit the latter, at least in part, and a decrement may subsequently be noted in the strength of the habit that subserves the inhibited response†. The most extensive

---

† It is worth remarking that some psychologists, for example, Maatsch, Adelson, and Denny (1954) argue that even the process of experimental extinction depends upon competing responses rather than upon a fatigue-asso-

work on the weakening effects of new responses upon previously established habits has been in the area of verbal learning. An association between one word and another is weakened if a third word is repeatedly made to follow the first (stimulus) word. Osgood (1948) was the first to recognize that this phenomenon, known as retroactive inhibition, is an instance of reciprocal inhibition. The earliest study utilizing competing responses to weaken responses with powerful autonomic accompaniments was reported by Pavlov (1927). (It has been referred to above in another context). A weak electric current was made a conditioned stimulus to feeding in a dog. During several experimental sessions, the strength of the current was increased by stages, and at each stage repeated feedings led to disappearance of all signs of anxiety and avoidance. Eventually, an extremely strong current elicited only a food approach response and no defense reaction at all. Apparently, at each stage of the experiment the occurence of feeding was accompanied by a reciprocal inhibition of such mild defense reaction as the slightly intensified electrical stimulus tended to evoke. This conclusion is, of course, based on the findings, recounted above, of the therapeutic experiments on neuroses of cats.

Reciprocal Inhibition in the Treatment of Human Neuroses

Since neurotic responses in human subjects, no less than in animals, most typically have anxiety as their principal constituent, making use of the reciprocal inhibition principle implies finding responses that will inhibit anxiety. Observation alone can determine what responses will have this effect, for although it is possible that certain mutual inhibitory arrangements are immutably established in the course of the physical growth of the nervous system, in other instances such arrangements are modifiable by the learning process, and also perhaps by further growth. For example, while feeding often inhibits anxiety in children and has been used to overcome phobias (Jones, 1928; Lazarus, 1959), it usually seems to have lost this effect in adults.

Up to the present certain responses have been found most useful in deliberate efforts to overcome neurotic anxiety response habits: (1) relaxation responses; (2) sexual responses; (3) assertive responses; and (4) respiratory responses (carbondioxide-oxygen mixtures used for pervasive ["free-floating"] anxiety).

The employment of relaxation responses in systematic desensitization (see below) most clearly parallels the treatment of animal neuroses described

ciated inhibitory state. It seems likely that, at the very least, in many instances competing responses are a contributory factor. The obscurity of the position is due to the fact that the great majority of studies on the weakening of habits have been concerned with extinction.

above. Closer experimental analogues for the use of assertive and sexual responses are given below. There is as yet no direct experimental parallel to carbon dioxide therapy. However, experimental precendents are available for the adjuvant use of other drugs for fundamental therapy (therapy that changes habit patterns in contrast to symptomatic therapy that merely cloaks them), and also for two less frequently used conditioning methods. All these will be discussed.

It must always be remembered, when studying special methods of therapy of the neuroses, that the effects peculiar to a specific method must be separated from the more general effects of interviews that give a measure of success to all psychotherapy.

Systematic Desensitization Therapy

Systematic desensitization is an example of "gradual approach" therapy, closely parallel in its essentials to the already described method of overcoming experimental neuroses. It is applicable to treating the neurotic response habits related to a wide range of stimuli, but is generally not used in connection with neurotic responses that lend themselves to treatment by changing behavior in interpersonal situations. It is, however, especially valuable for treating phobias and habits of responding with anxiety to many relatively complex situations, such as being rejected or being watched, whose basic similarity to the phobias is far greater than is generally realized.

Systematic desensitization, which has been described in detail elsewhere (Wolpe, 1958, 1959, 1961b), involves three sets of operations: (1) training the patient in deep relaxation by an abbreviated form of the method described by Jacobson (1938) (who was the first to demonstrate (1939, 1940) that the autonomic effects of relaxation are the opposite of those of anxiety); (2) during the same sessions, identifying the "themes" of stimuli to neurotic reactions, e.g. heights, crowds, situations of rejection, listing a considerable number of situations on each theme, and then ranking these situations in order of the intensity of anxiety each arouses (the ranked list being called an *anxiety hierarchy*); and (3) at the session following the completion of the foregoing operations, causing the patient (usually hypnotized) to relax deeply and then asking him to imagine the least disturbing item in the list. If, according to expectation, the anxiety evoked is of low intensity, the strength of its evocation will progressively decrease, eventually to zero, in the course of several further presentations of the item. The next item in the list is then presented, likewise repeatedly until it ceases to evoke anxiety. Proceeding in this manner, the therapist is eventually able to present the "strongest" item in the hierarchy without arousing any anxiety. At every stage it has been found that freedom from anxiety to an imagined stimulus confers freedom from anxiety upon confrontation with the real equivalent (though sometimes the latter lags behind).

It is crucial to note that, just as in the animal studies feeding can counteract only relatively weak anxiety, ralaxation can counteract anxiety only if the latter is relatively weak. A stimulus that evokes anxiety strongly may be presented many times to the relaxed patient without the strength of anxiety diminishing in the least. But if the anxiety response is weak, then from one presentation of the stimulus to the next the anxiety declines in strength and at last ceases to be in evidence. There is, in fact, an inverse relationship between the magnitude of anxiety a stimulus evokes and the ease with which the anxiety-response habit can be overcome by the inhibiting effects of a given degree of relaxation.

Once a "weak" stimulus has stopped eliciting anxiety, a somewhat "stronger" one on the same theme presented to the fully relaxed patient will evoke less anxiety than it would have done before. Successive presentations diminish the anxiety aroused by this also to zero. Stimuli at ever-rising levels in the hierarchy are thus brought within the anxiety-inhibiting capacity of the subject's relaxation. To put the matter in another way: If there are ten stimuli which, in their variations along a dimension of generalization (see below), elicit in a subject quantities of anxiety which vary from 1 to 10 and if through the inhibiting effects of relaxation the anxiety aroused by the stimulus evoking one unit is reduced to zero, the stimulus that orginally evoked 2 units of anxiety will be found to be evoking only 1 unit. Take, for example, a subject who has a fear of heights in places where there is no danger of falling. He has 1 unit of anxiety on visualizing himself looking down from a height of 10 ft, and 2 units when the height is 20 feet. Reduction of the anxiety from the 10-ft level to zero will have the result that the amount of anxiety evoked by 20 ft will be diminished to 1 unit. This in turn will drop to zero upon the repeated presentation of the 20-ft height to the imagination of the deeply relaxed subject; and then 30 ft will evoke one unit of anxiety. In this gradual fashion, anxiety reponses can be eradicated from any height. It must be emphasized that these decrements of response are not transient, but lasting. As in the animal experiments, they are indicative of decrease of strength of anxiety-response habits.

Desensitization amounts to a systematic deconditioning of anxiety responses along a stimulus dimension of generalization (Hull, 1943) from a central conditioned stimulus. The applicability of the generalization principle to complex configurations was first demonstrated by Miller (1948b). Since each stimulus in a continuum shares features with "adjacent" stimuli, the elimination of anxiety responses to a stimulus remote from the central stimulus involves the elimination of whatever fraction of the anxiety evoked by related stimuli is attributable to the shared features. The situations to which the subject is "exposed" in desensitization are imaginary, but there is evidence that responses to imaginary stimuli are similar to real ones (Stone, 1955).

The use of systematic desensitization is not confined to "simple" classical phobias. It can be applied to almost every case where the subject is disturbed by the mere presence of stimulus situations which contain no objective threat. It will usually be found that each stimulus situation, however complex, is one of a class of situations whose members evoke anxiety in different degrees. The coherence of a class very often does not depend upon the outward similarity of the situations but upon some core or theme that they share. Themes commonly found are being rejected, being disapproved of, aggressive behavior of others, or being watched. In constructing hierarchies based on such themes, all situations that embody the theme are first listed; and then the patient ranks the situations in order of the magnitude of the reaction he anticipates he would have on exposure to each. The following is a young woman's hierarchy of situations on the theme of "devaluation by others," ranked in descending order of intensity of her reactions.

1. An argument she raises in a discussion is ignored by the group.
2. She is not recognized by a person she has briefly met three times.
3. Her mother says she is selfish because she is not helping in the house. (Studying instead.)
4. She is not recognized by a person she has briefly met twice.
5. Her mother calls her lazy.
6. She is not recognized by a person she has briefly met once.

In a recent survey of a randomly selected sample of sixty-eight phobias and allied reactions in thirty-nine patients treated by desensitization, it was found that sixty-two of the areas of disturbance were either totally overcome or markedly improved in a mean of 11.2 sessions per hierarchy (Wolpe, 1961b).

Experimental Bases of Other Therapeutic Techniques

Each of the experimental findings given below has a clinical parallel in the form of new psychotherapeutic techniques. Reciprocal inhibition appears to be the effective process in each of the instances in which lasting changes of response have been observed.

The addition of a stimulus increasing the probability of a response antagonistic to anxiety: The effectiveness of such a stimulus was first demonstrated by Masserman (1943) and confirmed by the writer (1952a). As already stated, hungry, neurotic cats will not eat meat pellets dropped in front of them in the experimental cage. But some of them *will* eat if the pellets are conveyed to them by a human hand, either directly or at the end of a rod. In my own experiments, the hand had become conditioned to evoke approach responses to food because food had been routinely given to the animals by the human hand in their living cages. These approach tendencies presumably summated with the approach tendencies evoked by the food itself, and in some cases the resultant drive strength was sufficient to overcome the anxiety-associated inhibition.

A summation of action tendencies analogous to the above is frequently operative in patients undergoing psychotherapy based on principles of learning (e.g., Salter, 1950; Wolpe, 1952b, 1954, 1958; Stevenson, 1959). Through such summation, the subject is enabled to perform certain acts previously impossible. For example, a patient may have been chronically inhibited by fear from expressing his resentment toward a person who has always taken advantage of him. The inhibition of its outward expression does not remove the resentment, which may have been evoked at every encounter with that person perhaps over many years. The therapist, having explained to the patient in a simple way the reciprocal inhibition principle, points out the value of assertiveness wherever there is undue fear in person- al relationships. He increases the tendency to assertive action by making it clear that it is not "wrong" to stand up for one's reasonable rights or to hurt the feelings of those who flout these rights; by emphasizing the in- justices that have been inflicted on the patient and by pointing to the social unattractiveness of weak and poltroonish behavior. The action ten- dency aroused by changes in attitude thus directly brought about summates with that of the unexpressed resentment to produce a total action potential great enough to overcome the inhibiting effects of the fear. The patient can in consequence express his resentment outwardly. Such action leads to reciprocal inhibition of the anxiety response that had been invariable in this kind of interpersonal situation, and eventuates in a weakening of the anxiety-response habit. It is important for the patient to be carefully en- joined to be discreet—not to be assertive when the act might be punished, by the loss of his job, for example.

By contrast with the above, but to the same effect, in a technique em- ploying sexual responses in actual sexual situations to overcome impotence (Wolpe, 1954, 1958), the therapist's intervention results in a *subtraction* of anxiety instead of an addition to the opposing impulse. It is made clear both to the patient and his partner that no particular level of performance must ever be *required* on any sexual occasion. A major source of anxiety is thus removed, and the sexual arousal is consequently more capable of inhibiting such anxiety as remains.

There is a feature of this technique that has another experimental ana- logue. According to the usual instructions, the patient lies with his partner in a relaxed way and waits for surges of sexual feeling as a basis for action. It would appear that these surges arise as a function of behavioral oscillation (Hull, 1943, pp. 304–21)—fluctuations in strength of different motivational states. Presumably, a high level of sexual drive now and then coincides with a low level of anxiety, and at such time sexual feelings "break through". The experimental analogue to this is a method of overcoming experimental neuroses described by Masserman (1943) and repeated by the present writer (1948, 1952a). This consists of placing a hungry, neurotic cat in the experi- mental cage, and then forcing it, by means of a sliding partition, toward the food box containing attractive food. After a delay, the animal may eat. Thereafter, eating takes place with increasing readiness and the neurotic reactions progressively decrease. It seems plausible that this technique succeeds because occasionally in some animals, through behavioral oscillation, the food-approach motivation momentarily exceeds the anxiety-*cum*-avoidance motivation in strength.

Diminishing the level of anxiety by drugs as an aid to reciprocal inhibition: Investigations in past years (Pavlov, 1927; Dworkin, Raginsky and Bourne, 1937; Masserman and Yum, 1946) have revealed that lasting improvement sometimes occurs in neurotic animals after more or less prolonged treatment with such sedative drugs as alcohol, bromides, or barbiturates. The first study to have isolated relevant variables is a recent one by Miller, Murphy, and Mirsky (1957). Using electric shock as the unconditioned stimulus, they conditioned a large number of rats to perform an avoidance response at the sound of a buzzer. The animals were then randomly divided into four groups for extinction studies. Two of the groups received injections of saline and the other two injections of chlorpromazine on each of four consecutive days. A saline-injected group (I) and a chlorpromazine injected group (II) received fifteen unreinforced presentations of the buzzer on each of the 4 days, while the other two groups were simply returned to the living cage. Group II made far fewer avoidance responses than group I on these 4 days; and on the fifth and subsequent days, when *all* groups were given unreinforced trials without any injections, it was found that group II had a much lower residue of avoidance conditioning than any of the other groups (as shown by a much smaller number of avoidance responses). That this outcome was related to autonomic effects of the chlorpromazine and not to a suppression of motor responses was indicated by repeating the experiment with injections of phenobarbital of a dosage that had previously been equated with chlorpromazine in terms of motor retardation effects. In animals given phenobarbital the level of avoidance responses was not diminished, in marked contrast to the chlorpromazine group.

The *lasting* consequences of completely or largely suppressing the autonomic responses conditioned to the buzzer may be accounted for as follows. Besides the buzzer, the experimental situation contained other stimuli that as a result of the animal's "life experience" had been previously conditioned to responses with autonomic accompaniments other than anxiety (e.g. curiosity responses [Berlyne, 1960]). Anxiety responses at full strength could inhibit these other emotions; but when chlorpromazine damped down anxiety to a low level, it permitted them to surge forth and reciprocally inhibit whatever anxiety or fraction of the anxiety-evoking process was activated. Each occasion of reciprocal inhibition of anxiety responses would leave behind some measure of conditioned inhibition of the anxiety response habit.

The clinical implications of Miller, Murphy, and Mirsky's experiments are likely to be considerable. There are already suggestive pieces of information regarding the effects of prolonged administration of chlorpromazine and other tranquilizing drugs. Winkelman (1954) found that after administration of the drug for 6 months or longer in doses sufficient to produce marked amelioration of neurotic symptoms, improvement persisted for 6 months in 35 per cent of patients in whom the drug was gradually withdrawn, even though they had received no psychotherapy. Unfortunately, no control study records the improvement rate in the same period among patients who, receiving no psychotherapy, were given a placebo instead of chlorpromazine; but the percentage of patients lastingly benefited seems greater than may perhaps be expected from the use of placebos.

. In a number of exploratory tests with individual patients, I have found that after administering codeine, chlorpromazine, or meprobamate in such doses that the drugs inhibit any substantial degrees of neurotic anxiety (even during repeated exposures to relevant stimuli), lasting improvement is often noted after discontinuing the drug. I have also observed that in certain patients in whom systematic desensitization is obstructed by an inability to procure sufficient muscle relaxation to produce emotional calm, the administration of a tranquilizing drug an hour or so before the session makes successful desensitization possible. The anxiety-suppressing action of the drug makes it easier for active muscle relaxation to inhibit the anxiety that verbal stimuli from the therapist tend to evoke.

Reciprocal inhibition of anxiety responses would be favored just as surely by chemical agents augmenting responses antagonistic to anxiety as by those selectively suppressing anxiety. In the case of neurotic anxieties elicited by sexual situations, it has proved possible preferentially to enhance the sexual response by the previous injection of testosterone so that the anxiety response is inhibited and its habit strength consequently weakened. A case illustrating this process was reported a good many years ago by Miller, Hubert, and Hamilton (1938); I have had two similar cases. An experimental rationale for using testosterone to heighten sexual drive is to be found in the observations of Beach (1942) that sexual arousal in relation to any of a variety of sexual objects increases with increases in circulating sex hormone.

Conditioned inhibition of anxiety through a dominating motor response. In 1948 Mowrer and Viek performed an experiment showing that when rats are repeatedly exposed to a continuous mild electric shock, those animals who are enabled to learn a definite motor response in relation to the termination of the shock develop very little anxiety when placed in the experimental situation minus the shock. In contrast to these, much greater anxiety is shown by animals who have no opportunity to learn such a motor response. In another context (Wolpe, 1953), I have explained this phenomenon as follows.

When an animal is subjected to continuous electric shock in a given situation, autonomic responses of anxiety and many musculoskeletal (motor) responses are evoked. A similar variety of musculo-skeletal responses will accompany the autonomic responses at every repetition of the electric shock unless there is one motor response that is repeatedly followed by cessation of the shock. If there should be a response thus repeatedly reinforced, it will become increasingly dominant over all the other "competing" response tendencies. This implies a gradual weakening of the latter, probably by conditioned inhibition based on reciprocal inhibition. It is not unreasonable to suppose that the weakening of "competing" response tendencies extends also to the autonomic responses.

This suggested the therapeutic possibility that if a mild noxious stimulus is applied on repeated occasions in the presence of a stimulus evoking neurotic anxiety responses, and if this noxions stimulus is at the same time conditioned to produce a well defined motor response, the neurotic anxiety may be gradually weakened. Since the practical application of this idea involves considerable difficulties, it has been considered only for certain cases that have not responded to simpler measures. Consequently, treatment based on this principle has been attempted in no more than half a dozen patients. Two of these have clearly benefited. One, reported in detail elsewhere (Wolpe, 1958), who had a fear of falling and a very severe agoraphobia, recovered completely and was still well 4 years later. The second, who had a fear of trembling while using cutlery or drinking tea in front of other people, experienced considerable improvement. In both cases, arm raising was used as the conditioned motor response to mild shock to the forearm, and graded neurotic anxiety-producing stimuli were presented to the patient's imagination.

Conditioning of "anxiety-relief" responses. Zbrozyna observed (1957) that if a stimulus is repeatedly presented to an eating animal just before the experimenter withdraws the food, that stimulus acquires the property of inhibiting feeding even when the animal is in the middle of a meal. This observation suggested that "anxiety-relief" responses may be directly conditioned to convenient stimuli and subsequently used to counter anxiety. By analogy, it was expected that if an uncomfortable induction shock were administered to a human subject for several seconds and were then made to cease immediately after a signal, that signal would become connected to such bodily response sas would follow cessation of the shock. Furthermore, these responses would be the negative of the anxiety that had been produced by the shock. This, it was hoped, would imply the acquisition of a weapon to combat anxiety due to *other* stimuli. The hope was encouraged by the fact that Coppock (1951) and Goodson and Brownstein (1955) had shown that when a stimulus is repeatedly presented at the moment of termination of an electric shock an approach response is conditioned to that stimulus.

The experimental facts have been applied therapeutically to some neurotic patients as follows. Silver electrodes connected to the secondary circuit of a Palmer inductorium are attached to the patient's left arm and forearm respectively. Using an inflow of 6 volts from a dry battery into the primary and starting with the secondary coil at 10 cm, we observe the patient's reactions to brief shocks whose intensity is increased step by step through approximating the secondary coil to the primary. When the shock is "very uncomfortable"—usually at about 7·0 cm—a suitable level is considered to have been reached. After a pause, the patient is told that the shock will be turned on continuously. He is to endure it until he feels it quite unpleasant. It will be switched off the moment he says: "Calm". As soon as he says the word, the current is switched off. This is repeated ten to twenty times in a session. Some subjects report a feeling of relief at the cessation of the shock and this seems attributable to termination of anxiety responses to the shock. After one to three sessions, these subjects find that using the word in disturbing situations or during their aftermath decreases the disturbed feeling.

I have used this method in a small number of cases, purely as a symptomatic measure, and in occasional individuals it has been a potent means of diminishing ongoing anxiety. Meyer (1957) has made an attempt to apply it to obtain conditioned inhibition of neurotic anxiety. The effects were not very impressive in his small-scale exploration, but the method seems to deserve more systematic study.

Concluding Remarks

Experiments on the production and cure of neuroses in animals have resulted, as described above, in new methods of psychotherapy and also in a new theory of the crucial process conceived to operate in most psychotherapy—reciprocal inhibition of anxiety responses. It seems from a good many studies (e.g. Eysenck, 1952) that most other forms of psychotherapy yield favorable results in approximately 50 per cent of the cases treated, irrespective of the theoretical framework employed by the therapist. This suggests that a common process perhaps generally unrecognized, is the real basis of success in all of them. On the ground of parsimony the possibility needs to be entertained that reciprocal inhibition is the basis of this common process, just as it seems to be the basis of the special effects described above. It has been proposed (Wolpe, 1958) that the source of inhibition of anxiety responses is the emotional responses other than anxiety that may be evoked in any kind of psychotherapeutic interview. It is presumed that these emotional responses reciprocally inhibit the neurotic responses evoked by verbal stimuli and thus gradually diminish the neurotic habit strength. If it is indeed the case that therapists who employ conventional therapies owe their successes not to the processes alleged by their theories but to learning mechanisms of which they are not cognisant, it will be a strong argument for the widespread use in psychotherapy of the specific techniques based on principles of learning. A number of studies are under way, and others are in prospect, which, it is predicted, will establish the position beyond reasonable doubt.

Increasing numbers of clinical reports, meanwhile, testify impressively to the efficacy of behavioral methods of therapy. I have reported (Wolpe, 1958) that nearly 90 per cent of 210 neurotic patients were either apparently cured or much improved after a mean of little over thirty sessions. Of forty-five patients followed up over 2–7 years, only one relapsed. Eysenck (1960) has assembled more than thirty studies by many authors demonstrating successful elimination of neurotic habits by therapy based on principles of learning. Several further reports have recently appeared (Lazovik and Lang, 1960; Bond and Hutchison, 1960; Freeman and Kendrick, 1960; Walton, 1961).

The allegation is frequently made that such methods of treating neuroses are only symptomatic and do not "get to the root." This allegation springs from an assumption of the correctness of the psychoanalytical account of the nature of neurosis. Leaving aside the fact that psychoanalytical theory contains logical inconsistencies (Wohlgemuth, 1923; Salter, 1952) and that much of the evidence by which it has been bolstered is inadmissible (Wolpe and Rachman, 1960), the practical implication of the question is whether recoveries obtained by conditioning methods endure and are free from repercussions to the patient. The answer, based on the evidence so far obtained, would seem to be in the affirmative. Psychoanalytical theory postulates that, in general, recoveries from neurosis without psychoanalysis are unreliable; but in a survey of follow-up studies of such cases (Wolpe, 1961a) only four relapses were found among 249 patients. This finding accords well with conditioning theory, which holds that the elimination of a neurotic habit is permanent unless there is reinstatement by specific new conditioning.

REFERENCES

ANDERSON, O. D., and PARMENTER, R. (1941) *A long term study of the experimental neurosis in the sheep and dog*, Psychosom. Med. Monogr. **2**, Nos. 3 and 4.

BEACH, F. A. (1942) Analysis of the factors involved in the arousal, maintenance, and manifestation of sexual excitement in male animals, *Psychosom. Med.* **4**, p. 173.

BERLYNE, D. E. (1960) *Conflict, Arousal and Curiosity*, New York, McGraw-Hill.

BOND, I. K., and HUTCHISON, H. C. (1960) Application of reciprocal inhibition therapy to exhibitionism, *Canad. Med. Assoc. J.* **83**, p. 23.

COOK, S. W. (1939) The production of "experimental neurosis" in the white rat, *Psychosom. Med.* **1**, p. 293.

COPPOCK, H. W. (1951) Secondary reinforcing effect of a stimulus repeatedly presented after electric shock, *Am. Psychologist* **6**, p. 277.

DIMMICK, F. L., LUDLOW, N., and WHITEMAN, A. (1939) A study of "experimental neurosis" in cats, *J. Comp. Psychol.* **28**, p. 39.

DWORKIN, S. (1939) Conditioning neuroses in dog and cat, *Psychosom. Med.* **1**, p. 388.

DWORKIN, S., BAXT, J. O., and DWORKIN, E. (1942) Behavioral disturbances of vomiting and micturition in conditioned cats, *Psychosom. Med.* **4,** p. 75.

DWORKIN, S., RAGINSKY, B. B., and BOURNE, W. (1937) Action of anesthetics and sedatives upon the inhibited nervous system, *Curr. Res. Anesth.* **16,** p. 238.

EYSENCK, H. J. (1952) The effects of psychotherapy: an evaluation. *J. consult. Psychol.* **16,** p. 319.

EYSENCK, H. J. (1960) *Behavior therapy and the neuroses,* New York, Pergamon Press.

FARBER, I. E. (1948) Response fixation under anxiety and non-anxiety conditions, *J. Exper. Psychol.* **38,** p. 111.

FENICHEL, O. (1945) *Psychoanalytic Theory of Neurosis,* New York, W. W. Norton Inc.

FONBERG, E. (1956) On the manifestation of conditioned defensive reactions in stress, *Bull. Soc. Sci. Lettr. Lodz,* Class III, Sci. Math. Natur. **7,** p. 1.

FREEMAN, H. L., and KENDRICK, D. C. (1960) A case of cat phobia, *Brit. Med. J.* **2** p. 497.

GANTT, W. H. (1944) Experimental Basis for Neurotic Behaviour, Psychosom. Med. Monogr. **3,** Nos. 3 and 4.

GOODSON, F. A., and BROWNSTEIN, A. (1955) Secondary reinforcing and motivating properties of stimuli contiguous with shock onset and termination, *J. Comp. Physiol. Psychol.* **48,** p. 381.

HENDRICK, I. (1958) *Facts and Theories of Psychoanalysis,* New York, Knopf.

HULL, C. L. (1943) *Principles of Behaviour,* New York, Appleton-Century-Crofts.

JACOBSEN, C. F., WOLFE, J. B., and JACKSON, T. A. (1935) An experimental analysis of the functions of the frontal association areas in primates, *J. Nerv. Ment. Dis.* **82,** p. 1.

JACOBSON, E. (1938) *Progressive Relaxation,* Chicago, Univ. Chicago Press.

JONES, M. C. (1924a) Elimination of children's fears, *J. Exper. Psychol.* **7,** p. 382.

JONES, M. C. (1924b) A laboratory study of fear: the case of Peter, *J. Genet. Psychol.* **31,** p. 308.

KARN, H. W. (1938) A case of experimentally induced neurosis in the cat, *J. Exper. Psychol.* **22,** p. 589.

LAZARUS, A. A. (1959) The elimination of children's phobias by deconditioning, *Med. Proc.* **5,** p. 261.

LAZOVIK, A. D., and LANG, P. J. (1960) A laboratory demonstration of systematic desensitization psychotherapy, *J. Psychol. Stud.* **11,** p. 238.

LIDDELL. H. S. (1944) Conditioned reflex method and experimental neurosis, in J. McV. Hunt, *Personality and the Behavior Disorders,* New York, Ronald.

LLOYD, D. (1946) Facilitation and inhibtion of spinal motoneurones, *J. Neurophysiol.* **9,** p. 421.

MAATSCH, J. L., ADELSON, H. M., and DENNY, M. R. (1954) Effort and resistance to extinction of the bar-pressing response. *J. Comp. Physiol. Psychol.* **47,** p. 47.

MASSERMAN, J. H. (1943) *Behavior and Neurosis,* Chicago, Univ. Chicago Press.

MASSERMAN, J. H., and YUM, K. S. (1946) An analysis of the influence of alcohol on experimental neuroses in cats, *Psychosom. Med.* **8,** p. 36.

MESSERSCHMIDT, R. (1927) A quantitative investigation of the alleged independent operation of conscious and subconscious processes, *J. Abnorm. Soc. Psychol.* **22,** p. 325.

MEYER, V. (1957) The treatment of two phobic patients on the basis of learning principles, *J. Abnorm. Soc. Psychol.* **55,** p. 261.

MILLER, N. E. (1948a) Studies of fear as an acquirable drive: 1. Fear as motivation and fear-reduction as reinforcement in the learning of new responses, *J. Exper. Psychol.* **38**, p. 89.

MILLER, N. E. (1948b) Theory and experiment relating psychoanalytic displacement to stimulus response generalization, *J. Abnorm. Soc. Psychol.* **43**, p. 155.

MILLER, N. E., HUBERT, E., and HAMILTON, J. (1938) Mental and behavioral changes following male hormone treatment of adult castration hypogonadism and psychic impotence, *Proc. Soc. Exp. Biol. Med.* **38**, p. 538.

MILLER, R. E., MURPHY, J. V., and MIRSKY, I. A. (1957) Persistent effects of chlorpromazine on extinction of an avoidance response, *Arch. Neurol. Psychiat.* **78**, p. 526.

MOWRER, O. H., and VIEK, P. (1948) Experimental analogue of fear from a sense of helplessness, *J. Abnorm. Soc. Psychol.* **43**, p. 193.

OSGOOD, C. E. (1948) An investigation into the causes of retroactive inhibition, *J. Exper. Psychol.* **38**, p. 132.

PAVLOV, I. P. (1927) *Conditioned Reflexes*, translated by G. V. Anrep, London, Oxford University Press.

SALTER, A. (1950) *Conditioned Reflex Therapy*, New York, Creative Age Press.

SALTER, A. (1952) *The Case Against Prychoanalysis*, New York, Henry Holt.

SHERRINGTON, C. S. (1906) *Integrative Action of the Nervous System*, New Haven, Conn., Yale Univ. Press.

STEVENSON, I. (1959) Direct instigation of behavioral changes in psychotherapy, A. M. A. *Arch. Gen. Psychiat.* **1**, p. 115.

STONE, D. R. (1955) Responses to imagined auditory stimuli as compared to recorded sounds, *J. Consult. Psychol.* **19**, p. 254.

WALTON, D. (1961) Application of learning theory to the treatment of a case of somnambulism, *J. Clin. Psychol.* **17**, p. 96.

WATSON, J. B., and RAYNER, R. (1920) Conditioned emotional reactions, *J. Exper. Psychol.* **3**, p. 1.

WINKELMAN, N. W., Jr. (1954) Chlorpromazine in the treatment of neuropsychiatric disorders, *J. A. M. A.* **155**, p. 18.

WOHLGEMUTH, A. (1923) *A Critical Examination of Psychoanalysis*, London, Allen and Unwin.

WOLPE, J. (1948) An approach to the problem of neurosis based on the conditioned response, unpublished M. D. thesis, University of the Witwatersrand.

WOLPE, J. (1952a) Experimental neurosis as learned behavior, *Brit. J. Psychol.* **43**, p. 243.

WOLPE, J. (1952b) Objective psychotherapy of the neuroses, S. *African Med. J.* **26**, p. 825.

WOLPE, J. (1952c) The formation of negative habits: a neurophysiological view, *Psychol. Rev.* **59**, p. 290.

WOLPE, J. (1953) Learning theory and "abnormal fixations", *Psychol. Rev.* **60**, p. 111.

WOLPE, J. (1954) Reciprocal inhibition as the main basis of psychotherapeutic effects, A. M. A. *Arch. Neurol. Psychiat.* **72**, p. 205.

WOLPE, J. (1958) *Psychotherapy by Reciprocal Inhibition*, Stanford, Calif., Stanford University Press.

WOLPE, J. (1959) Psychotherapy based on the principle of reciprocal inhibition, in A. Burton, *Case Studies in Counseling and Psychotherapy*, Englewood Cliffs, N. J., Prentice-Hall.

WOLPE, J. (1961a) The prognosis in un-psychoanalyzed recovery from neurosis, *Am. J. Psychiat.* (In Press.)

WOLPE, J. (1961 b) The desensitization treatment of neuroses, *J. Nerv. Ment. Dis.* **112,** p. 189.

WOLPE, J., and RACHMAN, S. (1960) Psychoanalytic "evidence": a critique based on Freud's case of Little Hans, *J. Nerv. Ment. Dis.* **130,** p. 135.

ZBROZYNA, A. W. (1957) The conditioned cessation of eating, *Bull. Acad. Polonaise Sci.* **5,** p. 261.

18

THE PHYSIOLOGICAL BASIS OF PSYCHIATRY: THE CONDITIONED REFLEX†

W. Horsley Gantt

In arranging this series of discussions Dr. Wortis is following the stand which he has taken for a number of years of supporting an objective psychiatry. I am glad to be a participant in this effort.

Psychiatry ranks, let us admit at the outset, as among the most complex of all subjects if it is taken as a branch of knowledge rather than simply as an empirical method of helping the mentally ill. It deals primarily with deviations of the function of the most complex relationships. My justification for presenting the experimental and theoretical material of this article to psychiatrists is that for the advance of psychiatric methods, as Bacon has well said for science in general, "knowledge is power."

In the natural sciences we have seen the full fruition of the experimental approach. Now, is the modern experimental method, dating from Francis Bacon and Galileo, applicable to the study of human behavior and its aberrations? In this article I shall attempt an answer by showing what has been accomplished in the field by a special type of experimental method.

One type of study does not necessarily preclude others having a sound basis in the same field. At first no one can say absolutely what approach will finally prove most successful. Time alone must be the arbiter.

Pavlov [36] was the first physiologist to show how the experimental method should be used to study psychical phenomena. His researches, under the name of the conditioned reflex, are now too well known among those of the medical profession to require recounting here, although when I was a medical student I never heard of Pavlov except as a physiologist of digestion. But in spite of the fact that many know his name, few even in medicine understand the significance of his work; indeed many books have been written on psychosomatic medicine without a single reference to or mention of Pavlov who, perhaps more than anyone else in the present century laid the basis for investigating the relations between the symbols of our subjective life and the physiological expression on both somatic and autonomic levels.

† By permission of Grune and Stratton, Inc., New York, from: *Basic Problems in Psychiatry*, ed J. Wortis, New York 1953.

Briefly, Pavlov showed it is possible by physiological, objective methods to investigate the function of symbolization, of how the individual acquires those responses during its life as a result of experience. He studied the animal over its life span under nearly normal conditions, thereby substituting the chronic for the acute experiment, a new departure for physiology. Pavlov furthermore demonstrated the experimental neurosis.

Pavlov gave a physiologic meaning to the words "excitation" and "inhibition," functions which can be partially measured and recorded by the usual physiologic devices.

I do not mean to indicate that I believe these simple measures are the most important features of the symbolic processes of excitation and inhibition, but without a simple measure that can be recorded, progress by the scientific method is difficult.

What is the meaning of the term "conditional reflex?" The term itself states baldly only what we have before generally recognized, viz., that the individual makes adaptions during its life on the basis of its own experiences. But the method represents a new advance. Before Pavlov we had no physiological means of studying the complex behavior of animals comparable to our own psychic life. Psychical phenomena were, and still are to a great extent, evaluated by reference to our own subjective feelings, and this evaluation varies from person to person so that no two people agree. The cr, however, when expressed in movement or secretion, has a quantitative characteristic which can be obtained by every trained investigator. Furthermore it can be recorded and compared from day to day as can any other scientific record.

The cr can be as accurately measured as can the UR; furthermore it is equally as regular, if the conditions are kept constant.

In this laboratory, it has not only been shown that there is a little daily variation (in a rigidly controlled situation) of the conditional reflex (cr) as of the unconditional reflex (UR), but the cr can be expressed in an equation as readily as can the UR. Thus for the salivary cr the formula is: $cr = a + b (1 - e^{-cQ})$, an exponential relationship, while for the UR secretion of salivation the formula $UR = a + b$ shows a linear relationship.[13]

These formulae simply mean that as the intensity of the stimulus is increased, the cr at first increases but soon stops increasing or increases very slowly with added stimulation; while within the same limits, the UR increases equally with each unit of added stimulus whether the unit is added to the basic large or small stimulus. Individual variations are accounted for by the constants (for a given individual), a, b, c.

The term conditional reflex (cr) can be used to describe two different types of behavior: first the specific response based directly on the unconditional reflex (UR)—the original use of the word in Pavlov's work, as the secretion of saliva to the symbol for food; or, second, it can be used in a broad, general way, where any activity resulting from experience, regardless of its complexity or of its relation to a UR, is referred to as a cr. Pavlov occasionally employed the second use as well as the first, though more as a hope for the future than as an achievement of the present. I prefer a stricter use of the term to designate patterns of behavior based on specific UR's and acquired by the individual as a result of its own experience.

Most of the early work by Pavlov was done with food used as the unconditioned stimulus (US) and salivation taken as a measure of the response, both UR and cr. The salivary measure had the advantages of being quantitative, of being out of consciousness and therefore less prone to anthropomorphic interpretations, and of having few connections in the life of the animal except with food.

Excitatory and Inhibitory CR's, Terms and Concepts

Most people are familar with the concept of the excitatory (positive) cr and the inhibitory (negative) cr. The positive cr to food is the total response that the signal for food produces after it has been followed by food a certain number of times in that individual, and the negative cr is the response to a situation or signal similar in some respects to that of the positive cr but which is never followed by food. Each of these processes, excitatory and inhibitory, have definite characteristics. For example, excitation, whether it be pleasurable as with food or painful as with a noxious stimulus, produces an increase of respiration, heart rate and activity, while inhibition, whether of a pleasurable response or of a painful response causes a relatively slight change in heart rate, respiration, etc., and is frequently followed by sleep.

This expression of our behavior in the simple terms excitation and inhibition is too schematic to describe completely so complex a phenomenon. But there are many advantages for beginning the study of a complex subject in the simplest way that includes some quantitative measures of an essential aspect of the phenomenon under consideration.

The Latent Period as a Measure of Intensity

In physiological reflexes it is generally recognized that the latent period of a muscular contraction is inversely proportional to the intensity of the stimulus. I and my collaborators (Otterback and Dykman) [2, 35] have shown that latent period is also a reliable index of the intensity of the cr. Otterback and Gantt, using the food cr, showed the latent period of the secretion to two signals representing 2 g and 12 g respectively of food was with the larger amount of food 1.9 sec and with the smaller amount 2.5 sec. The latent period of the motor cr's to food was less reliable. In a study of latent period of the cardiac component of the cr to a painful stimulus, we found that the latency of the cr was inversely proportional to the intensity of the UR. It thus

appears that the latent period of the secretory cr is like the latent period of
the muscular contraction, a measure of intensity of the response, whether cr
or UR, and inversely proportional to the intensity of the stimulus (US).

The Components of the CR

The cr has a specific component related to the UR on which it is based,
e.g., salivation with the food reflex, movement with the pain reflex. Besides
this, there are general, supporting, or emotional components, e.g. cardiac,
respiratory, metabolic.[11, 14, 15, 24, 25, 28, 37, 38] Perhaps many other manifestations of the response will be detected in the future.

My collaborators and I have worked especially with the cardiac component because (1) of its great sensitivity, (2) the importance of the cardiovascular system in clinical medicine and (3) on account of the role of the heart
in the emotions‡. The sensitiveness of the heart rate in human subjects
has been demonstrated by Whitehorn, [41] and the cardiac conditional reflex
in dogs is one of the most interesting to show a quantitative relationship to
the conditional stimulus.

The Cardiac Component of the CR

In 1934, E. C. Andrus and I [38] began to study the possibility of forming
cardiac conditional reflexes to peripheral nerve stimulation, and in 1939
Hoffman and I, [24] and in 1942 Dworkin and I, [25] established the fact that
the heart rate changed regularly during the action of a conditional stimulus
signalizing either food or pain; in other words, that there is a definite cardiac conditional reflex subject to general laws of learned behavior.

After I had shown in this laboratory that the salivary conditional reflex
can be expressed quantitatively by an exponential formula, $cr = a + b$
$(1 - e^{-cQ})$, Hoffman and I investigated the changes in cardiac rate accompanying positive conditional reflexes (crs) of different intensities and inhibitory conditional reflexes (crs), in comparison with the heart rate changes
accompanying the reflex act of eating. A number of workers (Gasser, Meek,
Miles, Whitehorn) had previously established the fact that the heart rate is
accelerated by slight degrees of exercise and with emotional states. But it
was not known whether or not the slight amount of excitation produced by
the conditional signal (e.g. sound of a metronome) had a specific influence

‡ Pavlov purposely chose the salivary gland for the opposite reasons, viz.,
because it had few connections with the usual reactions and could be easily
isolated. For the early studies this isolation was an advantage because of the
need for simplicity in the initial steps of a new type of study; but the time has
come when this objective method can be extended to other fields such as emotions
and psychogenic cardiovascular disease.

on the cardiac rates. We have established the fact that, beside the slight change in heart rate that may be produced by any sensory stimulus, there is a marked and specific change in the heart rate in the cr. Furthermore, there is another specific alteration of heart rate accompaying inhibition. This is probably true for any form of cr, for we have shown that it holds not only for the food crs but for crs based upon painful stimuli.

Cardiac cr's to painful stimuli are, like the cardiac crs to food, proportional to the intensity stimulus ("motivation"). The latent period of the cardiac cr is short—within one or two heart cycles. The variations in cardiac crs depend upon the individual. Although the cardiac cr's have not yet been shown to bear an exponential relationship to quantity of unconditional stimulus, they are, like the secretory crs, at least grossly quantitatively related to unconditional stimulus, as regards both motor and secretory reflexes, involving defense and food. Because of the lack of a standard method of quantitating cardiac responses as yet no precise quantitative relationships can be stated.

When Hoffman and I first began the systematic investigation of the cardiac component of the cr, we did not recognize that there was a definite cardiac component of the response to a new stimulus or new situations (called by Pavlov the "orienting reflex" (OR) and by Whitehorn the "questioning reaction", referred to by Liddell as an index of alertness). Robinson and I, [38] making special studies of this response in 1945, found that the orienting reflex was characterized not only by directed muscular movements, but by respiratory, cardiac, and sometimes salivary reactions, which were present even in dogs deprived of most of the cortex. The cardiac is the most definite, the most constant and the most easily evaluated of all these measures. The OR disappears in most individuals (both dog and human) after several or more repetitions of the neutral stimulus; its persistence, a sign of hyperreactivity, is seen in both animals and patients.

As we have demonstrated that the above specific changes in heart rate are indepedent of any overt muscular movement of the animal and frequently in excess of that produced by a muscular movement, one is justified in speaking of a cardiac component of the cr which is as regular as the salivary cr, and even more delicate a measure of the nervous activity. It is a much more accurate and reliable index than the modifications in respiration accompanying the crs, although these also show the relationship but are cruder and more difficult to analyze. Thus in a dog whose crs had not been tested or exercised for 2 years, there was a complete loss of salivary and motor food crs but 100 per cent retention of the cardiac component, a demonstration not only of the stability of the cardiac reflex but of the fact that memory is selective and relative rather than absolute. [3, 22, 29]

The change in heart rate during the cr is not always acceleration but sometimes retardation, depending upon the individual; the pattern is the same in a given individual. On account of this individual variation, perhaps, the results of previous investigators were inconsistent.

The fact that the heart rate changes specifically and quantitatively during given cr (according to the intensity of the stimulus), even where there is no external evidence of emotion, indicates that bodily changes similar to those of the recognized overt emotions occur during all mental (as well as physical) activity in spite of the fact that the changes are not so great as in the more violent emotions.

Cardiac crs can be used as measures of the normal cr as well as a gauge of emotional tension. When this becomes too great, the relations are chaotic, and this state is characteristic of psychopathology. The pattern of the change is constant for a given individual. For each individual there is a certain change in the heart rate accompanying each type and intensity of excitatory cr, and another change in the heart rate accompanying inhibition. That the cardiac cr is a more delicate measure of activity is convincingly shown by its persistence in dogs after a long period of rest when the other components (motor and secretory) have disappeared. Thus the heart rate is a reliable measure of the intensity of conditional excitation and inhibition. This seems the more remarkable when we consider that these measures of heart rate are made for very short periods while the conditional stimulus is acting, viz., 3–10 sec.

To what Inborn Responses Can CRs Be Formed?

In answer to this question two errors of opposite nature are made, the first by those who are inclined to deny that functions generally considered visceral can be conditioned, and the second by those who facilely admit that any process in the body can arise through experience. In spite of the fact that Pavlov began his researches by forming a cr to an autonomic function (salivation), medicine today is reluctant to recognize that the whole autonomic system may, under certain circumstances, be conditioned. Some of the Russian followers of Pavlov, as well as many American psychiatrists, make the opposite error of assuming that any function whatever can be conditioned. The truth lies somewhere between these two extremes.

A great variety of functions have been conditioned in the last 50 years, from the "involuntary" secretion of urine to the "voluntary" skeletal movements.

In Pavlov's inital work with conditioning the salivary and gastric secretions, both food and acid were used. Most of the exact, quantitative research has been in dogs with the salivary cr to food; this cr becomes established usually in 10–100 reinforcements of a given signal with food. Conditioning of skeletal muscular movements, the initial work of which was done by the Bechterev school in Russia, is accomplished just as rapidly.

Bykov [17] has worked with a variety of visceral responses. Especially important is his work with the kidney. In order to study the urinary conditioning, he brought the ureter out upon the skin so that the urine could be collected directly without passing throught the bladder. Thus he was able to observe the secretion of the kidney with the same degree of accuracy that Pavlov had seen the secretion of the salivary glands in the dog when he was fed. Bykov and his collaborators could produce a psychic or conditioned secretion of the urine in the following manner: water injected into the rectum is ordinarily quickly followed by an increased flow of urine. However, by going through the procedure as if it were injected, there occured a conditioned secretion of urine. This urinary conditioned reflex could be inhibited and differentiated just as could the salivary crs. In general, a conditioned secretion of urine obeys the same laws as does the cr secretion of saliva.

The mechanism of the urinary cr involves both the pituitary and the nervous system; if either one is extirpated, the other is able to function, but if both the pituitary and the peripheral nerves to the kidney are destroyed, there can be no urinary cr.

In a similar manner, crs have been established for the secretion of bile, the contraction of blood vessels, the respiratory exchange, the heat regulation of the body, the amount of sugar in the blood, etc.

We have extended the work of Pavlov and Bykov to other autonomic functions, viz. the cerebellar movements, [1] the vestibular function of equilibration, [34] to intraneural stimuli (i.e. those arising within the nervous system instead of the usual ones applied to the external receptor organs) and to sexual stimuli. [21]

Anatomy (Phylogeny, Ontogeny, Structure and Function)

Investigation of the relation of structure to function is not new. As regards the brain, the question received an impetus from the experiments of Fritsch and Hitzig in 1870 (stimulation of the cortical areas), from the extirpations of Munk, Ferrier, and Horsley, as well as from the study of the relationships of the cortex to acquired responses (crs) by Pavlov. William James, in his *Principles of Psychology*, was a nineteenth century champion of the dependence of function on structure. Recently the matter has been further resolved by electrophysiology, e.g., in the investigation of Adrian, Bard, Woolsey *et al*.

By focusing attention on a specific type of response, viz. the cr, the importance of structure can be somewhat further elucidated. The ability to form a cr may be considered both from the phylogenetic and from the ontogenetic point of view. Phylogenetically, animals very low in the scale with very primitive nervous systems and without a brain, e.g., of insects, have been shown to have the ability to modify, to some extent, the inborn responses as a result of individual experience. This function, however, seems to be of little importance when compared with the strength of their instinctive, inborn responses. But as the nervous system increases in complexity, there is an increasing proportion of the acquired functions.

Ontogenetically, we see a similar phenomenon; infant mammals can form crs before the development of the cortex, but in the very young this ability is greatly restricted and retention is much shorter than in the adult. [9, 10]

From both the phylogenetic and the ontogenetic consideration, it appears that the ability to form the cr does not depend solely upon any specific type of nervous tissue, but that the function is greatly facilitated by the presence of a well developed cortex.

Extirpation experiments in the mammals have also brought out the dependence of the cr on the cortex, though the matter has not been finally settled. The view ranges from that expressing complete dependence on the cortex (early work of Pavlov), through the intermediate position of some (Zeliony, Culler, Bard, Bromiley), to those who claim that crs can be formed in the spinal animal (Shurrager, Dykman [17]). One explanation of the differences is to be found in the fact that Pavlov drew his conclusion from the study of the salivary cr, while others claiming the existence of the cr without the cortex have used the motor cr to pain. Practically all the experiments, however, show that the cr function is grossly impaired by cortical damage and that the higher we go on the zoological scale, the greater is the impairment until, in the human, the impairment of cr function can be used even as a means of differentiating the organic from the psychogenic psychoses.

Elements of the Conditional Reflex Arc: Intraneural Conditional Reflexes

Most of the stimulations for the crs of the laboratory and many of those for the acquired reactions of daily life begin with the exteroceptive analyzers (i.e., where the surface comes in contact with the environment), and link this stimulation with others originating either in other exteroceptive analyzers or in the interoceptive analyzers, e.g., a sound used as a signal for cutaneous pain or for food. A few cr's have been elaborated on the basis of stimulations proceeding from the proprioceptive analyzers; much of motor learning makes use of proprioceptive stimuli.

We have used stimulations whose points of origin are within the nervous system. For conditioning of such stimulations, I suggest the term "intraneural", in contrast to ordinary or extraneural conditioning, in which the stimulation arises outside the nervous systems, to which it is transferred through a specialized receptor.

The simple reflex arc in vertebrates is composed of the receptor cell and the afferent element, the central connection and the efferent nerve.

In an effort to relate structure to function, to determine the anatomic elements on which the conditional reflex is based, I attempted, in collaboration with Drs. Loucks, [32, 33] Light, [31] and Brogden, [1] to eliminate successively the various parts of all the structures involved. We aimed at temporary elimination rather than permanent destruction of the various elements. The trauma of extensive destruction of nerve tissue, as in cortical ablation, was avoided, although we did not entirely obviate the situation analogous to the three-legged stool described by Adolf Meyer—the stool falls if any one of the three legs is destroyed. [5]

Elimination of the Efferent Structures

Previous experiments with paralytic drugs, such as curare and morphine, led to conflicting results: the results of Crisler and Culler were in favor of the central connection as capable of functioning in learning without participation of the peripheral structures; the early results of Harlow and Stagner with curare were against this view. We avoided the poisonous systematic action of drugs by employing a surgical method, that of producing temporary paralysis by crushing the anterior nerve roots. After regeneration the conditional signal was given always without shock, and it was followed by withdrawal of the formerly paralyzed leg—the appropriate and specific conditioned movement but one which was never possible during the period of training. [31]

We concluded that for learning simple acts, exclusive of complex movements depending on chains of proprioceptive reflexes from successive peripheral situations, the effector response (muscular movement or glandular secretion) is unessential; such learning is within the nervous systems. This conclusion parallels the theory of Cannon and Bard of emotion as essentially central mechanism.

Elimination of Successive Parts of the Analyzer

I shall discuss the problem first from a strictly physiologic point of view. First, how much of the afferent arc of the unconditional reflex (UR) can be omitted and the response still serve as a basis for the elaboration of the cr? Second, how much of the afferent arc, i.e. of the analyzer, of the cr can be eliminated with preservation of the function of making connections with executer organs, i.e. of synthesis?

(1) Elimination of the afferent member of the unconditional reflex (UR)

A reflex movement of the hind leg was obtained by stimulating directly the dorsal root of a lumbar nerve to furnish the UR (movement of the leg), instead of, as in the usual experiment, applying a shock to the skin of the leg to cause a withdrawal. As in the ordinary cr experiment, the shock to the dorsal root was preceded by a buzzing soud. After a few combinations the signal (buzzer) evoked the same movement as the induced shock to the dorsal root; that is, a cr can be elaborated to a central excitation as easily as to the corresponding peripheral stimulus.

Similar experiments were performed on three dogs, using stimulation of the posterior columns of the spinal cord at about the level of the sixth lumbar nerve. The induction shock to the cord was preceded for 1 sec by a conditional stimulus (buzzer). The UR was a movement, usually flexion of the ipsilateral hindleg, to stimulation of the cord by the induction shock. In all these dogs, there was a conditional reflex to the buzzer, consisting of general tension plus movement of the hind leg, which appeared first on reinforcement 107 (sixth day), reinforcement 120 (seventh day), and reinforcement 422 (twenty-second day) in the various animals, respectively. [7, 33]

Cerebellar Conditional Reflexes

The integration of reflexes arising from cerebellar stimulation in thirteen normal dogs was investigated by the method of conditional reflexes. Induction coils were permanently inserted and insulated electrodes run into the posterior cerebellum between the cortex and nucleus dentatus. Stimulation of the normal dog through such inserted electrodes produced a variety of ipsilateral movements—turning of head, flicking of ear, protrusion of tongue, raising of foreleg. The stimulus was sufficiently weak not to be accompanied by pain, struggling or evidence of spread. When limb movements were elicited, the electrodes were found in the cortex or subcortex of the medial aspect of the crus primum; in movements of the deep neck muscles they were in the ventral lateral vermis. Not all movements evoked by faradization could be conditioned; most readily conditioned were movements of the foreleg and neck muscles. In most animals, rapid conditioning was obtained, with other evidence of higher nervous integration: extinction, differentiation, retention for days or weeks—comparable to the speed of ordinary conditioning through external sense organ with an intact cerebral cortex—indicating that the conditioning of reflexes arising within the cerebellum and having the characteristics of cerebellar movements is not different from ordinary conditioning.[1]

Stimulation of the sigmoid gyrus to give a leg movement was performed in this laboratory by my former collaborator, R. B. Loucks. [32, 33] In three dogs which received about 600 reinforcements of the conditional stimulus with the faradic shock to the motor cortex, there was no evidence of the formation of a cr.

(2) Elimination of the afferent member of the conditional reflex (cr)

Where, along the route of the afferent nerve and its various segmental and suprasegmental connections, may one apply the stimulus to be conditioned without destroying its function as a signal? In other words, to what internal stimulations can the organism make the union with the UR? By the methods described in the preceding paragraphs and the use of the buried coil technic, we found it possible to elaborate conditional reflex signals from stimulation of the dorsal roots, the area striata and even the motor area of the cerebral cortex.

Experiments undertaken in collaboration with W. J. Brogden indicated that stimulation of certain parts of the cerebellar cortex, may also serve as an adequate signal for a cr.

On the psychobiologic side, signals arising from various activities within the central nervous system (as well as proprioceptive stimuli) can function as conditional stimuli as readily as stimuli falling on the external sensory organs. This laboratory is now concerned with determining the efficacy of stimuli arising inside the central nervous system, in the sympathetic and the parasympathetic systems, as signals for acquired reactions, i.e. crs.

What Responses Can Be Conditioned?

I began to occupy myself with this question in the early 1930's. From a survey of the foregoing experiments on the autonomic functions, we see at once that the range of functions is so wide that we could be led to think any function in the organism can be made into a cr by the appropriate procedure. Neither does the ability for conscious control or even for a representation in consciousness determine whether a function is conditionable; for the HR and urinary secretion can be as readily conditioned as the movements of a finger.

Since most of the behavior (both conscious and unconscious) in the living organism has a survival value and is directed toward goals in a more or less organized way, i.e. is teleological, it seemed reasonable to invoke the ideas of usefulness, needs and purpose to explain conditioning. The prediction, however, of whether any given function could be conditioned on this basis broke down, and it became evident that we had to look elsewhere. Thus the knee jerk can be conditioned, though it fulfills no need and perhaps no useful purpose, and even the same function, e.g. gastric secretion, can, under certain circumstances, be conditioned and, under others, not; this will be described subsequently.

The objection can be raised that perhaps we cannot say definitely whether these functions may or may not be useful. But if there is no criterion for deciding whether a function is useful, when one says it is and another with equal vehemence says it is not, such an explanation is valueless for science. Another point raised is that the function may have been useful in another age. This, however, is relegating the question to an area where only speculation is possible. Here again, if the decision has to invoke such uncertainties for which there can be no criterion for a decision, it is of no value, and we should look for a more precise law.

Hedonism, Thorndike's law of effect, the pain-pleasure principle—all fail to explain either the formation of the cr or its persistence: in any psychiatric clinic we are aware of the pathological persistence of at least some useless responses. Any act whatever may be claimed to be satisfying or pleasurable under the circumstance in which it occurs, but this it usually only giving a name to what happens; for it cannot be predicted ahead what is pleasurable, and often the sole evidence that it is pleasurable is that it occurs, and conversely, if it occurs, it must be pleasurable, reasoning from a statement that has not been established. Obviously if we have to wait to see whether a response occurs to know whether it is pleasurable, then the term pleasurable has no meaning other than being another word for "it happens."

I do not wish to deny that pain and pleasure, biological need, and use generally determine the persistence and conditioning of a function, but the exceptions are so numerous that these are not acceptable explanations if we can find a better one.

We shall begin at the lower level in the higher vertebrates; in order to test the general hypothesis, whether reactions which do not involve "consciousness" and are apparently on a non-neural level can be modified by the experience of the individual ("taught", or conditioned) we chose a response that is easily produced, lends itself to quantitative measurement, and is independent of the central nervous system—the rise of blood sugar after the injection of adrenaline. Although the mechanism of adrenaline hyperglycemia is not exactly understood, the generally accepted view is that adrenaline stimulates breakdown of muscle and liver glycogen into glucose, and that it may also prevent utilization of glucose by the individual cells. Nevertheless, experiments with such an internal secretion should be important not only for the general hypothesis, but also in endocrine therapy, to show whether we may expect any modification from usage, similar to the conditioning of sleep by morphine when saline is substituted for the drug.[26]

The results of Hans Häusler from Graz, reported in the discussion of our data at the Fifteenth International Physiological Congress in Leningrad 1935, agree with ours that *non-neural conditioning in the higher animals cannot be obtained*. He saw no conditioned hyperglycemia from the injection of 1cc. adrenaline per kg, nor a conditioned hypoglycemia from the injection of insulin in dogs, nor did he get a conditioned fever from the use of beta-tetra-hydronaphthalamin.

The *origin* of the hyperglycemia that is being conditioned is a crucial point. The hyperglycemia accompanying a central psychobiological state might become conditioned as a component of this state. The same is true of salivary or gastric secretion; [30] it can be conditioned only when it is a component of a central state, such as nausea or food excitation. Thus one must think of the origin and meaning of the reaction as well as the reaction itself when he speaks of a "conditional reflex." The hyperglycemia of fear, as shown in Cannon's work is an example of such a central state of excitation. But the procedure in our experiments was not sufficient to cause such an hyperglycemia.

We selected other drugs which produced a secretory response through peripheral action on the nerve endings rather than through a central state— salivation through pilocarpine injection and gastric secretion "histamine"— and we found that the pilocarpine salivation and the histamine secretion cannot be conditioned. But we know salivation and gastric secretion when part of a food excitation is readily conditioned.

Teitelbaum and Gantt recently performed a similar experiment with cardiac conditioning, i.e. using a drug whose effect was produced by peripheral rather than by central nervous system action. Acetylcholine produces a change in heart rate (first slowing and then accelerating) through direct action on the intrinsic nerve endings and heart muscle, and subsequent compensation. When acetylcholine is injected from outside the room *without the presence* of the experimenter, its effect cannot be conditioned.

Some contrary experiments have been reported, e.g., the conditioning of leucocytosis and antigen formation by Metalnikow in Paris. However, when similar experiments were repeated in my laboratory (experiments of Sanford Stone), [39] no conditioning of leucocytosis was obtained in rats (on being plunged into cold water).

Adrenaline evidently regulates the carbohydrate metabolism essentially through direct action on body tissues and not through provoking a psychobiological state which would cause stimulation of the subcortical vegetative centers and of the whole chromaffin system. This view explains our failure to provoke conditioned hyperglycemia when adrenaline is used as the unconditioned stimulus.

Also, comparing our experiments with those using centrally acting (morphine) and peripherally acting drugs (pilocarpine, atropine) to affect salivation, and the failure to obtain a conditioned salivary reflex in the latter, it appears that the action of adrenaline in producing hyperglycemia is peripheral, which accords with its ability to cause a rise of blood sugar in the perfused liver, or when injected into decerebrate and decapitated cats, and also after removal of the sympathetics.

All these results agree with the theory that the *effects which have a central (usually cortical) representation through afferent fibers (even though enteroceptive) as well as an efferent control, can be conditioned,* while those without such adequate representation or those having no efferent connection with the central nervous system cannot be conditioned.

The second corollary of these experiments is that *we should speak of conditioning specific reactions rather than employ the loose and vague expression, a "conditional reflex to a drug."* The conditional response to an agent may be selective, consisting only of part of the original reflex action, thus varying from the latter qualitatively as well as quantitatively. Hence, conditional responses may differ considerably from the original reactions on the basis of which they were formed. [3] Conditioning is a filtering process rather than a duplication *in toto*.

Thirdly, from the fact that some of the effects of adrenaline can be conditioned, it is necessary to remember that one and the same reaction may be conditioned at one time and not at another. Thus it is understandable why the hyperglycemia accompanying a central excitation such as fear might be conditioned to the stimulus for the central state, albeit the final mechanism of the hyperglycemic production is through the action of adrenaline and is non–neural; for the liberation of adrenaline is a result of the central state. But where adrenaline is introduced artificially, the difference is analogous to that which exists between the production of salivation *peripherally* (by the injection of pilocarpine which cannot be conditioned) and the production of salivation *centrally* (by the eating of food). In the former, there is no central excitation involved in the salivation, whereas in the latter instance the salivation is preceded by and is an expression of the central excitation.

Teleology, Feeling and Conditioning

With the conditioning of food reactions and some others, it is known that a certain emotional tension (related to hunger, pain or sex) is necessary for the formation of the cr. For conditioning within the central nervous system (intraneural conditioning), there is no basis for asserting that an emotional tension, urge or feeling is essential. The current that my colleagues and I employed was fairly weak, so that we never saw evidence of pain in the animals. Furthermore, except in some instances in which an external movement occurred, there was no clear indication of any feeling. The dogs did not lift their ears, turn their heads, become alert or give any sign, even of orientation, to the stimulation of the cerebral cortex, such as one sees in ordinary, extraneural conditioning on using any new signal or unaccustomed change in environment; that is, from close observation of the external behavior, one may assume that the dog had no feeling—certainly none that could be classified as pain or pleasure or as that generally associated with defense. Conditioned contraction of the spleen and conditioned diuresis, demonstrated by Bykov and Alexejev-Berkman for dogs, can hardly be based on feeling, for the human subject certainly is not aware of the secretion of urine by the kidneys not of splenic contractions, nor are these reactions concomitants of a feeling or urge at the basis of the conditioning.

It would be much easier to think of conditioning on the grounds of biologic importance to the animal, of teleology in the sense in which Driesch employed it. Undoubtedly, many acquired reactions have their foundation here and also involve feeling, but my experiments do not fit into such a category; neither does conditioning of the knee jerk or of the pupillary responses. At present one can go no further than to assert that, as a general law, there is an association of function with certain nerve structures, so that when a stimulus arises in any of the sensitive units in definite time relationships with another activity, the two activities tend to recur together. What determines which of the many coincident reactions become functionally linked and the laws governing them remain to be discovered. Adaptation between the periphery and the center *(Anochin)*, the principle of integration as shown by Sherrington for segmental reflexes, also tends to keep the organism in equilibrium, but there is operative this other force of *function inherent in structure*, which may or may not pull toward a successful adaptation. By force of circumstances and structure, functions may become dysfunctions, a fact of which students of psychopathology are aware. Contractions of smooth muscle, having once begun, proceed *nolens volens ad finem*, as pointed out by Adolf Meyer in describing the automaticity of sexual acts. Adaptation, equilibrium, integration and evolution are powerful factors, but not always is it true, as Pangloss taught Candide, *que tout est nécessairement pour la meilleure fin dans ce meilleur des mondes possibles.*

A striking example of this relation of function to structure, irrespective of the needs of the organism, is the response of the fetus in utero (shown by Snyder and Rosenfeld [40], before it can have any purpose for the organism and even when it may lead to disastrous results (drowning or pneumonia). In the present state of knowledge of these events, one cannot say more than that function is related to structure in such a way that when the respiratory units reach a certain development, they begin to function, regardless of needs and external stimuli.

The Experimental Neurosis

Beginning in 1931, three dogs were put through a training (lasting for several years) involving one or more difficult or impossible differentiations between two tones. Parallel studies were conducted throughout the lives of these animals. All of them showed a disturbance of behavior in the situation of conflict, but of varying degree; in one it was only temporary, in the second it was of longer duration and more severe, and in the third there was, in addition, a spread to many physiological systems, suggesting the involvement of the "whole personality" perhaps similar to a major psychosis, which continued until 1939. A gradual amelioration of most symptoms occurred, probably because of certain factors in the treatment, but possibly also to other factors such as age.

Nick was a mongrel male introduced into the laboratory in early 1931 and kept in the paddocks with the other dogs. For about a year before any work was done on him, he was brought into the experimental room for casual observation. Nothing was noted then that impressed one as remarkable; in fact he was selected with Fritz and Peter for laboratory work, as being,

according to general appearances, normal. He seemed to be lively and playful, perhaps even more companionable and easy to make friends with than
other new dogs. [13]

No careful and detailed examination was made on him prior to experimentation, but it is significant that casually and by the means of ordinary
observation he appeared normal. The contrast between the results of casual
observation and the subjection to the rigidly controlled and delicate measurements in the routine of the laboratory deserves emphasis. It is only by the
latter method that we can detect the individual that will show a breakdown
under stress. The early symptoms seen in the laboratory situation which
gave us a clue to the constitutional instability in Nick were: (1) refusing to
eat; (2) the absence or inhibition of the cr when the differentiation became
hard, the slight cr at first and the easy setting in of inhibition; (3) the lack
of differentiation; (4) the striking increase of muscular activity and restlessness.

It is remarkable in Nick not only that the nervous symptoms continued
for 10 years without repeating the original conflict, but that the spread to
the urinary and sexual systems did not occur till after 1935, several years
after the conflict. That they were related to the conflict is shown by their
appearance only in the experimental environment and by other relationships to the original stimuli, as will be discussed.

Among the most interesting symptoms of the many pathological ones
which Nick showed were the sexual. The appearance of the pronounced
sexual manifestations and the reciprocal relations to nervous disturbances
constitute a definite and important chapter in experimental neuroses. Sexual
excitation as an expression of nervous disturbance has been seen in several
of our laboratory dogs, but most prominently in Nick. It may occur either
during the actual period of strain, or may be absent then and occur months
later from the trace of the conflict. [8, 13, 16, 19, 22]

The sexual manifestations may be summarized as follows: (1) the environment of conflict, including the isolated elements of the environment as well
as the people involved, provokes abnormal sexual excitations; (2) conversely, the effect of the environment inhibits normal sexual function produced
either by artificial or by natural stimuli; (3) paradoxically, the effect of
natural sexual excitation—as well as human companionship—dissipates the
neurotic manifestations as well as the artificial crs; (4) reciprocal time relations are seen between sexual excitation and other physiological excitations,
such as food excitation; (5) neurotic sexual symptoms are chaotic in character (irregular, etc.); (6) pathologically conditional sexual excitation differs
from the normal sexual crs.

These pathological reactions, instead of disappearing with time, became
firmly fixed and more frequent. However, they were never observed except
when some element of the old environment was present. It would therefore
seem that they were specific reactions. The other interesting sexual symptoms

in Nick cannot be described in detail here; the reader is referred to my monograph. [13]

Since the study of Nick, we have had even a more marked case of experimental neurosis with extremely abnormal sexual symptoms of an opposite character, viz. greatly diminished sexual reactivity (impotence) with a catatoniclike state in the experimental environment.

V_3 was a very shy fearful animal about 3 years old, reared in the laboratory. After months of handling, he persisted in running away from all the people who worked with him as well as from others, in spite of there being no history of mistreatment. When put into the experimental Camera he became practically cataleptic, and often fell to the floor, as if in an hysterial seizure. During these attacks he exhibited flexibilitas cerea, allowing his limbs to be put into various unnatural postures. Although absolutely no sexual erections could be induced by peripheral stimulation in this dog before alcohol, after a dose of 2 cc of alcohol per kg body weight, he showed a spontaneous erection when brought near the Camera and partial erection (without ejaculation and orgasm) lasting for 37 min. This dose is large enough to inhibit sexual erection in normal dogs, but in this extremely pathological animal, the most persistently neurotic of any dog we have had, erections appeared for the first time.

In spite of the favorable action of alcohol on these two opposite types (Nick, V_3), neither one of the dogs would voluntarily drink the alcohol (diluted in milk to 10 per cent), in contrast to Masserman's self-selecting-therapy cats. [21, 22]

Schizokinesis and Autokinesis

Western science has its roots in the greatest of known cultures, that of the Greeks. The idea of an ordered universe obeying laws rather than the caprices of spirits and the confidence that the human mind could divine these laws were so ably expressed by Plato that they have permeated Western thinking. Without any desire to belittle the great value of our heritage from Greek thought, I shall attempt to show the general idea has often resulted in a detriment to clear thinking in psychopathology. It has perhaps been overemphasized, not only by the Scholastics but by the moderns. The terms integration, holism (Smuts), equilibrium (Pavlov), adaptation (Darwin), homeostasis (Cannon), and many similar ideas adopted by psychiatrists express a general truth, but when believed in too implicitly they result in the neglect of definite and specific mechanisms, and even in the desire to adhere to concepts contrary to the facts. If my emphasis on the opposite phase—that of the disharmony on which pathology is based—seems too great, it is because of my desire to correct the excesses that have been built up on the concept of perfect functioning.

There is a normal physiological basis for maladaptation and even conflict. First, even in crs demanding little or no physiological or external activity, such as to the sound of a metronome symbolizing only 1 gr. of food, there is a marked overactivity of the visceral system and especially of the heart; the heart rate increases out of all proportion to the physiological need. Secondly, the heart, this vital organ for the maintenance of the life and health of every living tissue every moment, does not adapt harmoniously, compared with the muscular and digestive systems, and may even show an increased activity in a situation to which the organism has long since made adaptation in its external activity.

The cardiac component is both more sensitive in appearing first and paradoxically more stable in persisting longer. Without reinforcement, it has endured as long as 2 years after the motor component has dropped out. If the cardiac acceleration represents the inner emotional aspect, and the motor cr the specific external component, we have the picture of an organism externally in adaptation to the environment but internally excited and reacting to the trace of a conditional stimulus which long since ceased to have its former significance. The animal has achieved external adaptation but emotionally it is maladapted. Thus, there is a kind of cleavage between the outer specific muscular and the inner cardiac expression. There is this normal physiologic cleavage, adaptive inhibition in the specific response with persisting excitation in the general emotional reaction. The latter may even become more pronounced than it was originally. Thus, through this built-in principle of dysfunction, the organism tends to become a museum of archaic emotional responses, tied to the past internally while exhibiting freedom externally.

In our study of abnormal behavior, we must reckon with this constitutional principle of dysfunction as well as with the acquired neurotic tendencies.

That life exists at all is a tribute to its power for adaptability, so beautifully evident in homeostasis (Claude Bernard, Cannon), in the preciseness of gastric secretion and salivary secretion, and even in the intake of food. Nevertheless the living organism wages a losing battle (though prolonged), ending in death. On the psychobiological level we see the basis of this failure to adapt in the lack of harmony between the circulatory mechanism, this phylogenetic veteran of the physiological systems, and the other systems of the body. Dysfunction, reaching into the highest cortical levels, is not a recently acquired characteristic, but probably as old as life itself. [22]

Besides the maladaptation of the visceral responses to the obvious requirements† of the organism, to which I have given the term *Schizokine-*

---

† *Obvious* is used here to indicate that we have as yet no absolute criterion for judging what is always the best response for the organism, and we have to judge on the basis of the obvious. While all that appears to be good adaptation and vice versa is not necessarily the same when subjected to a more thorough

sis†. there is another property of the organism having to do with an inner development on the basis of old stimulations, but occuring without the presence of any external stimulation. This function I now call "autokinesis", a word suggested to me by John Dos Passos after discussing with him the phenomenon. This concept is based chiefly on the following two series of laboratory facts:

(1) The development of pathological symptoms in the experimental neurosis months or years after the original stress. In the 12–years' study of the dog Nick, and in shorter studies of other dogs, it was seen that the most severe expressions of the neurosis arose not during the period of active experimentation, but after a considerable interval during which the dog was rested. Thus, in Nick, the pollakiuria, the fully developed asthmaticlike breathing, and the very marked sexual symptoms did not appear for one or two years after the stress situation, but designed experiments showed that these symptoms were definitely based on the old conflict. [13] Also, in the dog V_3, the marked catatonia did not appear until about 2 years after what seemed to be the stress situation for him, and after a rest period.

(2) Retention in normal dogs. A study of retention of the motor, salivary and cardiac crs has been made in a series of dogs. [26] These experiments were done in two ways: some dogs were given a rest from the active experimentation, and brought down for testing after an interval of a few months to 4–5 years; in other dogs, the excitatory crs were extinguished by repetition of the conditional stimulus without reinforcement, until the cr disappeared and the dog was tested after a few months to see if it had returned.

Figure 1 shows that in the dog, Crazy, who had been completely decorticated on one side and partially decorticated on the other, the motor cr of withdrawing the foot was as strong, after 6 months' rest, to the signal for the shock on the first trial after the rest as it was while he was being actively worked with. On October 12, 1949, after the rest, he showed even better differentiation between the excitatory and inhibitory signals than he did on April 27 before the rest.

Figure 2 shows the retention of the cardiac components of the cr to a painful stimulus in a dog in whom the motor cr was also retained after a 4-year rest, during which the dog was not brought down to the experimental room. A comparison of the cardiac cr in 1952 after 4 years rest, with that in 1948, before the rest, shows that on the very first time the dog heard the tone after the 4-year intervals, his heart rate increased as much to the signal as during the active experimentation.

analysis, to make the opposite assumption that whatever the organism does is *always* in the direction of a perfect adaptation is to neglect contrary facts.

  † *Schizokinesis* has been suggested to me in discussion with my collaborator, Dr. John E. Peters, as a more accurate term than the general one *dysfunction* which I formerly used for this phenomenon.

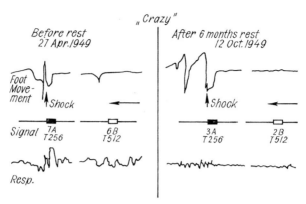

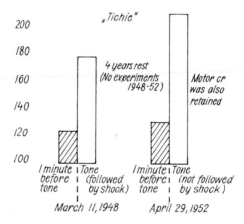

FIG. 1. Retention of respiratory and motor cr

FIG. 2. 4-year retention of cardiac cr

In the dog Billy (Figure 3) the experiment was performed in another way. The signals for two amounts of food (Wh for 12 g and M60 for 0·5 g) were repeated without reinforcement by food for several weeks until the conditional secretion not only dropped out for that day but did not reappear on the next day. As referred to previously, latent period is a good measure of intensity of the cr, the shorter the latent period, the stronger the cr. Experiment 1 on July 3 shows the normal latent period during active experimentation. In experiment 2 on July 19, after 2 weeks of daily extinction by repetition of the signals without reinforcement, the crs became very much weaker; this is shown by the long latent period. Between July 19 and October 16 Billy was given a complete rest without being brought down to the experimental room. Experiment 3 demonstrates spontaneous restoration: the crs have returned to an intensity even exceeding their normal, shown by the

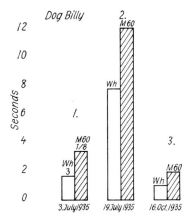

F𝐈𝐆. 3. Change in latent period of salivary cr: 1, during routine re-enforcement; 2, two weeks after extinction experiments; 3, after 3 months' rest without any experimentation

very short latent period, and differentiation between the two conditional stimuli has been preserved.

The function of autokinesis can be a therapeutic value as well as a pathological one. Not only can the individual develop pathological symptoms on the basis of previous conflicts, but a single therapeutic procedure or a single experience in life may initiate a development that is far beyond the expectation of the psychiatrist.

Application to the Study of the Patient

The Pavlovian methodology has been modified by me and my collaborators, as well as by a number of other workers (Krasnogorsky, Lashley, Finesinger, Sutherland, Muncie, Fleck, Reese [4, 6, 20 23, 27]) as an important aid in the evaluation of the psychiatric patient, as well as in discriminating between the psychogenic and the organic psychoses. By the cr method it is also possible to form a basis of determining which individuals are susceptible to nervous breakdown. The development of this field would lay the basis for a rational preventive psychiatry.[12]

Conclusion

Studies by the conditional reflex methodology help us to establish an objective psychiatry, and aid us in the understanding of both normal psychobiology and of psychopathology.

REFERENCES

1. BRODGEN, W. J., and GANTT, W. H. (1941) Intraneural conditioning: cerebellar conditioned reflexes, *Arch. Neurol. Psychiat.* **48**, pp. 437–55.
2. DYKMAN, R. A., and GANTT, W. H. (1951) A comparative study of cardiac and motor conditional responses, *Am. J. Physiol.* **167**, p. 780.
3. FLECK, S., and GANTT, W. H. (1949) Fractional conditioning of behavior based on electrically induced convulsions, *Fed. Proc.* **8**, p. 47.
4. FLECK, S., and GANTT, W. H. (1951) Conditional responses in patients receiving electric shock treatment, *Am. J. Psychiat.* **108**, pp. 280–88
5. GANTT, W. H. (1936) An experimental approach to psychiatry, *Am. J. Psychiat.* **92**, pp. 1007–21.
6. GANTT, W. H. (1937) Application of conditioned reflex methods to psychiatry, *Contributions Dedicated to Dr. Adolf Meyer*, Baltimore, Johns Hopkins Press, pp. 78–80.
7. GANTT, W. H. (1937) Contributions to the physiology of the conditioned reflex, *Arch. Neurol. Psychiat.* **37**, pp. 848–58.
8. GANTT, W. H. (1938) Extension of a conflict based upon food to other physiological systems and its reciprocal relations with sexual function, *Am. J. Physiol.* **123**, pp. 73–74.
9. GANTT, W. H. (1938) Impairment of the function of adaptability as measured by a simple conditioned reflex test in certain psychogenic contrasted with organic diseases, *South. Med. J.* **31**, pp. 1219–25.
10. GANTT, W. H. (1938) A method of testing cortical function and sensitivity of the skin, *Arch. Neurol. Psychiat.* **40**, pp. 79–85.
11. GANTT, W. H. (1942) Cardiac conditioned reflexes to painful stimuli, *Fed. Proc.* **1**, p. 28.
12. GANTT, W. H. (1943) Measures of susceptibility to nervous breakdown, *Am. J. Psychiat.* **99**, pp. 839–49.
13. GANTT, W. H. (1944) *Experimental Basis for Neurotic Behavior*, New York, Hoeber.
14. GANTT, W. H. (1946) Cardiac conditional responses to time, *Trans. Am. Neurol. Assoc.* **72**, p. 166.
15. GANTT, W. H. (1948) Cardiac reactions in partially decorticated dogs, *Trans. Am. Neurol. Aassoc.* **74**, pp. 131–2.
16. GANTT, W. H. (1948) A physiological basis for nervous dysfunction, *Bull. Johns Hopkins Hosp.* **82**, p. 416.
17. GANTT, W. H. (1948) Physiological psychology, *Ann. Rev. Physiol.* **10**, pp. 453–78.
18. GANTT, W. H. (1949) Emotional state on acquired and inborn reactions: satiation on cardiac conditional reflexes and unconditional reflexes to food, *Fed. Proc.* **8**, p. 52.
19. GANTT, W. H. (1950) Disturbances in sexual functions during periods of stress, *Life Stress and Bodily Dis.*, A. Research Nerv. and Ment. Dis. Proc. Chapter LXVII, pp. 1030–50.
20. GANTT, W. H. (1952) The conditional reflex function as an aid in the study of the psychiatric patient, in Hoch, P. H. and Zubin, J. *Relation of Psychological Tests to Psychiatry*, New York, Grune and Stratton.
21. GANTT, W. H. (1951) Effect of alcohol on the sexual reflexes of normal and neurotic male dogs, *Psychosom. Med.* **14**, pp. 174–81.
22. GANTT, W. H. (1953) Principles of nervous breakdown: schizokinesis and autokinesis, *Ann. N. Y. Acad. Sci.* **56**, pp. 143–64.
23. GANTT, W. H., and FLEISCHMANN, W. (1948) Effect of thyroid therapy on the conditional reflex function in hypothyroidism, *Am. J. Psychiat.* **104**, pp. 673–81.

24. GANTT, W. H., and HOFFMAN, C. (1940) Conditioned cardio–respiratory changes accompanying conditioned food reflexes, *Am. J. Physiol* **129,** pp. 360 to 61.

25. GANTT, W. H., HOFFMAN, W. C., and DWORKIN, S. (1947) The cardiac conditional reflex. *XVIIth Internat. Physiol. Cong., Oxford,* p. 15.

26. GANTT, W. H., KATZENELBOGEN, S., and LOUCKS, R. B. (1937) An attempt to condition adrenalin hyperglycemia, *Bull. Johns Hopkins Hosp.* **60,** pp. 500–11.

27. GANTT, W. H., and MUNCIE, W. (1941) Analysis of the mental defect in chronic Korsakov's psychosis by means of the conditional reflex method, *Bull. Johns Hopkins Hosp.* **70,** pp. 467–87.

28. GANTT, W. H., THORN, G., and DORRANCE, C. (1949) Anoxia on conditional reflexes in dogs, *Fed. Proc.* **8,** p. 53.

29. GANTT, W. H., and TRAUGOTT, U. (1949) Retention of cardiac, salivary and motor conditional reflexes, *Am. J. Physiol.* **159,** p. 569.

30. KATZENELBOGEN, S., LOUCKS, R. B., and GANTT, W. H. (1939) Attempt to condition gastric secretion to histamine, *Am. J. Physiol.* **128,** pp. 10–12.

31. LIGHT, J. S., and GANTT, W. H. (1936) Essential part of reflex arc for establishment of conditioned reflex: formation of conditioned reflex after exclusion of motor peripheral end, *J. Comp. Physiol. Psychol.* **21,** pp. 19–36.

32. LOUCKS, R. B. (1938) Studies of neural structures essential for learning: II. The conditioning of salivary and striped muscle responses to faradization of cortical sensory elements and the action of sleep upon such mechanisms, *J. Comp. Psychol.* **25,** pp. 315–32.

33. GANTT, W. H. (1938) The conditioning of striped muscle responses based upon faradic stimulation of dorsal roots and dorsal columns of the spinal cord, *J. Comp. Psychol.* **25,** pp. 415–26.

34. LÖWENBACH, H., and GANTT, W. H. (1940) Conditioned vestibular reactions, *J. Neurophysiol.* **3,** pp. 43–48.

35. OTTERBACK, V. L., and GANTT, W. H. (1947) Latent period as an index of the intensity of the conditional reflex, *Fed. Proc.* **6,** p. 173.

36. PAVLOV, I. P. (1941) *Lectures on Conditioned Reflexes,* 2 volumes (*translated* by W. H. Gantt), New York, International Publishers, p. 414.

37. PETERS, J. E., and GANTT, W. H. (1948) Effect of graded degrees of muscular tension on human heart rate, *Fed. Proc.* **7,** p. 92.

38. ROBINSON, J., and GANTT, W. H. (1947) The orienting reflex (questioning reaction): cardiac, respiratory, salivary and motor components, *Bull. Johns Hopkins Hosp.* **80,** pp. 231–53.

39. STONE, S. H., and GANTT, W. H. (1953) Adaptation to cold stress in Wistar rats, *Fed. Proc.* **12,** p. 139.

40. SNYDER, F. F., and ROSENFELD, M. (1937) Direct observation of intrauterine respiratory movements of the fetus and the role of carbon dioxide and oxygen in their regulation, *Am. J. Physiol.* **117,** p. 153.

41. WHITEHORN, J. C. (1939) Physiological changes in emotional states, *Research Publ., A. Nerv. Ment. Dis.* **19,** p. 256.

ACKNOWLEDGEMENTS

Acknowledgements are due to the following for permission to publish extracts in this volume:

AKADEMIJA NAUK SSSR

Pavlov, I. P. (1951) An Attempt to Understand the Symptoms of Hysteria Physiologically, in *I. P. Pavlov: Polnoe sobranie sotchinenii*, Tom III, Moscow–Leningrad.

AMERICAN JOURNAL OF PSYCHIATRY

Gantt, W. H. (1943) Measures of Susceptibility to Nervous Breakdown, 99, pp. 839–49.

BASIC BOOKS, INC.

Wolman, B. B. (1965) The Need for a Philosophy, in *Scientific Psychology* (ed. B. B. Wolman), New York, pp. 17–23.

Wolpe, J. (1962) The Experimental Foundations of Some New Psychotherapeutic Methods, in *Experimental Foundations of Clinical Psychology* (ed. W. Bachrach), New York, pp. 554–75.

CHEMICAL PUBLISHING CO., INC.

Bykov, K. M. (1957) Conditional-reflex Connections of th Kidney, in *K. M. Bykov: The Cerebral Cortex and the Internal Organs* (ed. W. H. Gantt), New York. pp. 39–54.

GOSUDARSTVENNOE IZDATEL'STVO MEDICINSKOJ LITERATURY

Sarkisov, A. S., Bassin, F. V., and Banstchikov, V. M. (1963) The Significance of Neurophysiological Terms for Psychopathology, in *Sarkisov, S. A., F. W. Bassin, and V. M. Bandstchikov: Pavlovskoe utchenie i nekotorye teoretitcheskie problemy sovremennoi nevrologii i psychiatrii*, Moscow, pp. 71–86.

GRUNE AND STRATTON, INC.

Gantt, W. H. (1962) The Future of Psychiatry. Pavlov's Contributions, in *The Future of Psychiatry*, New York, pp. 93–102.

Gantt, W. H. (1949) Psychosexuality in Animals, in *Psychosexual Development in Health and Disease*, New York, pp. 33–51.

Gantt, W. H. (1953) The Physiological Basis of Psychiatry. The Conditional Reflex, in *Basic Problems in Psychiatry* (ed. J. Wortis), New York, pp. 53–89.

INTERNATIONAL PUBLISHERS

Pavlov, I. P. (1928) The Discovery of the Conditioned Reflex, in *I. P. Pav-*

lov: Lectures on Conditioned Reflexes (translated by W. H. Gantt), New York, pp. 37–42.

JOURNAL OF AMERICAN MEDICAL ASSOCIATION

Alexander, L. (1962) Differential diagnosis between psychogenic and physical pain, **181**, pp. 855–61.

JOURNAL OF THE NERVOUS AND MENTAL DISEASES

Birch, H. G., and H. Demb, (1959) The Formation and Extinction of Conditioned Reflexes in „Brain-damaged" and Mongoloid Children, **129**, pp. 162–70.

PHYSIOLOGICAL REVIEWS

Gantt, W. H. (1960) Cardiovascular Components of the Conditional Reflex to Pain, Food and Other Stimuli, **40**, pp. 266–91.

PITMAN

Broadhurst, P. L. (1961) Abnormal Animal Behaviour, in *Handbook of Abnormal Psychology* (ed. H. Eysenck), London, pp. 726–63.

PSYCHOLOGICAL REVIEWS

Watson, J. B. (1916) The Place of the Conditioned Reflex in Psychology, **23**, pp. 89–116.

TRANSACTIONS OF THE AMERICAN NEUROLOGICAL ASSOCIATION

Gantt, W. H., H. Löwenbach, and C. Brown (1953) Acquired vestibular balancing responses, pp. 212–15.

UNIVERSITY OF KANSAS

Lindsley, O. R. (1960) Characteristics of the Behavior of Chronic Psychotics as Revealed by Free-Operant Conditioning Methods, *Diseases of the Nervous System*, in *Monograph Suppl.* **21**, pp. 66–78.

VERLAG VOLK UND GESUNDHEIT

Pickenhain, L. (1959) The Higher Nervous Activity of Man, in *L. Pickenhain: Grundriß der Physiologie der höheren Nerventätigkeit*, Berlin, pp. 116–29 and 149—55.

AUTHOR INDEX

Abraham, K. 13
Abramson, H. A. 215
Adelson, H. M. 291, 302
Adrian 311
Alexander, L. 5, 52, 53, 93, 235, 249, 329
Alexeev-Berkman 96, 106, 318
Allen 90
Allport, G. W. 13
Altmann, M. 172, 208
Anderson, O. D. 163, 166–175, 186, 207, 208, 216, 219, 287, 301
Andrews, R. C. 200, 221
Andrus, E. C. 308
Andy 91
Anochin, P. K. 319
Anrep, G. V. 303
Apter, I. M. 177, 208
Arieff, A. 188, 217
Armstrong, E. A. 208
Astrup, Ch. 3
Azrin, N. N. 271

Babinsky, J. 30
Babkin, B. P. 162, 163, 168, 208
Bachrach, A. J. 284
Bacon 305
Bagchi, B. K. 249
Bajandurov, B. I. 200, 208
Balakshina, V. L. 100–103
Balonov, L. Y. 94
Banstchikov, V. M. 4, 55, 328
Bant, J. O. 302
Bard 311–313
Barker, R. G. 13
Barnett, S. A. 199, 202, 208
Bassin, F. V. 4, 55, 63, 328
Bastock, M. 202, 208
Baxt, J. O. 183, 184, 210, 286
Bayne, T. L. 163, 166–168, 172, 216
Beach, F. A. 112, 163, 187, 200, 209, 298, 301
Bechterev 17, 39, 40, 107, 274, 310
Beer 16
Bekkering, D. 148
Benua 142, 147
Bergson 9
Berlyne, D. E. 297, 301
Bernard, C. 50, 92, 271, 322

Bernheim 31
Bethe 16
Bevan, W. 153, 209
Bijou, S. W. 196, 209
Binswanger 60
Birch, H. G. 5, 223, 233, 329
Birk, L. 93
Bolles, M. Marjorie 157, 215
Bond, I. K. 301
Borodavkina 105, 106
Bourne, W. 184, 211, 286, 289, 297, 302
Bowers, M. 233
Bowlby, J. 173, 209
Brady, J. V. 191, 201, 202, 209, 219
Bridger, W. H. 93, 278
Bridgman, P. W. 13
Brisset, Ch. 63–65
Broadhurst, P. L. 5, 153, 197, 199, 201, 202, 205, 206, 209, 220, 329
Brogden, W. J. 312, 315, 326
Bromiley 312
Brown, C. 121, 328
Brown, J. S. 206, 209
Brown, R. 208
Brownstein, A. 299, 302
Brozek, J. 94
Brückner, G. H. 200, 209
Bunch, M. E. 198, 215
Burch, G. 71, 74
Burmakin 38
Bykov, K. M. 2, 4, 49, 71, 74, 93, 95, 106, 147, 310, 311, 318, 328

Cain, J. 191, 209
Cameron, D. E. 200, 209
Campbell, A. A. 132, 133, 147
Campbell, D. 189
Cannon 38, 50, 92, 313, 316, 321, 322
Carleson 38
Carmichael, L. 154, 195, 210
Carrison, D. 233
Cason, H. 132, 143, 147
Cavanaugh, E. B. 202, 211
Chance, M. R. H. 163, 210
Chernigovsky 48
Citovich 132
Cohen, M. R. 13
Cole, J. 131, 147

330

SUBJECT INDEX